KILLING TIME

AN 18-YEAR ODYSSEY
FROM DEATH ROW TO FREEDOM

JOHN HOLLWAY
AND
RONALD M. GAUTHIER

Skyhorse Publishing

Skyhorse Publishing books may be purchased in bulk at special discounts for sales promotion, corporate gifts, fund-raising, or educational purposes. Special editions can also be created to specifications. For details, contact the Special Sales Department, Skyhorse Publishing, 555 Eighth Avenue, Suite 903, New York, NY 10018 or info@skyhorsepublishing.com.

www.skyhorsepublishing.com

10 9 8 7 6 5 4 3 2

Library of Congress Cataloging-in-Publication Data

Hollway, John.
Killing time : an 18-year odyssey from death row to freedom / John Hollway and Ronald M. Gauthier.
p. cm.
ISBN 978-1-60239-974-7 (hbk. : alk. paper)
1. Thompson, John, 1963- 2. Death row inmates--Louisiana--Case studies. 3. Murder--Louisiana--New Orleans--Case studies. 4. Suppression of evidence--Louisiana--New Orleans--Case studies. 5. Trials (Murder)--Louisiana--Case studies. I. Gauthier, Ronald M. II. Title.
HV8701.T58H65 2010
364.66092--dc22
[B]
2009047908

Printed in the United States of America

CONTENTS

TO THE READER

THIS IS A true story that we have decided to tell in a narrative style. Some of the dialogue between individuals in conversation has been estimated, though in every instance the substance has been verified by at least one, if not all, of the speakers, through various methods including court transcripts, oral and video depositions given under oath during court proceedings, documents collected during court proceedings, public media reporting, and interviews with the participants themselves. The dialogue from all courtroom scenes is contained in court transcripts, although some grammatical changes have been made, including modifications to spelling and grammar, and exchanging pronouns for proper nouns where it would enhance the reader's understanding. Letters written by John Thompson enclosed herein are actual letters, although some have been edited by the authors. We are indebted to Nancy Wohl, John's spiritual advisor, both for keeping these letters over the years and for sharing them with us.

1

WHY DID HE HAVE TO SHOOT ME?

DECEMBER 6, 1984
12:39 AM

Ray Liuzza slowed for the stop sign at Josephine, drifting slowly through it into a left turn, and scanning up ahead to Baronne for a parking space. The steering wheel slid through his fingers as he swung left from Brainard, the BMW's blinker clicking off as he gently accelerated down the one-way street. He was tired, and he had work tomorrow. He wasn't drunk, but he drove carefully anyway. He and Susan had made the rounds—the 4141, a couple of drinks at Lenfant's. No point in asking for trouble.

He'd tried to get Susan to let him stay, or maybe bring her back to his place. She didn't like coming back to his place—didn't like the neighborhood. Sure, it wasn't a gated community in the Garden District, but it wasn't a bad place to live, right in the center of the city, close to restaurants and bars and shops, close to work. He thought the place was real, with good working people.

He'd lived here for about two years, since his friend Frank had renovated the place. They had been friends at Tulane, and Frank had given him a pretty good deal on the nicest apartment in the building. He'd also let Ray help design it during the construction, so it had a little bit of Ray's style. It looked good and fit his personality.

Ray was a guy who paid attention to looks. Looking good was important. He'd lived in New Orleans his whole life, and New Orleans had style. Ray tried to bring a little of his style to the city, too. He had run a men's clothing boutique for a few years, bringing European fashions to town. Even though he'd gone on to join the family hotel business, he still kept up his European fashion sense. Anyone with an eye would see not just the silver BMW and the Italian suit, but the Cartier watch and the custom-made English shoes. He caught a lot of shit from the guys for those. They cost a small fortune and it took eight weeks for them to arrive, but they were worth it. You see a guy with a nice suit and bad shoes, it registers.

He saw a parking spot on the left side of the street, a couple of cars back from the corner. Luck was on his side. It was fairly cool, even for December, so close was good. He backed into the space and straightened out the car, turned off the lights, got out, locked the door, and started walking across the street to his apartment.

12:40 AM

PAMELA STAAB WAS in bed. She had been trying to finish a book she'd been reading, but sleep got the better of her—until now.

Her apartment, on the corner of Josephine and Baronne, was on the ground floor. It had been renovated pretty recently and was in good shape, but the walls were made of wood, and you could hear the street conversations pretty clearly as people walked by. She'd get this "life by Doppler effect" sort of thing, and sometimes she'd sit in her room and try to figure out whatever she could about people's lives as the volume rose, peaked, and faded as they walked by.

The noise she heard now, though, was different. The voices had a sense of urgency and brought her out of her sleep. She lay in bed, eyes open, listening.

A man was yelling at another man, but it wasn't aggressive yelling or catcalling, or a too-loud drunken story from someone walking home from a bar. This had a different tone to it—it was pleading.

She didn't make a sound. Whoever it was, they must have been right outside her window. With her blinds down she couldn't see anything, but one of the guys kept repeating something, his voice rising. "Take my watch!" That's what the man was repeating—"Take my watch!"

She heard another man's voice respond but couldn't make out his words. The first voice said it again. "Please, go ahead, take my watch. Please. Here, you can have my wallet." The other man replied, audibly this time: "No, man, I've got to shoot you."

The first man started to say something, and then she heard a *pop*, like a bottle of champagne, and then there was this silence, this silence that sounded all wrong. Then another *pop*; then a few more. No more voices now, just the sound of someone running away, feet beating on the pavement.

Pam sat up, listening, and finally realized whom the first voice had belonged to. She got out from under the covers and ran into her roommate Nora's room. "Nora! Ray's been robbed outside! He's been shot!"

12:40 AM

PAUL SCHLIFFKA CLOSED the front door of his apartment and stepped onto the sidewalk. He liked the feeling of the chilly evening, the quiet of the early morning air. He walked through the front yard toward his car parked on Baronne. He had his key in his hand and was about to get into his car when he heard it.

Pop. Pop. Poppop.

It sounded like gunshots, or what he imagined gunshots might sound like. Without thinking about it, he moved toward the sound, toward the corner, unconsciously craning his neck, his car keys still in his hand.

He was still about fifteen feet from the corner when a man appeared, a big guy with short hair. He ran quickly past Paul, who flinched. The runner continued down the street, swerving from left to right, heading away from where the shots had been fired, up Josephine toward Dryades.

Paul thought it was a good thing that the guy was outbound, seeing that the other thing he had noticed was the enormous bluesteel pistol in the guy's right hand—a long-barreled pistol that Paul wanted no part of. He stopped short and didn't move as the guy tore down the street, away from St. Charles. Maybe he had been seen, maybe not—Paul was pretty close but hadn't been standing in the light. Paul let him go without a sound. That gun. He waited a few seconds and then he moved up to the corner, looking down Josephine where the shots had been fired.

There was a man in a suit lying facedown next to the sidewalk.

Paul ran over and rolled the guy over. *Oh, man.* It was Ray who lived upstairs. He was badly hurt, bleeding and moaning.

Paul ran back around the corner and screamed toward the front entrance of his building. "Call the police—call 911! And get some blankets!"

12:40 AM

ROSEMARY CASH WAS asleep with her boyfriend in their apartment on the corner of Josephine and Baronne, on the Dryades side. She wasn't a real deep sleeper, and the unfamiliar noise snapped her awake. She bolted up, trying to figure it out. She reached over and shook her boyfriend. "Steve. *Steve.*" They were on the ground floor, and God only knew what might come bursting through their door.

He woke up, drowsy. "What? What's up?"

"Listen. I think I heard gunshots."

12:40 AM

SHERI HARTMAN LIVED on the north side of Baronne, at the corner of Josephine. She was up late, sitting in her living room, relaxing, and watching some crappy late-night TV show. She was new to the neighborhood, having just moved in a month earlier. It was on the edge of safe, only a few blocks from the St. Thomas Project, but it was affordable, and had a big second-story terrace, one of those ornate wrought-iron ones with French doors that she could open to let the air in.

She heard the shots, loud enough to get her out of bed. Six shots, to be precise. She turned off the lights in the apartment and ran across the living room to her terrace, making some noise as she threw open the doors.

By the time she got to the edge of the terrace and looked over the rail, there was a big black guy running across the street, up onto the sidewalk below her. He didn't slow down, but he looked up, and their eyes met, briefly. Then he kept running up the street and out of her field of vision.

Sheri looked back down across Baronne, where a man with blond hair was in the grassy section between the curb and the sidewalk, kneeling over the body of someone—a man in a suit. The blond man got up, walked to the corner, and screamed at someone in the building across the street to call the police.

Sheri turned and ran back inside, grabbed a sweater, and hit the stairs, running down to the street to see if she could help.

12:43 AM

NEW ORLEANS POLICE Department officers Clyde Angelo and David Carter were driving along St. Charles when the radio jumped: "Ten-seventy-one, shooting at 2103 Baronne." Carter grabbed the radio and responded as Angelo turned on the lights and hit the gas.

They got to Baronne and Josephine in less than sixty seconds. There was one streetlight on Josephine, and in the edges of its light, in a grassy patch next to the sidewalk, a man was lying on his back. From inside the car, the officers could see the man's blood emptying into the grass, his chest heaving.

Angelo parked the car, lights still on, and Carter got out. The victim was awake and afraid. He'd been shot more than once, looked like chest and back from a quick scan. His breathing was rapid and ragged, but steady. He was saying, "Why did he have to shoot me?"

Carter told him help was on the way. Some other guy, must have been a nearby resident, appeared with blankets, set them down next to Carter, and backed away. Angelo was already calling the ambulance.

The victim looked up at Carter, blood coming out of his mouth. From the way he was breathing, one of the bullets must have gone through a lung. The man panted, "He robbed me. Why did he have to shoot me? He told me he was gonna shoot me. You've got to take me to a hospital."

"We can't move you," Carter said. "Gotta wait for the ambulance—it's on the way. Couple minutes, that's all." The victim grimaced. "You saw the guy who shot you?" Carter asked. "What'd he look like?"

The victim shook his head. "No. You gotta get me to the hospital. I'm gonna die here." He inhaled, exhaled, coughing up some more blood. "Why'd he have to shoot me?"

Carter tried to study the victim's injuries. One bullet wound in the upper chest, near the shoulder, probably nonfatal. There was another bullet entry near the front of the hip. That wouldn't kill him either, unless it had hit an artery. He spoke to the victim again. "What did the guy who shot you look like?"

The victim's breathing got faster and shallower as he strained for air. "Put me in your car. Take me to the hospital. I'm not talking until you get me to the hospital. Help me."

The ambulance pulled up at that moment. The paramedics got out of the truck and hustled over. They bent over the victim and went to work. Carter got out of their way, walking over to help Angelo secure the area. In seven minutes, the paramedics had loaded the wounded man into the ambulance and peeled off to Charity Hospital, only three minutes away with the sirens.

Carter walked around the area, checking for clues and waiting for the crime tech to arrive. He kept replaying the victim's question in his head: *Why'd he have to shoot me?*

1:04 AM

FRANK MASELLI HAD gotten in bed and turned the light off but hadn't yet fallen asleep when his phone rang. It was Angie, the building manager of one of his buildings. She told him Ray Liuzza had been shot outside of his apartment. Frank got out of bed, grabbed a nylon jogging suit he had worn earlier that evening, and headed toward his car. *Christ,* he thought. *I just had a drink with him.* They had been celebrating Ray's promotion to vice president at the hotel.

Frank and Ray had gone to Tulane together. Ray was a funny guy, and they would go out together from time to time, taking in the sights, scouting the talent, a couple of young guys with some cash in their pockets and nothing holding them back.

Frank had offered Ray an apartment in 1979, in the first building he renovated, about four blocks off St. Charles. It was a pretty crappy neighborhood, truth be told, but they were all young and invincible then, and the building was in good condition. New Orleans had always been nice blocks next to run-down blocks. To compensate for the neighborhood, Frank had given Ray the nicest apartment in the building. Ray loved the place, and he loved the neighborhood. It had always seemed to Frank that Ray knew everyone around his neighborhood; he'd always talked about how important it was for people with his background and the people who lived in this neighborhood to get to know and understand one another.

Frank got to the building quickly. The ambulance was already gone, and a few cops were walking around the intersection. There was nothing for him to do at the scene, so he made his way through the cool evening air over to Charity Hospital.

Frank's and Ray's fathers were good friends themselves— wealthy New Orleans Italians who did business together. Ray Liuzza

Sr. ran the International Hotel and was active in the Chamber of Commerce, while Frank's father was a liquor distributor. Walking toward the hospital, Frank thought about how maybe Ray had started to make too much money for the neighborhood, with his flashy clothing and import car.

Frank could see the events of the night unfolding as he walked. Ray was probably looking flashy, and a robber saw the suit, the car, and the jewelry. The robber would probably get pretty angry when he opened Ray's empty wallet—he never carried any cash.

I should have told him, Frank thought. *He should have been out of that house and into another one in a better neighborhood.* He had tried, of course, but Ray hadn't listened. *Stubborn SOB,* Frank thought.

He walked into Charity's ER to find his friend. The news was as good as could be hoped: Ray was in surgery and hadn't been shot in the head. Frank used the pay phone to call the Liuzzas at home. He tried to stay calm as he explained what had happened, and sat down to wait for their arrival.

1:42 AM

IT TOOK DETECTIVE Don Curole twelve minutes to get to Charity Hospital from Homicide after he got the call. It wasn't a homicide, yet, but it sounded like the victim had been shot up pretty good. Better to get what information he could as quickly as possible. God knew he didn't need any more open files.

Curole walked into the ER and tracked down a nurse he knew from many similar trips to Charity. The victim had multiple gunshots to the chest and back. He'd lost a fair amount of blood and had shown signs of shock, but he was hanging in there in the OR. Both he and his doctors wouldn't be available until later.

Leaving the hospital, Curole headed over to Josephine and Baronne. The victim's name was Liuzza. There was a restaurant near the Quarter called Liuzza's—a down-home New Orleans place popular with locals and tourists. Curole wondered if there was a connection.

1:46 AM

NOPD CRIME TECH Anthony Cusimano pulled up at the corner, grabbed his camera, and walked toward the scene. There weren't any onlookers. Most people in this neighborhood—or any neighborhood in New Orleans, really—didn't want to get involved in these types of crimes.

It looked like a pretty straightforward shooting. The beat cops had stayed out of the area pretty well and things weren't too disturbed, so he got a few pictures and then started carefully moving around the scene.

Carter walked over to Cusimano and told him that the victim was found lying on the ground with multiple gunshots to the chest and back. Cusimano tried to figure where the shooter had stood. *He—or she—could have come from behind the building,* Cusimano thought. There was a small parking area and a wrought-iron gate that separated the sidewalk from the lot and the back door of the building. Cusimano walked through the gate, scanning the ground. No pellets or cartridges in the parking lot. Maybe the shooter had come from the other direction.

Cusimano walked back to the street and turned to look at the wall of the building. There were three bullet holes. The shots had either missed the victim or had gone through his body and into the wall.

Cusimano pulled a penknife out of his pocket and carefully pried a pellet out of one of the holes in the outside wall. Large-caliber; .357 probably. He put it in a baggie, then went and knocked on the door of the first-floor apartment. The woman who let him in gave her name—Pamela Staab. She was pretty shook-up, as the bullets had been embedded into her bedroom wall. From the inside, he could see a wooden door that had once led out into the street, a bullet hole all the way through it. Not far from the door, on the floor, was a bullet. Cusimano bagged it.

He told Ms. Staab that another officer would be along to interview her; his job was just to get any evidence out of the scene intact, keeping the chain of custody clean.

All in all, not a bad night: There was no gun, but two bullets—one that looked pretty good for a ballistics test. He hoped the victim pulled through, as it would make solving this case a whole lot easier.

2:20 AM

IT TOOK ABOUT forty-five minutes for Ray's family to arrive at the hospital. They arrived in true Italian-family style, with ten or more people making the trip in from various suburbs around the city.

In the hallway, Frank saw the doctors coming out of the OR. He walked up to them and asked how Ray was. He could see the answer in their faces even as the nurse explained what had gone wrong. They thought they had repaired all the wounds, but as they were sewing Ray up, his blood pressure had dropped. They reopened him and found another wound, one they had missed the first time. The blood loss had just been too much.

Frank didn't know if he was going to faint or throw up. He had to struggle just to breathe, had to tell himself, *You can handle this*. He thought about his drink with Ray just hours before, pictured Ray's excitement at having made VP at his father's hotel. And now . . .

He collected himself and walked over to tell the Liuzzas that Ray was gone. It was an odd experience, knowing that what he was going to say would change their lives forever. Ray's mother screamed, the others groaned, and Ray Liuzza Sr., as tough a businessman as Frank had ever seen, looked as though his face had been torn off. He just froze, then fell to the ground. Frank thought perhaps he'd suffered a heart attack. Thankfully, he had only fainted. Still, seeing the grief set in, Frank realized: *Your life stops when your child dies.* Maybe it would start up again in time, but it would never be the life they'd known before.

Not for any of us, he thought.

2

CARJACKING

MIMI LAGARDE PUSHED against the silver crash bar and opened the exit door at the New Orleans Superdome, walking out into the night air. The cool of the evening was refreshing compared to the stale, hot air from the crowd inside. She hesitated for a second, holding the door for her brothers Jay and Michael. Jay, nineteen, adjusted the camera strap around his neck as the three of them walked across the limo access road and toward the car, the boys talking excitedly about the game, a close loss for UVA, where Jay had just finished his freshman year. It was especially nice for Michael, who was only twelve, to be out on the town with his older siblings, but all three were thrilled to be in the city without their parents. Their mother would never have let fifteen-year-old Mimi go into town unless she was with Jay.

They reached the car and started to pile in. Jay popped the trunk, walking to the back to put his camera away. Mimi looked around—she didn't feel safe, suddenly. As Jay closed the trunk and walked to his door, she noticed a man walking up LaSalle in their direction, and he was moving pretty quickly. He had on a loose jacket or a zippered sweatshirt, with the hood pulled up, and a T-shirt underneath. Something about him was unnerving to Mimi.

Jay got in the car and popped the locks, and Mimi opened her door quickly and got in. She put her seat belt on as Michael got in on the passenger side behind her. Mimi was about to tell Jay to lock the doors when the man from the street jumped into the car, shoving Michael across the seat into the other door. "I've got a gun, and I'm takin' your car."

Jay tried to look at the man, but turned back quickly as the man yelled at him not to look back. Mimi jumped at the man's booming voice, her heart pounding in her chest as he threatened to kill them all if they looked at him. Jay flinched and gripped the steering wheel tightly.

He's gonna kill us, Mimi thought. She was petrified. She could see that Jay was trying to figure out what to do. He finally took his hands off the wheel, holding them open, palms toward the windshield as he told the man that he could have the car; they'd get out and he could just drive away. But the man told them he wanted their wallets, keys, jewelry—everything. He told Jay to start the car and drive.

Jay again offered to give the man the car if he'd just let them go, but the man said, "Start the car, and go right."

"Okay. No problem. No problem." Jay fumbled with the keys, got them in the ignition, and started the car. He looked over his left shoulder to check oncoming traffic and pulled out onto Poydras.

It took them about two seconds to cover the 100 feet to LaSalle, where the guy had told them to go. To the right was a dark, narrow side street with no people in sight. *He's going to kill us there,* Mimi thought. She braced for the right turn and was flung against the car door as Jay suddenly swerved hard to the left across the median gap, slamming sidelong into another car that was waiting to turn and coming to a screeching stop. Before Mimi could react, the man was thrusting his hands with the gun into the front seat, yelling, "I'm gonna kill you, fool!"

Jay had a split-second head start on the guy, turning and putting his hands up to block their captor. He and the man wrestled with the gun for a few seconds. Mimi jumped out of the car, noticing that Michael was pinned in the backseat. The man had pushed himself forward into the space between the seats. He was above Jay, trying to get leverage, both of them struggling for the gun, Jay somehow getting on his back and pulling his feet up. He was kicking the stranger again and again in the knees, stomach, and face. Finally, Jay's feet pushed the man through the passenger-side door.

The man stood up and ran down LaSalle, away from the crowd gathering around them and into the darkness. The Lagarde children watched him run away, then turned to make sure Jay was OK after the fight in the front seat. Jay walked around the car and picked up the gun, which the carjacker had dropped as he was falling out of the car. He held it up and looked at Mimi, then dropped it on the ground again. Both of them jumped as *bang!*—it fired. Neither of them were shot, but they realized that the gun had been loaded and cocked the entire time. They were lucky to be alive.

The Superdome security guards got to the scene first; the New Orleans police arrived a few minutes later. All of a sudden there were lots of cars, their flashing lights coloring the street as the cops talked into their radios. The police removed the gun from under the car and talked to each of the siblings in turn, asking them to describe the stranger. Their descriptions were each a little bit different; it had been dark, after all, and the man had been wearing a jacket with the hood up. They told the cops he was between five-foot-seven and five-foot-ten, pretty thin, had an Afro under his hood, and was wearing a loose dark jacket. They described his scraggly beard and said that he was twenty to thirty years old. That was the best they could do.

One of the officers came over to Jay, pointing to the bloodstains on his pants and shoes. "You bleeding, son?" he asked.

Jay looked down and saw that the policeman was right. There was blood on his pants and on his shoes. He felt around himself. He was all right, except for a large cut on his left hand. A few minutes later, one of the officers brought over a black man in handcuffs. "Is this the guy?" he asked.

Mimi looked at the man, who had a scraggly beard and was wearing some kind of shower cap. This guy was a lot bigger than their carjacker. Jay and Michael agreed; this wasn't the guy.

One officer, wearing gloves and holding a pair of scissors, approached Jay. He cut a hole in Jay's jeans, removing a section that had blood on it, and put the denim in a glass tube. He took Jay's bloody sneaker as well, and told the three kids that someone would call them to come to the station, answer questions, and look through some mug-shot books. He said they would need to fingerprint Jay to compare his prints to those found on the gun.

Mimi sat with Jay and Michael on the curb together, Jay in his cut jeans and one foot clad only in a sock. They waited together for their parents to come pick them up while the cops walked around, illuminated by the flashing lights of the police cars.

3

FINDING A KILLER

DECEMBER 6, 1984
10:30 AM

CUROLE SAT AT the corner of Josephine and Baronne, looking out the window of his car. He had the *Times-Picayune* on the seat next to him, the headline ROBBER KILLS HOTEL OFFICIAL DESPITE PLEAS peeking above the fold with a picture of Ray Liuzza Jr. Liuzza wasn't a bad-looking guy, Curole thought as he studied the picture: Italian, a slicked-back haircut, and a sort of dead-eyed, heavy-lidded look.

Curole wanted to close this case quickly. Liuzza Sr. had friends in high places—and he wouldn't be the only one pushing to find his son's killer.

Curole had been a cop for a long time, and he had seen this cycle before. The city was getting revved up, Son-of-Sam style, by a series of unconnected murders. Folks were getting pretty twitchy, talking about all the violence and deaths. The *Times-Picayune* was doing its share, publicizing a string of other murders and violent crimes around the city. Around Labor Day, a funeral home owner got himself shot and killed for no reason at all. On Thanksgiving, that Posey kid had been killed in some dumb name-calling fight. You could say it was good they were unrelated. Or, you could say it was horrible that so many people were killing each other in New

Orleans. Curole just wanted to arrest however many people he had to arrest to keep the body count down.

It happened from time to time, usually started by a string of murders or rapes in the white or tourist parts of town. The politicians would compete for newspaper time; the councilmen would hold press conferences for their new anticrime initiatives; Harry Connick—the district attorney for Orleans Parish and father of singer Harry Connick Jr.—and Mayor Morial and Chief Morris would talk about what they were doing to bring the criminals to justice. It all rolled downhill to him and his partner, making their job harder.

Curole got out of the car, closed the door, and walked over to the corner. The crime scene had been handled cleanly by the responding officers and the crime tech. Between them and the autopsy, done ninety minutes ago by the parish coroner, Curole had a pretty good idea of what had happened, but it always helped to go back to the scene, walk it through again, figure out who might have seen things, and make sure it all added up.

He stood on the sidewalk looking at the bloodstains. Liuzza's blood was still on the grass. He had taken five shots from a .357, none of them close enough to leave powder burns. That meant the shots had been fired from at least five feet away.

Well, it's not a suicide, he thought.

The autopsy said that one shot had hit Liuzza in the chest, below the right nipple. *That's the first one; it spins him around*, Curole thought. He was an unarmed victim, now with his back turned to the shooter. *But the shooter keeps shooting.* The next shot would have been the one that hit Liuzza in the back below the left lung, coming out his front abdomen. It wasn't a fatal shot, cleanly avoiding the chest cavity. Then came the one that hit him in the side of the buttock, exiting mid-thigh. *Second shot knocks him down; third one hits him on the way down.* Somewhere in that scenario were the two shots that did the serious damage, one hitting him mid-back, catching the spinal column, part of the right kidney, and the liver before exiting the right side of the chest. The other entered in the left rear abdomen, went through his small intestine and liver, and came out the chest.

One in the front; one in the side; three in the back. According to Carter's interview of the women in the downstairs apartment, Liuzza had been talking to the shooter, so the first two shots were probably from the front. He acted it out, miming where Liuzza had stood and how he could have turned, to make sure it made sense. *First shot in the stomach, so Liuzza bends and turns to run. Second shot in the hip; Liuzza falls. Maybe he's still trying to crawl away? Maybe he's just lying there? Either way, he's down, and that's when the shooter makes up his mind to finish the guy off.*

The beat cops had found Liuzza lying in the grass with his head north, toward Lake Ponchartrain. So the shooter probably came up from the south, from St. Charles. Liuzza hadn't put up much of a fight. He wasn't beat up at all, and the women in the apartment—and the article in the paper—said he'd been begging for his life.

Curole considered the scene some more. Maybe Liuzza had already given him the wallet when he got shot. He must have, since Paul Schliffka, the neighbor from next door, told Carter that right when he heard the shots he went to the corner. That's when he saw the shooter run past. He wouldn't have had time to go through any pockets.

It appeared to be a simple robbery/murder, nothing more sinister. That actually made the investigation harder. If there was a motive, the number of suspects would be smaller. But a random robbery and shooting? That could be just about anyone in this town.

Curole had one near eyewitness—Paul Schliffka. He had seen a six-foot-tall black guy with close-cropped hair in a jacket and jeans running by on the dark street. Even though the shooter had been within six feet of Schliffka, he still couldn't pick him out of a lineup or a mug-shot book. Further, Curole had no weapon, no ID from the victim, nobody with any motive, and absolutely nothing that linked anybody to the shooting. He was looking for a wallet, and maybe some jewelry; Liuzza Sr. said his son always wore an expensive watch and a gold ring with an "L" on it.

Curole would watch the pawn shops, send out info, interview whomever he could, and hope that something clicked. He got back in his car. Whatever clicked, he hoped it clicked fast.

DECEMBER 23, 1984
3:45 PM

Ray Liuzza had been dead for two weeks now, and Curole had nothing to go on. He'd interviewed everyone he could find in every house with a view of the crime scene, most of them twice. None of them could really give him anything. His best lead was a call-in to the Crimestoppers hotline, a woman named Mary Wells. She said some guy named Charles Bradford Ricks was the shooter.

Curole went to see her, asked her a few questions, sat back, and let her do the talking. She knew a lot of details about the crime—the way Liuzza had pleaded for his life before he was killed, how many shots were fired, where they hit him, and what he was wearing—things you'd usually have to be there to know. There was always the chance that she'd called Crimestoppers for the reward money, but this didn't feel like that. In the first place, her initial call to the police had been anonymous; he had only found it by going back and looking at the Crimestoppers reports after she mentioned it. In the second place, she seemed legitimately scared that the killer would come for her.

It was also possible that she could have gotten her story from the papers. The case was getting a lot of media attention, with the family putting out ads on the radio and flyers up in the neighborhoods. Still, she wasn't stumbling over her answers or reading some script.

Curole had brought Mary Wells's information, along with some information he'd gotten from a local FBI informant that was pretty similar to Wells's statement, to Eric Dubelier, the assistant district attorney working this case. Dubelier had authorized a polygraph, but they couldn't get it scheduled until January 9. In the meantime, the Liuzza family had collected money for a reward and they were advertising this fact around Ray's neighborhood.

The Liuzzas were political donors. The chief, the mayor, the DA—they all received money from the Liuzzas. And the Chamber of Commerce also had some pull. If the family felt like they had to beat the bushes themselves, had to help the police do their jobs, that couldn't be good. Tell the truth, though, any lead was a good lead at this point.

The other concern was Dubelier, the ADA. He had a pretty good reputation with the cops as a guy who turned their arrests into convictions and helped them hit their numbers. But he was coming off a high-profile case that the DAs had blown by mishandling evidence. More to the point, he was married to Connick's niece. Curole could see how all this was going to play out: It would be political football with him and his partner, Marco Demma, as the ball. If they arrested someone, Dubelier would prosecute, Connick would get double credit for that, and all would be well. If not, Connick could say to the Liuzzas that he had done his part and that it must have been that dog-ass NOPD who couldn't find a suspect.

All in all, it had the potential to be a first-rate shit show. *Happy holidays,* Curole thought.

DECEMBER 31, 1984
10:30 PM

"CRIMESTOPPERS HOTLINE, CAN I help you?"

"Uh, yeah," said the voice on the other end. The caller sounded like a young black male. "I'd like to report . . . I got information about a robbery and, uh . . . murder."

The operator kept her voice cool and calm. Don't ask for a name—that was rule number one. "Okay, sir, I'm so glad you called. How can I help you?"

"Uh, you know that murder been on the news, that murder of that Lalooza dude—the rich white dude? I know who done it."

The operator pulled the Crimestoppers "questionnaire" pad over and clicked on the end of her pen. "Okay, sir. You know we haven't solved that one yet, so it's really good that you called. You say this was a murder? And what was the name of the victim?"

"It was, uh, Lalooza—something like that. I don't know how to spell it. Lalooza."

"Okay, sir, thank you for that. Now, I gotta ask you some questions, have you tell me what you know, okay? You don't have to tell me who you are or nothing like that unless you want to."

"Uh, okay. What you want to know?"

"Well, first thing, do you know where this murder took place?"

"Uh-huh. Right there on Josephine and Baronne."

"That's great. And who did it, sir—do you know that?"

"Girl, why you think I'm calling? Man that did it was a dude name of Nut, live over there on Simon Bolivar."

"Does Nut have a real name?"

"Yeah, his real name John Thompson."

"Okay, sir. You said he lives on Simon Bolivar. Do you have an exact address?"

"Yeah, he live at 1302 Simon Bolivar, with his grandmother."

"Can you describe him for me?"

"Yeah. Black man, prob'ly twenny-three, twenny-five, something like that, prob'ly 'bout, you know, six feet tall, maybe 130 pounds."

"Any distinguishing features?"

"Naw, not really."

"Okay, sir, that's great. What happened?"

"Nut and Kojak, they were driving, see, and they saw this Lalooza dude on the street, and they decided they gonna rob him.

Nut had to shoot the dude, but he did it. It was an accident, see, while they were robbing him, and Kojak was in the car waiting. But they done it."

"Great. Thank you, sir; you did the right thing, calling us. Does Kojak have a real name?"

"Kevin Freeman." The caller was getting more comfortable, the "uhs" disappearing and his answers becoming more decisive. "He live at 2220 Felicity Street."

"And you said Mr. Freeman was waiting in his car? What kind of car was it?"

"Kojak's driving a '75, maybe '76 Chevy two-door, black and burgundy."

"Okay, sir. Is there anything else you can tell us about the incident? This is great information."

"Naw, that's all I know. How I get the reward?"

"Well, sir, the first question is, do you want to remain anonymous?"

"Yeah. These guys dangerous. One of them's already scared the other dude's gonna kill him. They find out I'm talking to you, I'm in some deep shit, you know. So yeah. Anonymous."

"Okay, sir. Well, I'm going to give you a number—292. And if your tip is accurate, and we arrest and convict Nut or Kojak, you can call us back and tell us that you're witness number 292, and we'll arrange a meeting place to get your reward money to you. We'll give you a check you can cash. No one needs to know your name, ever."

"Okay, that'll work," the caller said.

The operator pressed down on the receiver, let it up, and dialed Homicide. "Who's handling the Liuzza murder?" She wrote "Curole" on the bottom of the form, putting it in her out-box along with the twenty or so other "tips" that had come in that day.

JANUARY 10, 1985
12:42 AM

CUROLE SHOULD'VE KNOWN. He had worked with Mary Wells for two weeks, checking out her story, and it seemed to hold together. She'd even passed the polygraph. It was a little different from her first statement—that made him suspicious—but she had passed it. That was enough to get an arrest warrant out of Dubelier, so he and Demma went out and picked up Charles Bradford.

Poor bastard. Curole shouldn't even have wasted his time taking the guy to the station. Bradford had been hurt at work a few years back, and he walked with a limp, which would have made it difficult for him to run away like Paul Schliffka had described—or, for that matter, like Mary Wells herself had stated. But when Mary Wells looked at Bradford at the station lineup, she suddenly had no idea who he was; the man wasn't the Charles Bradford she had gone to school with.

It turned out that none of the schools Mary Wells went to even had a Charles Bradford enrolled, and the bus she said she'd been on had dropped off at a different time that night. It was all bullshit.

So now they had no Mary Wells, no strong leads, and they were following a trail that was thirty days cold and getting colder. They posted the Crimestoppers flyers in the neighborhoods, and every day, Curole would get some more worthless tips. But the hotline kept ringing—and criminals sometimes talk.

JANUARY 13, 1985
6:00 PM

CUROLE CHECKED HIS messages, picked up one from another Homicide officer who had fielded a phone call from Liuzza's landlady. She said that some guy had made contact with her, knew who had killed Liuzza, and wanted to tell the family. The landlady told him to come back later and she'd tell him what to do. She had set up a meeting between the man and Liuzza Sr. at the International Hotel at four o'clock the next day, and the landlord wanted Curole to be there.

JANUARY 14, 1985
4:00 PM

CUROLE GOT OVER to the hotel, found the head of security, and got the entire story. He and Demma were allowed to set up a recorder to tape the conversation, and Curole went into a back room to listen while the security chief met with the informant—a young black man, a projects kid. The kid didn't want to give his name or any of the particulars to the security chief. He said he'd written everything down about the crime, and his friend would show up later with the information, once he could see Liuzza Sr.

This kid is here for the reward, Curole thought. Well, that was why a reward was posted—to give someone a reason to come forward and tell the truth. Curole hated that defense-lawyer tactic of saying that since someone had gotten a reward, they weren't telling the truth. Maybe Liuzza Sr.'s money and connections couldn't bring his son back, but they sure as hell could help him find the boy's killer.

Suddenly the kid said something that caught Curole's attention: "The one that sold the man the gun, they sold him the watch and the ring, trying to set up another friend of mine, you know. He don't know where none of that stuff's from. He's in a bind, you know."

Ray Liuzza had lost a wallet, a watch, and a ring that night. Now this kid was telling the security chief that he knew who had bought them?

Then the informant was asked about the gun, asked if it was from a gun shop in the neighborhood on Howard. He said he didn't know, but it was a big, new gun; the kid had gone with the murderer to sell it to someone else. "He didn't sell it. I went and sold it for him. I didn't know it had no charges on it or nothing, until after it came on TV that the man's son was shot dead and I realized he brought me this empty gun."

"What was his name?"

The kid drew back a little, realized he'd maybe gotten ahead of himself. "Uh, I just got his nickname. I bring all that back. I got it wrote down."

He paused a moment. Then he added, "It hurt me to see what they did, shootin' him so many times with a gun that big. And they didn't get nothin' off him. Man didn't carry no money on him. They got a wallet full of credit cards, a watch, and a ring."

He knows a lot of shit about the murder, Curole thought. He said the shooter was a drug user, smoking clickems. Curole knew a little about them—joints dipped in PCP. They were pretty new in town. Screwed you up pretty good, too.

Finally, the kid gave his name—Richard Perkins. But he told the security chief to call him Funk.

Funk told the security chief that he and his friend would be back within an hour to meet with Liuzza Sr. He didn't deny wanting the reward, but also mentioned that he wanted this all to be cleared up as soon as possible, since there were two people involved.

Two people? Curole thought.

The security chief had caught that too, and asked Funk about it. Funk squirmed a little.

"Yeah. All the person there saw was one—the one that ran. That dude who ran didn't have too much to do. All he did was went on that street, ran, and left this other person, 'cause he panicked. He didn't touch the man or nothin'."

"Oh, I thought it was just the guy that did the shooting."

"No, there's two of them. One went with him, but he didn't touch no one; he just ran off and panicked and left him."

The security chief asked for Funk's social security number and then told him to give it to the operator when he came back later that evening. Funk handed over his card and his number was recorded.

It was an impressive audition. The kid, Funk, seemed pretty credible and knew his facts. Curole didn't think the papers had mentioned an eyewitness—but the kid did. If his story panned out, maybe they'd close this case after all.

JANUARY 13, 1985
9:40 PM

WHEN FUNK came back to the hotel, the security chief and Ray Liuzza Sr. were waiting. He came in with another black guy who sounded more educated, like he had a decent job. The man introduced himself as Greg Dawson, a friend of Funk's from the neighborhood. Dawson said he was an insurance agent. It made sense to Curole, Funk bringing along his professional friend who was used to negotiating with white people.

Dawson handed over some handwritten notes as they spoke. According to Funk, they had called Crimestoppers twice but hadn't gotten the response they had hoped for. Funk identified two men, Kevin "Kojak" Freeman and John "Nut" Thompson, who were involved in the killing. Funk said that Thompson told him he hadn't meant to shoot anybody but the gun had just gone off. *Yeah. It just went off, and then it just went off four more times,* Curole thought. Apparently, Thompson told Funk he was scared about the "heat on the street."

Curole turned the story over in his head. Funk's story made some sense: Thompson talks to him because he's high and scared; Thompson does the murder, and now he needs to put some distance between him and the gun, so he gives it to Funk Perkins. Funk puts two and two together and realizes he's now connected to the murder. He's pissed at the setup, and now he has a reason to come forward. In Funk's mind, since he's setting up a guy that tried to set him up, he's probably not a rat. Plus, there's the reward offered by the family, so he comes forward to the family and not to the police.

Funk was asked who he sold the gun to. It was someone in the projects—a man named J.R.; Funk said J.R. was also supposed to have the watch and the ring, but that J.R. didn't know anything about the murder connection. And when asked what color was the gun that he sold, Funk said it had a brown handle and was black— might have been a .45.

Funk claimed that Freeman and Thompson had each confessed to him. The two men had been driving around one night with the gun and saw a rich-looking man. They parked the car a block away and went to rob him.

Curole had been right—no more sinister motive than a robbery of a well-dressed guy in the wrong place at the wrong time. The story's logic held together, but best of all, the facts could be tested. If they found J.R. and the gun, everything else would pan out.

Funk agreed to give the police a signed statement and tell them the story he had just revealed (and which Curole had already gotten on tape without Funk's knowledge). Funk was to come to the station and ask for Curole.

JANUARY 14, 1985
3:55 PM

Curole pulled the records on Thompson and Freeman before Funk Perkins came in to the station. Both men had records—nothing violent, just some drug offenses. He made copies of each man's Bureau of Investigation photos and showed them to Perkins, who didn't have any trouble picking the mug shots out of an impromptu photo lineup.

Perkins signed a statement that was almost identical to the story he'd told the day before: Three days after the shooting, he said he'd gone with John Thompson to J.R.'s house to sell the gun. Thompson had stayed outside while Perkins went in and sold the gun to J.R. for $75 and some weed. A few days after that, Kevin Freeman told Funk about the murder, while both of them were high, and while Thompson was in jail for something. Perkins didn't know what Thompson was in jail for, but it wasn't anything serious, as Thompson had been out again less than a week later. With Thompson now out of jail, Perkins got him talking too. Thompson told Perkins he and Freeman had done it; he said they had just intended to rob a rich guy and they figured they'd find someone near St. Charles. The robbery went bad, and Liuzza ended up dead.

Funk said he knew where J.R. lived and could take Curole there.

JANUARY 15, 1985
2:30 PM

FUNK WAS WORKING out better and better. They were waiting for Dubelier to get them a search warrant for J.R.'s house, now that Funk had pointed it out, and the address matched a Junior Lee Harris, so that was looking real. In the meantime, Curole had gone through the pile of Crimestoppers questionnaires, and voilà—another John Thompson lead. Ken Carr, a concerned and impartial citizen, had told Crimestoppers that he was alone in Harry's Bar on New Year's Eve and had overheard two guys talking. One of the men was clearly agitated—said he'd shot and killed a white man and now the cops were all over the neighborhood, posting flyers for a reward, and he was scared. The speaker told his companion that it was an accident—he had to shoot the white man because the victim was trying to take the speaker's gun—but now the heat was getting pretty heavy and he was scared.

Curole looked at the form for any given names and they found *Nut* written under "Alias," and *John Thompson* recorded further down.

He smiled. Maybe this Funk kid was gonna work out after all.

4

ARRESTED

JOHN THOMPSON OPENED his eyes and looked around in the darkness. His initial confusion was softened by the realization that his arm was around Denise, he was sleeping in her bed, and their three-year-old son, John Jr.—known as Tiger—was in the next room.

The phone, which was what had woken him up, rang again. John rolled his body a little and reached his free hand to get the phone, trying not to wake Denise. "Hello?"

"Nué," his grandmother said, "where you at?"

John looked at the clock. "Momma, what you callin' me at three AM for? You know where I'm at—you callin' me here."

"Baby, the police was here lookin' for you."

John rubbed his eyes, a little exasperated. He tried to keep his voice down. No sense getting angry at his grandmother. "Uh-huh. What they want?"

"Man say he want to talk to you. What you done, baby?"

"Momma, I ain't done nothin'. Who was it? What they say to you?"

"They just say they want to talk to you, ask me when you gonna be home. I told 'em you weren't here, that I didn't know where you were, but when you came home I'd call 'em. Man left his card. Baby, it says Homicide. What you got yourself into?"

John sat up a little at that, not used to being questioned by Homicide. "Naw, Momma—nothin' to worry about. They must think I saw somethin' on the street or somethin'."

"You comin' home in the morning?"

"Yeah, Momma, I'm comin' home. Just here with Denise and Tiger."

"Okay, baby. Good night."

"Good night, Momma."

He hung up the phone and moved his body back into the bed, pulling Denise closer to him. He liked the way she felt against him. She calmed him down. Still, he heard the worry in his grandmother's voice, and he fell back asleep wondering why a policeman from Homicide was knocking on her door.

IT HAPPENED AGAIN an hour later—the phone ringing and waking John up. He rolled over and grabbed it. "What."

"John? Why the cops tearin' up my house lookin' for you?" It was his mother this time.

"What you mean?"

"You know what I mean. You know why they been here. Four police. They just came and beat on my door, woke me up, came in here lookin' for you. What you done?"

"What? Nothin'."

"Don't even tell me. You sellin' that shit, now I gotta deal with the police knockin' down my door middle of the goddamn night."

John's irritation got the better of him, and he raised his voice. "So you gotta call me here? Now? It's the middle of the damn night. We can't talk about this in the mornin'?"

"Police didn't want to talk about it in the mornin', did they?"

"Okay, okay," John said. "I'll deal with it in the mornin'." He hung up the phone, thinking, *Shit.*

WHEN JOHN WOKE up again, it was morning. He was alone in the bed and could hear Denise in the front room with Tiger. Tiger was laughing, a belly laugh that made John smile. He was playing with some toy that made a lot of noise. The boy loved that toy. It always made him laugh, and he'd keep pushing those buttons forever. John listened to the boy playing with his mother, heard the love between them, and rolled out of bed.

He put on jeans and a T-shirt and walked into the front room with a "Hey, baby." Denise looked up and smiled. "Hey yourself," she said. "Say hello to your son."

"Hey, Tiger," John said. Tiger looked up, then back to the toy. He pushed a button, made the sound, and laughed.

Denise smiled. "See how smart he is?"

John stood next to Denise, cradling her head into his stomach, and said, "I see." He stepped away from her, saying, "I gotta go home, see how Momma is. I'll come back later."

"Don't be long; we gotta go to the store today."

John reached down and picked Tiger up, holding him in one arm. It was getting harder to do; Tiger was getting big fast. The boy gave John a one-armed hug but was still focused on the toy, so John put him down again.

"Why don't you all come with me?" he said to Denise.

She smiled, pleased to be invited. He waited for a few minutes while she put together a bag of things for Tiger. She wasn't asking why there were phone calls in the middle of the night. *She probably thinks it's like usual, people looking for late-night fixes*, he thought, and he didn't tell her any different.

It took about twenty minutes to get to John's grandmother's house, where he lived when he wasn't sleeping at Denise's. His grandmother was awake, watching TV in the kitchen when they came in. John kissed the old woman on the forehead and said, "Sorry, Momma. Sorry those police woke you up. What they want?"

The look he got from the old woman was like a kick in the stomach. It was a look that you can only get from a woman you love who wants you to be better than you are. She said, "Nué, baby, what you done?"

"Nothin', Momma. I'm gonna take a shower." He kissed her cheek, turned to go upstairs.

His grandmother said, "I told the police I'd call them when you came home."

He stopped walking and turned around. "Momma, you can call them if you want. You want to call them, go right ahead. I got nothin' to hide."

"This the man who came," she said, handing him a business card. Detective Donald Curole, New Orleans Police Department, Homicide Division. John put it down on the counter. "Okay, Momma. I'll call him. I'm gonna take a shower now."

He walked upstairs and turned the shower on, letting it heat up. When it was hot, he stepped in, letting it rain down on him, wishing it could get into his brain and rinse out his thoughts, free them up like the steam.

DON CUROLE SAT in his car outside Thompson's grandmother's house. The old lady had called him, like she said she would, and told him John was home. That sort of thing always made Curole scratch his head—family giving up family like that. Had she given up on the boy, given him to the streets, or did she think that he was so good he couldn't possibly have done anything wrong—that he didn't need any protection from the police?

Curole patted his chest pocket, feeling the folded arrest warrant.

It had been pretty straightforward once they'd found Funk. Funk took them to J.R.'s house, then they let him go. They got a warrant for J.R.'s house and had gone back around midnight last night.

J.R. was there. His name wasn't really J.R.; it was Junior, Junior Harris. Once Junior realized they were looking for a murder weapon, he was pretty eager to help and get the hell out of the way. He told Curole he didn't have the gun anymore, that he'd sold it, and that he'd never used it. What he did have, though, was a ring on his pinky finger—a gold ring with an "L" on it.

Curole asked him where he got the ring, and Junior said he'd bought it from John Thompson; he had paid six dollars for it. Curole pulled the ring out from an envelope beside him on the passenger seat and rolled it in his fingers. *Six bucks,* he thought. *Not much to die for.*

Junior had sold the gun to another guy down the street, a guy named Jessie Harrison. He walked them over to Harrison's house. Like Junior, Harrison didn't want any part of a murder weapon, either, and he didn't want to piss off Curole and Demma; he let them look around without a warrant.

Their search of Harrison's house turned up two guns, one of which was a .357 that matched Funk's description of the gun he had sold. They'd have to see the ballistics test to be sure, but Curole figured that it was most likely the murder weapon. And the gun, along with Funk's story, had been enough to satisfy Dubelier, who got them arrest warrants for Freeman and Thompson. By 3:00 AM, they were back on the street looking for their killers. They found Freeman at home and arrested him without a problem, and now they were back at Thompson's place.

A squad car pulled up next to Curole's—the backup he'd called for. Curole grabbed his gun, put it on his hip. He got out of the car and strolled up the walk while the uniforms went around to the back.

JOHN HEARD THE police downstairs, speaking to his grandmother, then calling his name.

He pulled on a shirt and a pair of shorts and walked down the stairs. There were four cops at the bottom waiting for him. The one in front, a big white guy, said, "John Thompson?" like he was confirming it.

John knew what was going to happen as he walked down the stairs. When he reached the bottom, Curole turned him around and put handcuffs on him. John sighed, wishing the cops could have done it outside rather than right in front of his grandmother, his girlfriend, and his son. The TV played the theme from *The Young and the Restless*. Denise said, "What you doing? Where you taking him? He ain't done nothing; why you arresting him? You ain't even asked him nothing. He ain't done nothing."

Curole turned John back around to face him, saying, "John Thompson, you're under arrest for the murder of Raymond Liuzza Jr. You have the right to remain silent." He reached behind John and got a hand on John's wrists and gently guided him to the door. The other cops watched cautiously, making sure John didn't try anything. Curole continued, "You have the right to an attorney. If you can't afford an attorney, one will be provided to you."

John turned to his grandmother, whose face showed both fear and sadness. She looked like she had known this moment was coming, and still, she couldn't avoid it. He said, "Momma, I ain't done nothin'. I'll see you soon."

He glanced over at Denise, who wore a different expression. Denise was mad. John didn't know if she was mad at him or at the cops. Probably both. He said, "Denise, I love you, baby. Take care of Tiger; I'll be back soon."

Then they were out the door, down the steps, and into the car.

THE COPS PUSHED John into Orleans Parish Prison for booking. It was an old, industrial building, filled with shouts and curses, the drab walls coated with sweat and layers of filth. The cops took his prints and his picture, and threw him into a holding tank along with every other drunk, addict, or banger they'd pulled off the street the night before.

John kept quiet, but he was scared. He hadn't ever been in one of these places before. He'd spent some time in juvey, but that wasn't anything like this. Then last month, he'd been pulled in for parking tickets, but that was just a quick hold, nothing serious. Now, here he was in OPP with probably sixty or seventy guys in a space that shouldn't have held more than twenty. There were guys passed out on the floor, sleeping off whatever had got them in here, some of them lying in their own mess, smelling up the room.

John tried to move forward, to find some space, but anywhere he tried to go he was moving someone else out of their spot in the crowd. He tried to figure out the right attitude to take. Should he say "Excuse me"? He felt like if he did that, he'd sound weak, and this wasn't the place to show weakness. Still, he knew he better be ready to show respect; he didn't want whatever guy he bumped into thinking he was starting something. He'd had practice on the streets with staying on the edges of fights, finding the balance between not staring down and not getting stared down.

A few minutes after they let him in, the door opened again, and the cops brought in breakfast. A guard pushed a cart of food in front of the door, and suddenly a line was forming. Grits, black toast, and stale coffee. There was nowhere to sit with it, and no one was moving to make way for anyone else, so John wedged his way over to the line, got his plate, let the line push him away from the cart, and ate standing up, trying hard not to spill in the jostling crowd.

He didn't know how long he had been in there, but at some point the door opened and a guard called his name. John walked outside the holding tank and the guard put cuffs and leg shackles on him. He walked down the hall—the shackles forcing him to take tiny steps—until he was told to stop in front of a door. The guard took off the cuffs and shackles and gave him a green shirt and pants with OPP emblazoned on the back in white letters. Then the cuffs and manacles were put back on, and he was walked into Tent City.

"Welcome to your new home," the guard said.

It wasn't even a cell. He couldn't believe it. They had sent him to jail and he didn't even get a cell. He asked the guard, "What's all this?"

The guard said, "We got too many of you dumb niggers breaking the law and getting locked up; don't have enough room for everyone to get a cell. So you get a tent here in the City, four guys to a tent, sleeping on the floor. And don't worry—it's all locked down."

Maybe you arrestin' too many niggers, John thought, but he figured there wasn't much point in saying that.

5

POSITIVE ID

STEWART **L**AGARDE **PULLED** the blue Honda Accord into the driveway nose first—the same car his children had been attacked in. It had been three weeks since the incident, and he was still calling the police every other day, asking if there was any new progress on finding the guy who had tried to carjack his kids. There never was; the only prints on the gun had been Jay's.

Today, though, Stewart thought his luck might be changing. He had a copy of the newspaper with an article titled TWO HELD IN SLAYING OF HOTEL EXEC. It had a photo of a black man, his hands behind him in cuffs and his head down, being escorted by two white cops, and a mug shot of a skinny black man with a pencil mustache and an Afro. The caption said the man in the mug shot was John Thompson, and that he'd shot and killed some hotel executive near Charles Street for a wallet, using a .357 magnum.

That's the guy, Stewart thought. *That's the guy who tried to rob and kill my children.* It was the same kind of gun, same period of time, and it happened when the black man just walked up to a white person on the street and robbed him. Thompson had the scruffy hair the kids had described—the whole bit. Inside the house, Stuart called Mimi over to look at the newspaper photo. She was fairly certain it was the guy who'd been in their car. He then showed the picture to Michael, who agreed. That was all he needed to hear.

Stewart picked up the phone and called the NOPD.

FEBRUARY 11, 1985
6:34 PM

Bruce Whittaker put one file in his out-box and pulled out the next from his never-ending in-box. *Let's see what we've got here,* he thought.

Whittaker was the armed robbery screener for the New Orleans district attorney's office. Screening was the first step toward "management" at the DA's office, and it came with a pay raise that was certainly welcome to anyone who was trying to make a living as an assistant district attorney.

It wasn't much of a life: long hours running stressful cases full of awful people doing horrible things, and all for crappy pay. But Whittaker had personally disposed of about 3,000 cases over the past couple of years, including fifty or so jury trials. It was important work—work to feel good about, striking back at the bad guys.

Whittaker had a personality and some street smarts, and he did well in court. He was a likeable, everyman kind of guy, with a face that showed exactly what he was thinking—which certainly worked to his advantage in front of a jury.

He hadn't exactly set the world on fire as a law student, but to tell the truth, the best students usually didn't join the DA. The criminal courts needed guys like Whittaker, guys who really only wanted to put away bad guys and didn't care so much about how much they got paid to do it. The violent crimes that made New Orleans a dangerous place and gave it a bad reputation—the murders, the rapes, the armed robberies—those were the cases he and his colleagues handled.

His job, screening cases to make sure there was enough evidence to convict, was a priority to his boss. Harry Connick had been DA for about fifteen years—long enough to implement his individual philosophy of criminology. Connick believed there were more criminals than there was time to prosecute them, so the key was to prosecute efficiently, only going to trial with the cases likely to win. There were exceptions, of course—high-profile cases that needed a trial so that the public would see justice being done. But in general, Connick relied on his screeners to make sure the cases were winnable, that the cops were doing their jobs, and that the arrests were strong enough to get a conviction before the DA's office charged anyone.

Accepting fewer cases could be seen as being weak on crime, though, so Connick didn't let anyone plead a case out. There was no deterrence if criminals thought they could cut a deal, and reduced sentences reduced faith in the system. This philosophy meant that Connick's office relied on the screeners, guys like Whittaker. He screened all the armed robbery arrests, decided whether to take the case, and determined what to charge. Once the criminal was charged, he or she either pleaded guilty or went to trial.

Connick tried to act like the cause of a case was bigger than the numbers, but numbers shaped public opinion, and Connick was a politician. The perception of his office was at least as important as its actual performance, and Connick was a master at understanding the temperament of the city. His roots ran deep into the city's culture, including its music; he and his wife still had a jazz record shop in the city, and he was known as "The Singing DA" for his regular nightclub performances, where he sang jazz standards. Rumor had it his son, Harry Jr., was a pretty fine performer too.

Even with his personal charm and knowledge of the city, the perception of the DA's office was pretty bad just now, with the city all up in arms over an upswing in violent crime and the office taking hits on a couple of tough public cases. One of those cases—involving a college basketball recruit—had been a disaster, attracting national media attention. A local judge had thrown the prosecution out of court when the player's defense lawyer uncovered some previously undisclosed evidence that the DAs had in their file but hadn't turned over to the court. Months later, they were still getting bad press from it. Whittaker certainly didn't want any repeats on his watch.

Whittaker refocused on the case report in front of him. Armed robbery, John Thompson, black male, twenty-two years old. There was a note saying this case was attached to a separate murder case, with Dubelier, a Special Prosecutor, on the murder. That caught Whittaker's eye. If it had a Special, it must be a big case. It made sense that it was the Liuzza murder, as the papers had been running with that for a while.

It was interesting, though not surprising, that this case was going to Dubelier. He was aggressive, macho. Connick would certainly want someone good on it, and Dubelier fit the bill. Dubelier was Whittaker's boss, and had the third-highest job in the office, behind Connick and the first assistant. He was a tough, aggressive, abrasive guy, hypercompetitive. Every motion, every objection, every moment in a case was a new chance for Eric Dubelier to win something. No issue was too small to fight. He wanted to win motion by motion, objection by objection, never giving an inch until the case was won and the criminals were in prison.

Dubelier was teamed with Jim Williams, the homicide screener, on this particular case. Williams was probably the most successful homicide trial lawyer in the office. He had a different style than Dubelier but wasn't any less aggressive. Dubelier was about winning, about beating the other side. Williams was a true believer, one of those guys who thought he was God's instrument of justice.

So Dubelier and Williams would be trying John Thompson for the murder of Ray Liuzza. Whittaker looked at the mug shot of the young black man, with his Afro and wide-eyed stare. Thompson was charged with Murder One in the Liuzza case; for Connick that meant they were seeking a death sentence. But, usually, to get the death penalty, the accused needed prior violent felonies, since most juries wouldn't send a first-timer to death. Whittaker looked at the rap sheet—a lot of minor crimes until this armed robbery, no other felonies.

Whittaker read the police report on the carjacking: three white teenagers outside the Superdome; one carjacker with a .357; no injuries. The kids had given a description that matched Thompson, but they hadn't caught him at the scene. No one had ID'd him until the kids had seen his picture in the paper for the Liuzza arrest.

To charge armed robbery, Whittaker needed to prove that Thompson used a dangerous weapon and that he took property by force or by threat of force. They had the gun on the scene and witness testimony, so the dangerous weapon was in place. There was a bullet fired, pulled out of the car, and ballistics would prove it was the right gun. And the attacker had gotten away with the driver's wallet, so that took care of the taking of property. All the required elements of the crime were present. What they needed now was a definitive connection to Thompson.

There weren't any prints on the gun, so that wouldn't work. There had been a fight between one of the kids and the attacker, and there were some fabric samples with blood collected—a piece of the driver's pants and a tennis shoe. They might want to do a blood test on those. Whittaker made a note of that on his screening form. If the blood was the attacker's and wasn't from one of the kids, and if Thompson had a matching blood type, that would be a slam dunk.

Without any physical evidence, they'd be relying completely on the IDs from the three kids in the car. They weren't great IDs, to Whittaker's way of thinking. Three white teenagers from the suburbs giving an ID on a black man three weeks after the crime based on a newspaper photo of a mug shot from a different arrest with a headline saying he was a murderer? Defense lawyers ate that kind of thing for breakfast, lunch, and dinner. But that was what they had. No one else reported seeing the guy, despite the fight in the car.

Whittaker rubbed his eyes, took off his glasses, and absentmindedly chewed on the earpieces. Eyewitness testimony was always dicey in court. People made mistakes; they were in stressful situations and wanted to catch someone, which made them suggestible.

Public defenders were used to this, and they'd take a purely eyewitness case apart. He'd have to dig deeper.

WHITTAKER CALLED JAY Lagarde in Charlottesville. He'd decided to do the ID legwork himself, even though he usually told the NOPD to do it themselves. This would be a little more complex than the usual lineup, since Jay Lagarde was a college student in Virginia and Mimi and Michael were minors.

Whittaker had sixty days, by law, to charge the case or drop it. Jay Lagarde was 1,500 miles away, and he wasn't planning on coming home anytime soon. Whittaker didn't have the budget to fly the kid to New Orleans for the ID, so he came up with a plan to use a photo lineup to confirm Jay's ID. The kid seemed pretty sharp, so Whittaker figured he could do it the way it needed to be done.

He put seven photos in an envelope along with careful instructions. He even thought about the order of the photos—if he made Thompson photo number 1, or number 7, he'd get crucified on the stand for drawing attention to him by the order of the photos. So he made him number 5, and put in the letter all the instructions necessary to ensure that nothing in the photos or the letter could prejudice Jay's ID.

If all three Lagarde kids independently identified Thompson in the photos, then the jury would see each of them separately ID Thompson in open court. The defense would still make the argument that the kids were tying the photo ID to the photo in the newspaper, but there was nothing he could do about that. All the men in the photos looked a lot like Thompson—the closest matches Whittaker had been able to find in the Bureau of Investigation books. He put the envelope in the mail.

MARCH 7, 1985

WHITTAKER PARKED IN front of the Lagarde house. He had waited to interview the younger kids until receiving Jay's response. Jay had passed that test, signing on the back of photo 5 that Thompson was the carjacker. *Let's see if the younger kids can do their job,* he thought. Thompson had been arraigned that day, had been assigned his lawyer, and so now was the time to make sure the DA was really going to take this case forward.

Inside, Whittaker laid out the same seven photos, in the same order he had sent them to Jay, on the living room table for Mimi. He asked her to look at the photographs and point out the man who had carjacked them, if she could. Mimi moved through the photos carefully. When she got to photo number 5, she said, "That's the man who robbed us."

Jackpot, Whittaker thought. Number 5 it was. After Mimi signed the back of the photo, she left the room and Michael came in. Whittaker showed Michael the same photos, and he pointed to both numbers 5 and 6. Michael said, "Number 5 looks like the man, and number 6 kind of looks like the man." To be careful, Whittaker asked Michael to write that down on the back of each picture.

Three independent IDs on the photo lineup— Whittaker was convinced. He drove back to the office to start processing Thompson for armed robbery.

6

GOOD COP, BAD COP

"Thompson."

The guard woke up John roughly, poking him hard with a nightstick, smacking him on the upper arms and shins to rouse him. "Let's go. Get up."

John didn't say anything. He was a little disoriented, which made him less aggressive than he would otherwise have been, but he'd seen this drill before and knew he'd have to play along.

They'd been sweating him for several days. They'd leave him alone during the day, letting him fend for himself in Tent City. At night, though, when he was tired or asleep, they'd come to get him for questioning. The guard would wake him up, not making a lot of noise, but enough that other prisoners would notice.

John had already had a couple of guys look at him funny when he was brought back to the tier. Maybe they thought he was snitching. They knew he was up against a murder charge. They thought what the guards wanted them to think: that he was getting pulled out of the tier on a nightly basis to keep the guards informed of what was going on inside. Isolating him from the inmates, making him a target. It was just another one of their games.

John's head cleared as they put the cuffs on him and pushed him down the hall and toward the interrogation room. It looked like another night of the same questions, asking John why he killed

Ray Liuzza, why he and Kojak did it, or to tell them the truth about what happened. *You might be a lot of things, but you're no rat,* John thought. If this was the worst they could throw at him, he'd be fine. Even if they got rough, he was all right with that. John wasn't a big guy—five-nine in sneakers, 165 pounds—but he was tough. He'd been in fights before, and knew he could take the punishment of getting slapped around by an angry cop if that's what it came to.

As he was led into the interrogation room, John found himself wondering what bruises from a beating would make the others think when he got back on the tier. Would they make him seem more like a tough guy who wasn't talking? Or would they make the other inmates think he was definitely an informant, going the extra distance to make it look real so no one would suspect?

It was a small room, with a steel table and three chairs, two on the same side as the door and one on the far side. The two cops that had arrested him were there, one sitting in the lone chair facing the door, the other standing defiantly in the corner, arms folded, like they'd been waiting for quite some time.

These guys had questioned John before, and John had given them his story. It was a simple one, and he'd said it again and again, the same words over and over: "I don't know. I wasn't there." John figured the simplest story was always the best, and how were they going to prove anything different? Did they have any witnesses? Did they have his fingerprints on the gun? If they had any concrete evidence, he figured they would have said so. It wouldn't have mattered if they did, since they got the gun from someone else. How could they connect it to him—and what if they did? Did having the gun mean he'd shot someone?

One thing was different, though. This time there was a third cop in the room, a black cop John hadn't seen before. The black cop was half sitting and half leaning on the table, one foot touching the floor, the other propped on a chair, which he now pushed out, scraping its legs against the floor and motioning for John to sit down.

The black cop smiled at John. "John, come on in and sit down. Sorry we had to wake you, but we got some new information on your case, thought we should talk it over with you soon as possible, you know?"

"Uh-huh." John had it figured out before he even sat down. Good cop, bad cop. Get the black cop to talk to the black folk, like John would just confess to this police just because he's black. *Stupid motherfuckers,* he thought. "I already told you each the last three days: I don't know what happened. I wasn't there. You think you get a new guy askin' the questions that's gonna change the answer? It won't. I don't know; I wasn't there."

The black cop seemed offended. He said, "Man, now, you getting all defensive right from the start. That's the wrong move. I'm here to help you. We know you didn't do nothing wrong. We know you didn't shoot Ray Liuzza."

The cop got up from the table and walked behind John, and John noticed for the first time that the cop had opened John's wallet and left it open on the table between them, revealing pictures of Denise, Tiger, and his other son, Dedric. Dedric was about two years older than Tiger, and the boys had different mothers. John didn't see Dedric as much, but seeing that cop holding Dedric's picture made John just as angry.

John held his anger in, though, and looked at the policemen and at the chair that had been offered. He stood an extra second, showing them that he didn't have to do whatever they told him unless he agreed, and then sat down. "You know so much, why don't you let me go the fuck home? You know so much, you know I didn't do it, why you got me in here right now?"

"Man, why you bein' so tough? This ain't even your fight." The cop put his hand over the wallet and the photos. "Listen up, now. You're gonna lose your family, John. This girl, I don't know if she's your wife, your girlfriend. But you gonna lose her, and you gonna lose these two young boys here. What for? To protect some dude from the neighborhood ain't gonna do nothin' for ya? Come on, man. Help me out so I can help you out. Tell us what we need to know to put Kojak away for this. You don't need to go down with him. You ain't gonna prove nothin' being all hard."

"You ain't got nothin' on me 'cause I didn't do nothin'," John said. "I got nothin' to say, and Kevin Freeman ain't tellin' you shit."

The cop nodded, like he knew this was coming, like he'd seen it all before. He said, "Yeah, okay, I hear you. You ain't done nothin'. That's good. I'm glad." He pulled a tape recorder out of his pocket. "Before you get all righteous, though, you might wanna listen to this." He pressed PLAY on the tape recorder and set it on the table.

The tape played Kojak's voice; Kevin Freeman described the scene. He said he was walking down the street with John Thompson—that the two were looking for someone to rob. Kevin explained that he and John saw a white man getting out of a silver BMW and described how John said, *Yo, man, let's go hit that dude. I got the heat here with me.* Freeman told the cops that this was the moment he'd learned that Thompson was carrying a gun, and it was the moment he had decided that he didn't want to have anything to do with whatever Thompson thought was going to happen. Freeman took off running down Josephine, away from the Lake, away from John Thompson and his armed robbery. He hadn't gotten too far away, though, when he turned back, seeing Thompson standing over the body of a man, holding the gun.

The tape stopped, and John looked around at the cops. The white cops were wearing these satisfied looks on their faces. John ignored them and talked only to the black cop. "Man, you know that don't mean shit. How I know that's even Kevin Freeman? Could be one of y'all's voices on that tape."

It was an act. John was far more shaken than he was prepared to let on. The voice was real. Kevin Freeman had turned on him. He couldn't deal with that now, though. For now, it was best to keep his story clean and simple and not to get involved in a back-and-forth with Kevin Freeman. "Y'all ain't got shit on me. You can't, 'cause I didn't do it, so fuck y'all sayin' I'm playin' it for a game."

At that, the nice, amused, helpful expression on the black cop vanished. He turned to the white cops and said, "You give us a minute?" They nodded and walked out. He waited for the door to close, and then turned back to John.

"Man, John," he said, "you ain't thinkin' this through real good. I know you all hard, and you ain't got to talk to no po-lice. But you gotta play ball here, man. Look at these pictures." He held up the photos of his family, one by one by one. "You got a good-lookin' girl, John; you got two beautiful kids. These men here, they don't give a shit about ruinin' your life. Way they look at it is, you can help them get a murderer off the streets, or you can spend the rest of your life in prison with him. It don't make one bit of difference to them. In fact, it goes the other way. You don't help them, you're no better than that murderer, and they are gonna *enjoy* puttin' your sorry black ass in jail for the rest of your life.

"I'm tellin' you, man, they got all they need to do it, too. Not just this tape. Your picture's in the paper for the arrest, man. You're famous. Guess what's next. White folks see a black man's picture in the paper for a murder, they look at him, and guess what? We all look alike, don't we? You know? So they start thinkin', that's the homeboy killed my son. Or that's the homeboy robbed my wife, or my kids. And they start callin' in, reportin' crimes, tellin' us you the man that did 'em all. You know that's how it's gonna be. And these guys"—he pointed his thumb at the door—"they are gonna take you out of this room here and walk you over and process you for a new armed robbery unless *you* start tellin' us what you know."

John looked at the mirror on the wall. He knew the white cops were there behind it, watching to see what he was gonna do. Like there was any question.

John started talking, but his voice didn't sound like itself. "Man, how you think you gonna bust me on some murder I didn't even do? You ain't got nothin' on me. You can't, because *I didn't do nothin'*. You know you got shit; that's why you guys are tryin' all this crazy made-up shit. You gonna try to get me talkin' with some other voice on a tape accusin' me; play that shit, I don't even care. I know what I didn't do, and I ain't got nothin' to tell you because I got no idea what Kojak did, or what anyone did to no one. I didn't do nothin'. I got no idea what happened. I got nothin' more I can say."

He sat there, waiting for any reaction, thinking about how he'd settle things with Kojak once he got back on the tier. How he'd settle it his way. He was a lot of things, but he wasn't a rat.

The cop looked at John and shook his head a little. He pushed away from the table with a theatrical sigh. "Okay, John. Have it your way." He opened the door to the room. The white cops came back in. The one with the beard said, "We make any progress?"

"No. Same story."

The cop smiled smugly at John. "Okay, tough ass, let's go."

John stood up from the table and walked toward the exit. The cops walked him down the hall, and just like the black cop said, they booked John for armed robbery.

As he had predicted, John was back in Tent City in time for breakfast, getting walked by the guards past the other tents and over to his so everyone could see him and think that he was ratting on Kevin Freeman. For the first time, though, John knew it was really the other way around.

7

ROBBERY TRIAL

APRIL 11, 1985

JOHN LOOKED AROUND as he was led into the courtroom by the bailiff. His mother was there, and Denise, both women dressed up in their Sunday best. They were clearly upset. John nodded at them confidently, and smiled. He was telling them not to worry. By the time the day was over, this would all be over, and the charge would be thrown out. He made an awkward thumbs-up motion, the best he could do without lifting his shackled arms.

He had met with his lawyer, Numa Bertel, for the first time two days before, and Bertel knew his defense. John thought he was the right lawyer to represent him, too. A longtime criminal lawyer in New Orleans, Bertel had been the first assistant DA to Jim Garrison, Harry Connick's predecessor, in the 1960s. When Garrison lost the position to Connick, Bertel had changed sides, going to work for the Indigent Defender's Office. Since then, he had defended thousands of guys just like John.

Bertel told John that the DA had three white teenagers who would ID him for the carjacking, but John wasn't too worried about that. He had an alibi, had given Bertel some names. Bertel had said he would round up the guys who could prove his story.

They spent the first few hours picking a jury—hours during which John sat in the courtroom, bored out of his mind. When they were finally done with that, the judge, a big bearded man named

Patrick Quinlan, talked to the jury about what they were going to do. And then the trial began.

There were two DAs running the case against John, an older one and a younger one. The younger one, Deegan, didn't say much. The older one, a tall white man named Jim Williams, was really in control. He didn't look like much to John, but he had a lot of energy as he described to the jury what he alleged had happened on December 28, when the kids came out of a basketball game and got in their car, and John attacked them. Williams focused on the girl, Mimi. "She'll tell you that that man, as they were getting into the car, ran up to them, and he produced a gun." Williams reached into a box and pulled out the .357 that Jay Lagarde had dropped under the car at the scene. "He produced this gun right there, and he told them all to get into the car. He said, 'I want everything you got,' and he said, 'I want the car,' and he told them where to drive."

Williams had a flair for the dramatic. "He had the gun—this gun—this big gun—this big black gun, pointed at the front seat, at these three young people."

He forgot to mention that the people were small and white, thought John bitterly.

Williams continued, describing the crime as it had occurred, covering the car crash, the fight between Jay Lagarde and the carjacker, and the carjacker escaping into the night. He described the scene and the evidence. John thought it was odd that Williams told the jury that the gun had no fingerprints on it, but the jury didn't seem to be too concerned with that. He also told the jury that Mimi had identified John because John's picture was in the paper, but he didn't tell them that it was because he'd been arrested for the Liuzza murder. *Figures,* John thought.

Williams droned on for a while longer, but John wasn't really paying attention. He figured the jury would smell what this big white guy was cooking easy enough, and that his lawyer would straighten things out.

When it was Bertel's turn, he said, "You will hear from the State's own witnesses that before they saw the so-called ID photograph, they had been shown pictures of my client. They know who he was, and they will testify, armed with that knowledge, they then proceeded to identify him in photographs. We do not propose to tell you that there wasn't an armed robbery, but we will produce testimony that will indicate to you that John Thompson was not the man who did it, and I'm sure that if you listen, that you would never convict somebody if they didn't prove this case beyond a reasonable doubt. I'm convinced you will not send that man to jail for a possible term of ninety-nine years. You will find him not guilty, and we will thank you for it."

Ninety-nine years? John thought. It was the first time anyone had told him the maximum sentence for his charge. *For robbery? It ain't like someone died,* John thought.

Mimi Lagarde took the stand first, looking nervous. The DA questioned her, walking her through the events of that night. She looked at the photos that Bruce Whittaker had shown her weeks before and told the jury that she was sure John was the man who had robbed her and her brothers at gunpoint.

John just shook his head. *We all look alike to you, I guess,* he was thinking.

Numa Bertel questioned the girl. He had a nice, Southern gentleman's way of walking around and asking questions, like it was a conversation, not like he was trying to expose her as a liar or anything. Mimi's description of her attacker had been pretty vague: the man was "short," but she wasn't sure exactly how short, and he was "probably an older man—in his thirties."

John smiled at that. No one would think that was him. After all, he was only twenty-two.

From there, Bertel got into the real situation. "Your father was quite interested in seeing that this man was caught."

"Yes," the girl said.

"Is it fair to say that he kept in contact with the police to determine if they'd caught the man?"

"He did try to keep in contact with the police," she said. "He brought me the newspaper, and told me to look at it, and for me to tell him if I thought that was the man who robbed me."

Bertel acted as if all of a sudden the case had been made clear to him, acting a little bit for the jury. "Ohhh, your father brought the newspaper to you, and said, 'Mimi, look at this, and see if this is the man that robbed you.' "

"Yes."

"Mimi, I noticed when you testified, you said you got a pretty good look at his face. Now, *pretty good* means not necessarily very good. Is that correct?"

"That's correct."

"When people say pretty good, it's not like very good. Is that right?"

"I got a good-enough look at this face for me to be testifying against him," the girl replied.

John looked up at that, looked over at the jury. They were all paying attention to the girl now, looking like they felt sorry for her. Bertel looked at him with an expression that said, *Don't worry. We'll get our chance.* All of a sudden, John wasn't as sure as he'd been before.

The girl's younger brother Michael took the stand next. He told the same story to the jury, except that he admitted to Bertel that when he had been shown pictures of possible carjackers, he had to pick two photos because he didn't remember well enough what the robber looked like. John looked over at the jury, giving them a look that said, *You see that? This kid has no idea who it was.*

They called the older brother to the stand next, the one who had driven the car and fought off the attacker. As he told his story, same as the other two, John watched the jury size him up. John could tell they admired Jay, the brave kid who had risked his life for his younger sister and brother.

The DA's office had sent the photos to Charlottesville, where the kid went to school, and they said he had ID'd John from those photos. The DA then asked John to stand up. He did, and the DA said, "Is that the man who robbed you?"

The young man said, "Yes."

"Is there any doubt in your mind?"

"There's none."

Bertel took over the questioning, his tone showing John and the jury that he didn't believe a word of this. He walked the boy through the attack in the car even more slowly than the DA had. "You were seated on the driver's side, with your feet up in the air."

"Well, basically, yeah, pointing toward him, with my hands on the gun, and my feet were in the air and on top of him as much as possible."

"So he was on the passenger side."

"Yes, sir."

"You were kicking at him."

"Yes, sir."

Bertel leaned in closer. "But at the same time, you had the gun."

"Well, I had two hands on the gun, yes, sir."

"You must have been in a very crouched position. Your knees must have been up in the air."

"Yeah, that's true."

"You have a stick shift in the car?"

"Yes, sir."

"Did that get in your way?"

"Uh, yeah. It was pretty much a tangled situation up there. I was pretty scrunched, and I got cut up in a bunch of places."

Bertel mimicked the boy's description, actually lying down in the courtroom, trying to show the jury what the boy described, to show them how unlikely it seemed. "Weren't you excited?"

"I was very tense, and my adrenaline was pumping a lot."

"But you were short of hysterical."

"No, I wasn't hysterical."

Just like the other two kids, the older one said he had ID'd John from the photos that had been sent to him. And just like the other two, he had seen the picture of John in the paper, handcuffed and being led away, charged with the murder of Ray Liuzza.

The jury took a break for lunch. John was led back into the judge's chambers, which contained a small holding cell. They led John into it and locked the door behind him. John sat on the small stool in the cell, the only thing there, and waited. They brought him a sandwich and a paper cup filled with water. John ate the sandwich, and when it was time, the bailiff came and unlocked his cage and walked him back into the courtroom.

The younger DA, Gerry Deegan, was straightening his papers and getting ready to talk. He called Bruce Whittaker to the stand.

Whittaker talked about all the things he did as the armed robbery screener. John looked at the court reporter, her fingers flying over the keys of her steno machine, taking down every word that was said. He looked at the jury. The courtroom had fans, but still, circulation was bad and it was hot. A few looked like they were paying attention, but some of the others looked like they were about to fall asleep in the heat, especially with lunch now in their stomachs.

Whittaker was droning on about how the photographic lineup had worked with the Lagarde children. John couldn't believe it.

No way they bust me on this, John thought. *No way.*

Whittaker was still talking, explaining that he'd used the same photos that he had sent to Jay Lagarde when he went to visit Mimi and Michael at their home. *You see?* John wanted to scream to the jury. *You gonna believe this ain't a frame-up? You think the lawyers didn't tell them it was me? These kids don't have any idea. They just signed what they was told to sign.*

Numa Bertel stood up to question Whittaker, and he was on it. "Mr. Whittaker, I noticed in your instructions to Jay Lagarde, you advised him as follows: 'Please take time to look at the photos away from all distraction and interference. It is recommended that no one be present when you view them.' Why did you do that?"

Whittaker replied, "There are always insinuations that the cops were pointing at a particular picture, and I didn't want that to be any problem here. I wanted him to look at the pictures alone, so nobody would be there saying, that guy looks pretty guilty, or something like that. I feel comfortable that he was not influenced by whatever people may have been around."

Bertel smiled knowingly. "Ohhh. You feel comfortable about that?"

"Yes, sir, I do."

"You were there?"

"No, I was not."

"So how do you know his roommates didn't influence him?"

"I take him at his word."

Bertel smirked at that. "You do not know what went on in that room."

It wasn't a question, but Whittaker answered anyway. "That's correct."

John looked back at the jury as Bertel kept asking Whittaker questions designed to show how flimsy the photo identification was. They looked as bored as John felt.

Deegan called a guy to the stand John had never seen before. His name was Anthony Cusimano, and he was the crime scene technician, the guy who came to the scene to collect evidence and test it. Cusimano testified that he had recovered the gun from the scene, and it had tested negative for any fingerprints. *Can't get me on that,* John thought.

And then, just like that, the older DA, Jim Williams, stood up and said, "Your Honor, the State will rest subject to its right of rebuttal."

I knew that's all they had, John thought. *Three white kids saying it was me.* He turned and smiled at his mother and Denise. *It's gonna be okay,* he thought.

Bertel called Clement Cambric to the witness stand. When they had met, two days ago, Bertel had asked John for his alibi. John told him: He was working. He worked as a valet for a carnival organization, called a *krewe*—the folks who dressed up in crazy Mardi Gras outfits for the holiday balls. It was a pretty good way to earn some cash, going down to the clubhouse and helping the guys get into and out of their costumes. He'd work for a few hours, get paid in cash under the table at the end of the night, and maybe get a tip from the guys whom he helped get dressed and undressed. Clement was the boss, the guy who made sure there were enough valets there to take care of all the partygoers, and to organize them as they traveled to different places around the city on different nights.

John told Bertel he was supposed to be there by 6:00 PM, but he'd been a little late that night. The job was to wait around until the ball was done, and that was after 11:30 PM—so how could he have been at Poydras and LaSalle, where the carjacking took place, before midnight? Plus, he'd gone in the uniform he was supposed to wear, a white shirt and black pants, and the guy who did the carjacking had on jeans and a sweatshirt. John had told Bertel that the people at his job didn't know him as John Thompson; they knew him as John Williams, because he had gotten the job from his stepfather, whose last name was Williams.

Bertel asked Clement, "You're not in a position to say that you saw John Williams there on the 28th, are you?"

"I couldn't be positive that he was there or not. According to the records, three Williams worked, but I can't tell which ones it was."

Bertel thanked him and told him he could step down. He called Nathaniel Williams, John's stepfather, to the stand. John had known Nate for about four years, and Nate confirmed for the jury that the valet service knew John Thompson as John Williams. "Now," Bertel continued, "are you in a position to tell us whether you remember working with him on the 28th of December?"

"I don't remember," Nate said. John groaned to himself.

"Is that because there were a lot of people there?" Bertel asked.

"It's not the idea of a lot of people there. I just don't remember the time. I don't remember making that day, or not. I don't know if he was there, or not."

"You worked them all, so one of these Williams in the notes is you."

"Should be me, the first one," Nate answered.

"But you don't know who the other two Williams are."

"No, I really don't."

Bertel motioned at John. "It could be this man."

"Could be," Nate agreed.

Bertel had gotten two of Nate's sons, Kenneth and young Nate, to testify as well. Both men agreed that John Thompson was known as John Williams, but Kenneth hadn't worked the ball on the night of the 28th, and young Nate couldn't confirm whether John had been there that night or not.

John's stomach was starting to tighten. How could none of these people be telling the jury that he was at the ball that night?

Then he heard Bertel call his name, and John stood up and walked to the witness stand.

JOHN LOOKED AT the jury when he answered Bertel's questions, like Bertel had told him to do. He told them he'd gotten to the ball at five minutes to six, and he had been there until about midnight. He'd made eighty dollars that night—ten from the service and the rest in tips. He didn't know why Bertel asked him about his record, but he told the jury the truth: He'd been convicted for marijuana possession, a misdemeanor, and for possession of a firearm, a gun that wasn't his, that he'd just picked up from the ground and a police officer was there to see it.

"Now, John, you've heard what everybody here has said went on. I want you to look at me, and tell me, on December the 28th, at approximately 11:40, or any other time that night, did you rob anybody at all?"

"Definitely not," John said, trying to smile a little.

"And on that night, how were you dressed?"

"Black and white," John said.

"Meaning the white shirt and the black pants?"

"Yes, sir, and I had a sweater on."

"Were you dressed that way when you left the Municipal Auditorium?"

"Yes, sir."

"What time did you leave the Auditorium?"

"About midnight."

"Where did you go?"

"Well, my grandfather has a barroom on the next block. I walked down to the barroom. It's on North Robertson."

"Is that close to the Superdome?"

"It's the opposite way. I stayed till my uncle closed the barroom and brought me home, about 1:30."

"Your Honor, I have nothing further," Bertel said, and sat down.

Jim Williams was already standing up before Bertel had sat down. "Mr. Williams, you seem to remember December 28th pretty well. How do you know you were there at five minutes to six? Not quarter to six, but five minutes to six, five months ago, you remember the time?"

"Yeah, because I was trying to be at the ball on time," John said. "They got a big old clock on the wall when you first come in the door, and I looked at it."

"Now, Mr. Thompson, you say you went to your grandfather's barroom after the ball. Did you know anybody at the barroom?"

"My uncle."

"What is your uncle's name?"

"Chiney Williams."

"Okay. Is he here today?"

John shook his head. "He went to California."

"So, nobody else? You didn't know nobody else at that bar?"

John said, "They had people in the bar. I didn't know them."

Williams nodded, like it was what he had expected to hear. "Okay. Mr. Williams, when you work the balls, do you have any friends that work there? Is there one single person that can come here and say that you were there on the 28th?"

"I don't know," John said.

"Well, you seem to know December 28th pretty well," Williams said again. "Let's see if you remember some other days just as well as December 28th. What about December 27th; what did you do December 27th?"

"I played with my little boy," John said. "It was two days after Christmas. I brought him out and let him ride his Big Wheel."

"What did you do on December 20th?"

"I couldn't tell you."

"What did you do on December 6th?"

John looked at the lawyer, surprised. "December the 6th? I couldn't tell you."

"What about December 7th?"

John shook his head.

"You remember where you were on December the 6th around one in the morning?"

"Yeah," John said. "I was by my house with my mother."

"With your mother?"

"Yes, sir."

Williams kept at him about December the 6th. When had he gone home that night? Had he been alone? Once he went in at 6:00 PM, did he come back out, or did he stay there the whole night? Who else was in the house? He wanted the names of everyone there. He wanted to know why John had stayed at his mother's house when he usually stayed with his grandmother. It went on for several minutes. Then he went on to other dates. Where had he been December 10th? November 14th?

John answered the questions as best he could, but said "I don't know" to most of them. Williams was getting frustrated. "Well, why do you remember that you were at your mother's house on December 6th when you don't remember any of these other days?"

"'Cause it was the day before my girlfriend's birthday," John said, feeling a little cocky. *Thought you had me, didn't you?* he thought.

Williams kept asking him questions that didn't matter at all. When had he seen Denise on the 28th? What was she wearing? Williams went on like this for another few minutes, and finally he said, "You know, the Lagarde family got up and testified, and all said you were the man that robbed them. Do you know them?"

"No, sir. I never knew them, but when they came into court yesterday."

"Well, can you tell this jury why they all got up here and identified you as being the man that robbed them?"

"No, I couldn't."

Williams stared at John. John looked back. Finally, Williams said, "I have no further questions." Bertel agreed.

John thought, *We got this.*

8

FORTY-NINE YEARS

APRIL 12, 1985

JOHN SAT IN his cell with his head in his hands, his heart racing. He tried to calm himself down, but nothing worked.

Forty-nine years, he kept thinking. *Forty-nine years.*

The jury had convicted him. They had believed the Lagarde children, and the white DAs, and they had convicted him. They weren't sure that he'd actually gotten away with anything, though, so they convicted him of *attempted* armed robbery. And for that, just for *trying* to rob someone, they said he should go to jail for forty-nine years. And Quinlan sentenced him without parole.

John ran his fingers over his face, over his head, and tried to tell himself this wasn't happening, that he hadn't heard the jury say the word "guilty." He had been so sure that he almost turned and lifted his arms to Denise in triumph before he realized they hadn't said "not guilty." The courtroom had become really hot then, and he thought for a second he was going to faint. He had looked at his lawyer, but Bertel just frowned and shook his head a little, like he was disappointed.

John thought, *He didn't get no forty-nine.*

It had gone bad from the second they had finished their closing arguments. Jim Williams told the jury about all the IDs from the Lagarde children, about how no one could say that John was really at the valet service, and no one could supply him with an alibi.

Bertel told the jury that John was innocent until proven guilty, and reminded them of the weaknesses of eyewitness identification, especially in a case like this one, where the procedure for the photographic lineup was so obviously biased against John.

John had thought it was pretty good, but when the jury walked out of the room, none of them looked at him at all.

DURING BREAKS IN the trial, John would be taken back into the judge's office and locked up in the small holding cell. The court police had led John back to this cell to wait while the jury deliberated. Not long afterward, the door to the room opened and Jim Williams walked in. He walked over to John with a smirk, saying, "I got you now, boy. Jury's gonna come back and get you in this case, and then I got you again for the murder you did."

John didn't remember what he had said in reply. Whatever it was, it was loud, and it was nasty, and he just kept shouting, telling Williams he didn't have shit, that John hadn't done shit. None of those three white kids had any idea who he was, and Williams knew it. They didn't know anything.

Williams sat there grinning. He said, "Boy, you don't get it, do you? When we put your picture in the paper, we got a dozen calls from people saying you did this, you did that to them. This case was just the one we took. All these people say you're the bad guy. So I don't care at all if I lose this case. It doesn't matter. I still got you on any one of nine other cases. I'll get you sooner or later, and then when I get you on those, I'll get you on the murder of Ray Liuzza, and then I'll get you in the electric chair. You're not going anywhere except death row and the chair. You're mine. And when you're there, and they put that on your head, and they strap you down, it'll be my face you see. You'll know it was me who got you after all you did."

Judge Patrick Quinlan walked in at that moment, alerted by the noise. He started yelling too, and even Williams knew better than to talk back to the judge. Williams left, shooting John a bitter look. John stood in the cell, his chest heaving, angry and scared. He waited for Quinlan to say something to him but the judge never did.

Just a few minutes after John's confrontation with Jim Williams, they led him back into the courtroom because the jury was already returning. It had been less than two hours since they went to deliberate. *'Cause they got no case,* John thought. John looked around at the columns, the benches, the police, the judge's people, and the people in the audience. He sat down in his chair, next to Bertel.

The jury came in, single file. John rose as they entered the room, and they walked right past him. Once again, not one of them looked at him. The courtroom got quiet.

They said he was guilty.

John's heart sank, but he thought, *Even if they think I'm guilty, they'll go easy on me.* It was his first felony conviction, and his first for a violent crime, and nobody even got hurt. John had thought, *Three to five.*

He had been terribly, terribly wrong.

9

BIG DADDY RED

MARCH 6, 1985

JOHN LAY ON his cot and looked up at the ceiling. He didn't know what time it was; sometime between lights out and morning—it didn't really matter. He was getting used to the waiting. They all did in prison. They waited for something to happen, and then when it did, they waited for the thing after that to happen. The problem wasn't the waiting. The problem was, what was he waiting for?

He was waiting for something that would get him out of jail, get him back to Denise and the boys. He couldn't sleep, not with the rats crawling around his feet and on his bed. He kept his things locked in a storage locker at the foot of his bed, but Orleans Parish Prison had been so dirty for so long that the rats were fearless; they'd chew through anything, even if you were kicking them or hitting them with something.

The past several nights had been like this: staring into the darkness, listening to the periodic screams of other prisoners in the dark, men living out their own nightmares. Every now and then, one of those nightmares would be real, and the next morning John would hear the other men talking about how the scream was from a knife, or a gun, or a homemade tempered-plastic spoon puncturing eyes, lungs, or throat in a burst of activity that ended as quickly as it started, except for the persistent moans of the loser.

Part of what he was waiting for was his lawyers to do something. He didn't have Numa Bertel anymore. Bertel had told Judge Quinlan that he was friends with Ray Liuzza's father, and so he couldn't represent John. In place of Bertel, the judge appointed two other lawyers. After meeting Rob Couhig and Pat Fanning, John figured that was part of the plan, too. Judge Quinlan used to be a DA himself, and had worked for Connick, so John had a pretty clear idea of where the judge's loyalties were.

Couhig wasn't even a criminal lawyer. He had told John straight up, right at the beginning, that he wasn't familiar with defending criminal cases. Fanning was a criminal lawyer, but that didn't mean he was any better than Couhig.

Both men had come to OPP to meet with John, though to John's mind it had taken a long time before they appeared. They sat down and started talking. Not fifteen minutes later, without even hearing John's story beyond his statement "I didn't do it," Fanning told John that if he pleaded guilty, Fanning could get him life instead of the death penalty. John got mad and started shouting at Fanning, told him in no uncertain terms what he thought of that idea. He couldn't believe that his lawyers decided right off the bat that he was guilty and needed to admit it.

Fanning stormed out of the meeting room and filed papers with Judge Quinlan to leave the case. The judge wouldn't let him out, so he stayed on, but John had not spoken to him since, and didn't really want to. No way would these men be his way out.

John kept thinking, turning things around in his brain. He had told Couhig what to do, but Couhig hadn't done it. He had given Couhig things to ask the witnesses, to check their stories, but Couhig hadn't done that either, and neither had Fanning.

So what you gonna do, John? he thought. *They got you all set up, a robbery charge and a murder charge, and Kojak and Funk gonna testify on you, and you got two lawyers set up by a judge who used to work for Harry Connick his own self. What you gonna do?*

MARCH 7, 1985

JOHN HAD TALKED to a couple of the other inmates who knew the law fairly well. They all told him he needed to change the venue, get the case out of New Orleans. He had discussed this with Couhig, but here they were, still in New Orleans, still with the judge who used to be a DA and who'd appointed his crappy lawyers.

So, John was done listening to Couhig, and done waiting for something to happen. He needed to take things into his own hands. He had paper and a pen, and he started writing:

> *What's Up, Big Daddy Red:*
> *Look, lil Daddy, I'm coming straight to the point; ok, look. I need your help like I never need it before "dig." I want you to come to court on the 21st of the month to tell that you seen "Kevin" give me a ring around Dec. 21 or later in the month. If you can found it in your heart to do that for me, I will be glad—just say we was on Euterpe Street when you seen him gave the ring to me, and don't change your statement, ok? I know you can do that with no problem at all. Tell your lil family hello for me, ok. Tell all the fellows the same. Do you see Funk anywhere? If you do, tell him if he come to court we is going to tell on each other; he know what I'm talking about. Please find him and tell him that before March 21, 1985, ok. Tell "Doie" and "Tue" to be cool. Well, lil daddy, take it easy and take care of your lil girl for me, ok.*
> *Later,*
> *Nut*
> *To his main man. Take care for me!*

John folded the letter, put it in an envelope, licked the envelope closed, and handed it to a prison guard to mail.

10

CONDEMNED

JOHN WALKED BACK into Judge Quinlan's courtroom and sat down in the same chair he had been seated in for his carjacking trial. Rob Couhig and Pat Fanning were seated next to him. Only three weeks had passed since his last trial, and already, here they were again. John looked at the DA's table where Jim Williams and another lawyer were sitting.

John didn't like Jim Williams, that was for sure, but even he had to admit that what Williams had done at John's robbery trial was clever. Williams knew he had John set up—that even without fingerprints on the gun, all he had to do was get those white kids to get up on that stand and say that the black man had held them up. By the time John got on the stand, Williams knew he had already won the case.

John hadn't really understood it at the time, but now he saw it clearly. He remembered Williams asking him where he'd been on all those dates, but he kept coming back to December 6th. And no one had noticed—not even Numa Bertel, since he wasn't representing John in the murder case. But now John knew it.

December 6th was the night Ray Liuzza was murdered. During the armed robbery trial, Jim Williams hadn't cared whether John did the robbery or not; what he really wanted to know was John's alibi for the night Ray Liuzza was shot.

John looked straight ahead and tried to calm himself down. Couhig had told him it was going to be a long and repetitive day, but he'd said if they were lucky, at the end of it, they would have a good jury selected, one that might be sympathetic to him.

He was half right, anyway. It was a long and repetitive day. John sat at the table for the entire day and listened to Fanning, Williams, and Dubelier. The room was initially filled with seventy-five potential jurors, most of them black. Quinlan sent most of the people outside, then he started bringing them back in groups of twelve. Williams or Dubelier would get to ask questions of the group, and then Fanning and Couhig would get their turn. Couhig, however, kept out of it, taking notes on each juror and letting Fanning do the talking.

Once they were done questioning each group of twelve as a group, they would knock a few out, the lawyers sometimes debating, sometimes in agreement, and the judge sometimes rejecting potential jurors. Then they brought back the remaining jurors from the group, one at a time, and asked them each the same questions. Dubelier and Williams wanted people who weren't afraid to vote for the death penalty and would move to eliminate those who were opposed to capital punishment.

They went through the entire group of seventy-five this way. Sometimes the DAs would start, sometimes Fanning would start. Then Judge Quinlan might ask the person a question or two. Only then would they decide whether the person could be on the jury or not.

They were there past ten that night selecting jury members—and this was after they had woken John up at about four in the morning to go stand in line for the van to take him to court. At the end of it, everyone was exhausted. Judge Quinlan told the jurors to come back the next day, and not to watch the news or read the papers.

Their jury panel had started with seventy-five people, fifty black and twenty-five white. Even so, somehow John's jury of twelve people ended up with eight whites and only four blacks. Of the blacks, there were three women and one man, and all of them were forty to fifty years old. *This could be bad,* John thought as he was walked back to his cell. *These women ain't gonna want to let me out.* John knew these women, could tell by the way they looked at him that they weren't sympathetic to his situation. These women were like his mother and grandmother. Looking at John, they would probably just see a young black man who had dropped out of school, sold some drugs, got into guns, and now had crossed the line and shot somebody for a handful of nothing. *Hell, most of them have already heard the story on the news,* he thought. *How many of those jurors today said they'd heard the news story and said Ray Liuzza had begged for his life and got shot and killed anyway? They'll see a murderer whether one is standing there in front of them or not.*

MAY 7, 1985

THEY STARTED EARLY the next morning, with Fanning again asking the judge to throw the case out of New Orleans, and objecting to the racial makeup of their jury. Quinlan noted Fanning's objections, but ruled against him both times.

"Your Honor," Fanning continued, "we went to the assistant DAs in this case, and we asked them if they would be willing to negotiate a plea bargain, and they said no. I just don't want anyone later on to say that the defense attorneys didn't make every effort to prevent their client from getting the electric chair." Couhig stood up and asked the judge to rule on another outstanding motion—they had moved to exclude the armed robbery conviction from the murder trial, to prevent Dubelier and Williams from using that conviction against John if he took the stand. Earlier, Couhig had explained to John the importance of this motion. If Quinlan allowed the DAs to use the armed robbery against John, Couhig said, they would keep John off the witness stand. The crimes were too similar, Couhig said, for John to testify. Dubelier would compare the murder case to the armed robbery case, and the jury would find John guilty, simple as that.

Couhig asked Quinlan for his ruling. Quinlan said, "Does the State have anything to say?"

Dubelier looked over at Couhig, then up at the judge, and shrugged. "Submit it."

"Okay. As to the issue of using the attempted armed robbery conviction in the guilt phase if the defendant takes the stand, the court is going to rule that the State would be allowed to question the defendant about that conviction if the defendant does take the stand. If the defendant does not take the stand, then obviously the State cannot use that. As to the issue of whether or not it can be used in the death phase, the court is going to rule that, in fact, it can be used in the death phase."

Couhig leaned over and whispered to John, "That means they can't talk about the armed robbery if you don't take the stand. If you get found guilty, though, they can use it and discuss it with the jury when they decide what your sentence is."

John thought, *I guess I don't get to tell my side of the story, then.*

With that, they brought in the jury. John did what Couhig and Fanning had told him to do and stood up when the jury entered, trying to catch each juror's eye, and look as sympathetic as he could.

Dubelier stood to give the jury his opening statement. "During the course of today, and possibly tomorrow, the State will prove beyond a reasonable doubt that Mr. Thompson, on December 6, 1984, in fact, killed Ray Liuzza. At the time of the killing, he had specific intent to kill or to inflict great bodily harm, and additionally, he was engaged in the perpetration or attempted perpetration of an armed robbery."

Dubelier went on for quite a while, explaining the case. He told the jury they would hear from Kevin Freeman, and he told them about Freeman's plea bargain in exchange for his testimony against John—a sentence knocked down to accessory after the fact, with a five-year sentence, or the opportunity to stand trial with a charge of second-degree murder. He then described the scene on December 6th, laying out a story for the jury—a story of John and Kevin Freeman driving in a car, running out of gas, and seeing Ray Liuzza on the street. Dubelier described John telling Kevin Freeman that he was going to kill Ray Liuzza, and Freeman running away, turning to see John fire the gun into Liuzza's body.

John just shook his head and looked down at his feet. He figured the jury would know Freeman was just talking to save his own ass, and what else could be expected from the DA, anyway?

Dubelier continued, talking about the ring and the gun, about Funk Perkins and Junior Lee Harris, and how all the evidence pointed to John. Then he mentioned that the coroner would testify that John's shots had been the cause of Ray Liuzza's death. "It's the State's belief that at the close of this trial, you will be convinced beyond all doubt that on December 6th of 1984, that man, John Thompson, committed first-degree murder. He killed—he murdered—Ray Liuzza, and you'll be convinced when you go out to deliberate that a verdict of guilty as charged of first-degree murder is the only appropriate verdict in this case."

Dubelier sat down and Couhig stood up. "Good morning, ladies and gentlemen. I'm Rob Couhig. We've been asked by the court to represent John Thompson. It is our absolute position that John is innocent." Couhig told the story that Eric Dubelier had not told—a story of witnesses, including Paul Schliffka, who described a six-foot-tall man with close-cropped hair as the killer.

Couhig was actually getting a head of steam going. He mentioned that the autopsy showed the bullets had not been fired at close range, which conflicted with what Kevin Freeman would say. And he said, "The conversation with Richard Perkins—you will have to judge what $15,000 in reward money means to a person, and why he would say somebody did it, or that he would put it on Kevin Freeman and John, and get away with it, knowing that the State might be prepared to cut a deal with Kevin, which is what they did."

Couhig finished by pointing out that whatever Kevin Freeman claimed he saw, he saw from two blocks away at 12:40 at night, and he closed by stating, "The presumption of innocence of John Thompson should not, in your minds, ever be altered."

Kevin Freeman took the stand. He avoided looking at John, who was staring at him with a heat that could melt steel. Each sentence Freeman spoke made John angrier than the last.

Freeman's story was pretty much what it had been on the tape recorder the cops had played for John in the interrogation room at OPP: Freeman was driving down the street, minding his own business on his way home late at night, and he picked John up in his car. Their car ran out of gas and they had pulled over on Josephine and started walking.

Freeman told the jury that he and John had seen Liuzza getting out of his BMW in his nice suit and crossing the street, and that John had said, "I got the heat with me; let's go rob that rich white dude." Freeman turned and ran, but turned back a couple blocks later to see John wrestling with Liuzza and then firing the gun.

John snickered a little but got a sharp look from Couhig, who had told him not to react at all in front of the jury.

Couhig spent a fair amount of time questioning Freeman, covering the statements he made to the police, asking him how he could be sure of what he'd seen from so far away. He also made the point to the jury that of the two men, Kevin Freeman and John Thompson, it was Freeman who more closely resembled the man described by Paul Schliffka.

Then Couhig went into great detail about whether Freeman actually saw John pull the trigger, questioning each fact, every step of the way.

Freeman said, "When Nut ran over here and grabbed him, I was about on the other side of Baronne Street, going toward Dryades Street."

"How far had you gone down the block toward Dryades Street?"

"About in the middle."

"Now, let's go over what you saw. You saw John grab this fellow."

"Wrapped his arm around the neck."

"And throw him to the ground?"

"Pulled him back to the ground."

"And John went over with him?"

"No, he didn't go down with him."

"Now, you saw them wrestling?"

"Well, that was what was told to me."

Couhig turned quickly. "Ohhh, no. I don't want what was told to you, sir. I want what you saw."

"I seed him grab him."

"Did you tell Mr. Dubelier that you saw them wrestling?"

"Yeah. With the gun, yeah."

"Did you tell the police officers that you saw them wrestling?"

"Yes, sir."

"Well, did you see them wrestling or not, sir?"

"Yes, I seed them wrestling, yes, sir."

"Fine. And when you saw these people wrestling from three-quarters of a block away, is that when the gun went off?"

"Yes, sir."

Couhig kept on Freeman, making him go through the scene in detail: how Freeman ran away from the scene toward Saratoga and looked back, and from two blocks away saw John run up the right-hand side of the street after the shooting. Once he was satisfied that he had sufficiently pinned down Freeman's story, he allowed the witness to step down.

Dubelier called NOPD officer David Carter to the stand. Carter, the first police officer on the scene, told the jury how Ray Liuzza had died, bleeding through his blue pinstripe suit and asking, "Why did he have to shoot me?" Fanning objected several times to the prejudicial nature of the testimony, but Quinlan overruled him each time.

Dubelier produced some photographs of the crime scene, photos taken of the sidewalk where Liuzza had lain after being shot. While Liuzza's body was not in the photos, his blood was clearly visible in the grass. Officer Carter described Liuzza becoming pale and sweaty, as if he were going into shock.

Dubelier asked, "Did you, at any time, move Mr. Liuzza prior to the arrival of the emergency unit?"

Carter replied, "No, sir. The only time that I moved him was to try to hold him in position, being that he had a gunshot wound near his spine. I kept telling him not to move because he was thrashing around."

With that, Dubelier's questioning ended, and Couhig rose. He asked Carter about Paul Schliffka's description of the single shooter, and Carter said that he had interviewed Schliffka, who had described a six-foot-tall person with hair that was "black and short, Afro style."

"Thank you, sir; no further questions," replied Couhig.

Jim Williams called Pamela Staab to the witness stand. She lived in the apartment on the ground floor where Liuzza had been shot, and she echoed Officer Carter's description of events. She called the building superintendent, reported the shooting, and went outside to try and comfort Ray.

Williams said, "What did you see when you came outside?"

"I saw Ray lying down there, and he had a blanket over him."

"Was he saying anything?"

"Immediately after I heard the shots, I heard Ray scream, 'God, I'm dead—call an ambulance!' But by the time I got out there, no, I didn't hear him say anything."

"You did not see anybody who was involved in the shooting, did you?"

"No, I didn't."

With that, Rob Couhig stood again: "Describe for me, if you would, the nature of the 'Take my wallet, take my watch.' Was it a plea, or more aggressive than that?"

After Couhig had established to his satisfaction that Pamela Staab had heard the brutal shooting of an unarmed man pleading for his life, his cross-examination mercifully ended, allowing Jim Williams to call Paul Schliffka to the stand.

Schliffka said, "As I was getting into my car, I heard one gunshot. There was a slight hesitation, then I heard two more. Between the first and the second shot I started walking toward the corner. I couldn't figure out what it was. Then I heard three more, and right after that, I saw a man running up Josephine with a gun, and by the time I got to the corner, there was a man running down Josephine, and Ray Liuzza laying on the ground."

"Can you describe that man to the ladies and gentlemen of the jury?"

"He looked about six foot, and had short hair, black, had a black leather or plastic jacket on because it was shiny. He had dark pants, and he had a gun in his right hand."

"Okay, Mr. Schliffka. Did the New Orleans Police Department attempt to have you pick out someone's picture from a photographic lineup?"

"Yes, but I was unable to do so."

"Why is it you could not pick someone out?"

"Because I didn't get a full image of the man running down the street. I got a profile."

"Do you think that today if you saw the man you'd be able to recognize him?"

"No."

"Thank you, Mr. Schliffka," Williams said. He raised his hand toward Couhig and Fanning and said, "Please answer their questions."

Couhig said, "The man who ran past you had a gun in his hand?"

"Yes."

"Did he have short hair?"

"Yes."

"No question in your mind about that?"

"No."

"How tall was the man?"

"Between about five-foot-ten and six feet."

"And he ran past you with the gun. And you told them one man—you saw one man."

"Yes, I did."

"And he was on the Josephine and Baronne side of the street."

"He was on the right-hand side."

Couhig turned to Judge Quinlan. "I have nothing further, Your Honor."

Quinlan said to the jury, "Ladies and gentlemen, let's break here, and we will start up again after lunch." They led John into Quinlan's chambers, to his holding cell, and fed him. John half-expected Williams to come in and taunt him again, but this time he was allowed to eat his lunch in peace, reflecting on the morning.

Couhig and Fanning didn't do all that bad a job, he thought. And if Red responded to his letter and came in to testify, maybe Red would get Funk to *not* testify. *That happens,* John thought, *I could get out of here okay.*

In the afternoon, the DAs focused on the ballistics evidence and the gun. They worked backwards from the discovery of the murder weapon, calling Jessie Harrison to the stand. Harrison briefly described buying a .357 magnum from Junior Lee Harris, and having the NOPD come to his door in the middle of the night asking for it. Then Williams called Junior Lee Harris to the stand.

Harris described buying the .357 in question from a man he didn't know, for twenty-five dollars, and later selling it to Jessie

Harrison. Williams said, "Did there come a time during the negotia-tions for the price of the gun that the person that sold you the gun went outside of your house?"

"Yeah, he went outside the house, and told me, he said, 'Let him go check with somebody out there.'"

At this Fanning objected, saying that whatever the salesperson of the gun had said was hearsay and inadmissible. Quinlan agreed, leaving the identity of the man outside Junior Lee Harris's house a mystery for the jury.

Williams moved on, unfazed. "Do you know a man named Nut?" Junior nodded. "Is he here in the courtroom today?" Junior pointed to John. "Okay. Did there come a time when he brought you something to sell to you?"

"Yeah, a ring. It was a gold ring with an 'L' on it."

"How much did he sell it to you for?"

"Six dollars."

"What did you do with it?"

"Put it on my finger."

"I have nothing further."

Couhig stood up to examine Junior. "Mr. Harris, were you arrested between January 17th and today?"

Dubelier stood up. "Your Honor, I'll stipulate that Mr. Harris was arrested on March 3, 1985, for rape."

Couhig said to Harris, "Were those charges refused by the DA's office on Friday of this past week?"

Dubelier, still standing, said, "Your Honor, I'll stipulate that the charges were refused on Friday of this past week."

Couhig kept his eyes on Harris, ignoring Dubelier. "Let me ask you this, sir. You admit that you spoke to the district attorney on Friday of last week about this case?"

"I talked about the rape charge at first, then he asked me about that."

"In order to talk to the district attorney, did they have to come over and get you out of prison and bring you to their office?"

"Yes."

"That's all the questions I have, Your Honor."

John looked at the jury.

Jim Williams said to Harris, "Mr. Harris, did Mr. Dubelier at any time ever promise you anything for coming here?"

"No, sir."

"Did he promise to drop those rape charges because you came and testified?"

"No, sir."

"Thank you, sir."

John watched Junior Harris step down from the stand. He walked past John and looked at him apologetically, but he did not slow down as he walked out of the courtroom.

Finally, Dubelier asked Funk Perkins to come to the stand. John just shook his head as Funk started talking. *I should never have given that boy the gun to sell,* he thought to himself. He had never expected Funk to turn on him like this. They had not been best friends, but they certainly hadn't ever been enemies. He and Funk had always helped one another on the street. Funk had gone out with one of John's sisters for a while, and she'd asked John to help him out sometimes, so John had done a little business with Funk now and again.

John had never told Couhig and Fanning that he had given the gun to Funk, saying instead, "Even if I had it, what would it matter?" Guns were just another kind of currency on the street, something easily traded for drugs, money, jewelry, or anything else in the street's barter economy. What did selling a gun to Funk Perkins have to do with shooting Ray Liuzza?

Dubelier said to Funk, "Where did you sell the gun?"

"At Junior's house."

"How much did you get for it?"

"Twenty-five dollars, a little weed, and some T."

"What is T?"

"Something you snort," Funk said.

"Who were you with when you sold the gun?"

"John Thompson."

"That's the man who gave you the gun?"

Funk nodded. "John Thompson."

Dubelier kept going, asking Funk about John's supposed confession to the crime in front of Funk, John telling Funk that he'd killed Liuzza accidentally, that he'd gotten a ring and a watch from the victim.

Then Dubelier said to Funk, "I'll show you what I've marked as State's Exhibit Eleven. Mr. Perkins, do you recognize this?"

"Yeah, I recognize it."

Couhig took a copy of the paper from Dubelier, looked at it, and shot John a look. He almost threw it across the table at John.

It was the letter John had written to Big Daddy Red from prison.

Dubelier said to Funk, "Do you remember giving it to me?"

"Mm-hmm."

"Where did you get it?"

"From Red."

"Who's Red?"

"Just a friend in the neighborhood."

"To your knowledge, does this man Red know John Thompson?"

"Yeah."

"Mr. Perkins, has anybody promised you anything if you testified today?"

"No, uh-uh."

"Did anyone promise you anything if you went to the police and provided them with information about this case?"

Funk shook his head. "Ain't nobody sent me to the police. When they come to me, I just went down myself."

John read his letter to Red again. Couhig hadn't asked any questions about it, but he had a feeling that Red wasn't coming to court if he had given the letter to Funk. Red must have thought John wanted Red to rat out Funk, and Red wouldn't want to be a rat. He must've given the letter to Funk, and that would just make Funk mad and ready to come in and testify.

Couhig was starting to question Funk now. "Where are you employed now, sir?"

"At the Hilton Hotel."

"How long have you worked there?"

"About three months."

"Isn't it true that you got the job at the Hilton Hotel after speaking to police on January 16th?"

Funk said, "No, no, I got the job after . . . I was going to get the job anyway; I had already put an application in."

Couhig changed course. "Is it fair to say, sir, that $15,000 is a lot of money?"

"What are you talking about?"

"Just that, sir; $15,000 is a lot of money, isn't it?"

"I ain't finished school. I don't even know nothing about that many numbers," Funk replied.

Couhig asked Funk a series of additional questions, but none of it really interfered with Funk's testimony—that John Thompson had given him the murder weapon, and that when Funk learned that the gun had been used in a murder, he'd called the police. John glared at Funk, who seemed totally unconcerned as he stepped off the stand. *Man, you turned on me,* John thought. *That ain't how it's supposed to work.*

Dubelier called a handwriting expert to the stand. The expert had asked John to conduct a handwriting test, and from that he was able to confirm that John had written the letter to Red. So now they had Funk testifying against John, and a letter in which John threatened Funk and tried to keep him off the stand. *Perfect,* John thought.

Dubelier's next witness was Ken Carr, whose testimony stayed true to his statements to the police. Carr said that he had called Crimestoppers and reported overhearing a conversation in Harry's Bar on New Year's Eve in which a man confessed to murdering a rich white dude.

Couhig poked fun at Carr for going to Harry's Bar at 11:30 on New Year's Eve, leaving his wife and kids at home. Couhig then suggested that Carr's story wasn't credible, because over a three-hour period, in a bar on New Year's Eve, Carr only admitted to drinking two beers.

Then Couhig asked, "Describe Harry's for me."

"It's a small place, a normal bar, you know. It's just a little place. It's, you know, a little place they can go to."

John sat at the table fuming. He didn't believe Couhig had even gone to Harry's Bar to check it out, to see if Carr was telling the truth. At that point, he stopped paying attention to the proceedings of the trial and simply sat and fed his anger while Eric Dubelier, and then Rob Couhig, examined Detective Donald Curole, the man who had arrested John. Curole described meeting with Perkins, finding the gun based on Perkins's tip, and splitting up with his partner to arrest both John and Kevin Freeman.

Then Ray Liuzza Sr. took the stand. Liuzza was supposed to be there to identify the ring that the cops had taken from Junior Harris, to prove that the ring in custody was the one his son had worn on the night he was killed. But Rob Couhig knew that the old man had offered a reward for information leading to the arrest and conviction of his son's murderer, and Couhig didn't go anywhere near that. He just asked him a few simple, innocuous questions and let the man step down.

Couhig sat down after he'd finished his examination. John whispered to him, "Why you ain't ask him nothin' about no reward?"

Couhig replied, "John, he's the father of the victim. If I try to make him look dishonest, it will do you more harm than good in the eyes of the jury."

"Yeah," John said. "Yeah, I'm sure. It ain't that you don't want to be the guy defendin' his son's killer, because he's a big shot in town, is it?"

Couhig gave John a look like he had gone too far, and turned back to the case without answering.

The day ended with the pathologist who had conducted the autopsy. He described the wounds suffered by Ray Liuzza, and his ideas about how the young man had died.

Once again, Rob Couhig stood up to try and combat the imagery of multiple gunshots pushing through Ray Liuzza's body. He was focused on one thing with the doctor, and that was "stippling"—the pattern of gunpowder residue from the muzzle of a weapon, which would generally be found on the skin of a murder victim who had been shot at very close range, as described by Kevin Freeman. "In this particular case, Doctor, you found . . ."

"No stippling around any of the wounds."

"A weapon of this sort—how far away would one typically need to be to avoid seeing any stippling?"

"You would need to fire the gun from a distance of greater than five feet away from the victim," the doctor said.

"Thank you, sir. That's all the questions I have."

Dubelier stood, and said, "Your Honor, the State rests." John looked at the clock above the judge. It was after 6:00 PM. He was suddenly exhausted and hungry. The lawyers talked about admitting various exhibits introduced during the day, and the jury was released. They would reconvene the next morning.

Maybe Red will come tomorrow, John thought. He wasn't expecting it, though.

MAY 8, 1985

THE GUARDS CAME to get John a little after 4:00 AM, to walk him over to the transport waiting area. He was already awake. *Let's just get it over with,* he thought. If this was how it was going down, he'd have to get tougher to prepare for it.

They got him over to the courthouse by about 8:00 AM, and he sat in the holding cell for a little while until Couhig and Fanning arrived at the courtroom. After that he was released into their custody, and he went and sat in the same chair he always sat in. He was starting to think of it as "his" chair.

A few people filed into the courtroom, and the lawyers and clerks paced around until Judge Quinlan entered, and then the jury came in from a different door in the capitol. The judge was all business, and they got started right away.

Yeah, John thought. *Don't want to waste the judge's time. I been waitin' five, six hours here.*

Since Dubelier had finished calling witnesses to attack John, it was time for Rob Couhig to tell John's side of the story. He started by calling Johnny Ferguson, a friend of John's, to testify that John had been at a party on New Year's Eve, and therefore he couldn't have been in Harry's Bar confessing to the murder, as Ken Carr had testified.

The party had been at Fourth and Liberty, at Denise's mother's house. Johnny testified that he had arrived at the party around 11:30 PM. He said that John was already there when he arrived, and that John had still been there at about 2:30 AM, when Johnny left.

Johnny held up pretty well under Dubelier's questioning, John thought, watching the prosecutor question his friend in his aggressive, clipped style. Dubelier tried to hurry witnesses with his questions, asking the next one on the heels of the previous answer, as if he wanted to keep the pressure on the witness.

Johnny kept up, though. There had been about ten of them at the party. Yes, they had gone all through the house. Yes, they had been drinking. Dubelier asked how far away Harry's Bar was, and Johnny estimated two miles. "Isn't it more like six or seven blocks?" Dubelier said. Johnny agreed, and that was pretty much it.

Couhig called Denise's brother, Reggie, who testified that he had also been at the party between the hours of midnight and 1:30 AM, and that John had been there the entire time. Dubelier asked Reggie a few questions, and Reggie said that he hadn't necessarily been talking to John the whole time. "You couldn't say that you knew exactly at all times where John Thompson was, could you?"

"No, I couldn't say that," Reggie agreed.

"He could have gone outside; he could have walked down the street."

"It's possible," Reggie said.

Reggie was excused.

Rob Couhig turned to John and said, "You still okay with not taking the stand?"

John shrugged. They had discussed this. Couhig and Fanning were very clear that if he took the stand, he'd be worse off. John didn't know about any of that, but he knew that his defense team hadn't said a lot of the things he'd wanted them to. Still, they were the experts, so he didn't say anything.

Couhig rose and said, "Your Honor, the defense rests."

Pat Fanning rose with him and said, "Your Honor, I have some objections I'd like to put on the record." Quinlan excused the jury and let Fanning talk. Couhig had explained this to John, telling him it was a way of making sure that later on, John could file an appeal on as many issues as possible.

Fanning went on and on about things Dubelier had done that he thought were unfair. Each time, Judge Quinlan overruled the objection, always siding with the DA. John shook his head. Couhig saw it and said, "Don't worry; this is what we expected. As long as it's on the record, we can appeal later."

As the court reporter tapped away, Fanning said to the judge, "Prior to the defense resting in this case, Mr. Couhig and I consulted with our client, Mr. Thompson, and discussed with him the possibility of him testifying on his own behalf. We advised Mr. Thompson that should he take the witness stand, the fact that he has prior convictions—including the prior conviction for attempted armed robbery—would come up before the jury, which it would not if he didn't testify. After consulting with us, Mr. Thompson concurred in our decision not to take the witness stand, Your Honor."

Quinlan instructed the bailiff to let the jury back in, and Eric Dubelier rose to present his closing argument. He paced back and forth in front of the jury, speaking clearly and loudly to make sure his voice projected and that everyone in the courtroom could hear him clearly.

Dubelier told the same story he had told in his opening statement, connecting each of the witnesses' testimonies together. He described the robbery and murder: "But, what did Mr. Thompson do when he realized what he had done? He committed an armed robbery, and he killed someone. He's got to get rid of any evidence that links him to this crime. So he goes and gets Richard Perkins, and says, 'Richard, I got a gun I need for you to sell for me.' He and Richard go to Junior Harris's house, and Richard goes in while John stays outside, and negotiates to sell the gun to Junior Harris for twenty-five dollars and a bag of weed.

"Then, a few days later, Thompson is desperate for more money, and he decides he's going to sell the ring that he stole from Ray Liuzza. This time he goes to Junior Harris directly, and sells the ring for six dollars.

"What has John Thompson accomplished at this point? Well, it sure makes it pretty easy to look like Junior Harris went out and killed somebody because he's got the gun and the ring. So Thompson has disassociated himself with the critical evidence in the case. He never expected that these people would come forward and testify against him because Richard Perkins was his friend, and Kevin Freeman was his friend, and Junior Harris is a criminal."

John thought, *You got that right*. He'd never thought that any of these people would have testified against him.

Dubelier picked up the gun. "You heard the physical evidence. What did the police find at the scene? Two pellets that passed through the body of Ray Liuzza. An expert has testified that those pellets came from this gun. This is the murder weapon. You're looking at it. This is the gun that Thompson took, and killed Ray Liuzza with. There's no question about that.

"Can we prove that he schemed to get out of this, to make it look like someone else did it? I think so. Read the letter that the man wrote to someone, we don't know who he is, named Big Daddy Red. He asked for Big Daddy Red, this unknown person, to come into court and testify that Kevin Freeman gave him the ring. That would make it look like Kevin Freeman did it. Now, where's Big Daddy Red? Well, Big Daddy Red wasn't going to come in here and lie. We don't know where he is, but he's not here. Thompson tried to get someone to come in and say something different, but the evidence is, he had the ring, and he sold the ring."

Dubelier went down the list of witnesses, telling the jury why they could be trusted to tell the truth. Ken Carr, he said, was totally neutral and disinterested, and had no motive to make anything up. He turned to Junior Harris, and said to the jury, "He's a criminal, no question. The issue is, though, when he took the stand here, did he lie?" He showed the jury Harris's statement to the police, taken on January 17th when the gun and ring had been found, and said, "Word for word, that statement was the same thing that he testified to here in court. So all this nonsense about us cutting deals with him, and us cutting him loose on a rape charge so he'd come in here and testify—throw it out. That's ridiculous.

"Detective Curole, the homicide detective, he's sitting over there. He worked on leads for six weeks nonstop. The important leads—the ring, the gun—where did they lead to? They lead to that man, John Thompson. All roads, all fingers point to him. Everybody who had anything to say on this witness stand—all the evidence points to him. He's a murderer.

"I'm going to ask you when you go up to deliberate to come back and convict that man for what he did, for killing Ray Liuzza. Convict him of first-degree murder. Thank you very much."

Couhig stood up to take his turn. He coughed, then took a drink of water. John could see he was nervous, that he was figuring out what he needed to say as he walked over to the podium. He began by thanking the jury: "I know when you go in there, you're going to weigh and consider every element of the evidence, and make sure that they prove their case, not just a little bit, but beyond a reasonable doubt, giving John every benefit—*every benefit*—of the doubt.

"Mr. Dubelier says that all roads lead to John Thompson. There is an important intersection that doesn't, and that is the intersection of Josephine and Baronne, where a man goes who shouldn't have, and another man saw him, and saw the man who did it. That witness's testimony is enough to create a reasonable doubt even if you said that someone must pay for this horrible thing, and this is who the district attorney and the police say did it. The district attorney may have prosecuted the wrong guy; they may have cut the deal with the wrong fellow; they may have taken all of this tremendous pressure that was building up on Officer Curole and rush forward with an accused accomplice who says he saw John do this thing a half a block away, on the other side of the street, when he was running.

"At the intersection of Josephine and Baronne, a man runs by, and another man stands there and sees him with the gun in his hand. He didn't have any problem describing the man. Short-cropped hair; dark complexion; a black man; about six feet tall. Any doubt in this man's mind? No. You'll have to decide for yourself whether John is six feet tall. John, could you please stand up?"

John stood up, all five foot eight of him, but he tried not to stand too straight.

"Richard Perkins came forward to the police, or the police went and got him. Which is it? Funk says, 'They came for me.' Officer Curole says, 'He came to us.' No big deal, but it tells you something about what Funk's doing here, perhaps. Officer Curole says, and Funk says, that Kevin Freeman told Funk he parked the car in the 1800 block of Baronne Street. Kevin Freeman's story was entirely different. Freeman says he parked down the street, on Carondelet. And then, of course, Mr. Innocent, Kevin Freeman, says, 'Man, I don't want nothing to do with that. I ran.' This innocent runs across Baronne before the shooting happens, turns around, and he sees this wrestling, this wrestling that Pam Staab never heard in her testimony. So Freeman continues running, and in the most ludicrous part of all, he says, on the corner of Saratoga and Josephine, he turned around, and he's able to see two blocks away and he can see John Thompson running.

"It's a put-up.

"So then, we come to Mr. Carr. The man who on New Year's Eve left his family at eleven o'clock, who went to a bar by himself, and had two beers on New Year's Eve in about three hours. If that's not the most incredible statement you're going to hear.

"So what do we do? We bring Mr. Ferguson, who has no relationship with Mr. Thompson, who's not family, and he says, 'John was with us that night.' Mr. Williams agreed. And of course they had some drinks that night. Any of us on a New Year's Eve might have a few drinks.

"Now, you heard Mr. Dubelier talk about the letter, and you read it. What does it ask? It asks for a man to come forward and tell what he saw. It doesn't say, come forward and lie. It doesn't say, come forward and distort the truth.

"Ladies and gentlemen, the district attorney has proven that a man died. They've proven that this weapon did it. They've proven that they made an arrangement with a guy for testimony. I'm not even going to talk about Junior Harris and the rape charge. You all have to figure out whether it's coincidental that they dropped it last Friday, or not. But ask yourselves another question: Reasonable doubt exists as to the description of this murderer. Recall that Mr. Schliffka looked at John Thompson's photograph and couldn't pick him out. Mr. Carr gave a tentative identification, so the police brought him a picture of Mr. Thompson with *long* hair, and he picked him out then.

"The State has fallen short in their task. Their failure to consult, to ask Mr. Schliffka to show them what they did, allowed the wrong man to cut the deal with the district attorney. You saw Kevin Freeman. You judge whether he had close-cropped hair. You judge whether he was taller than John Thompson at approximately six feet. You judge whether he had the darker complexion. You judge his motivation, then you judge the attitude of Funk, Rickard Perkins. You question in your own mind the motivation of Mr. Carr and the $15,000, and Mr. Perkins and the $15,000, and probe deep into your heart what went on."

Couhig smiled a little to himself. "There's nothing worse than a lawyer who talks too long in argument. All I can ask you now is to consider those things and return a verdict, please, of not guilty."

John watched the jury as Jim Williams stood up. The courtroom was quiet, and the jurors unreadable. Williams adjusted his glasses, glaring out of them at the jury. His posture was stiff, almost soldierly, and his tone dripped with righteousness.

For the most part, Williams covered the same ground Dubelier did—the rules of what was first-degree murder, the murder itself, the evidence that the gun was the murder weapon, the letter John had written to Big Daddy Red, and the fact that Perkins and Carr were disinterested witnesses.

Williams said, "Let's talk about the reward money. You've heard that talked about, mostly out of the lawyers' mouths. Ladies and gentlemen, not one single person came and took that stand and told you anything about any reward money. There is not one word of evidence in this case from people who took this stand regarding reward money. If there had been, you'd have heard the defense put somebody on and discuss a claim made on the money. All this reward money is just hearsay. So when the witnesses came and said, 'I don't know anything about any money, I'm not getting any money,' they were telling you the truth because there was no evidence to show otherwise. So you can put that outside your scope of consideration in this case. No reward money involved—not at this point, anyway, and not as far as those witnesses were concerned.

"Ladies and gentlemen, when you go to the jury room, you will sift through the evidence, and you will say, it just all points to one thing. It points to the fact that John Thompson, while armed with this gun, took the life of a person who was loved by all of those people sitting in the front row—took it, and snuffed it out.

"Ladies and gentlemen, come back with 'guilty as charged.' Thank you."

John watched the jury look past him at Ray Liuzza's family, then look back at him. He glared back.

Quinlan began to speak, telling the jurors the different legal rules for what was first-degree versus second-degree murder, what was robbery versus attempted robbery, reminding them that John had the right to remain silent and not take the stand, and on and on. John looked at the clock—it was still only a little after noon. It wasn't even lunchtime. His entire defense plus three closing arguments, and now Quinlan talking to the jurors, had taken less than three hours.

THE VERDICT CAME quickly, right after lunch. The jury walked in, and one of them, an African-American woman, handed a piece of paper to one of the judge's clerks. The clerk with the paper stood up and said, "We, the jury, find the defendant, John Thompson, guilty as charged."

The courtroom exhaled, with John's family dropping their heads while the Liuzza family began quietly shaking hands and hugging, neither family wanting to make a display before the jury, but everyone overwhelmed with emotion. For John's part, he sat back down, his face expressionless and his head spinning. He felt like the world had started spinning a million miles per second, and as he looked around the room he swore he could hear each person's thoughts, each of them looking at him and thinking, *murderer*, like his conviction was a beautiful thing.

John looked and found his mother in the benches behind him. She had Dedric in her arms and was crying. Denise was next to her, holding Tiger on her lap. And then he turned around and faced forward, and wouldn't let them see his face again.

With the guilty verdict rendered, it was time for the jury to decide John's fate. Would they give him the death penalty, life in prison, or something more lenient?

It don't matter, John thought. *It don't matter. I got my forty-nine years already. How they gonna make it any worse?*

EVEN AT THE sentencing hearing, Couhig and Fanning told him not to take the stand. John wasn't sure why, since the reason he'd stayed off before was that the carjacking conviction would come up. Now that they were talking about sentencing, the jury had a right to know about John's past crimes, and even though the carjacking happened after the day Ray Liuzza was killed, Quinlan had ruled that Dubelier and Williams could talk about it. But Couhig and Fanning told him not to talk, and so he followed their direction.

Jim Williams stood up and told the jury that the armed robbery showed that John was violent and a career criminal. Mimi Lagarde was also brought to the stand, where Dubelier and Williams asked her questions about the carjacking. She cried, describing how John had put a gun to her face and fought with her brother.

Fanning had brought in some "expert," a scientist from Tulane, to talk about what kind of person John was. The doctor, if that's what he was, admitted on the stand that Fanning had called him only days before, on the Friday before the trial, and he had only met with John once. Still, he said that this had given him enough information to make a sound assessment of John's character. The scientist told the jury about John's father, a drug dealer who had spent a lot of his life in prison. He told the jury about his stepfather, abusive with John and abusive with John's mom, and he reminded them that John's mother had really been a child herself at the time of his birth, just fifteen years old.

The expert's conclusion, given what he knew of John, was that John was a career criminal whose only life would be on the street committing acts of violence.

He's right about that, John thought. *Got no other way to make a livin'. If that's what gets me the death penalty, they gonna need to execute the whole Sixth Ward.*

Next, Couhig put John's mother on the stand and questioned her about John and his childhood—about whether there were any redeeming qualities that the jury should know about. John hated watching her up there, being forced to defend him in front of all those people, knowing that they all thought she was partly to blame for her son turning out to be this monster. And it would get worse if they sentenced him to death—she'd surely feel as though her testimony wouldn't be enough to save her son.

Fanning and Couhig asked her how old she was when she had John, and whether she'd known how to take care of a child at the age of sixteen; with that done, they asked her to step down and called Denise to take the stand. She said she loved John, and that was pretty much it.

That was the end of John's character witnesses—his mother and his girlfriend, nervous and unprepared, answering a few vague questions.

John didn't stand a chance, and he knew it.

Jim Williams stood up, righteous and powerful. He had been focused on the evidence in his last argument, but now that they were in the sentencing phase, he had more leeway to get the jury's emotions involved. He described the brutality of the murder. He told the jury that Ray Liuzza did not have to die, that it was the shots in the back of an unarmed man that had been the cause of death. He described Ray Liuzza pleading for his life, and about how long he'd been conscious after he was shot, knowing that he was dying. Williams said it was John's plan to have the gun and to find someone to kill that night. He told the jury that life in prison wasn't enough punishment for John. He said that if the jury gave John life in prison, he'd be able to start fresh in the state pen at Angola. Williams made it sound like summer camp, saying that John would make new friends, be able to visit with his kids. He said John could even join the prison softball team. In the meantime, Williams said, the Liuzza family had a dead son, and nothing would ever change that.

After Williams, the only thing left was a brief word from Patrick Fanning. Fanning simply talked about himself, saying, "I'm not going to put a guilt trip on you about the death penalty. We're court-appointed counsel, and whatever somebody might say in the future about the case, we tried. We tried. John Thompson never got a break in his life, and now we're asking you to give him one. Send him to Angola Penitentiary for the rest of his life—lock him up, throw away the key—but don't kill him."

Send me to prison for life but don't kill me, John thought. *Some break.*

QUINLAN TOLD THE jury what was required of them—unanimous agreement on the sentence. They could sentence him to death if they thought the murder was particularly heinous or brutal, or if they thought the robbery was an aggravating factor. They could also sentence him to something less. According to Louisiana State Law, however, if the jury's recommendation on sentencing was less than unanimous, Judge Quinlan was required to sentence him to life imprisonment without benefit of parole.

The jury was out for two and a half hours—time that John and his family spent waiting nervously, John in the holding cell in Judge Quinlan's chambers while his family waited in the hall outside the courtroom. John wondered what they were thinking. Would they come to visit him? He was never going to be out of prison again. Would he ever be able to hold his sons? Would Denise leave him? Would his momma turn away from him?

You got bigger problems, he thought. *You might get fried in the electric chair.* Then he thought, *Actually, that might be the best news you get all day.*

THE JURY CAME back in, looking serious. John stood as they walked by. They sat, and Quinlan asked, "Have you been able to come to a unanimous decision?"

The foreperson, the woman who had had the piece of paper that said John was guilty before, stood. "No, Your Honor, we have not been able to come to a unanimous decision."

"Can you tell me this—without saying which way it is, do you have any idea how split this decision is?"

"Eleven to one, Your Honor."

"Do you believe that further deliberation might result in your ability to reach a decision?"

"No, Your Honor."

Quinlan called the lawyers to the bench and spoke to them. John couldn't hear what they were talking about, but he remembered Quinlan's rule. If the jury wasn't unanimous, he wouldn't get the death sentence. It would be life in prison.

The lawyers returned to their tables and Judge Quinlan said to the jury, "Ladies and gentlemen, so that we can be very clear: It's my understanding that you feel that even if you were to go back out now to deliberate some more, that it would be futile—that there would not be a chance of you reaching a verdict. Would that be correct?"

At this, the foreperson turned back and looked over the jury. Her gaze landed on one juror, in the second seat in the back row, one of the African-American women. All the other jurors looked at her. *She's the one,* John thought. *The one who doesn't want to kill me.*

The woman shifted nervously in her seat as the others looked at her, their unspoken question hanging in the air. Slowly, she closed her eyes and tightened her fists, and then she nodded, without saying a word.

The foreperson turned back to the judge and said, "We'd like to go back in." Quinlan nodded. "Ladies and gentlemen, if you would go back in and attempt once again. If after a reasonable time you're not able to reach agreement, well then, let the sheriff know, and we will come back out."

Couhig and Fanning looked at each other with amazement in their eyes as the jury left. The door had barely closed behind the jury when Fanning rose. "Your Honor, it's clear to everybody in the courtroom what's going on right now. Miss Chaney, the juror in the second seat of the back row, was the holdout; it was eleven to one, and she stuck to her opinion in the back. They announced they were ready to come out and she still stuck to her opinion. When the foreperson of the jury looked over to her, and it became obvious to everyone who Miss Chaney was—that she was the lady who wouldn't vote for the death penalty—she looked around the courtroom and saw the sea of faces, and she succumbed to the pressure of all the people in the courtroom."

Dubelier jumped up, objecting to Fanning's description. Quinlan let him finish, and then said, "When the Court questioned the jurors as to the possibility of them reaching a verdict, the foreperson, at first, indicated no, but as the jurors did look around, the Court asked again, and the jurors said, 'Yes.' So the Court has allowed the jurors to go back to attempt to deliberate again to reach a unanimous verdict. The Court believes that after a three-day trial like this, the jury should have every opportunity to reach a verdict if they think it is at all possible."

Fanning was lodging an additional objection and asking to poll the jury on their recommended verdicts, both of which Quinlan rejected, when the bailiff appeared. The jury was ready to return.

They filed in, most with their eyes to the ground. Quinlan asked again, "Have you been able to reach a unanimous decision?"

The foreperson rose. "Yes, we have, Your Honor." She handed it to the clerk, who read, "Having found the statutory aggravating circumstances, and after considering the mitigating circumstances offered, the jury recommends that the defendant be sentenced to death."

Fanning renewed his request to poll the jury, as John sat back, stone-faced. *If this is how it's gonna be,* he thought, *y'all ain't gettin' the satisfaction of seeing me react.*

Each juror was asked, "Is this your verdict?" by Judge Quinlan. One at a time, each juror answered, "Yes." Leola Chaney was the second juror asked, and this time she did not hesitate. "Yes."

He had started the day as John Thompson, the accused. He was ending it as John Thompson, the condemned. He looked at Couhig and Fanning, but they had nothing to say, except for Couhig's "I'm sorry, John."

The sheriff stood him up and turned him toward the door. As he walked, John looked at Denise and his mother, at the tears running down their faces, and scanned the Liuzza family, saw their joy and relief on the other side of the courtroom.

He followed the sheriff out of the courtroom and back to jail.

This ain't right, he thought. *This ain't right.*

11

PAY IT FORWARD
<hr/>

WHEN JOHN WAS waiting for his murder trial, sitting with his forty-nine-year sentence for armed robbery, the other inmates at OPP would tell him not to worry, he could handle the time. They all said the same thing: "There's only two days you spend in prison. That's the day you go in, and the day you get out."

They stopped saying that after he got the death sentence. It wasn't true anymore. John wouldn't get that second day. He got one day, and that day was over.

Still, today would be different from the others. John was finally leaving OPP for where he should have been since June, 1985—Angola.

John couldn't decide whether he was looking forward to the move or not. He'd been told by other inmates that Angola was a much better place to do time than OPP. He knew a couple guys on death row already, and they wrote letters telling him he was crazy to stay in OPP when he could be treated right on death row, where he could get some privacy in his own cell.

There wasn't any privacy on the tier in OPP, that was for sure. John had all his stuff in a footlocker, with a lock any idiot could pick or break in seconds, and sides that the rats could eat right through. And there was no place to get away from the other inmates. Guys got raped, stabbed, beaten to death. John saw all of it.

Staying out of that violence was a full-time job. On the street, he remembered talking to people about how prison couldn't be as bad as they said. He knew now he'd been wrong. It was just as bad as they said.

He had been in OPP two years, seven months, and two weeks—since January 16, 1985. But his murder conviction and death sentence were on May 15, 1985, so by John's reckoning, he'd been in OPP two years and three months longer than he should.

The reason was plain, if you looked at it. OPP was funded based on a per-prisoner fee, so everyone could be fed and clothed and guarded. But there was a twist. OPP was funded by the parish and the state, but it wasn't funded to handle state prisoners. So when a prisoner came into OPP for a trial or hearing in the parish, that prisoner counted as a state prisoner, not a city prisoner, and OPP got paid a premium for that prisoner—maybe something like three times more per day than they get paid for housing the regular inmates. After his conviction, John counted as a state prisoner for funding purposes, and OPP got a premium to keep him.

He didn't know what had changed to make them send him up to Angola now—after all, the economics hadn't changed. One of John's friends at OPP had been in the same situation, sentenced to death but held over at OPP. He got out by causing a ruckus, standing on a table and breaking lightbulbs and starting fights until he was more trouble than he was worth, so they shipped him up to death row in Angola. That's when he started writing John letters, telling John, "Get your ass up here, son." He said Angola was cleaner, private—a better environment than OPP.

John hadn't created the ruckus that his friend had. He was in no hurry to leave OPP, no matter how bad it was. It wasn't that he had a problem with death row. He had to agree with his friend—any private space would be better than Tent City, or even a shared cell in OPP. Even the isolation cells at OPP had three other guys in them. The other men in there were always the crazy ones, the ones who would tear at their own skin, scream, yell, make noises. A person could be in there with those crazy men for as long as the guards decided.

BAD AS OPP was, though, it was closer to John's family, or at least to his grandmother and Denise. Dedric would be ten in December—the third birthday John would miss—and Tiger was six and a half. They were too young, and weren't allowed to visit him.

John's mother didn't really like to visit that much; neither did Denise. It was easy to see why. For a while, though, they made the effort. Denise would walk up to the visiting benches, facing John through a wire-mesh wall. The wire was pretty thick, so no one would try to cut it or poke holes in it to make physical contact with their visitor, so it was hard for them to see each other. Talking was easy enough, if you could talk loud enough to be heard over everyone else's conversations and crying and yelling, and so that's what they'd do.

John had known he would have less contact with Tiger and Dedric. They couldn't visit now, and later, when they got old enough, they wouldn't want to visit. Staying at OPP would make it easier, but he knew how it would go. It would be the same as it had been for him and his father. He should have been ready for what happened with Denise, too, but he wasn't.

When John first went in, Denise visited him every other day. She kept that up for a month or so, but soon her visits slowed down. As her visits became fewer and farther between, John felt his connection with the outside world slipping. His panic showed as anger—anger he would take out on her when she did visit. That made things worse. It quickly got to the point where John would start every visit by being angry that she wasn't coming more regularly. He'd tell her that he had all this pressure about the trials that were coming up, and she didn't care enough to even visit. She'd get all defensive, tell him he was lucky she came to see him at all since he had deserted his family. It would just get worse from there.

About two months after he was arrested, Denise shut him up in the middle of one of his tirades by saying "I'm three months pregnant."

John was stunned. He thought, *How the fuck could she do that to me? How could she tell me we're gonna have another baby? Don't I already have enough to worry about?*

They both knew John wasn't getting out. Still, Denise kept coming in, trying to do the right thing and to stand by him. But it got harder and harder to talk, and he finally figured out why. During a visit in early fall, John looked at her through the mesh and said, "Denise, you know that baby's not mine."

She had tried to protest, but he had done the math. He had been arrested in January, and Denise was clearly not about to give birth. Any child of his would have been born by now. That meant another man, and that meant she'd slept around before his convictions, before she knew he wasn't coming back.

Denise had broken down, wailing that she was sorry. John wasn't interested in her apologies. He was interested in hurting her. He pounded on the wire mesh, yelling at her, calling her a bitch and a whore. John asked her, "How the fuck you do this shit and come here, fuck me over while I'm stuck in this motherfucker?"

She straightened up at that. "I didn't have to come tell you. I coulda just stayed away."

"That's just what you ought to do," he said. "Lucky I can't get outta here, too, or I'd fuck you up, you and that ignorant man you sleepin' with."

He could barely see her face, but her voice cut right through his soul. "Fuck this shit," she said. She stood up, said, "I'm leaving right now," and walked out of the prison.

John yelled, "Fuck you, then!" to her back, but he waited by the screen, straining through the mesh to watch her leave the room. He turned and almost walked right into one of the old, veteran inmates. The old man was just standing there, looking at John through his wrinkled face.

John said, "What you lookin' at, old man? You lookin' to get your ass kicked too?"

The man just chuckled. "Young buck, you don't want to fuck with me. I'm nothing to you but a little good sense you oughtta listen to."

"Man, the fuck I want to listen to your tired old ass for?"

"I tell you what, you oughtta listen to me. You wait a few years, you're gonna learn some stuff I could tell you now. I'll tell you this—you run that woman off with the time you got, you ain't gonna have nobody while you doing this time."

John stopped. The man said, "I been doing time for a while. I been out to Angola three times. I was there in the seventies, when the white-boy guards had shotguns and shot a nigger if he even looked the wrong way. We were working in them fields, and fighting in them dorms, and hoping a nigger didn't cross you out or you get shot by one of them guards.

"You do time long as I done time, you learn this. And you, you gonna do time as long, maybe longer than I done. Don't fuss with your woman, youngblood. Ain't no one else gonna stick with you while you do this time. Your daddy and mommy, they gonna get old and die while you here. Your kids, they too small, they gonna get a life of their own. They ain't coming. You ain't got your girl, you ain't got no visitors at all. You just got my pretty face to look at."

John said, "Man, you don't know what she went out and done to me."

"All I know," he said, "is she might be all you got. I ran mine off and ain't nobody visiting me now. Hate to see you fuck up like I did."

He had walked away without another word, and John went back to his bunk. *What the fuck am I gonna do now?* John thought.

JOHN WAS SNAPPED out of his memory by the guard walking in, telling the men on the loading dock to get in the bus. John crammed in the back with a bunch of other convicts, the men talking to each other as they walked in. "Glad to be outta that hellhole, bruh," one said. "Ready to get out to them fields, do my time."

Another one said, "Yeah, man, that Warden Foti's a cold motherfucker. Inmates sued his ass before about that shit in there. Won, too. But nothin' changes in OPP, man."

The driver started up the bus and put it on the highway. John kept quiet. He'd heard inmates talk shit all the time, talking about shit they didn't know anything about, going on about life sentences and death sentences. "Life sentence just like a death sentence," one of them said. "How's it different? Both take your life away. Death sentence is easier, you ask me. A way out. Rather be lying in that ground than dealing with this shit every day."

John just looked out the window as they hit the interstate.

He thought about California, where he'd lived when he was six years old. His mother had taken him out there, put him with another part of the family while she tried to find some work. He lived in Los Angeles for a year until she found a new husband, then he came back to New Orleans to live with her. Her new husband was okay, but got a little mean when he was drinking. Once, when John was about seven and a half, he got after John with a belt. After that, John's grandmother stepped in. She said, "I'm taking Nué," and that was that. From that time on, John's grandmother became the center of his world.

Nué. No one ever got that right. It was "new-ay," with the "a" like in "escape." Everyone, even the cops, called him "Nut." Not his grandmother. She said it was an Indian word. She said, "That's a name for a warrior chief—because that's what you are, a warrior chief." But everyone on the street heard her calling him, they said, "Man, the fuck that old lady calling you 'Nut' for?" And so he was Nut on the street.

But he was Nué with his grandmother. She was strict and kept a close eye on him, a closer eye than his mother did. He called her "Momma" and thought of her as his mother, made sure she knew where he was all the time. She knew what was going on in the neighborhood, tried to keep John away from it. But the streets eventually called to all the kids in that neighborhood.

There was a boy who lived two doors down from John, and they started hanging out. They got a little older, and their world got a little bigger. They'd go out the back fence unseen and walk around the neighborhood, exploring the Third Ward—the drugs, the guns, all of it. Soon after that, John had started hanging out with other kids, messing around like kids do. They'd break into cars, drive them around; smoke some grass; nothing else major besides that. And there were definitely no guns.

Guns had always made John uncomfortable. On a day just like any other, when John was eighteen, he walked out of his house and turned to walk up the street. A car came around the corner, driving slow. He saw the looks on the boys in the car, and then saw the shotgun come out the back window. He turned to run, but it was too late. Shots rang out as the car peeled away, leaving John with a serious wound in his left leg.

To that day, he still had no idea why he'd been shot.

THE PRISON VAN came to a stop and the doors opened. John stood up as much as he could and shuffled out with the other men, the guards helping him down so he didn't fall in the shackles.

The building set apart for death row didn't look like anything special. It was cinder block and only a couple of stories high. Someone kept it up—it had a nice lawn, with flowers in front. It didn't look like a place where the worst of the worst lived.

John sat in the front room, the two guards still watching him while they filled out all the paperwork. They walked him from the processing area to the guardroom for the tier, two more guards behind a wall with a window, in front of a door made of iron bars.

His first thought was, *Man, death row smells.* It smelled like shit, grease-fried shit, mixed with sweat and dirt and something else he couldn't place, something strange and unsettling. They walked him down six cells, and as he walked he realized that it wasn't just the smell that was bothering him. It was the noise, too. *How does anybody fuckin' think in this place?* he wondered.

There were two TVs along the wall outside the cells, spaced down the tier. Each one was tuned to a different program, blasting at peak volume. He couldn't tell exactly how many, but probably twenty or twenty-five inmates were on the tier, talking to one another, to the guards, or to themselves. Some of the guys had radios, and they were playing music on top of that. All of it vibrated back and forth, bouncing off the cinder block and concrete.

John had been on death row for less than three minutes, but he already knew his friend had been wrong. There would be no privacy here.

The guards opened a cell door and John walked inside. It was too small to be a closet. John could maybe lie down in it the long way, but it would be hard to lie down across it side to side. There was a cot on the right side, bolted to the wall, and a sink that he could probably squeeze both hands into at once and a toilet next to that, both bolted into steel plates on the back wall. The pipes, John knew, were way back in the wall so there was nothing he could rip out and use as a weapon. There were cinder-block walls on three sides and bars on the wall he had just come in through. The bars were maybe the width of a silver dollar, with flat bars across every foot and a half or so, and a space across a few bars where a meal tray or a book could be passed through.

Across the hall was a dirty window, up high, that let in some light. The rest of the light was from tube lights in the hall ceiling.

The cell bars locked behind John and he was left alone.

Hold on, John thought. *This cell ain't empty.*

It wasn't that there was another person in the cell. He was definitely alone. But there was a bedroll on the bed, and as John sat on the cot and looked underneath, there was a chest on the floor under the bed with a pair of pants folded on top. John slid the chest out and looked at it for a second. *They must be fuckin' with me,* he thought. *This must be some hazin' shit, put the new man in the cell of a crazy man, see what happens. He'll come back and see me and lose it; maybe he tries to kill me right off, or some guard'll step in, save my life, and then I start off owin' him somethin'.*

John yelled for a guard. Nothing happened, so he yelled again. That set the other prisoners off screaming and yelling, hooting and laughing.

The guard came to the door at the end of the tier. "Thompson. You got a problem already?"

"Yeah. This somebody's cell. Y'all done made some kind of mistake. This somebody's cell."

"Ain't no mistake, and ain't nobody's cell. It's all yours for a long time. Enjoy it."

John hoped his voice was calm as he said, "Motherfucker, I'm telling you there's somebody's shit in here. How you got somebody's pants in here this ain't somebody else's cell?"

John didn't know what he said that was wrong, but all of a sudden all the noise, all the talking, yelling, jeering, taunting—it stopped. The TVs were still going, but everything else was quiet.

The man in the next cell finally spoke up. "Your name's John?" He was quiet, calm, serious.

"Yeah."

"Yeah, so, uh, that cell belonged to another inmate. Sterling. Sterling Raults was his name. He ain't gonna be needing that stuff no more; you can do with it what you want. He ain't coming back."

"What you mean, he ain't comin' back?" John said, then immediately wished he hadn't.

"You one of the ones they send sometimes, one of them's not so smart? Maybe that'll be good for your appeal. They fried him last week."

John was sitting on the cot with the trunk between his feet on the floor. His stomach flipped, looking at the dead man's stuff, feeling the dead man staring at him from the chest.

It was as if John suddenly realized exactly who he was for the first time. He wasn't John Thompson. John Thompson was as dead as Sterling Raults, as dead as Ray Liuzza, as dead as all the other guys on the tier. It was just that the warden hadn't gotten to his execution yet. When he walked in, he thought the cell was smaller than a closet. He was right—it was the same size as a coffin.

He pushed the chest away from his feet, pulled his body into a ball on the bed, sweating and shaking. He fought not to make a sound, knowing that everyone would hear it. He said, as tough as he could manage, "Guard. Man, get this shit outta my cell. Sitting in here with a dead man's shit in my cell."

The guard strolled back down the tier. "Why, it's a present for you, John—from him and from us. You think he needs it where he's gone? He don't want any clothes, it's so hot where he went." He paused, then said, "Hey, I got it. Someday, you can do a favor like that for someone else. Pay it forward, you know?" The guard chuckled to himself at this.

Slowly, John unwrapped himself from the cot, his feet pushing the chest away again, as far away as he could. He couldn't take his eyes off the chest, and couldn't hear anything except the guard's laugh. He was still shaking, feeling cold even though it was hot on the Row.

He was able to place it, now, the strange sensation he'd felt as he walked onto death row, the thing that had made him uneasy.

It was the realization that he was dead.

12

PHILADELPHIA LAWYERS

Philadelphia lawyer. n. A shrewd lawyer adept at the discovery and manipulation of legal technicalities. (*American Heritage Dictionary, 2008*)

MICHAEL BANKS PULLED into the valet station and handed the car keys to the teenage kid in the waistcoat who came around to the driver's-side door. Another valet opened the passenger door for his wife, Lori. Michael walked around the car and extended his elbow with playful gallantry to escort his wife into the tastefully appointed lobby of the Wyndham Franklin Plaza Hotel. They rode the escalator up to the ballroom, site of this year's Andrew Hamilton Ball, the Philadelphia Bar Association's annual charitable fund-raising dinner.

The Hamilton Ball raised a lot of money every year for altruistic legal activities for a wide variety of community causes: the underprivileged, arts organizations, and others in Philadelphia who truly needed legal help but lacked the resources to pay for it.

Michael was a strong advocate of pro bono work, and always made sure there was at least one pro bono case on his docket at any given time. On his commute from East Falls (in the northwest part of Philadelphia) to the Center City offices of Morgan,

Lewis & Bockius, Michael could see the whole gamut of social opportunity, from burned-out drug houses to huge, multimillion-dollar estates.

Michael's office, on the twenty-eighth floor, with its antique furniture and plush carpeting, provided him with an unobstructed view of Logan Square and its elegant Alexander Calder fountain. But the view also took in the other side of that same square, less than two hundred yards away from the building. Homeless men gathered there, wandering aimlessly around the soup kitchen, along with the battered women and abandoned children whose cases were heard at Philadelphia's Family Court. The city provided Michael with daily reminders of how lucky he was, and the obligation he and his colleagues at Morgan, Lewis—widely considered Philadelphia's premier corporate law firm—had to the community around them.

Michael had been groomed since birth to go further than his parents. He had a JD from Columbia, and had gotten his undergrad degree at Cornell. Even so, Michael felt, and perhaps even nurtured, a certain amount of outsider status. He'd seen the trust-fund babies at college and law school, and he was acutely aware of how different their lives were compared to his father's—how hard his father worked as a sole practitioner. His father took all comers, represented folks in the neighborhood on a variety of cases, rarely turned a case down—even if it was a case for good people who couldn't pay.

The practice of law at Morgan, Lewis was a little different. Morgan was a century-old Philadelphia institution, an international law firm with a "who's who" client roster, including the world's most successful businesses. Michael worked in the Labor & Employment Law group, specializing in representing business owners in employment matters in the United States. His cases were complicated, nuanced, and challenging, and he defended some of the most powerful executives in the country.

It was a rewarding job, financially and intellectually. He loved the competitive aspects of litigating and the aggressiveness of negotiating. It fed his mind and his ego, and it paid very well. On the other hand, Michael rarely got to pick his clients. If a key executive in a Fortune 500 company did something wrong, the firm would defend that as vigorously as it would a frivolous lawsuit against the company. The lawyer inside Michael prized that professionalism, but there was still a part of him that wished from time to time that he had a little more leeway with his clients and cases.

Morgan, Lewis helped address that frustration by encouraging Michael and its other lawyers to take on pro bono work, recognizing that the obligations of its lawyers extended beyond the Four Seasons and the Wyndham Plaza. It was this part of the firm's culture that Michael truly appreciated. *Never forget,* Michael's father had said; *The law is a service profession, and people truly need the services you can provide.*

As Michael and Lori approached the bar, they spotted Gordon Cooney, Michael's colleague and good friend. Gordon, a handsome, athletic man with strawberry blond hair, a freckled face, and a ready smile, was accompanied by a new date, someone Michael had not met before. He chuckled a bit, knowing that Gordon was not yet ready to settle down with just one woman.

Gordon was the favored son of the firm's Litigation section. He had grown up on the Main Line, playing lacrosse with the sons of society at the Episcopal Academy. Like Michael, Gordon's father was a lawyer, though his practice was more white-shoe than blue-collar.

With Gordon's considerable natural talents and all of his economic and social advantages, he could have been another one of those law students who coasted on his family's prominence. It was to Gordon's credit, and to his family's, that he was not at all that way. In fact, Michael was constantly impressed by Gordon's complete lack of a sense of entitlement. He was not only a brilliant lawyer, but also a man who managed to live up to the highest standards of professionalism and ethics without being "holier than thou."

As the cocktail hour wound down, Michael and Gordon sat down for dinner. Joining them at the table was another young lawyer from the firm's Litigation section, Andy Leipold. Andy had only been with the firm for a few months, but word was already spreading fast that the firm had a superstar-to-be on its hands.

Even by Morgan's lofty standards, Andy had an impressive résumé: summa cum laude at Boston University; high honors at Virginia Law and editor in chief of the *UVA Law Review;* a clerkship with Judge Mikva in the D.C. Court of Appeals; and a coveted spot as a law clerk in the U.S. Supreme Court for Justice Lewis Powell. Andy smiled a lot, and his voice had a smooth sincerity—a pleasant baritone with a low-key, flattened Maine timbre that conveyed a kind and caring quality.

Clerking had really helped Andy understand how he wanted to use his law degree, showing him firsthand how the law could be an instrument for justice and social change. Given that passion, some had questioned his decision to practice at a large corporate firm, but Andy firmly believed that firms like Morgan, Lewis could have high-quality and stimulating legal work and also maintain a social conscience, and he was determined to try to combine the two in his practice.

As they ate, the talk at the table centered on the pro bono cases each man had previously worked on, and what sorts of cases they might do in the future.

"You know what nobody has done at Morgan that would really be worthwhile?" Andy asked. "A death penalty case."

The table grew quiet with surprise. Morgan's lawyers weren't typically involved in defending violent criminals. Still, the thought captured Michael's attention, as capital punishment had always seemed barbaric to him—an indefensible and amoral state-sanctioned murder of its citizenry. It had always amazed him that the United States, of all places, was one of the last developed nations in the world to allow capital punishment. But Michael also knew that taking on a case like that would require a lot of time—and it would push the Morgan lawyers into an area of the law quite unfamiliar, with extraordinarily high stakes.

Andy continued, saying, "I reviewed dozens of petitions when I was clerking. The death row inmates who aren't representing themselves are being represented by appointed counsel who are well-intentioned, but they aren't any more familiar with this area of the law than you are; they don't have your legal skills, and they don't have anywhere near the resources of a firm such as Morgan, Lewis backing them up. The quality of the representations overall, from what I've seen, is a real problem."

Lori was watching Michael as Andy talked, and she recognized the look in his eyes. He wanted to do it. She said, "I don't know, Andy. You want to represent rapists and child molesters, mass murderers? With all the wonderful causes that you could spend your charitable time on? I mean, I'm not saying you can't do a better job than their other options. I'm just saying, do you think that's the best use of your charitable time?"

Michael knew what Lori was really saying. They had two kids and two careers, no spare time, and he was coming up for partner soon. This might not be the moment to take on a time-consuming charitable obligation. Nonetheless, he was drawn to the idea. What if Andy was right? Maybe a firm with Morgan's resources could really make a difference in a capital punishment case—especially if it were not entirely certain that the client was deserving of that sentence (or of incarceration at all).

Gordon seemed to be reading Michael's mind. "I don't know how you decide among charitable activities, either. There are so many worthwhile things. But the death penalty is an area where our skills as trial lawyers might be uniquely useful. And in some way, it's particularly valuable because it's so unpopular. If we're going to have a system that puts people to death, we have to have confidence that the system isn't making mistakes. It's a situation where it would be better to have a guilty man go free than an innocent one put to death. And if our participation ensures that the system is forced to not cut corners here, I think that's useful, even if you're representing someone who actually committed one of these horrible crimes."

Lori wasn't quite done. "Okay, but Gordon, do you really want to represent a convicted rapist, or a child molester? I mean, these are bad people, whether or not they should be put to death."

Michael said, "I think we're getting a little ahead of ourselves. We're not saying they're paragons of society, but that isn't the point. The point is to make sure they're guilty before carrying out the ultimate punishment. No one is saying we'll take on one of these cases, and even if we did, it would be our choice. If we don't like the client, if it's so horrible it offends us, we don't have to take the case."

Gordon raised his glass. "Well, this is a pretty appropriate conversation for the Andrew Hamilton Ball, since Hamilton himself was famous for taking on—and winning—a major pro bono censorship case against the King of England in pre–Revolutionary War Philadelphia. In fact, it was his creativity and passion for what was thought to be an impossible defense in the service of the law that coined the term 'Philadelphia lawyer.' So I offer a toast—to Andrew Hamilton, to pro bono cases, to great lawyering, and to the Philadelphia lawyer."

NOVEMBER 22, 1987

MICHAEL WAS STILL mulling things over on the train ride into work the next Monday. Why *not* take on a death penalty case? He had always hated the death penalty. Why not put himself on the front lines? He agreed that people on death row deserved the best representation they could get as much as the CEOs Michael usually represented.

And didn't he have an obligation to fight against the things he thought were unfair in society? Wasn't that why he had become a lawyer in the first place?

Still, Lori wasn't all wrong. Michael had a family and a career to think about. Representing a convicted murderer or rapist might not be the best plan for a senior associate gunning for partner at a conservative law firm. The partnership, and a lifetime of financial security, was his to lose—and taking on a huge case representing a man convicted of a detestable crime would siphon huge amounts of his energy and cost the firm money.

Sitting on the train, he knew what his father would say: *These people deserve the best representation they can get. This is America. It's everyone's right. Let's make sure at least one of them gets what each of us deserves.*

GORDON WAS HAVING a similar debate with himself on his morning run. He had represented schools, battered women's shelters, and local groups in Philadelphia on less-controversial issues. Working to free a death row inmate was a different kind of challenge. He was far from an expert on death penalty law, and his views on the death penalty weren't as tightly held as some of his colleagues. Was representing a convicted criminal how he wanted to spend his free time?

The answer worked itself out as he jogged. It wasn't the ideology behind the death penalty that concerned him. Instead, it was the procedural safeguards that ensured the right person was being executed. How could the benefits of capital punishment—the deterrent value, the fundamental fairness of punishing wrongdoers—be realized if the rules of law weren't strictly followed? The ultimate punishment deserved ultimate certainty.

As Gordon continued to think about it, he began to find the thought of taking on a case like this more interesting. It would be hard to find an area of law where Gordon's love of legal procedure would have more of an impact. If he needed to work longer hours to make sure his "paid" cases didn't suffer, that would be fine. *You never know*, he thought. *Maybe we'll represent a person who's actually innocent.*

MARCH 12, 1988

IT HAD TAKEN a few months for Michael, Gordon, and Andy to put a proposal together and get approval from the firm's management for their pro bono case. The delay was actually more related to their existing cases than anything else, as the senior managers had been extremely supportive of the idea. The three men were amazed at how few questions had been asked about the time or monetary commitment, which they knew could get into the thousands of hours and millions of dollars. The only question posed to them was from the firm's managing partner, who simply asked, "Is this something you feel strongly about?"

Gordon had answered, "Yes, sir," and that was that.

Approval in hand, the three men began looking for a specific case to work on. While Pennsylvania technically had a death penalty statute, the governor was personally opposed to capital punishment, and had announced that he would not sign any death warrants while in office. As a result, all the local death penalty cases were on hold, and they needed to look elsewhere to find an active case.

As it turned out, finding a case wasn't very hard at all. Ninety-six people had been executed since 1976, and ninety of the executions had occurred in the southeastern United States.

Texas was far and away the most aggressive about thinning out its death row population, but Louisiana was rapidly making a name for itself as well. Since January 1987, "Old Sparky," as the electric chair at Angola Penitentiary was called, had really been blazing, killing eleven men—including three in a ten-day span that summer. Even Texas wasn't matching that pace.

Andy was given the name of the executive director of the Loyola School of Law's Capital Defense Project, a legal clinic in New Orleans that coordinated death penalty appeals throughout the state. One case in particular seemed perfect for them. It was a case that no one in New Orleans wanted to touch, as the accused had been convicted of killing the son of a well-off and well-connected businessman in town. The timing was right, as it was heading into mandated post-conviction relief appeals that were unique to the death penalty, so the original lawyers on the case were happy to leave it. And as Andy and the director talked, Andy realized there were several procedural issues that would be of interest to investigate. The executive director said she'd send up the transcripts and police report, and if they wanted to represent the defendant, they could let her know.

The name of the condemned man was John Thompson.

13

TRUTH IS WHAT THE JURY SAYS IT IS

MICHAEL SAT WITH Andy and Gordon in a conference room on the twenty-seventh floor of One Logan Street. The conference room overlooked the Ben Franklin Parkway and most of North Philadelphia. It was a spectacular view, although no one was looking at it. Instead, they were focused on their discussion. Several copies of the John Thompson trial transcript lay in front of them, along with the typical mess of notepads, diagrams, markers, and coffee cups that made up a case file in disarray. Andy stood in front of two easels at one end of the large mahogany table, holding a big black marker. One easel was labeled STRENGTHS, the other WEAKNESSES.

Andy had started the meeting by comparing the transcript in *State of Louisiana v. John Thompson* with other capital punishment cases he had reviewed in past jobs. To put it bluntly, Andy had seen worse. Generally, in Andy's experience, if freeing your client was your goal, representing death row inmates on appeal would rarely be a satisfying experience. Andy didn't really think that freeing John Thompson was their goal—he would be satisfied with representing the man professionally and making sure the system operated according to Louisiana law and the U.S. Constitution—but he was pleasantly surprised to see that there were a lot of issues they could work with, and also, that their client was not a totally unsympathetic human being.

It was a cold-blooded murder, no doubt about that. Liuzza had been unarmed, Thompson had fired multiple shots, and the DAs had used all of this nicely in the trial. In the autopsy report, the medical examiner had pointed out in loving detail the path of each bullet that had entered Liuzza's body. And the trail of evidence leading to Thompson and Freeman as the men who had committed the robbery was compelling.

Still, the DA's case was weak on physical evidence tying Thompson to the murder. While the evidence against him was substantial, it was also circumstantial. Kevin Freeman was the only eyewitness, and he was most certainly biased. The only unbiased observer, Paul Schliffka, had not seen the actual murder being committed, had described a much taller man to police, and had not been able to pick Thompson out of a lineup. The evidence linking Thompson to the gun and the ring was testimonial, not objective physical evidence like fingerprints. Did it mean that Thompson was innocent? Of course not—and a jury that had seen the evidence clearly thought he was guilty. But to a trained litigator, this was far from a slam-dunk case.

Gordon said, "Andy, you're right, and if you're looking for an emotional place that lets you defend Thompson as a convicted murderer, I think it makes sense. But we can't retry this case. We can't prove to an appellate court that John Thompson is innocent. He's guilty. That's been decided. The truth is what the jury says it is, and they've said John Thompson is guilty."

Michael added, "Gordon's right, but it's actually harder than that. We can't go in there splitting hairs and expect to walk away with Thompson's freedom. Whether or not he's innocent—and I agree with Gordon that so far, he's not—and whether or not Freeman's telling the truth, we're not going to win this by saying 'The evidence was circumstantial.' We're Northern lawyers waltzing into New Orleans to tell a local district judge, who's also a former DA, that he blew a criminal conviction with huge political ramifications.

If we don't have something pretty compelling, we don't stand a chance."

"You're both right, of course," said Andy, "but to Michael's point, I think it's important to remember that no appeals court is going to want to overturn a case on a legal technicality if they believe Thompson is truly guilty of the crime. We'll have an uphill battle unless we can find a way to say that this guy is pretty clearly innocent. So, let's focus on the legal arguments while keeping the facts in mind."

They could not reopen the facts, so they needed to figure out where the trial had been unfair to Thompson, or where exactly the judge had made mistakes. Andy outlined two ways to get their client off death row. The first was to show legal, procedural flaws in the way the trial had been conducted. Andy turned around and wrote LEGAL ISSUES on the first pad. The second way was to discover new material facts about the trial that the jury hadn't known about, thereby justifying a new trial. On the other pad, Andy wrote NEW EVIDENCE.

Any material fact significant enough that it might have caused the jury to decide the case differently could be used to get a new trial. However, they would have to convince Judge Quinlan of these material reasons to retry the case, and that wasn't necessarily going to be so easy.

Gordon asked if they had received the transcripts from the jury selection process, known as voir dire. The new director at the Loyola Death Penalty Resource Center, Nick Trenticosta, had indicated that he thought there might have been some issues with this process, and Gordon wanted to review the transcripts to see for himself what the issues were.

The transcripts had not been received yet, but Andy wrote *Batson* under LEGAL ISSUES. This was shorthand for the landmark Supreme Court case of *Batson v. Kentucky*, which established the logical view that it was unconstitutional for jury selection to be based on the race of the potential jurors. Thompson's murder trial had predated the *Batson* ruling, so they'd have to fight about whether the case applied to Thompson's jury selection, but fortunately, Pat Fanning had objected to the use of peremptory challenges in the choosing of the jury at the trial, so perhaps they could look at that angle.

Gordon said, "What about the timing of the two separate trials—the armed robbery and the Liuzza murder? If I've got the timeline right, the murder occurred on December 6, 1984, and the carjacking on December 28th. Thompson and Freeman were arrested on January 17, 1985, for the Liuzza murder. The next day, John's picture appeared on the front page of the newspaper. The Lagardes saw the paper and called the cops, saying that Thompson was the guy who'd carjacked their children on the 28th, and Thompson got an armed robbery trial as well.

"Somehow the armed robbery case was tried first in Quinlan's courtroom, and the murder case came after," Gordon continued. "Can trial schedules be manipulated that way? If I'm Couhig or Fanning, there's a big change in how I handle the case with or without that armed robbery conviction. The DAs couldn't even go for the death penalty without it, because Thompson wouldn't have had a prior violent felony. And with it, they have to keep Thompson off the stand, and he can't testify in his own defense. Plus, the armed robbery gave the jury aggravating circumstances that suggested John should get death instead of life in prison for the Liuzza murder. The DAs could depict Thompson as a career criminal with a history of violent crime, when, in fact, at the time of the Liuzza murder, he'd never had a violent crime arrest or conviction."

Andy wrote *Order of Cases? Trying armed robbery first?* on the LEGAL ISSUES pad.

Michael didn't say anything, but he thought the carjacking case was a real weakness for their arguments. He agreed completely with Andy that the DAs had manipulated the calendar, and why they had done so. He also agreed that getting the armed robbery conviction removed from the murder trial should, as a matter of law, get Thompson a new trial for murder. But the armed robbery case was pretty open and shut, in his view: Three teenagers had identified Thompson in the newspaper, in a photo lineup, and in open court. To say the armed robbery should not have been used in the sentencing phase amounted to saying, *Sure, he might be a career criminal, but that career started after December 6th. When he killed Ray Liuzza, it was his first violent crime, so he should just get life in prison.* It would be hard to make that a compelling argument to an appeals court. Still, the three men had agreed to represent Thompson in appealing both the armed robbery and the murder cases, since the two cases were clearly related.

Andy wrote *Armed robbery* on the LEGAL ISSUES page. He turned back to Michael and Gordon and said, "Okay, we'll have to dig on the carjacking and see how we can leverage the murder case from there. But let's move on to the details of the murder: Liuzza gets out of his car, walks across the street to his house, but is stopped by someone with a gun. They have a confrontation, and Liuzza pleads for his life loudly enough to be heard through the wall of the house near him before being shot five times. The shooter gets away with Liuzza's wallet, watch, and ring; only the ring is found. A witness saw a six-foot-tall man running from the scene with a gun but couldn't identify him. Those facts are undisputed. Everything else comes from a witness who might have a bias, and not all those biases were made clear at trial. Plus, Freeman's testimony doesn't completely make sense to me. I'd like to take a closer look at him, and his plea bargain."

"Like Gordon said, the truth is what the jury says it is," Michael pointed out. "We can look at it, but the jury saw Freeman testify. Dubelier made sure they knew about the plea bargain. The jury heard Couhig challenge that, and they still thought that Thompson pulled the trigger, and that Thompson killed Ray Liuzza, and that he should get the chair for it. This is going to be a tough road." *Tough doesn't really cut it. More like nearly impossible,* he thought to himself.

They were dealing with a death penalty supported by a murder case built completely on circumstantial evidence, and an armed robbery case built completely on eyewitness testimony from three teenage witnesses. It was a high-profile, black-on-white cause célèbre murder involving New Orleans' first family of business. It had been prosecuted pretty aggressively by two experienced DAs, in front of an ex-DA judge. And all of that would be useless to them in the appeal.

Still, it was their job to find the arguments that would work, not to obsess about how difficult their job was going to be. Michael started thinking about the reward that Couhig had brought up at trial. It sounded like the cops, or the DAs, might have promised some reward to Perkins and Carr in exchange for their testimony. No reward had been disclosed at the trial; if indeed such a reward had existed, that alone would probably be material enough to get a new trial.

Andy wrote *Reward* on the NEW EVIDENCE pad. Andy and Michael were going to meet with John's trial lawyers on their visit to New Orleans. Hopefully they'd learn more about the purported reward in a few days. If the jury didn't know about the reward, it would be a good bet they could get a new trial. Michael agreed with Gordon, and with the speculation that each witness had a potential bias.

All three agreed that they had to make an "ineffective assistance" claim, an argument that Thompson's lawyers were so bad during his trial that he was effectively deprived of his constitutional right to a lawyer. Ineffective assistance was put forth in almost every death penalty case, and was generally the first argument made when inmates represented themselves. The argument almost never succeeded, but since every death row inmate believed passionately that his lawyers hadn't represented him well, it was included in almost every appeal. It was clear to all three men from the transcript that Fanning's closing argument was seriously lacking, beyond any reasonable expectation. In addition, Couhig and Fanning had also never done their own ballistics test on the supposed murder weapon—this point could also be contested as malpractice.

The "expert witness" chosen by Couhig and Fanning to vouch for Thompson's character had also been less than ideal. First of all, he was a sociologist, rather than a clinical psychologist, so there should have been some question about whether his conclusions would be legitimate. Second, while the expert had painted Thompson as a product of his harsh environment, which seemed fair, the conclusion that Couhig and Fanning let him share with the jury was that Thompson was destined to be a career criminal, which obviously didn't do Thompson any favors in the eyes of the jury. It was all well and good to show the jury Thompson's dysfunctional relationship with his father, and to link that troubled past to his more recent drug hustling and street fencing. But the expert had gone further, stating that Thompson was a savage, feral man completely out of control with his emotional impulses. This had essentially confirmed the jury's worst fears. The "expert" told the jury that if Thompson went back into society, he would continue committing crimes, as that was all he knew, and all that he had been taught by both his father and his own experiences. It had not been a sympathetic picture. Quite the contrary, Michael thought this opinion had played a big part in the jury's decision to impose the death sentence.

Who is the real John Thompson? The thought ran through Michael's head. *He must have seemed pretty horrible to the jury if they gave him death without any real priors.*

Michael looked at his watch. They had been at it for two hours. They ended the meeting, with Michael agreeing to write up a memo with their thoughts. They'd return to it in a couple of days.

8:35 PM

MICHAEL WAS BACK in the conference room, where the two large white pads were still standing, along with a DO NOT REMOVE sign fashioned from a file folder stretching across both easels. He was thinking about their discussion earlier—about making a judge feel that Thompson had been wronged, while subtly arguing that *maybe* he was innocent. These were two very different things. One was a question of guilt: John Thompson didn't kill Ray Liuzza. The other one was a question of justice: Whether or not Thompson was guilty, his trial hadn't followed the rules. If the system wasn't held accountable, especially in a death penalty case, it would all fall apart.

It was a professional necessity for any lawyer to find something about his client that he could believe in, something about him that was worth fighting for. Michael needed to find that now for a cold-blooded killer. He needed a core belief to inspire his creativity, sustain his energy, and anchor his morals as he defended the indefensible.

He skimmed the white flip pads with Andy's block-lettered argument outline. Was John Thompson innocent? Michael doubted it. Was he not guilty of these crimes? Michael didn't know. What was the truth?

Who saw John Thompson pull the trigger and shoot Ray Liuzza? According to the trial, only Kevin Freeman did. But Freeman had a reason to lie. Michael remembered Benjamin Franklin's quote: "Two men can keep a secret if one of them is dead." Only Ray Liuzza Jr. and the shooter knew who had pulled that trigger, and Liuzza was dead.

Michael accepted that he'd probably never know whether Thompson actually pulled the trigger—although if he were forced to make a wager, he would bet that Thompson had done it. It was in this belief that Michael found his anchor, the thing that would allow him to represent John Thompson: Capital punishment was wrong, both in thought and in action. He hated the thought of capital punishment, and he always had; state-sanctioned murder could not be condoned. But it was the fact that Michael would never know the identity of Ray Liuzza's murderer that galvanized him now. *Forget what the jury said,* Michael thought. *The truth is the truth, not what the jury says it is.*

Michael knew people would think he was using lawyer tricks to get a convict freed. In fact, it was precisely the opposite: He was holding the system accountable to its principles to ensure the guilt of a man sentenced to death. Since the system couldn't sustain that burden, John needed to be represented, needed to be defended until what had really happened that night could be proven.

He looked at the pads, writing down the argument headers, the road map for their defense of John Thompson: stranger, drug dealer, teenage father of two toddlers, convicted carjacker of teen-agers, and convicted murderer of a defenseless man pleading for his life while being robbed for a watch, a wallet full of nothing, and a six-dollar ring.

Michael tore the pages off the pads, folded them, and put them under his arm, making a silent promise. No one was going to kill John Thompson until they *knew* he was the murderer. Michael flipped off the light switch and walked down the hall to his office.

14

NICK TRENTICOSTA

THE DOOR TO the Loyola Death Penalty Resource Center was open, if one could find it. The LDPRC was part of the Loyola University New Orleans School of Law, but its facilities were off-campus, downtown, next to the ACLU, where Nick Trenticosta had been able to parlay some connections and some federal funding into a cost-conscious office space. Michael and Andy walked through a cheap, lightweight door and stepped gingerly into the room, careful not to step on a tidal wave of encroaching documents.

The thin, worn gray carpet on which they stood was just about the only flat surface throughout the room that was actually visible. A fair amount of the floor, and all of the table and bookshelf space, was covered by a startling number of case files and other ragged piles of paper. *I guess the Thompson case isn't the only capital case these guys are chasing,* Michael thought. An almost-empty coffeepot sat in a small coffee machine next to an open door leading into another similarly overwhelmed room.

Across the room, a slender man in T-shirt and jeans looked up from behind a table, his body concealed to the chest by file folders. He gave a high-pitched but enthusiastic "What's happening!"

Nick Trenticosta was a tall, skinny, academic-looking guy with a thick salt-and-pepper mustache and round wire-frame glasses. A turn of his head revealed a long, carefully groomed ponytail. His voice was pleasant, with that distinctive New Orleans accent—not country enough to be a twang, too smart to be a drawl, too open and hospitable to be Northern.

"The boys from Philadelphia," he said. "Come on in."

Nick had once been a public housing advocate in the city, in the St. Thomas Project. The Louisiana Coalition of Jails and Prisons had an office near the Projects, and one of the guys who worked there was organizing folks opposing the death penalty. The Louisiana Coalition Against the Death Penalty, he called it, and he started educating Nick.

Nick was naturally drawn to the work, learning fast how the system worked. He read and researched the cases of many of the men on death row at Angola and started using his community organization talents on the biggest need—talented and well-resourced lawyers to even the playing field against the cops and prosecutors. He was articulate and persuasive enough that one of the lawyers he was recruiting invited him up to Angola in 1983, to actually see the conditions on death row.

Nick went to Angola, met Antonio James, and drove back to New Orleans. Before going home, though, he stopped at LSU and applied to the law school.

Immediately after graduating from LSU in 1986, Nick moved to Florida, where he got a job with the Capital Collateral Representative in Tallahassee. Nick and his colleagues centralized the management and legal review of the cases and assigned lawyers to work them pro bono. When he couldn't get lawyers, he worked the cases himself.

He worked in Tallahassee for a year, but by working twenty-four hours per day he got three years' worth of experience, then returned to New Orleans in 1988 to open the LDPRC after Congress passed a bill that gave federal funding to other regional death penalty clearinghouses.

It was a good match—Loyola supplied cheap, talented, idealistic law students, and Louisiana provided plenty of condemned inmates. Too many, in fact—all the cases for every man on death row were managed by Nick and only one other lawyer. What Nick really needed, what the men on death row really needed, were experienced lawyers from big firms who could run these cases the way they deserved to be run—lawyers who had the time and the talent to dig into those issues and the money to tie up every loose end.

From what Michael had heard of Nick, he was a "true believer," a crusader against capital punishment. A lot of true believers were terrific advocates, lawyers who made passionate arguments and simply would not give up on their cases. On the other hand, Michael had seen both defenders and prosecutors bring that kind of singular focus to bear, and it could be damaging to their case. Absolute conviction often caused a righteousness that could over-look objectivity. That took away credibility and wouldn't play well with a less-zealous jury.

Michael wondered whether Nick had this problem. Having met him now, he decided that Nick probably did see himself as a Robin Hood type. In Nick's version, DA Harry Connick played King John. Nick was bringing together a band of Merry Men to harass the Realm and restore civil rights. *Hence the ponytail—hairstyle of swashbucklers everywhere,* Michael mused.

Nick's job was to make sure that death row inmates had the best counsel they could find, and to provide lawyers like Michael and Andy, who were inexperienced in the law of capital punishment, with tools that would make their lives easier—relevant case law, access to investigators, and strategic recommendations on defense, to name a few.

Michael quickly appreciated Nick's directness. The man was clearly not afraid to address questions head-on. When Michael asked what they needed to know about Thompson's trial lawyers, Nick snorted.

"Rob Couhig and Pat Fanning—not bad lawyers, but not the right guys for this case. Couhig, he's a smart guy, but not a criminal lawyer—more of a businessman and a politician. He ran for Congress here. How far do you think a guy who wants to be a congressman is gonna go to defend the accused murderer of Ray Liuzza's son? Shoot, I don't have to tell you. You read the transcript. The man wouldn't even question Liuzza Sr. on the stand. The Liuzza family had a reward posted and on the radio for weeks. Couhig could have asked him all about the reward if he wanted to, and he didn't."

"Why do you think he stayed away from talking about the reward?" Michael asked.

"Well, partly he didn't want to upset the man, and partly he couldn't get straight answers about it from Dubelier. You gotta give Dubelier credit. Boy's known for withholding evidence. It's really the calling card of the Connick DA's office."

Andy leaned forward. "What do you mean?"

Nick laughed. "Well, down here, there's violations, and then there's *violations*. If you're asking whether the New Orleans DA's office withholds exculpatory evidence to get convictions, there's nothing in any opinions you'd read that says so.

"Harry Connick is a politician. He gives the people in his office room to get the job done. On John's case, Dubelier and Williams made an interesting choice as prosecutors. You know they were Specials, right? Williams was chief of homicide trials at the time, but Dubelier wasn't the guy usually assigned to Quinlan's court-room. It's possible Dubelier was put on the case so Connick could control it from behind the scenes, but I'm just speculating there. As for Jim Williams—well, that man's about as bad as they come. He's got a mini electric chair in his office, battery-operated—an actual working electric chair. He cuts out the mug shots from the people he's put on death row and he clips them to the chair. He's almost literally collecting scalps. I don't know another DA—hell, I don't know another human being—who gets as much of a thrill from putting people to death."

Andy and Michael looked at each other, letting Nick's comments sink in.

"Nick, do you think there's an appealable issue on the scheduling of the armed robbery trial and the murder trial? How can they flip the trial schedule and use a later act as an aggravating factor for an act that was committed earlier?" Michael asked.

"Nah. I mean, you're right, but I'm not sure that dog'll hunt," Nick said. "Case law around here is all lined up behind the prosecution. DA and the judge have huge discretion to manage their calendars; nobody's gonna overturn that. It gets worse. Couhig kept asking for more detailed police reports. The police keep a daily report and then at the end of the case, after an arrest is made, they change that into a summary report. Dubelier provided the summary report only, and wouldn't give us the dailies. Quinlan never made him, either. And Louisiana law supports Dubelier, says that the police and the DA aren't the same party, and if the police have evidence in their possession, that isn't the same as the DA having it, even if they are both part of the government."

Michael nodded. "Yeah, we did that research. Figured we'd argue it, but it would be a loser, unless there's some problem with the robbery conviction."

"You need to get an investigator to help dig up stuff and find the witnesses," Nick stated. "I brought in a mitigation investigator to do a report on John already, to create a profile that might make him more endearing to the higher-court judges. I can get you that report as a starting point."

Nick took a sip from his coffee mug, a white ceramic mug with a red NO circle on top of a noose. He swallowed, and said, "You'll like John. He's a rare one. He's smart."

"What's his alibi?"

Nick smiled. "He doesn't have one. That's what I mean about John being smart. He's not like these other guys who get caught up in some fancy lie, or cling to some strained nonsense about why they're innocent. Not John. He won't make up some story for where he was that night. He just tells you the truth."

Michael noted Nick's use of the word *truth*. He said, "One of the people we'd like to speak to is Kevin Freeman. Do you know where he is?"

"Yep," Nick said. "Prison. He spent ten months in jail on the Liuzza plea bargain, got out, and resumed his old lifestyle. Got busted for drugs or car theft or something, and he's in OPP, I think."

"I thought Freeman's plea bargain was five years. How did he get out in ten months?"

Nick leaned back and put his hands behind his head. "Dubelier gave Freeman a choice: accessory after the fact and five years, or roll the dice and stand trial for second-degree murder. Freeman testified that he'd stand trial for second-degree murder, which let Dubelier tell the jury that Freeman believed in his own innocence, and the plea deal wasn't that great, so obviously Freeman was telling the truth.

"The jury bought it, and they convicted John. And Freeman went to jail. But here's where it got interesting: After Freeman testified, he changed his mind on the plea, and Dubelier let him plead to accessory after the fact. He pled guilty, but instead of five years, he got one of the better criminal lawyers around town. The lawyer got the DA to support a release for time served instead of the five years. Quinlan agreed, and Freeman served ten months; he was home by Christmas. Meanwhile, John's on death row in Angola." He looked across the table at Michael and Andy. "You see what you're dealing with here?"

"We're beginning to get the idea."

"Seen John yet?"

"We'll be heading up there day after tomorrow."

"Like I said, he'll surprise you. He's rough around the edges, but he's got something. A charisma. He knows he needs help, but he's got his pride. You ever seen death row?"

Michael and Andy shook their heads.

"Well, John's stuck up in a six-by-nine concrete box twenty-three hours a day. Gets an hour out of his cell a day, gets outside three hours a week if he's lucky. He's got to shower, make phone calls, whatever he needs to do outside his cell, during that one hour. Other than that, he's in solitary. It's pretty grim, I'll tell you that. And it's scary. This governor, he's an executioner—wants to increase the deterrent value of the death penalty, as if there was one. They've killed eleven inmates, *eleven,* since last June. You know that weighs on a man."

Nick handed them a couple of files full of reports his office had put together on John's background and a list of jurors in the voir dire. Michael put the folders in his briefcase and he and Andy thanked Nick for his help before leaving the office.

Nick watched the door close and considered his two new colleagues. *Philadelphia,* he thought. *Big firm from the Northeast. Well trained, firm'll support it so they'll have enough money, and they won't be run off by the politics, at least.*

Still, he thought, *those boys have no idea what they just bit off.* He got up and went to pour himself another cup of coffee.

15

GUILT OR INNOCENCE

MICHAEL AND **A**NDY walked up Poydras Street toward the Law Offices of Adams and Reese, Rob Couhig's law firm. It had been a good morning. At the recommendation of the concierge, they had walked a couple of blocks to Mother's Restaurant for breakfast, where they stood in line with the locals for the specialty of the house, the "debris omelet." Michael didn't know what DAY-bree was, but it sure mixed well with eggs.

As he walked, Michael chuckled to himself. "You know what Lori said to me the other night?"

"What's that?" Andy asked.

"She said, 'Michael, you want to go running around playing Clarence Darrow on this case, I'm behind you all the way. But if you get this murderer off on some technicality, don't expect me to have him over to this house for dinner.' "

Andy laughed out loud. "Sounds tough."

"Yeah, she's tough. You always know where you stand with Lori. I told her not to worry—the statistics on getting death row inmates acquitted were pretty grim. Let's handle that first, and then I'll worry about changing her mind on dinner guests."

THEY WALKED INTO Rob Couhig's office. Adams and Reese was one of the nicer law firms in town, and from Couhig's office, on one of the top floors of a skyscraper, you could see everything from the Superdome over across the Quarter to the Mississippi, with the barges moving up- and downriver.

Michael wasn't at all surprised by Couhig's appearance, or his charming manner. He had spoken to Couhig on the phone, and a bespectacled, gregarious, polite, charming New Orleans corporate lawyer in shirtsleeves and suspenders was just about what he'd expected.

The three lawyers sat down at a table off to the side of Couhig's desk, Michael and Andy each taking out pads of paper from their briefcases while Couhig waited. Once they were situated, Couhig took the lead, telling Michael and Andy that losing the Thompson case was the biggest legal failure of his career. He was very clear that, in his opinion, Dubelier and Williams had kept things from the defense.

"We didn't have all the information we needed to try that case," said Couhig. "And I take some of the blame for that. I'm not sure what I could have done differently, what I should have done differently. But let me tell you something you need to know right up front: If you guys need, or want, to make an ineffective assistance claim, I won't fight it one bit. You do what you need to do, and you just tell me what I can do to help you. Now, what do you want to know?"

Couhig's generosity and candor, and his obvious anger toward the prosecutors, surprised and gratified Michael. A lot of lawyers, having lost a high-profile case, would fight like hell to stay away from it. Couhig appeared to be the opposite; he was actually embracing the appeal, hoping it would succeed where he had failed.

"Well, Mr. Couhig, I guess what I'd like to know is what else you think we should pursue?"

"Well, look—the case wasn't perfect. To tell you the truth, John's a mean sonofabitch."

"We've read the transcript and the report from your sociologist."

"Well, then, you know that John's had a rough past. He's no choirboy. And for him, it was like a test to see if we believed him. No alibi, no nothing. John truly believed that just saying he was innocent would be a good-enough defense. Plus, he didn't click at all with Fanning. Pat Fanning is one of the best criminal defense lawyers in this town, and John alienated him right off the bat.

"Look, God knows I didn't prove it at the time, but my view is that Eric Dubelier couldn't *prove* that John was guilty without stacking the deck against him. We asked Dubelier at least a dozen times for a whole lot of evidence we never got—police reports, the information on any rewards, the DA's files. Dubelier wouldn't give us any of that, and Quinlan wouldn't make him. Quinlan wouldn't even review it himself to be able to tell us that there was nothing material in there. You combine that with Thompson not wanting to talk to us, and it's hard to make any real defense."

Michael was concerned that John fought with his defense lawyers. He asked Couhig about it, and was told that John even filed his own change-of-venue motion—he didn't believe that Couhig was arguing with the judge about that. He thought Couhig and Fanning were in the pocket of the Liuzza family.

"But the real kicker was the Big Daddy Red letter," Couhig said.

"Yes, that seemed to be a big deal in Williams's closing at the murder trial," Andy said. "What's the story there?"

Couhig shook his head. "I told John not to talk or write to anyone about the case, as there were too many people watching him. So what does he do? He sends that goddamn letter from jail. Of course, they grab it in transit, and now Jim Williams has a blackmail letter from John to Funk Perkins. Williams had a field day with that letter. John claimed that he wasn't telling anybody to come in and lie; he was just telling Big Daddy Red to tell the truth. Of course, John didn't know Red's last name, and Red never came to trial, so we'll never know."

Andy asked about the ballistics test—or lack thereof—and Couhig shook his head, saying that they didn't have the time or money.

Couhig also encouraged them to visit Numa Bertel, the defense attorney for the armed robbery trial. He would be better able to answer their questions about the proceedings of that trial. He also said they should try to track down Leola Chaney, one of the jurors on the murder trial. He said, "We thought we might have a hung jury, but it looked like the other jurors put some pressure on her in front of Judge Quinlan. Fanning put it on the record in an objection; you can find it in the transcript."

Michael wrote down this information while asking, "What do you think of Quinlan?"

"I've known Pat for a lot of years. Pat Quinlan is a decent human being. He was a good choice for judge, and he's a credit to the bench. He sees the world a certain way, and it's no surprise that a former DA and a former State's Attorney is going to be prosecution-friendly. But that was his first murder trial, and he played it straight and ran a clean trial. I didn't agree with him on everything. We argued a lot about whether the armed robbery was admissible. I thought then, and I think now, that since John was appealing the conviction in that case, his conviction wasn't final. Quinlan rejected that argument several times. But he was direct and truthful about his reasoning."

Couhig got up from the table and walked to the window, looking outside. He ran his fingers through his hair, sighed, and turned back to them. "Look," he said, "maybe if I'd been a more experienced criminal lawyer, or if Pat and John had gotten along better, or if John had a better story—probably all of those things contributed to what happened. In my mind, we did the best job we could, and lost. I've looked at myself in the mirror, and I truly believe that. Now, I have no real idea if John is truly guilty. But like I said, he's no choirboy. Really, he's not even all that nice a guy. But I think you've got some real grounds for appeal, and I'll certainly help you if I can."

16

MEETING AT THE FARM

AUGUST 17, 1988

THE DRIVE FROM New Orleans to the Louisiana State Penitentiary at Angola—"the Farm"—took them almost three hours. It was a pretty drive, northwest on Interstate 10 to Baton Rouge through rich green countryside; then north on Interstate 110; then Louisiana Route 66 for the last twenty miles. Angola was a working farm—a plantation, really—in the middle of nowhere; 8,000 acres surrounded on three sides by a bend in the Mississippi River.

They had driven their rental car in from the east, traveling along two lanes of blacktop that slithered back and forth like a snake for twenty miles through a tall deciduous forest clotted with rotting underbrush and kudzu. It was the only road in or out of Angola. The suffocating plant life, and the length of the road, ensured that it would be no easy task to escape from the Farm.

Eventually the fenced towers and barbed-wire barriers of Angola rounded into sight. They coasted to a stop in front of a muscle-bound guard with sunglasses and a severe crew cut, the open gate the only visible break in an otherwise endless twenty-foot-high chain-link fence, lined top and bottom with thick coils of razor wire.

While the guard stood motionless in front of the car, two more armed guards approached. Michael could see the tower nearby with another guard at its top.

While Michael's driver's license and Bar ID cards were checked against the "guest" list, he looked through the gate into the prison grounds. *Actually,* he thought, *it's kind of pretty.* It was lovely country, empty of people, with only a few small buildings within view.

The guard returned and gave them directions to Camp J, the home of death row. They drove about a mile into the farm, passing two teams of men dressed in white short-sleeved shirts, long white pants, and work boots, working in the fields as a uniformed guard paced back and forth holding a rifle. Michael turned to Andy and said, "It's like a scene from *Cool Hand Luke.* Who knew that movie was real?"

Camp J was a two-story building set off from the main road with its own small parking lot. They parked the car and walked in through an unlocked double door into a cinder-block entryway with a guard at a desk. Once again, they showed their identification cards. The guards led them down a hallway painted the same dirty institutional beige as the rest of the building. Michael wondered if professional consultants had been used to find this precise shade, thinking how perfectly it conveyed a mood of ineffable grime and sadness.

The guard led them to a windowless beige door that he unlocked using a key from his belt and held open for them. Behind the door was a tiny interview room with a steel table and four steel chairs. They walked in and waited for their first visit with their new client. Stretching from wall to wall across the room was a thick steel screen made of dense mesh.

Andy put his briefcase on the table and loudly dragged one of the steel chairs over toward the mesh screen. Michael sat down as well, as the door closed and locked behind them.

Ten minutes later, there was movement on the other side of the screen, and John Thompson walked through the door.

Whatever Michael was expecting, John Thompson wasn't it. It was hard to see through the screen, but it seemed that John was casually dressed, wearing a T-shirt, baggy jeans, and a pair of white sneakers. His clothes weren't striped; he wasn't wearing a jumpsuit; and there was no uniform identifying him as an Angola inmate. The only evidence that they were talking to a convicted murderer was the shackles on John's wrists and ankles, the chains coming together in a steel loop at his waist. John walked easily into the room, grabbed a chair, and sat down.

He's small, Michael thought as he stood up to introduce himself to John. It hadn't really occurred to him before, but he had always thought murderers would be big. John was small, and thin.

Whatever John's thoughts were about his new lawyers, he didn't say. Instead, his first words to them were soft-spoken and direct, looking them in the eyes and calmly saying, "Look, I didn't do it. I didn't do none of it. I wasn't even there."

Michael and Andy sat in silence for a moment and Michael realized his surprise at the lack of emotion in John's voice. John talked as though he was completely disinterested in his case and situation. It was as if he really didn't care whether Michael or Andy believed him or not.

Michael had been rehearsing the start of this conversation for weeks. He explained to John that they weren't there to prove his innocence or guilt, because in the eyes of the State of Louisiana, John was guilty, and there wasn't any more debate on the issue. Instead, their job was to try and get John off death row. Michael also assured John that whether or not John actually killed Ray Liuzza really didn't matter. He just wanted to get his appeal moving and to have the courts reopen his case.

Andy then asked John where he was the night of the murder. John looked at the two men. "I don't know."

Andy pressed more. "You must have thought about where you might have been that night."

John shrugged. "I don't know where I was. I wasn't there. Simple as that. You askin' me about somethin' happened almost four years ago. By the time I got arrested and even knew what night the crime was, it was six weeks after the murder. Maybe I was high, maybe I was with my girl. I don't know. That's it."

Michael pointed out that the police had tracked the murder weapon and the ring taken from Ray Liuzza's hand to John. His only question, for now, was how John had gotten these items in the first place. John didn't answer directly, saying only that Kevin Freeman was lying to save his own ass, and that Funk and Ken Carr only wanted the reward. He would have set them up in court if his lawyers had let him take the stand. He didn't believe the ring was authentic, and he insisted his prints hadn't been on the gun.

John said that he had done exactly what Couhig and Fanning had told him to do—stay quiet. He said they were bad lawyers, citing both their failure to follow up on Ken Carr's testimony about Harry's Bar, and Fanning's "weak" closing argument.

Michael thought to himself, *He's certainly not stupid.* John's assessment of Fanning was right on, from what Michael had been able to gather. Certainly the trial transcript made plain that Fanning's cross-examination was little more than a concession speech that actually did far more harm than good.

Michael, Gordon, and Andy were planning on filing a claim that John's lawyers were ineffective. They cautioned John not to file his own petitions anymore. Michael promised to always ask John his opinions and to always tell him the truth. But in exchange, John had to play it their way.

John smiled. He explained that every three months, he had been writing letters to lawyers listed in a magazine, and not one of them had ever contacted him. Three hundred letters every three months, and no response until Michael and Andy had shown up. So he was ready to work with them and do as they suggested.

Michael gave John a list of the people he wanted to try and meet with—Couhig and Fanning, John's relatives, jurors, and Kevin

Freeman. John didn't disagree, but he didn't add anyone to the list, either. Michael waited in awkward silence, hoping for some more feedback, but none came. John seemed content to let him do the talking.

To fill the silence, Michael talked about some arguments they'd been forming after reading through the trial transcripts, specifically issues with the jury selection, and with some of the things Dubelier and Williams did and stated during the trial. John followed along, nodded from time to time, said "uh-huh" and "all right" in a quiet voice, but didn't add much input or ask any questions.

After about an hour—what felt to Michael like a one-way monologue to a fairly disinterested client—he said, "Well, John, I guess that's about all we've got for today. Is there anything else we can do for you, anything you need that we can help you get?"

At this, Thompson seemed to straighten up a little. He looked at them through the mesh and said, "Yeah, man. I need a lawyer. I needed someone to represent me and take care of me out there, you know? Y'all not from N'awlins. Y'all don't know how it works down here. This game here, it's rigged. I need someone gonna represent me, gonna work to get this sorted out right. That's what I need." He looked at both of them, steady and unimpressed. "I need a trip out of death row."

Michael nodded, unsure of what to say.

Thompson looked and them and said, "Until then, though, I could really use a radio."

17

THE KITCHEN SINK

WITH AN AWKWARD half-Frisbee-throwing motion, Gordon launched the final draft of John's post-conviction release appeal brief—affectionately called the "Kitchen Sink" because it had every argument they could think of in it—onto the crowded table in the conference room. It hit with a satisfying thud, the weight of the document quite impressive, surprising Michael, who had been leaning back in his chair with his feet up on the table. The brief, 141 pages in length, laid out a series of arguments that Gordon hoped were powerful and compelling in a clear, crisp, authoritative style. *It better be good,* Gordon thought. *For the first time, I've written a brief that really is life or death.*

Gordon wished they'd had more time. Now that it was done, six months didn't seem like nearly enough time to thoroughly examine and argue all the issues they were worried about. On the other hand, he knew that deadlines had to be set. In this case, their deadline was Thompson's current execution date, set for February 22, 1989. They had to file the brief now to keep the appeals moving and John's execution stayed.

It had been a challenging brief to write. The law allowed them to make as many arguments as they could, and in fact encouraged them to do so, since any arguments they left out would be forever unavailable for them to address—unless they found new factual evidence that could not have been discovered earlier.

Still, they didn't have a lot to go on. They didn't have any great scientific defenses, and they had no objective proof of John's innocence. As Nick had informed them, DNA evidence was only available in about 10 percent of death penalty cases, and this was one of the other 90 percent. No DNA had been collected from the crime scene, and no fingerprints had been left on the murder weapon. The DA's ballistics test had been accepted by Couhig and Fanning at the original trial, so Michael and Gordon couldn't argue that point now (except to say that Couhig and Fanning were ineffective lawyers for accepting the test, and that argument wouldn't go anywhere).

With the majority of objective arguments unavailable, the Morgan, Lewis team had been forced to look for more subjective forms of new evidence; they needed new witnesses who had not been available at the first trial.

In order to track down any potential witnesses, Nick Trenticosta helped the team hire Garry Eldredge—the best fact-based private investigator in New Orleans. He was put on a retainer, and Michael asked him to do some digging, which was good. Even the money to cover Garry's fees—which Morgan was paying—would have been beyond the scope of most lawyers willing to do this sort of work.

New facts or new evidence could be brought before Judge Quinlan anytime, and did not have to be found before they submitted their brief. So while Garry looked for new facts in New Orleans, the Philly lawyers had turned their attention back to what they knew best: harassing opposing counsel. They started writing letters and lobbing phone calls in to Connick's staff, seeking the complete files for both the murder and carjacking cases, and they started compiling the arguments they had for the brief.

The result of that work lay strewn before them now; the war room was in its full glory, a hub of frenzied legal research and analysis. Andy had just pulled the last of five copies of the Kitchen Sink off the printer, sprinted out of the office, and jumped into a cab. They had missed the Fed Ex deadline for that evening, so now their only chance at getting their brief filed was to take it to the FedEx cargo center at the airport before midnight, ensuring it would be on the last plane leaving from Philadelphia.

The room they had practically lived in for the past week and a half was trashed. Pizza boxes and half-empty containers of Chinese food lined the edges of the room and piled up near the trash cans. Soda cans and cups of coffee were littered across tabletops, land mines for the carelessly tossed binders, file folders, and case law that the team was analyzing, debating, and quoting from as they composed, edited, and re-edited the brief. Drafts of various arguments, typed up by Morgan's word processing department and marked up by each lawyer, were in complete disarray.

Gordon walked around the table past Michael, who was in perfect concert with his surroundings. Normally well put-together, Michael was leaning back in one of the conference-room chairs, his tie askew and hair disheveled. His stockinged feet were up on the table and his shoes were in another chair.

Michael's eyes had closed but Gordon knew he was still awake. Gordon walked farther down the hall to the room that held supplies for the conference rooms. He pulled two beers out of the refrigerator and returned to the war room, nudging Michael with one of the bottles. Michael opened his eyes and took the beer without a word, too tired to speak.

With the Kitchen Sink out the door, the only thing left for them to do was sit and worry about the arguments they had probably failed to include. *It always happens this way,* Gordon thought, *no matter how long you give yourself to prepare.* He wanted each of their arguments to be perfect, impervious to criticism, and articulated in the simplest, most powerful language possible. As a result, the fine-tuning and tinkering on a brief like this could go on forever, with the analysis filling up whatever time was available until the brief was due. Without the deadline, the arguments would never be finalized, but it always felt like there was something more he should have said, like he could have done things better, or differently. They called it "writer's remorse" around the firm. As the pressure of finishing the brief dissipated, it was replaced with self-doubt, even in cases where a man's life wasn't at stake.

Michael twisted open the beer, tossed the cap behind him in the general direction of the trash can, and leaned back in his chair. He took a long swig and closed his eyes. "You think it's good enough?"

Gordon sat down heavily and opened his own beer, letting out a deep, tired breath. He couldn't think about how to make it better. After all the chaos, all the hand-waving from the DAs, all the investigations and interviews, the lawyers had agreed on eleven separate arguments. Any of them was, technically speaking, sufficient to justify a new trial for John. Even Nick, with all of his experience in death penalty law, had been unable to come up with any other arguments that had even the slightest chance of success.

Was the brief good enough? Gordon didn't know. He loosened his tie and undid his collar button. He said, "I guess we'll find out, but that's not really the question you're asking. You're still asking yourself if he's innocent, aren't you?"

Michael shrugged. "Aren't you?"

Gordon didn't know how to respond. He wanted to believe that John was telling the truth. He also wanted to believe in the system. He didn't know what the truth was any more than the jurors did, and his information was limited to the transcript and a few meetings, while the jurors had seen and heard all the testimony firsthand.

Michael sat up. He wasn't content to do all this work as a tactic to delay the inevitable. They needed to get John off death row for good. The bar for that was high; he rated their chances at less than 25 percent. Their brief was a good piece of work, but it was still a death penalty defense in a case without an obviously innocent defendant.

There were eleven arguments in the Kitchen Sink. Michael only gave four of them any chance at even delaying John's execution. Most of what they had written was fairly standard anti–death penalty arguments. They were well made in the brief, but they weren't novel ideas. Every judge in Louisiana and all the way up to the Supreme Court already knew those arguments inside and out, and they were losers, even if Michael believed they were right.

They called those arguments "the seven sisters." They included arguing that Couhig and Fanning had been so ineffective that John had been deprived of his right to counsel; the argument that holding the trial in New Orleans was unconstitutional because the crime was so inflammatory that there was no way he could get a fair trial; and the argument that John's armed robbery conviction should not have been used in his murder case because the armed robbery was still under appeal, and since it could have been reversed, it should not have counted against him in the murder case and sentencing. It also included more generic arguments that were guaranteed losers, like "The death penalty is unconstitutional as cruel and unusual punishment."

Still, there were four arguments that Michael thought might get them somewhere. The one Michael liked best was the coercion of Leola Chaney. To Michael, the transcript clearly showed that Ms. Chaney had been publicly revealed, in open court, as the lone holdout against John's death sentence, and that she had changed her vote as a result. That was a clear error in the trial, and it was an error that Pat Fanning had caught and objected to at the time, which supported their appeal. Finally, its importance could not be disputed. Ms. Chaney had become the swing vote that sentenced Thompson to death. If her vote had been pressured in any way, that alone should be enough to argue that the death sentence was invalid and should be reversed.

Michael and Gordon liked this argument because it was unique to the facts of the case and therefore couldn't be used by other death penalty inmates to secure their releases. As a result, Quinlan could support Thompson's argument without worrying about its impact on other cases. The downside, though, was that reversing the sentence of death wouldn't impact John's guilty verdict; the best result they could achieve would be a resentencing to life imprisonment, and it was possible that all they would get would be a new sentencing hearing, which could result in the reimposition of the death sentence, a sentence that would likely be iron-clad and unassailable. Either would be an improvement, but only marginally so.

They made the argument stronger, they hoped, with sworn affidavits—one from a TV reporter who had been in court that day and believed that Ms. Chaney had been coerced, and one from Leola Chaney herself.

Michael thought back to the day he and Andy had met her. They had gone to her house, a narrow, unassuming two-story row house in the Eleventh Ward that faced onto a large parking lot. It was a neighborhood not too dissimilar from Thompson's.

They rang the bell, and waited. The front door opened to reveal a middle-aged black woman. She looked at them through her screen door and, even though they had not called ahead, seemed to know who they were. She said, "I been wondering when y'all would come, I knew you would sooner or later," she said. "Come on inside."

Michael and Andy had looked at each other, surprised by this woman's prescience, and walked into the house. They followed Ms. Chaney into her living room, where she offered them each a cup of hot tea and sat down in a chair, giving Andy and Michael the couch.

"You know, I ain't been right since that trial," Mrs. Chaney said. "That was my first jury I had ever been on. I told those men before

147

the trial started, when they asked all of us all those questions, that I could find for the death penalty if I had to. But you know, you see lots of stories in these parts, and boys 'round here, they do some things you can't hardly believe they do, horrible, violent things that don't square with the nice, sweet boy you see walking down the street and helping people with their groceries, that sort of thing. Some of these boys, it's true—they got trouble written all up and down them, and you know they the ones to stay away from.

"Now, Mr. Thompson, he looked rough, to be sure, and when he wasn't looking confused he was looking angry, but I've had children, you know, and I know what their faces say. And Mr. Thompson's face, he didn't give much away, but when the judge told us in his instructions about 'mitigating circumstances,' I started thinking about all of the testimony. I mean, we had heard a lot about this young man in the past three days. That boy was beaten all the time when he was a child, beaten by every parent or older child around. No wonder he ended up being the kind of guy who could father a son and then go out and kill a man in cold blood.

"I started listening to that, and I thought to myself, 'The boy may be a murderer, Leola, but are you going to send him to the chair for something a lot of boys only go to prison for, especially when he's got that raw hand dealt to him like that?' So I decided that his growing-up situation, that was a mitigating factor."

Andy said, "Were you the only one who felt that way on the jury?"

"At first, in the jury room, there were three of us who didn't want to give the death penalty," she responded. "The group kept talking and talking, and wore down the other two, and they decided they would vote for death. They all said he was a career criminal—he held up those white kids outside the Superdome. But I just didn't feel right sending that boy to his death in that electric chair. So I held out, and we went back out to ask the judge what to do.

"The judge didn't want to let us just stop there. I remember I was in the back row. So the leader, she stands up, says 'Judge, we are deadlocked.' The judge, he asks what is the vote. She says 'Eleven to one.' So now everyone knew that there was only one person who could stop the death sentence, and the rest of the jury, they got all quiet and turned and looked at me.

"There was no sound at all and everyone in the courtroom was just staring at me, waiting for me, almost like they were judging me. Every single person in there. They all knew I was the holdout, just me, and that I was the person who would decide the sentence.

"The judge, he talked to the lawyers privately for a few minutes. When they came back, the judge asked whether we should go back in and talk some more. Everyone turned to me again. It was horrible. I got all emotional. I started to cry in front of everyone.

"The foreperson of the jury actually turned and whispered to me, 'Could we go back in?' I said yes, we could go back in. I would have said anything, I think, to get out of that courtroom and all of that attention.

"The judge must have wanted me to change my vote, or he wouldn't have sent us back, right? So we went back in there, I thought about things, and agreed to change my vote. I was intimidated."

Michael looked over at Andy. Both men were thinking the same thing: *We've got to get her to testify to this.*

Ms. Chaney continued, "Since that night, I haven't slept real well. I get headaches. It's been real hard. Still, I bet it's nothing compared to what Mr. Thompson's going through, and that makes it worse, even if he is a murderer."

She paused and got up from the couch. She went into another room and came back with a Kleenex, which she used to dab at her eyes. She sat back down, looked straight at them, and said, "Can you help me make it right?"

MICHAEL TOOK A sip of his beer and looked around the war room. He didn't know if the affidavit that she had given them, along with the rest of the Kitchen Sink, would "make it right," but they had taken their best shot.

If the Leola Chaney argument didn't work, they had a strong argument that the DAs had improperly excluded blacks from the jury because of their race, in violation of the Supreme Court's 1986 decision in *Batson v. Kentucky*. This was Nick Trenticosta's favorite argument, because unlike the Chaney argument, the *Batson* argument would probably be useful in overturning dozens of capital punishment cases in the future if they could make it work here. Michael had taken the lead in writing this part of the brief, relying heavily on an expert statistician to back up the discrimination claim.

Statistics were important in this type of claim as objective evidence of discrimination. The Supreme Court said that the first step was for Thompson to show that "more likely than not," race was a factor in the prosecution's decision to exclude certain jurors. The statistics supported this view: In a city that was two-thirds black, with a similarly distributed jury pool, the Thompson jury managed to be only one-third black. If the Court agreed, it would turn its suspicious eye on the prosecutors and ask them to justify their jury selections in a race-neutral way.

One problem with their argument was that Quinlan had already allowed Dubelier and Williams to put race-neutral justifications for their juror selections (and rejections) on the record. Michael's hope was that their statistical analysis would show that that justification was fictional—that there was no way, based on the prevalence of blacks in New Orleans and in the jury pool, that those justifications could be accurate, and that decisions based on race were the only plausible explanation.

The statistician's analysis was straightforward and powerful: The original pool of potential jurors had been seventy-four people—forty-eight blacks and twenty-four whites. From there, he examined each phase of the jury selection process, assessing the likelihood that such a pool could become a jury of twelve that was made up of four blacks and eight whites. Jurors could be removed from the pool either for cause (because there was a problem with their objectivity), or by using a peremptory challenge (meaning that one side or the other simply wanted to remove them). Peremptory challenges could not be questioned, but each side was only allowed eight of them.

The most telling fact, according to the statistician, was that Dubelier had used every one of his eight peremptory challenges to exclude an African-American person from the jury. The statistical odds that this occurred with race *not* being a factor in the prosecution's decision was less than three in a thousand.

Michael wasn't sure whether approaching a highly emotional, race-based death penalty case with statistics like these would be persuasive, but he liked having a legalistic and procedural argument as a counterpoint to the factual unfairness presented by Leola Chaney. It would be hard for the same court to use technical, legal analysis to get rid of this *Batson* argument and then use a softer "feel" to dispose of the juror coercion argument.

The third argument claimed that it was improper to use the armed robbery conviction as a factor in Thompson's sentencing, and Michael thought this was pretty solid. Citing the Supreme Court decision in *Johnson v. Mississippi*, they argued that Thompson's armed robbery conviction could be used as a factor in his sentencing for the murder of Ray Liuzza only if the conviction was "final," meaning that it was no longer under appeal. Clearly that was not the case in this instance. To underscore this point, the Morgan team filed a separate appeal in the armed robbery case and would pursue that appeal in tandem with the death penalty case. They would challenge the photo ID conducted by Bruce Whittaker in the armed robbery case and push the "final appeal" issue in the murder trial.

As with the other arguments, this one had its own challenges. Couhig and Fanning had already lost on this issue with Quinlan, and again with the Louisiana Court of Appeal in the armed robbery case, so the odds were against them. Still, if they got the armed robbery either reversed or ruled inadmissible in the murder case, the aggravating factor Dubelier had used to secure the death penalty would be gone. From there it would be straightforward to argue that John's sentence should be downgraded.

The last of the four arguments had been the most challenging because it centered on Rob Couhig's fervent belief that the DAs had not turned over all the evidence in their possession, denying Thompson his constitutional right to mount his own defense.

In the landmark case of *Brady v. Maryland*, the Supreme Court recognized that prosecutors had an obligation to give defense lawyers any information that might be material to the defense and that might be useful in proving that the defendant was not guilty of the crime charged. The Brady argument for John's appeal was pretty simple: The lawyers argued that both Funk Perkins and Ken Carr had agreed to testify because they expected to get a reward. In their view, the DAs had repeatedly denied the existence of such a reward. If it turned out that Perkins or Carr had an expectation of payment in exchange for certain testimony, then the DAs had deprived Thompson and his lawyers of important information showing Perkins and Carr as biased, placing their testimony in a different light and possibly leading to a verdict of not guilty at Thompson's trial.

Couhig was adamant that there were facts to support this argument, and they had since turned up some information that suggested Couhig might actually be right. They had sent a private detective to track down information about the reward, an ex-NOPD cop who had gotten Curole to talk to him about it. Curole said that the Liuzza family had sponsored a $15,000 reward that was posted all over the neighborhood where the murder had occurred, and was even broadcast on the radio. More telling was the fact that Curole had been involved in the payment of the reward. He said that the majority of the $15,000 had gone to Funk Perkins after the trial, and the rest had gone to "a black man who called Crimestoppers," which was almost certainly Ken Carr. Thus, two of the three apparently disinterested witnesses in Thompson's murder case had been given cash money in exchange for their testimony, and none of this had been disclosed at trial.

Of course, in order to meet the *Brady* standard, the Morgan, Lewis team needed to show that the evidence withheld had a material effect upon the outcome of the trial. Simply showing that Perkins and Carr had expected to get a reward wasn't the same thing as showing that their testimony was false. They had to convince Quinlan that if the jury had been given the information about the reward payments, they might have discounted the two men's testimony and reached a "not guilty" verdict. Complicating this further was the very troubling fact that Couhig had specifically asked Perkins and Carr about any reward expectation. If Quinlan decided that Couhig had raised this issue at trial, they would be barred from arguing it now in the appeal, and it would be a lost cause.

Still, the fact that Perkins and Carr had actually received money suggested a pretrial agreement, something that Perkins and Carr—along with Dubelier and Williams—had denied during the trial. If they had testified with the expectation that a reward was going to come to them, that alone might be material enough to get John a retrial.

Four strong arguments and "the seven sisters" weren't a lot to save Thompson's life, but that was the hand they'd been dealt. They only needed one of the eleven arguments to turn in their favor, and this brief would almost certainly buy them some time to find new facts on the murder case.

Still, Michael knew he had to be realistic. A jury of twelve independent citizens had decided that Thompson shot Ray Liuzza in cold blood for practically nothing. John's lawyers hadn't committed any substantial malpractice. Perhaps the reason they weren't finding any clear evidence of innocence was because there wasn't any to find.

Gordon was right, he decided. Was the Kitchen Sink good enough to win? No. But it was sufficient to fight another day. For now, that had to be enough.

Michael stood up and turned to Gordon: "I'm packing it in. Good work—we'll see where it goes from here." Gordon nodded wearily. The two men shook hands, each acknowledging the other's efforts, and Michael walked out of the room.

Gordon's eye lingered on a list of names taped to the war room wall, a list someone had posted as a reminder of what they were up against. There were eleven names on the list, each one a man who had been electrocuted between the date of John's conviction in 1985 and now. Eleven men executed in the same chair in four years—the highest rate of executions in the nation. And it was escalating, with four of those eleven occurring in the last year.

Louisiana had been working hard, and John Thompson was firmly in its sights.

18

ISOLATION

EXACT DATE UNKNOWN, 1990

THE CELL DOOR closed behind John and the guard said, "We'll see you whenever you learn how to act like a human being instead of a fucking animal." He walked off and John was alone in solitary, in the dark. He considered his situation—no radio, no clock, no letters or books, just the cell with the cot and the toilet. But there were also no TVs, no noise, and no Michael Perry. And now everyone on the Row would know what happens when you fucked with John Thompson. All in all, he'd take this trade.

Michael Perry had fucked with John, and so John had had to make an example of him. It had been a visiting day, and John's mother was coming from New Orleans. His cell, and the others on the Row, faced out over the front of the building, and they could see the bus arrive and the visitors step off and walk into the building.

When the bus pulled up, all the men stood in front of their cells and looked out across the hall and out the windows, scanning the visitors, hoping that someone would come to see them. John knew that everyone was watching—the men really couldn't help it, even if they didn't expect anyone to be coming off the bus. They were all hoping that someone would surprise them, and at the same time worried that someone would disappoint them by not being there.

John shared the same sense of excitement and nervousness. He desperately wanted to see his sons. At the same time, he was scared to see Dedric's or Tiger's little-boy legs coming down the steps of the bus.

Slowly, painfully, John's mother stepped down out of the bus and began laboriously moving up the walk toward the death row building. A stroke several years before had left her partially para-lyzed, making walking difficult for her as she moved her right leg and dragged her unresponsive left leg. John watched her walk, his heart swelling as he considered the effort she was making to pay him a visit.

That was when he heard Michael Perry say, "Who this cripple bitch coming to see?"

Everybody on death row knew that Michael Perry was crazy. The man had no idea where he was half the time. He would sit in his cell and talk to himself; he'd yell and scream. He refused to shower unless he was forced to by the guards. Sometimes he would scratch and claw at himself. John thought putting a crazy person like him on death row with the rest of them was a joke, even if Perry did kill his whole family, which he did.

Still, crazy or not, the man just couldn't say that about John's mother, and yelling it that way across the tier for everyone to hear, that couldn't pass. John said, "Man, Michael, best not to talk like that; that's my momma."

So Michael knew. But he said it again: "Who this cripple bitch coming to see?"

John listened to the rest of the men as they hooted and hol-lcred, but he thought, *Well, that's all there is to that, then.* He said, "Michael, I'm gonna deal with you when I get back. Remember that." He wouldn't do anything before the visit, but Michael and everyone else needed to know that something would be done.

He waited for two days before he saw his opportunity when he got his exercise hour. He put some clean clothes in a bowl, grabbed his lighter and a pack of cigarettes, and walked to the shower. On the way, he walked past Michael Perry, asleep in his cell, shirtless.

John went in to the shower and cleaned himself. He turned the shower as hot as he could get it, beyond scalding, placed the bowl on the floor, and pushed it gently with his foot under the water. With his dirty clothes, he picked the bowl up with both hands and walked casually out of the shower and down the hall.

As he passed Michael Perry's cell, John casually tossed the bowl of scalding water through the bars. The water landed squarely on Michael's back. John kept walking calmly back to his cell, listening with satisfaction to Michael's screams. No one responded—neither prisoners nor guards. Michael kept screaming, and everyone simply assumed he was having one of his episodes.

John walked back into his cell, leaving the door open. He put the bowl down and lit a cigarette, exhaling contentedly as Michael's agonized yelling filled the tier.

It took the guards longer to figure things out than he had thought it would. Nobody said anything to them, except Michael himself, and the guards didn't listen to him because he was crazy. It was two days later, when his smell finally got to be too much even for the guards and they took him to take a shower, that they saw the burns on his back. Then they listened, and now John was here, by himself.

Everything was a trade-off. John lay down on the cot and closed his eyes, trying to use the topic of the New Orleans Saints to distract his brain and drift off sleep.

19

FIGHTING CITY HALL

THE KITCHEN SINK was filed, but there was still a lot of work to do. In particular, Michael and Gordon wanted to fill in some of the gaps in the *Brady* arguments. Nick Trenticosta and Rob Couhig believed there were other documents that the DA had never turned over to John's defense, and since any new documents would extend and enhance their appeal, Michael and Gordon were working hard to make sure they had everything on hand before they moved forward.

Their efforts to get the complete prosecution file began with a letter from Michael to Jeff Bridger, the ADA in charge of the appeal. Bridger had had no role in the trial, but Michael expected the DA's office to fight hard to avoid providing any additional information about either case. It would be a blot on Harry Connick's record if the conviction in the Liuzza case were overturned, and it would have ramifications for him in both the white and black sections of New Orleans come election time. Plus, Bridger and Connick knew that with Thompson's life hanging in the balance, Michael and Gordon would be looking for any advantage, however small, to reopen the case, or, at a minimum, to slow down his execution. The obvious strategy was for Bridger to refuse to provide any information unless and until ordered to by Judge Quinlan, and then, to provide information only minimally and begrudgingly.

Assuming Bridger acted as expected, the question would be whether Quinlan was predisposed to force the DA to open the files. He certainly had not supported Couhig and Fanning in their pretrial discovery requests, and Michael assumed Quinlan would be the same way in the appeals process. That said, Quinlan had certainly talked as though he would play ball with them at their first meeting, instructing Bridger to provide the defense with "every scrap of paper" related to the case. Michael had smiled at that, the judge using evocative language that Michael would make sure everyone remembered anytime there was a delay or a refusal to provide information.

With Quinlan's telephone order at the front of everyone's mind, Michael wrote to Bridger, officially requesting that the DA provide any information in its files or those of the NOPD within sixteen categories of information, including "the complete files of the police and the district attorney relating to the Liuzza murder and the investigation and prosecution of John Thompson and Kevin Freeman." He reminded Bridger in the letter of Quinlan's "every scrap of paper" admonishment.

To make sure nothing was missed, Michael also asked for more specific information across broad areas of the case, including any and all statements made by prosecution witnesses to the police or the DAs; any arrest or search warrants for any other suspect in the murder or armed robbery cases; any materials related to Kevin Freeman's plea agreement; any documents related to jury selection in either case; any audiotapes of either trial; and a list of depositions for people that might have additional information about the case.

Bridger's response was telling, if not particularly surprising. He provided a single-page response two months later stating that Thompson was not entitled to any of the information that they sought. Despite his prior verbal ruling, Quinlan had not seen fit to respond one way or the other to Bridger's letter, so their motion was in limbo. They'd keep knocking on the front door, but it was time to send someone around back to see if they could get in that way.

Nick had a paralegal, a good-looking woman with a British accent. She was dating an NOPD officer, and with a little persuading, she had gained access to the police file on the Liuzza murder. According to her, there were quite a few documents that weren't in Thompson's defense file. In particular, there were written statements from Funk Perkins and Ken Carr to the police, statements they would need to analyze and compare against the trial transcript. Any factual difference between the statements and the trial testimony could be grounds for a new trial.

There was also a document signed by Curole that sounded like it could be one of the "dailies" that Trenticosta had spoken of—the police reports regularly filed throughout the ongoing NOPD investigation. The highlight, though, was that the police file apparently had a notarized document stating the terms of the reward offered by both the City of New Orleans and the Liuzza family. Each reward recipient would be given 50 percent of their total reward upon the arrest of the murder suspect, with the other 50 percent to be paid upon that person's conviction. It sounded pretty different from Jim Williams's arrogance at trial, his whole "no evidence has been presented that suggests these people have received any reward money" stance.

Michael wasn't a criminal law expert, but he was considerably more experienced in getting documents from lawyers who didn't want to provide them. He picked up the phone and dialed Judge Quinlan's chambers.

AUGUST 5, 1989

MICHAEL AND GORDON sat in the office, reading the file that Nick's paralegal had identified for them. It didn't have the dailies, but it was interesting reading, including police statements that Funk Perkins had given prior to the trial, statements that had never been provided to Rob Couhig or Pat Fanning. Michael thought the existence of the statements alone might get them a new trial, and it certainly bolstered their *Brady* arguments in the Kitchen Sink, but in order for them to really make that claim, they'd have to show that whatever new information was material and that it would likely have caused a jury to rule differently.

Michael scanned each page quickly, expectantly, waiting to find the new information that he knew had to be there. He flipped from one page to the next, his frustration growing page by page. Gordon, on the other hand, seemed to have infinite patience, reading each page carefully before calmly turning to the next.

Finally, Michael found what he was looking for. "Gordon, look at this—on page six. You remember Freeman's testimony at trial? He swore up and down, fought with Couhig on it, that he had parked his car on Carondelet and Josephine, *south* of the shooting by several blocks, and that he had then run *north* to get home. But you look at this now: Funk tells Curole that Freeman parked his car in front of Katie's Beauty Salon, *north* of Baronne, on Josephine."

"So?"

"Well, I don't know, but if Freeman and Perkins have different stories, then something's up somewhere."

"Not necessarily. One of them just got it wrong. Probably Funk."

Michael kept reading. "Here's another one. Funk says here that Thompson went to pick Kevin Freeman up and they had gone to look for someone to rob. Freeman's story was that he had been driving home in his car and had just happened to pass Thompson on the street, where he decided to give Thompson a ride."

Gordon said, "Yeah, but the fact that Perkins and Freeman have different stories doesn't mean Freeman is lying. It could mean Perkins is lying or manipulating little facts to get the reward, which is actually part of our argument. Plus, Perkins said that Freeman was confessing all of this when they were both high. Who knows how credible any of his facts are?"

Michael nodded. It was unlikely they could use these facts to get a *Brady* reversal from Quinlan. They were too far from the center of the case, and Gordon was right: If Perkins was wrong, Freeman's story would stand up. Still, it bugged him. Little details like this were what lies were built on. They'd need to file this away for use later on.

20

TUGGING AT THREADS

SEPTEMBER 19, 1989

MICHAEL SAT IN Gordon's office, looking across his colleague's desk and spitting out the contents of Bridger's latest letter with an amazement that had quickly shifted into fury. Bridger was jerking them around: First, he said that the lawyers couldn't have anything, and then he'd responded to Quinlan's request to furnish the document by saying that it didn't matter whether the DA's office could produce anything, because all the documents had already been turned over. They had asked whether that only applied to the DA or NOPD, and were told it was just the DA's office, and that Bridger didn't know what the NOPD had.

Michael wasn't sure how a DA could put a case together without a police report, or how Dubelier or Williams could have satisfied their obligations to provide all evidence about the case without reviewing the complete police file, but if Bridger didn't have the file, it wasn't because it was impossible to get. Michael and Andy had walked into the NOPD to ask for the file, and while they couldn't take it with them or copy it, it had been handed over to them with no questions asked. Not long after that, the DA's office had sent over some new statements, which had mysteriously been found and brought to their attention. Now, Bridger's latest letter revealed that there were audiotapes of interviews related to the case that had been recorded on January 14, 1985—one at 4:20 PM and one at 9:40 PM.

The tapes had not been transcribed yet, and Bridger had not provided copies, but both Michael and Gordon were certain they contained confidential statements of unidentified witnesses. Michael found it laughable that the DA's office and Bridger hadn't listened to these tapes previously; how could they not want to know what was on the tapes and whether it helped, or hurt, their case?

The more he read Bridger's letter, the angrier he got. In addition to the statements and the audiotapes, Bridger further stated that the DA's office had some attorney-client privileged material, or attorney work product materials, that the DA's office was not required to turn over to Michael and Gordon.

Gordon expressed the proper sympathy and outrage for his colleague, although in reality he wasn't terribly surprised or offended by Bridger's delay tactics. Bridger had a job to do, and his job was not to make their job easy. Besides, all of this back-and-forth provided more ammunition that they could use to position themselves within the larger realm of the case. They could use this, and the police file, and the other information they were gathering. Each little piece of information was like a piece of thread. If they pulled on it, a little bit at a time, and kept pulling until they'd pulled it out completely, maybe they could make the DA's case unravel altogether.

He was already mentally composing another letter to Judge Quinlan, thinking about how they could take the moral high ground regarding the city of New Orleans' "questionable and dilatory tactics" that "stretched the rules of discovery, evidence, and ethics to, and perhaps beyond, their breaking point," or something like that. Maybe that would help swing Quinlan over to their side a little bit.

21

LIFE IN ANGOLA

JOHN PULLED OUT the typewriter from under his cot, inserted a sheet of paper, and started to type, putting his name and cell number at the top, along with the date. *Dear Nancy . . .*

He always stopped at this point, to figure out what he was going to say. He wrote to Nancy, his spiritual advisor, fairly frequently, and had a pretty good idea of how the letter would go, but it made sense to take a little more time. Paper and typewriter ribbon weren't easy to come by, and it wasn't like he didn't have the time to write carefully.

Letters were the easiest way for John to communicate with people outside Angola. He was only allowed two calls a week, except to his lawyers—unless a guard was irritated, or someone on the tier had done something, or one of the other dozens of reasons why they might limit phone time. If he bribed a guard with something, maybe he could get an extra call, but that was expensive. Even so, the calls were collect, and the phone time limited to his one hour of exercise. So letters were better; even so, John liked to make sure his thoughts were organized and that he knew what he was going to say before he started typing.

He pulled out Nancy's last letter and read it again for about the fiftieth time. She was feeling low right now, and so was he, but he decided to keep his feelings to himself and to try to cheer her up for a change. Nobody wanted to read a sad letter. Nancy didn't, and John wanted—no, needed—Nancy to write him back.

Nancy was the biggest surprise to come out of death row for John. He'd been in his cell, and the mail had come in. A trusty (an inmate who had been given the job as a reward for good behavior) threw a letter in through the bars of his cell. John had picked it up, but he hadn't recognized the handwriting. The return address was a P.O. box.

When he tore open the letter and read it, it was short and polite, from a woman who lived in New Orleans. Nancy said that she had been given his name by Sister Helen Prejean. Everyone in Angola knew Sister Helen—the nun who fought against capital punishment. Sister Helen had held some sort of community meeting on the topic, Nancy had attended, and Sister Helen had asked Nancy to be a pen pal for a death row inmate.

The letter hadn't said much about Nancy, which John understood. If he had been writing to a murderer, he would have used a P.O. box himself. He wrote back quickly, though, as it gave him something to do to pass the time.

They had exchanged a number of letters since then, and she had opened up a little bit over time. He still didn't know where she lived, but that was okay. He was never going to see her house anyway. He did know that she had two daughters, which she told him after he'd confessed that the hardest part about death row was not getting to see his boys grow up.

He kept reading Nancy's letter and her apology for the time between letters. That made him smile—this generous woman was donating her time to him and apologizing for not doing it more often; she clearly understood how much her letters meant to him. So he continued typing, writing about his mother's birthday, and asking Nancy a little more about herself.

His fingers moved one at a time but fairly quickly over the typewriter keys. *Tell you a close secret that I don't share with many people,* he typed. *I wasn't a child of God when I was a free man.* He told her about being shot in the leg, the drive-by with the shotgun, and how he now took that as a sign from God—a sign he had ignored, that he should have changed his ways.

The shooting had cost him nine months in the hospital. It was right after John Jr.—Tiger—was born, and he hadn't been able to play with his son. The doctors had said he might not ever walk again. He proved them wrong within a year, but learning to walk again had been the hardest thing he'd ever done in his life.

He looked down and realized that his fingers had stopped typing. He noticed it happening more and more—how hard it was for him to concentrate on one thing. He kept drifting into the same memories over and over. He wasn't sure why. Lately, it had been guns, and how they'd come to him and then left him.

I just bought and sold them sometimes because they were good for money; somebody always wanted one, he thought. *It was business—somethin' you could trade to get drugs or money.*

Another thing he always thought about, something he couldn't shake, was the way Kojak and Funk had sold him out. Kojak he guessed he understood. He'd wanted to stay out of jail. If he'd just kept quiet, neither one of them would have been convicted. But Funk . . . . Funk was a different story. He just went out to get John for money. And now John was in here, and he had absolutely no way to confront either Kojak or Funk about it.

John started typing to Nancy again. He wanted to tell her that he was on death row for nothing other than being a black man in New Orleans when a white man got shot, but he didn't. She wrote like she was white, and he knew she probably thought he was guilty, too—that he'd killed a man and robbed some kids. But she kept writing to him, like he was somebody worth her time. So he told her he hoped there would be some progress on his case. He told her that he respected her, and that it was hard to find someone like her. He wrapped up the letter by talking about sports, a nice, upbeat, neutral ending. He signed the letter by writing, *Give your husband my best, and take care of yourself and the girls. Peace and love, Your Friend Always, John.*

Peace and love. *You get right down to it,* he thought, *what else is there to hope for?*

JUNE 16, 1991

JOHN SPENT TWENTY-THREE hours a day in his cell. He had to find ways to occupy himself; otherwise, he'd just waste entire days doing nothing. Michael and Gordon had gotten him the radio he asked for, so he'd listen to music, read books, write a letter, or play chess— each inmate using a sheet of paper with a board on it, each square representing a number. The inmates would call out the moves back and forth.

He tried not to watch TV, but the two TVs on the tier were on all day long. Sometimes the shows made his mind wander; other times they made him think about what he was facing, about his situation. He'd watch the world news: war in the Middle East, people afraid to go home, and kids in refugee camps. John would watch that, and think, *I'm not in too much of a different situation than they're in over there. We're both fightin' for our life, and the government is responsible for both our situations.*

Sometimes the talk shows would be on, and he'd have to listen to those severely disturbed people. They probably thought he was the crazy one, and maybe they were right. After all, he *was* on death row.

Sometimes the guards turned the TVs to shows about the death penalty. It was their idea of a joke, forcing the inmates to listen to people arguing about how terrible they were and how good it would be for the world if they were killed.

From time to time, John thought about both Ray Liuzzas—the dead man and his father. How would Liuzza Sr. react to seeing the man who killed one of his sons? The older Liuzza wouldn't come to see John, and John refused to get involved with the case, now that he'd seen how rigged the system was. If Ray Liuzza Jr. had been a black man in New Orleans, instead of a rich white man's son, John wouldn't be on death row. The cops wouldn't even have tried that hard to look for the gun. Just another dead black man; probably wouldn't have even been in the paper. Not on the front page like Ray Liuzza was, anyway.

It was self-serving, he knew, but that was how he felt. He wouldn't put anyone on death row, no matter what they did, knowing what it's like and what it does to people. Of course he'd want justice if someone hurt his own boys, but he'd need to be sure that the right person was getting punished.

He knew life didn't mean a thing to those DAs—Dubelier and Williams—who had the power to give it or take it away. To them, John was just another black criminal. Maybe he killed Ray Liuzza, maybe not, but they figured that if he wasn't guilty of that particular crime, he was certainly guilty of something. They took a case off their books and served the greater good.

At the same time, John had come to realize he hadn't been very smart. He had believed what his father had told him: If he stayed away from violent crime, stuck to dealing and fencing, he'd only get short time. He thought he could count on his lawyers and the jury to know the game. Now he knew, his lawyers didn't care, and the jury believed the cops and the DAs.

In prison, he read *The Prince* and realized how stupid he'd been, how much of the game he had missed. Machiavelli, or Sun Tzu, they weren't writing short-time books. They would have played it smart, like Dubelier and Williams.

There was another side of it too, the side he focused on in his letters to Nancy. Death row had changed John. First, he was alive. If he had stayed on the street, he would probably be dead by now. Even if he had stayed alive, he would never have thought about it the way he did on the Row—wouldn't have appreciated his freedom, or thought about whether he was doing things the right way. Being on death row changed everything.

The truth was, John had been on a path. Petty theft to drug use to violent crime—that's how it went. He'd dropped out of school, and he wasn't able to join the army without a high school diploma. Stealing things, selling drugs—that was what he'd had to do to support Dedric and Tiger and his family. He started with weed, but he'd moved on to clickems, joints dipped in PCP. The PCP had made him feel so damn strong, he'd believed he could do anything. John had wanted to walk up to a man and punch him in the face, or walk into a store and steal things, or walk up to a man and rob him, and he'd believed that he could just do it and walk away. It was only a matter of time before that would have led to something serious and irreversible.

Looking back, he knew he'd made the prosecutor's job easy. John could see that he had lost control of his life. He'd let the outside world steer him down a path—the drugs, the petty crime, the trials—doing whatever his lawyers or the Court had said, without question. That was his mistake. He knew it was probably too late, but he needed to do something now. John thought to himself, as he did every day, *If I ever get out, I got to turn my life around into something good.*

JULY 7, 1991

JOHN HAD BEEN looking forward to this day for weeks. Now it had come and gone, and he sat in his cell, reflecting. The typical noise was going on—offers to bet on the games that night, guys wanting to play chess, the usual. John ignored it all, lost in his thoughts.

He didn't know why the days that were supposed to be good always ended up being so hard. Every time he thought that he might actually have some happiness, or a feeling that he was connected somewhere, something would happen that would take it away, reminding him where he was: living in his deathbed.

The good part of the day was that John Jr.—Tiger—had come to visit him. He had been three when John was arrested. Now he was ten. Twelve-year-old Dedric, John's oldest son, had also come for a visit, five hours from New Orleans on a bus. He got all the way there, off the bus, and into the security line for the visiting room, on a trip that had been planned for weeks. But when he got to the head of the line, the guards told him he couldn't come in. They made the boy wait outside for two hours because he was wearing shorts. Tiger had been wearing shorts, too, but the rule was that if you were ten, you were still considered a child, and shorts were permitted. If you were twelve, you were too old, and couldn't come in wearing shorts.

Dedric had made this trip by bus, in the Louisiana summer, to visit his father in prison, a trip he probably didn't want to make in the first place, and now he had to stand outside. Both boys knew that there was nothing John could do about it. He couldn't protect Dedric, or any of them. All three of them knew it, what kind of a father he was.

It had taken John's mother months to get the money together for this visit. She had told John that Dedric was already becoming a problem. He was getting involved with older kids, paying a lot of attention to girls, hanging out on the corners. Drugs were everywhere. By Dedric's age, John had already tried a lot of what was out there; there wasn't any reason for Dedric to be any different. John didn't know if his son was getting involved with dealers or gangs. He couldn't get Dedric on the phone most times, and when he did, the boy didn't want to talk to him. *Hell*, John thought, *what twelve-year-old wants to talk to his pops anyway, let alone through a prison phone?*

I'm probably lucky he didn't get in to see me, John thought. He would have said something wrong, or asked a question the boy didn't want to answer, or gotten angry at something Dedric did or said because he was twelve, and twelve-year-old boys made their fathers angry. John didn't have any idea what to tell that boy. Still, if he could have seen Dedric, just laid eyes on him, and have the boy see him, maybe Dedric would have understood that he was what John lived for—for Dedric and Tiger. Even better, maybe Dedric would have seen how that small-time shit can catch up to you. Maybe he'd think twice before starting as a runner. *That would have been all right,* John thought.

He had tried to explain that to Tiger, but he'd probably fucked that up too. Getting to see Tiger, to talk to him—it was amazing how a kid could give you so much without even knowing he was giving it. Everything that boy did had *joy* in it—joy for the things around him. Death row had just about every other emotion. There was hope, and charity, and wisdom, friendship, loyalty, and honesty. Not everywhere, not all the time, but they were there. But they didn't have any joy. The only time John ever felt joy was when he could see his kids. It helped him to overcome the frustration and disappointment of not being able to touch them, of only seeing them through a screen, of spending the entire time worrying about the fact that every second that went by brought the end of the visit closer. Or now, thinking about his two boys on their bus driving through Baton Rouge, believing in their hearts that he was a murderer, no matter what he said to them.

John missed all of the boys' special days and special moments. He missed their birthdays and holidays. Worse than that, he missed those moments in the middle of the day, the nothing moments of going to the store to get a dozen eggs and having one of the boys ask a question about something only a kid would think to ask. But one thing he'd learned in prison: There was no sense in trying to make up for lost time. Once it was gone, it was gone.

All John wanted to do was get out of prison and live his life with the people he loved. He didn't want to steal or smoke or shoot anybody, or even talk to anyone. He just wanted to take his boys swimming.

Michael and Gordon had gotten a stay in the case by filing a brief, but since then nothing had progressed. It was moving slowly, and John was getting frustrated.

He had taught himself the Twenty-third Psalm, and he tried to pray the Serenity Prayer, asking God for the courage to change what he could, to find the serenity to accept what he couldn't, and the wisdom to know the difference. It helped. Maybe he was a dead man walking. Maybe he just needed to let go of the idea that any of it mattered. None of it did. He'd end up dead in the chair, and his sons would live and die, and that would be that.

Yeah, he thought. *I'm ready for my date whenever it comes.* It would, that was for certain. The Lord would see him through.

John liked Michael and Gordon, but they weren't getting him anywhere. They didn't have any reason to try and hurry things—he wasn't paying them, and they weren't the ones sitting on death row.

The TV pierced his thoughts, and he looked up at it. *Man, I wish football season would get here.* Football was his favorite sport, and it would give him something to look forward to, the Saints and Bobby Hebert and Ironhead, instead of this image in his head of Dedric, in shorts, walking away from him.

JULY 21, 1991

Dear Nancy:

Well, hopefully when these few lines reach you, they will find you as well as the rest of your family, all doing very well. As for myself, I am doing about the best I can in health. This isn't a good day here, as you're probably already aware of the execution that is going to take place here within 11 hours from now—unless the governor has a change of heart.

I was pretty close to Andrew Jones, so it's pretty weird to watch him leave off the tier knowing it's a good possibility that I will never see him again. I know we're here to die, but

I try really hard to believe that the people wake up to what's really happening. But looks like we is a long way from that. But it's a part of life here on death row. The only thing you could do is try to keep your faith and pray. But every time someone is put to death, it tear into that faith a lil by lil. Just the thought of knowing that pretty much well could be you next time, with executions taking place. These kind of thoughts flow through your mind, whether you want them or not. The key here is to control your thoughts, don't let them control you.

But I must admit, there is a bright part of this weekend that lifted me up from this miserable feeling. I received the pictures of you and the girls. I can't tell you how much I appreciate them; and what timing. I needed something right now to help get me out of this mood. When I looked over at the pictures, I thought about how I needed to answer your letter, which was something to occupy my mind. To try and stop focusing on what's to happen tonight. Looking back over this letter, I really didn't do too well, huh?

Well, it's almost that time of the year once again for football season to start. It's good to hear that most of the team is in camp early this year. As far as quarterback goes, I don't think Steve will start this year, or he might play the first two games. But Bobby is what will get them where they want to go. I can't wait to see what they look like. TV is very dead right now.

Well, it's time to eat this nasty food they is about to give us. I am ready to eat something. I don't eat much of what they bring us, but at the moment I haven't ate nothing today.

Well, hopefully I will hear from you soon. I will end here for now, but will write you soon. Kiss the girls for me, tell Mike I said hello. Until next time, take care of yourself.

Peace & Love Friends,
JOHN

22

POWERLESS

JOHN WAS BACK in his cell after some time in lockup. The amazing thing about it wasn't that Angola thought taking him out of solitary confinement and putting him in a cell with the uncontrollable crazy dudes was punishment. The amazing thing was how much he felt like one of those dudes in the sitcoms, like a Ricky Ricardo or one of those guys who comes home from work and feels like he's got to deal with everyone else's problems.

He'd been taken off of death row and moved to Camp J for no reason he could tell. The guards just came and got him one day, no warning. They said he was a threat to security, packed him up, and moved him in there with the crazies, and took away all his privileges. It wouldn't have been that bad, really, except that he couldn't have his radio. He missed the football on Sunday, but on the other hand, he didn't have the noise either.

The guards said he did it to himself. A group of the inmates on death row had been complaining about the conditions, and writing letters about it to anyone they could think of. What really got him in trouble, John figured, was when he talked to Judge Quinlan about it at the end of a hearing in New Orleans. Quinlan had sent someone out to look at the conditions, and, lo and behold, John got packed up and moved out to someplace the prison thought was worse.

There were some good things, including getting his first hot meal in about two years. Hot food was typically prohibited on death row. They said it was because they didn't have a stove or an oven in the kitchen there, though John didn't believe that. And even though they wouldn't deliver his mail to him, they let him write letters and said they'd mail them for him.

The situation had changed as suddenly and randomly as it had started. But John wasn't thinking about the cold meals and rotten conditions in the prison, or the blaring television. His thoughts were elsewhere.

Now that he was able to use the phone again, he was hearing more about the situation with his family back at home. It wasn't good. John's mom was having a hard time with Denise, and both women wanted him to fix it, as if he could do anything from Angola. Denise didn't want Tiger to talk with his grandmother on the phone, and wasn't letting him visit her either.

John could imagine how it happened. His mother probably told Denise she wasn't living right, wasn't doing right by the boy, and Denise would have gotten pretty mad about that. He could hear her saying to him in that tone she had, *If that old woman is going to criticize, she can stay the F away.*

Still, it was taking its toll on his mother. With John unreachable in lockdown, his mother had gone to see a lawyer about visitation rights. Thankfully, nothing had happened there yet, or Denise would just dig in more. But now, to top it off, John's mother told him that Tiger had called her even though he wasn't supposed to, to tell her that Denise's new husband was beating him.

John had told his mother to get the lawyers moving, even though he knew it would take a lot more than one woman claiming abuse to get lawyers to take Tiger away from his mother, especially with his father in jail. And the fact was that his mother couldn't really take care of Tiger herself, half-paralyzed as she was after a stroke.

John ran his fingers over his scalp, trying to figure out what to do. He was supposed to get his hour exercise time in four hours. Maybe he'd try to use the time to call Denise, see what was going on.

He looked down at his hands and was unsurprised to see hair from his head in them. He knew it was the stress.

He wasn't the only one feeling tense on death row. Another inmate had gone from the Row to the Death House last week. Somehow, he got a last-minute stay, and came back to the Row again, but people were still recovering from the reminder that one day, it would be them going to the Death House. It was the sort of thing that made tempers flare, and tempers in prison were always dangerous.

He made himself think about the Saints—or maybe the Saints just came into his head to save him from himself? The team was looking good right now. They were learning how to sit on a lead. Steve Walsh, he looked like a real quarterback. He was young, but he'd get better, and maybe they'd start winning some of the big games.

It was so stupid that he was even on death row in the first place. Why did they even have the death penalty anyway? New Orleans had more murders in the last year than they had the year he was supposed to have killed Ray Liuzza. Why? Because of the high sentences they gave for violent crimes.

John couldn't figure it out. It wasn't that he thought the criminals shouldn't be punished, or that slaps on the wrist would deter murderers. But if they were going to give sentences like his—forty-nine years for a first violent crime, an *attempted* armed robbery where no one even got shot—then of course you were going to see more murders. What was the difference between forty-nine years without parole and a life sentence? John was twenty-two when he'd received that sentence, and now he was twenty-eight. He couldn't even imagine being seventy-one years old. If the carjacker had shot those three kids, there wouldn't have been any witnesses. If he got caught for the murder, it's basically the same sentence. Why couldn't any of those DAs figure that one out?

On top of everything else, it was getting to be holiday season. Commercials for Thanksgiving were starting to appear on TV. Christmas wasn't much good on death row. People wanted to come up and visit, but everyone outside always had so much going on, and it was hard to get to Angola. He knew there wouldn't be any visits for him. In some ways, it was okay. No visit or phone call would make him feel better when he started remembering being with his mother and grandmother on Christmas, and remembering how he'd felt when his father wasn't there, or knowing exactly how his boys felt about his own absence.

He reached under his bed and fished around in his trunk, pulling out a picture of himself. The prison sent a trusty in to take pictures of the inmates every three months. They could buy a few of these photos for $1.50 and send them to people. John looked at himself. He didn't think he had changed all that much, but when he got a newspaper in the cell and read about all the killings and the crime in New Orleans, when he thought about who he was now and who he would have been, and where he would have gone with his life if he'd never been put away, he knew there were changes. Most of the guys he had hung out with were dead now—killed for drugs or by drugs or with drugs. Young kids now—Dedric's age, Tiger's age even—were selling and using. He had been part of that, feeding that behavior and making a living off it. Outside now, if he hadn't changed his life, he would be dead.

Of course, he was dead in Angola, too.

He looked at his clock. Three more hours before his exercise hour. He reached under his bed, grabbed a book, and lay back on his cot, trying not to think.

23

LEMMON V. CONNICK

NOVEMBER 10, 1992

ALTHOUGH **Q**UINLAN **HAD** originally scheduled the discovery-status conference in the Thompson case for June 20, 1990, it was clearly not a priority for any of the people involved. Bridger and Quinlan had made multiple requests for delay, and while Michael, Gordon, and Andy knew John wanted things to move more quickly, any delay kept John alive and gave them more time to find additional evidence or new arguments for John's case.

Even so, the magnitude of the delay was surprising to Andy. The hearing changed dates nineteen times, but finally took place on November 10, 1992. From a strategic perspective, the delays were a boon to the defense, because Andy had found their path around the DA's brick wall.

NOVEMBER 5, 1992

S**ARAH** D**AVIES** S**TOOD** in front of the copy machine with her law book, placing each page on the glass and pressing COPY. She pulled the copy of the Louisiana Supreme Court's opinion in *Lemmon v. Connick* from the side of the machine and headed up to the Morgan, Lewis law library.

Sarah had only joined Morgan, Lewis a few months before, and she hadn't worked on the Thompson case very long, but already she knew that she'd most likely find Andy in the library. He was a researcher at heart, with a temperament that didn't lend itself to the sharp-elbowed practice of high-stakes corporate litigation. Andy felt more comfortable surrounded by books and case law, away from the phones and secretaries, the paralegals and document clerks. He called the cubicle he permanently squatted in his "satellite office," and it was stocked with various volumes of legal reference books amid signs instructing the librarians not to refile them.

Andy wasn't in his cube when Sarah arrived, and as far as she knew, he hadn't yet seen what she had in her hands: volume 590 of the second edition of the *Southern Law Reporter*. She left the book, opened to page 1,574, on Andy's desk, along with a Post-it square on which she had written: *Call me—Sarah*.

IT HAD BEEN nearly four years since the Kitchen Sink had been submitted to Judge Quinlan. John's original execution date of February 1989 had been stayed when they filed their brief. So far, there had been no official ruling on any of the eleven arguments they had made in the brief, but the important ruling came in March of 1989, when Quinlan agreed to allow them to expand their investigation into the case and to seek documents and other information from the DA and the New Orleans Police Department to help support the arguments in the brief.

Not surprisingly, the DA's office had been extremely unhelpful. Michael had assumed that Judge Quinlan would intervene at some point to force the DAs to produce either the information they'd requested, or proof that the information they'd requested didn't exist, but apparently New Orleans judges operated differently than those in Pennsylvania. Quinlan just ignored them, providing no guidance or rulings to the attorneys on either side. He seemed content to let Michael and Bridger send angry letters back and forth.

In May of 1990, Michael thought he had finally made some progress. He couldn't see the documents himself, but he was able to convince Judge Quinlan to personally review the complete file of the DA's office privately in his chambers, and to evaluate Michael's document requests with the file in front of him.

Unfortunately, if not surprisingly, Quinlan sided with Connick and Bridger. He informed them that after his personal review of the DA's files in chambers, there was nothing more that he would compel the DA to turn over. There would be no new evidence. Quinlan set a status hearing for June 20, 1990, to discuss how the appeal would proceed.

Since then, Andy had spent days in the Morgan, Lewis library, trying to figure out how to get at the DA and NOPD files. He had tried everything he could think of—the DA's office directly; the NOPD directly, and through a private investigator; and Judge Quinlan. He had even researched the Louisiana Public Records Act to see if a public request for information might compel the government agencies to turn the files over. Nothing had worked. It had all seemed hopeless until Andy walked into the library and found Sarah's note.

LEMMON V. CONNICK was decided in December 1991 by the Louisiana Supreme Court. The case was in regard to a criminal defendant (Lemmon) seeking information from the New Orleans District Attorney regarding his case file. Lemmon had tried to use the Louisiana Public Records Act to pry the records free. As in Thompson's case, the DA had argued that the disclosure was improper. Lemmon didn't take no for an answer, however, and pushed his appeal to the Louisiana Supreme Court, which expressly overturned the DA and ordered the release of the documents.

The Court had clearly and directly ruled that cases of post-conviction relief, like John's, were not considered "criminal litigation." In the *Lemmon* case, the Court ordered Connick to turn over the requested documents. *Lemmon* gave the lawyers a new legal basis with which to access these files. It was a good reason to go back to Quinlan, but Andy was still dumbfounded as to why the DA wouldn't just give him and his team the files.

Certainly, it was not unheard of for lawyers to fight over the production of documents. You couldn't lose if your opponent didn't have the information. But in this case, the DA had already won. Dubelier, Williams, and Connick had their conviction and their death sentence. Didn't they want to have the execution happen now? And yet, by fighting so hard not to produce the actual files, they delayed that process rather than accelerating it.

Andy had a few theories regarding why Connick might be behaving this way: The DA didn't want to set a precedent of having open file discovery in criminal cases; or maybe he was being sincere and truly was concerned that witnesses for the prosecution could be discovered and injured. Maybe that precedent was important enough to them that they could live with delaying the appeals process of a convicted man on death row.

Or maybe the DA was hiding something.

Either way, the *Lemmon* case gave them a new reason to discuss the issue with Judge Quinlan, and a new opportunity to ask Quinlan why the DA was being uncooperative in providing the file.

They sent several letters referencing *Lemmon* to the DAs. Michael had taken the lead on that, and the letters reflected his aggressive style—a belief that the best defense was a good offense. Written carefully to cover any possible piece of information that could have been used to prove John's guilt, Michael asked for complete NOPD and DA files for the murder case, including the "dailies" that were regularly filed throughout the ongoing NOPD investigation. They also asked for any statements made to "representatives of the State," using that phrase carefully so that the DAs couldn't pull their standard finger-pointing trick, saying, "We can't control the police; you've got to ask them—it's in their files."

They also requested any grand jury testimony related to Kevin Freeman or John Thompson, testimony that would have been used to get the original indictments and criminal charges. And, because the Louisiana Public Records Act allowed them to get documents from *any* case that was in post-conviction relief, they asked for records involving jury selections in previous capital cases that had been tried by Eric Dubelier or Jim Williams, including the cases of John's fellow death row inmates at Angola. They also asked for documents related to the armed robbery case, including the audiotapes of the closing arguments that had never been transcribed. And finally, remembering Couhig's outrage at the DA's deception regarding the reward money offered by the Liuzza family, they asked for documents related to any such reward offering. It was a comprehensive list, and it asked for a lot of material.

Even with the mention of *Lemmon*, the DA did not respond to their letter, although a private attorney named John Keller, who represented the DA's office, did send Michael a letter stating that some of the documents sought by the Thompson defense team might be in the possession of Judge Quinlan himself. On February 11, 1993, Sarah wrote a letter to Judge Quinlan, informing him of their efforts to obtain all of the information permitted by the *Lemmon* decision, and attached Keller's letter.

The move worked. Judge Quinlan ordered the DA and the NOPD to turn over any information they had. And in April, a box showed up in Michael's office from the New Orleans District Attorney's Office, starting a chain of events that would take a full decade to resolve.

MAY 17, 1993

THE DA's DELIVERY of new documents yielded some information that Michael thought might blow their case wide open. But one key issue remained: The DAs continued to resist providing any physical or tangible evidence in their possession to the Thompson defense team, in either the murder or the armed robbery case. As a result, Michael and Gordon had no way to conduct any independent testing.

Even more than the documentary evidence they had fought so long and hard to get, Michael was amazed at how difficult it had been to get this information, and how Quinlan had allowed the DAs to ignore request after request, in writing and by phone. Michael had asked for the gun that was used in the murder case, and for any physical evidence collected in the armed robbery case. These were standard requests that would be made in any criminal case, and while he understood the DA's desire to not comply with the requests, it was astonishing that Judge Quinlan had permitted it.

It certainly wasn't the fact that there was too much physical evidence, meaning that turning it over would be a burden to the DA's office. The amount of physical evidence linking John to either the murder or the armed robbery was very small, particularly when compared to many other death penalty cases. The evidence that had been the most persuasive against John at trial was the testimony of Kevin Freeman and Funk Perkins. It was Funk's testimony, rather than any physical or scientific evidence, that linked the gun that shot Ray Liuzza Jr. to John. Dubelier and Williams had been able to craft a chain of custody that connected John to the murder weapon through Funk Perkins, Junior Lee Harris, and Jessie Harrison, but it really was the eyewitness testimony that proved John's guilt, while the gun only functioned as a useful prop at trial.

In the armed robbery case, the gun had been similarly unconnected to John by any scientific evidence, and it was the tearful eyewitness identification by Mimi Lagarde and her brothers that had sealed John's fate with the jury. Unlike the murder case, though, the police evidence log showed that the crime scene technician had taken a tennis shoe and a section of Jay Lagarde's pant leg, both of which had blood on them, from the scene of the crime. The DAs had not used either the shoe or the pant leg in the armed robbery trial, but it was hard to know what that meant. Just to be thorough, they had made a request years ago, asking the DA to turn over both the samples and any tests; Michael had assumed Connick's office

John had watched a lot of guys get led off the Row and out to the Death House. When that happened, no one knew which way it would go. John had to assume he'd never see that man again, and he'd want to say his good-byes and make it meaningful. Even if he hated the guy, some things rose above that. He didn't want to see anyone executed.

On the other hand, having a date and getting executed weren't the same thing. Everybody on death row was on their third, or fourth, or seventh, or however many dates, and usually got a stay. Most times a guy went to the Death House and he'd come back a few days later. So John didn't want to make a big deal about that, wanted to stay positive, both for himself and the guy going to the Death House.

Still, they all knew the score. Everybody knew everyone else's legal case and their defenses. They all talked about their cases every day, trying out new theories, sharing tips about things that had worked, sending around newspaper articles about guys in other states who had been released. So when a guy went to the Death House, everybody on the Row had a pretty good sense of whether or not he was going to come back. John had known, and Thomas had too, that this trip was probably his last.

John was thankful, actually, that he had been in OPP getting ready for a hearing when it was Thomas's time to go. It meant he hadn't really had to say good-bye.

Thomas had used his time the way he'd preached it. He admitted his crimes to John and explained how he got to Death Row on the very first day they met, and he never once hid from it or put it off on someone else. Thomas never told anyone he was innocent, never asked for anything better than what he got. In John's mind, that made Thomas better than most of the criminals in jail at present, let alone most of the men on death row.

What Thomas had wanted was to bring his family back together. He had been living in California with his wife and eight children,

knew that no conclusive evidence had been provided by these items. If they had proven John's guilt, he knew Williams would have used them in court. If they had provided conclusive evidence of John's innocence, Williams would have been ethically bound to reveal them.

Even though it would likely lead to a dead end, they had to follow it and be sure. Physical evidence would be the best way for John to prove his innocence—if they could find any. Michael certainly wasn't going to stop asking just because the DAs and Judge Quinlan had not yet done what he wanted, and he was emboldened by their success with documentary evidence after *Lemmon*.

It was becoming perfectly clear to Michael that Judge Quinlan really didn't care what happened to John. Still, the fact that it was an uphill battle didn't change his job, or how he would go about it. Sarah brought him the motion she had typed up, asking—again—for the turnover of all physical evidence. Michael signed it and handed it back.

Maybe this time, he thought.

24

DEAD FOR GOOD

MAY 14, 1995

"**I**N THE END, you know, it don't make no difference. Death is comin', and none of us is gonna run fast enough. It's not this cell that keeps me from runnin', either. None of them guards is gonna escape it. Hell, lookin' at some of those fat crackers, I might live longer than they do. It's somethin' else. And the question you gotta ask yourself is, if it's somethin' outside of this cell that controls life or death, then how are you gonna act inside this cell?"

The question had been directed at John by one of his fellow death row inmates, Thomas Lee Ward, not long after John had arrived at Angola. At the time, John hadn't answered it. He had been a young man then, had wanted to show these motherfuckers on death row that he wasn't nobody's bitch—didn't need to talk to Thomas, or anybody.

Thomas was okay with that. He just said to John, "Once you got that question answered, you be all right in here." He used to talk to John a lot, since their cells were next to one another. John never asked him why, but whatever the reason, Thomas decided to try and educate John about the larger issues of life, as only a prison philosopher could.

Thomas had seen clearly who John was when he arrived at Angola: an angry, wounded, scared street tough. He told John that he was like that due to a failure of responsibility.

Thomas told John he had two choices: one was to keep being angry at everyone and everything—Denise, the DAs, the guards, his lawyers, Funk, Kojak, the other inmates. If he did that, he'd be killed, by the guards if not by another inmate. More important, Thomas told John that all of his anger would make sure that whatever time he did have on earth would be miserable. Thomas said, "Man, death row gives you the greatest gift a man can have. Time."

John had laughed at that. *Time.* How could any time in Angola be a good thing?

Thomas wasn't put off by John's laughter. He kept talking to him, day after day: "Death row is a beautiful thing. We got no distractions. We got our lives, and our deaths, and that's all. And in between, we got to figure it all out.

"You figure, if death comes to all of us, rich or poor, white or black, innocent or guilty, then what makes one man different from another?" Thomas asked. "What kind of life did you lead? The only thing that matters, the only thing, is what you learned from the day you was born to the day you died. Maybe you made mistakes, but if you learned what you did and what you should have done and how to live better from there, then you changed. And that change, that's your control, that's who you are." He'd say, "John, we all got a gift here. We got the time to figure ourselves out, make our rules to define who we are. We aren't just reacting to some action, some stimulus out there every day. We been cut off from all that."

John didn't say anything, but Thomas kept at it, day after day. And one day, John had to agree. No one can run from death.

Not even Thomas. Death happened for Thomas Lee Ward the same way it happened for others John knew on the Row. The only difference was that while previous inmates got fried in the chair, Thomas Lee Ward got stabbed in the arm with a needle. To John, that didn't make any difference at all.

and his wife had returned to New Orleans, where she was from. She took the kids with her. He begged her not to leave, and when she did, he followed her, trying to get her to come back with him.

It came down to a confrontation in her mother's house in New Orleans. Her stepfather told Thomas he would never see his kids again. Thomas was upset, angry, and confused. He went to a bar to clear his head, got loaded up on booze and coke, and went back to the house. He asked his wife's stepfather to let him see the kids one last time. When the man said no, Thomas pulled a gun out and shot the man, and his wife.

Thomas never asked whether his crime of passion deserved a death sentence—whether he was a worse criminal than a drug dealer who shoots someone for business. He figured he was paying for what he did, and he was learning how to change himself on the inside, the only thing that made a difference to him.

When one of the inmates was in the Death House, the guards wouldn't put the news on the TV in the Row. They knew it would excite the inmates. Even without the news, the inmates knew. They knew what day it was, and when the appeals were due, and all of that, and they knew if the condemned was on the Row or in the House.

They knew what was happening outside the prison, too. People would be gathering outside the prison like they always did. Sometimes they could hear the chanting at the front gate: "Amazing Grace" and other songs would float up through the barred windows on the tier. When Thomas was in the waiting room in the House he'd be surrounded by people—the executioners, his lawyers, his spiritual advisor, the warden. A TV crew was there, too. *Dateline*, *Nightline*, *Primetime*—one of those shows had decided to monitor the proceedings.

John pictured Thomas in there, waiting, killing time with his lawyers and the warden, or just sitting around like he was used to doing in his cell back on the Row. He had gone to the House before, and gotten a last-minute reprieve. He had even finished his last meal. The stay came through thirty minutes before his execution.

John wondered: *When it was his time, would he lose hope, and when?*

After his last trip to the House, a close call where he had gotten a last-minute stay, Thomas had explained to John how the night before the execution, they ran him through a rehearsal of the execution, so he wouldn't make a scene or screw it up in front of the people that had come to watch him be killed. He had known what it would feel like, walking into the gray room with the black leather medical bench with arm and leg straps to hold him down. He had known as he walked into the room that it was the last room he'd ever walk into, that lying on that medical bench would be the last thing he'd ever do, that the people in this room would be the last ones he'd see, the last ones he'd speak to, and this would be his legacy, before he was taken off the planet for good.

For good, John thought. Was that right? Was that what it was all for?

John had seen six other guys go to the Death House and not come back. He knew them, like he knew Thomas. Thomas wasn't some crazy person who couldn't learn how to behave right in society. He wasn't some sick bastard, hell-bent on killing people as long as he was a free man. Maybe he'd been that sick bastard for a moment, just one instant when he'd been fighting for time with his kids. And maybe he would have done other things that deserved the death penalty if he'd stayed out.

But on the Row, Thomas had set a moral code for himself, one that he followed. Death row made him a different man. He was at peace with himself and the world. He knew right and wrong. Prison had done what it was supposed to do for Thomas, taking away all the noise and confusion and desires and replacing it with time and contemplation, reflection and religion. And once he knew what they had been trying to teach him his whole life, they executed him.

Another death row inmate, Leslie Dale Martin, once told John that the only thing keeping any of them alive was the irrational hope of survival. Even if they changed, like Thomas, they were dead anyway. What kept John alive was the belief that somehow he would get out—even though none of them ever did.

One step at a time, Thomas's chances for a stay vanished. His sentence was upheld by the Court of Appeals. The Pardon Board ruled against him, three to two. Given his conduct in prison, he might have gotten that one swing vote, but his wife, the one he had followed to New Orleans, testified to the Pardon Board that he should die for his crimes. Then the governor declined to issue a pardon, and all that was left was to clean up the dishes from Thomas's last meal and let him sit for the last hour of his life in a locked room with a guard there to prevent him from killing himself.

Thomas used to tell John about his brother, who got stabbed to death on the streets of Harlem at age twenty-six. Thomas's view was that he was lucky compared to his brother's fate. Even though a lot of his years were spent in prison, Thomas made it to fifty-nine years old. That's a pretty long life, he'd say to John.

John imagined Thomas walking into that execution room and sitting on the chair, looking back at all the people waiting for his death. As the needle went into his arm, John pictured him thinking, *Maybe the world will be a better place without me after all.*

They put Thomas's last words in the newspaper: "I am leaving the world at peace with myself and with the Almighty. I feel remorse for the things that I did. I hope that young people today will learn that violence is not an answer. I hope the legal system learns that lesson, too. The death penalty is not a solution."

Harry Connick thinks it's a solution, John thought. *He says it's like a war. If that's what it is,* he thought, *it's the kind of war where you walk in on an unarmed man in chains and kill him.*

KILLING TIME

These were the worst times for John, the times when the irrational hope of survival left him and he saw his destiny. Thomas didn't buy that. He'd say John was hoping for the wrong thing. He'd say John couldn't hope to live forever. He needed to hope that he could make himself a better man on death row. "You do that," he'd say, "and they lose. Death row isn't there to improve you; it's there to exterminate you. And if you get better before they get to exterminating, you've gone and won no matter what they do."

Maybe John was a better person, and maybe he was just killing time before his killing time. Either way, he had his hearing in a week and then he'd return to Angola. There would be someone new in Thomas's cell, and they'd all sit and wait for their next date.

25

REWARD

JUNE 23, 1995

GORDON SAT UPRIGHT in his bed in the dark hotel room. He looked at the clock and groaned—early morning. He stretched, moving his head from side to side and puffing up the polyester-filled hotel pillows.

It had taken five years, but the Louisiana Supreme Court had finally decided that there might actually be some merit to their argument that the DAs had systematically withheld evidence from Thompson's lawyers. True, the Court had denied the other ten claims for relief set out in the Kitchen Sink, but, as they'd been saying since day one, they only needed one claim to win.

Gordon had read the decision in his office on that shiny, rolled fax paper like some archaeologist trying to decipher a scroll. It was several pages long, but the important part was just a few lines, a single paragraph:

> This case is remanded to the district court for purposes of conducting an evidentiary hearing on relator's claim that the State knew or should have known that Richard "Funk" Perkins lied at trial about his knowledge of, or the benefit he hoped to derive from, the reward offered by the victim's family, and that the State did nothing to correct the witness's testimony disavowing any motive or bias in the case.

The Supreme Court hadn't gone as far as it could have. There was no ordering of a new trial, and the remand to the trial court meant that they'd have to present the information again to Quinlan, which would be a high bar. After all, the man had not only seen it happen the first time, but he'd also already rejected their arguments once. They also hadn't specifically said that Thompson could dig into the reward issue on Ken Carr, or the Kevin Freeman plea bargain.

Still, it was continuing a positive trend, following the *Lemmon v. Connick* motion and discussions with Quinlan, which had finally gotten them the audiotapes taken in the International Hotel—the statements that Funk Perkins had made, recorded by Curole.

Gordon liked their chances. They now had a pattern of deceptive behavior to show Quinlan that might give the "DAs were bad" angle some teeth, and with this remand, Quinlan would know that the state Supreme Court was watching, which might make him a little less likely to blow them off again.

It had taken nine months from the Court's opinion ordering the hearing to this moment, a night of tortured near-sleep in New Orleans before a scheduled 9:00 AM hearing with Judge Quinlan. Now that they were here, to win they'd first have to show that Funk and Ken Carr had not been truthful in their testimony concerning the reward and what they had expected to receive for testifying. Then they had to show that the information the DA's office had failed to disclose was significant enough that it could have changed the jury's verdict in the case.

Their biggest problem would be Couhig's failure, at the trial, to press anyone about the reward itself, especially with Ray Liuzza Sr. Couhig would testify that he'd asked about the reward and was told that there was none, so there had been no evidentiary foundation that would have let him ask those questions at trial. Gordon was worried that this might not be enough. They'd have to finesse it. On the state-sponsored reward, they had the

Crimestoppers questionnaires for Perkins and Carr, which were certainly state-sponsored and never disclosed to Couhig and Fanning.

Gordon gave up trying to sleep and pressed the button at the base of his bedside lamp. The days were gone where he'd throw up before an argument, but no matter how many of these he had under his belt, he never felt 100 percent prepared. He'd argued about tens of millions of dollars at a time, but he'd never given an argument that someone's *life* had depended on before. John would be there, and he'd be watching, seeing his lawyers in action for the first time. He would know whether Gordon was prepared, and he would know if Gordon was fighting for him tooth and nail, or just going through the motions.

For better or for worse, Gordon wasn't a go-through-the-motions kind of guy. He grabbed the folder off the nightstand that contained the DA's response to the reward argument and started to read.

JUNE 24, 1995

ON THE DAY of the hearing, the guards woke John up hours earlier than usual. They took him to a loading dock where he waited with the other prisoners going to court that day. That's where he was now, waiting to go to the hearing about the reward.

He'd been on this loading dock before, every time he had to go to court for his trials. All the prisoners were there, and he realized it had been ten years since he'd stood on this platform with Kevin Freeman as the two of them went to Quinlan's courtroom, the day he'd tried to get Freeman to stop telling stories.

He tried to explain it to Freeman, tried to tell him that the cops had nothing on either of them; they had nothing but Funk, and Funk wasn't fingerprints or an eyewitness or anything. He tried to tell Freeman that if they just hung tough and trusted each other, they'd both get out of this, but Freeman had told John straight up that he couldn't take the heat and was gonna say what he was gonna say to save his own sorry ass.

He wanted to get Freeman at this hearing, too, wanted to hear what Dubelier and Williams had promised him, hear about how the five-year sentence that Freeman was supposed to get became less than a year. But that would never happen, since Kojak had gotten himself shot and killed on the street.

Still, Gordon didn't think they needed Freeman for this hearing. While he was biased, the bias was caused by his plea bargain, which had been clear to the jury in testimony. Funk Perkins and Ken Carr were different. They had testified for money and lied about it.

If Gordon and John could win this hearing, they'd get a new trial. Once they had that, they could use the newly found audio-tapes to compare against Freeman's statements at trial, showing how Kevin's story had changed every time he told it.

THE GUARDS LOADED John into a van, even though the courthouse was connected to the prison, and marched him to the little holding cell in Quinlan's chambers. He stayed there for some time, until the sheriff came and got him and led him into the courtroom, a different courtroom than Quinlan had used during the murder trial.

Gordon was already there, seated at a table in the front of the courtroom with Nick Trenticosta. He seemed pretty calm, and definitely looked calmer than John felt. John was nervous. He didn't really want to talk to Gordon, both because he didn't want to show nerves and because he didn't want to distract Gordon from the task at hand.

The lawyers for the DA were not Dubelier and Williams this time. Gordon had told John that one of them, the one in charge, was named Solino. Gordon said he was a good guy. John didn't react much to that, just smiled a little at Gordon's naiveté. Gordon still hadn't seen how these guys really operated. The other lawyer was a woman, junior to Solino.

One of the court officials stood up and said, "All rise." John stood up and the judge came in. There was no jury, so they got right into the hearing. Gordon and Nick started talking, but John wasn't listening. He was focused on Judge Quinlan. *No way this ends well while that man's makin' the decisions,* he thought. Whatever he saw in the judge's eyes, it wasn't a new trial.

GORDON HAD DECIDED that Nick should handle the first part of the hearing. It let Quinlan see the local lawyer first, instead of the carpetbaggers, and it gave Gordon the chance to see Nick operate. Nick had an impressive grasp of death penalty law and seemed to know where the bodies were buried, so to speak, in New Orleans. Since the first order of business was a request to Quinlan to expand the scope of their hearing from the reward given to Funk Perkins, which was what the Supreme Court had ordered, to include the reward given to Ken Carr, the risk was pretty contained.

As it turned out, Nick was impressive in court. He was deferential to Quinlan, knowledgeable about the facts and the argument he was making, and he had a low-key style, calm but passionate, and quite persuasive. Given Nick's single-issue death penalty focus, there was a risk that his obvious lack of objectivity on the existence of the death penalty could be interpreted by a judge as clouding his judgment. Put differently, John might be better served if he didn't have a perceived anti–death penalty fanatic on his defense team. For now, though, they seemed all right.

They had found Ken Carr in prison, doing time for some unrelated crime, and had sent a private investigator down to interview him. The PI had returned with Carr's sworn affidavit that he had known about the reward when he'd come forward to Curole, and that he'd gotten paid after the trial. The meeting also yielded an unexpected benefit—a confession, of sorts, from Carr that when the reward was paid out to him, he was told not to tell anyone about the payout. Given the affidavit, Quinlan agreed to expand the argument: Today's hearing would reevaluate both Perkins and Carr.

It was a good way to start the day. Including Carr made the DA's actions look more like a pattern of malpractice than an isolated instance. Most important, the material impact of Carr's and Perkins's testimonies together was bigger than either of them individually, so their chance of getting a new trial out of it was improved. Gordon looked at the written outline of his argument and carried it with him to the podium. He felt the familiar butterflies in his stomach, the dryness in his mouth that always accompanied him in front of a judge. There was no other sound in the courtroom as he smoothed out his tie, absently checking the straightness of the knot and making sure there was some water up there with him.

"Good morning, Your Honor. The defense calls Rob Couhig to the stand."

Gordon had a lot of ground to cover with Couhig. Gordon needed Couhig to describe the efforts made by Thompson's defense team to learn about any and all reward payments. Couhig and Fanning had asked Dubelier and Williams in writing to disclose any reward, and Couhig had asked Perkins and Carr on the stand whether they were expecting to receive a reward, and each time he was told that there was no reward—that no one had any idea what he was talking about. There wasn't much Couhig could do from there, especially since he didn't have the audiotapes that Gordon and Michael had been given, and he hadn't seen the Crimestoppers questionnaires they had received. As a result, there had been no indication to the jury of any potential bias from either witness.

Proving those facts was the first part, but Gordon needed Couhig to take him even further. As the lead defense attorney in Thompson's murder trial, Couhig could say, in his own words, how he would have tried the case had Dubelier and Williams's nonresponsiveness or deception not limited what he was able to ask of various witnesses. That made Couhig's statements crucial to proving that the DA's failure to turn over the audiotapes, questionnaires, and information about the rewards had a "materially adverse effect" on John's case.

Couhig sat in the witness stand, angled in his chair so that he could see both Judge Quinlan and Gordon. He spoke clearly and calmly, directing his responses to Judge Quinlan as the key audience. Gordon asked short, open-ended questions that let Couhig give long, detailed answers. They went on this way for about ninety minutes—building the argument in logical, stepwise style—leaving bread crumbs for Quinlan to follow to the conclusion that Thompson's trial had been ruined by hypercompetitive DAs who had gone too far in withholding evidence.

Gordon started by asking Couhig about the formal, written requests for information he had given to Dubelier. The documents had asked for "any and all inducements such as financial rewards" that would be given to any State witness for their testimony. Couhig described how Dubelier had waited for a month before responding to his requests, and how the response, when it finally came, was that the only inducement given to a State witness was Freeman's plea bargain. Dubelier had provided no information at all in response to Couhig's request for evidence related to a reward paid to witnesses in exchange for their testimony. And yet, somehow, immediately after the trial, Funk Perkins and Ken Carr had gotten richer.

Satisfied that the foundation was laid—*We asked for this information, Dubelier had it, and he failed to give it to us*—Gordon moved into the trial testimony. He asked Couhig to read specific sections of Funk's testimony at the murder trial, and Couhig reminded Quinlan of Perkins's statements under oath: that the cops came to Perkins first, and that his testimony wasn't motivated in any way by a reward payment.

From there, Gordon turned to Jim Williams's closing argument, the crowning irony of the murder trial transcript. He asked Couhig to read Williams's statement. Couhig played the part well, putting a sarcastic, self-important tone into Williams's self-congratulatory statement to the jury: "Not one single person came and took this stand and told you anything about any reward money. There's not one word that's in evidence in this case from people who took the stand regarding reward money. If there had been, you would have heard them put somebody on and say, 'So this person has made a claim on the money.' "

Gordon let that hang in the air a minute, let the Court hear how nervy Williams was, telling the jury in his close that there was no evidence of a reward payment, which both he and Dubelier knew existed. Gordon thought this was a level of deception beyond the pale, a clear violation of legal ethics. He would have loved to put Williams on the stand, to tear him a new one in front of Quinlan. Still, a low-key approach was more persuasive, so he simply said to Couhig, "And to you, sir, as trial counsel, what was the significance of that statement?"

Couhig, however, was not under the same constraints as Gordon and felt burned by Williams. He'd taken a hit to his reputation and risked a lot of friendships in New Orleans defending John Thompson, and he was angry. Couhig turned to Quinlan and said, "Your Honor, we had no evidence presented at the trial about a reward. We asked for it and were not provided with any, and we could not get any. The witnesses had denied any information about a reward. As a result, in my closing, I was unable to attack their credibility on that basis. Mr. Williams accurately sums up the situation in his rebuttal. He talks about Mr. Perkins. He said he is the one that made the break in this case. Did he show any reasons why he would come here and lie? No. No prior convictions. And he was right. The way it was presented was the way Mr. Perkins came across. Mr. Williams specifically comments on Mr. Perkins's statement that he was not getting any money—that he was telling him the truth—and I think those were his exact words because there was no evidence to show otherwise."

It was exactly the answer Gordon had wanted. Externally, he showed nothing, asking Couhig, "Were there oral requests for this information?"

Couhig nodded. "Mr. Dubelier spoke, Mr. Williams and I spoke, very often with repeated argument in front of his Court both on and off the record about whether Mr. Dubelier was forthcoming with his discovery."

Quinlan interjected—an unusual step for a judge during testimony—and said, "I still remember that."

Gordon decided to capitalize on that, to bring the audiotapes to the forefront. It would be hard to argue that Dubelier and Williams had been operating on the level with the audiotapes. The tapes had been in the police file, and no matter what Dubelier claimed today, what line of nonsense he served up about the DA's lack of control over the police file, Gordon knew that there was no way any halfway respectable DA wouldn't have reviewed the entire police file, and the failure to acknowledge the existence of those tapes was hard to ignore.

Gordon asked Couhig, "Now, sir, we have provided to the Court copies of certain audiotapes that were made. Prior to trial, did the State inform you that they had these audiotapes?"

"No, sir, we were not provided with the transcripts."

"Were you told that the prosecution had copies of any audiotapes?"

"No, sir."

"Looking at those transcripts, Mr. Couhig, do you find any material that would have been useful to you to impeach Mr. Perkins?"

Couhig straightened up and leaned toward the microphone. "In general, it seems to me there was an inquiry of Mr. Perkins seeking some assistance or help in exchange for his testimony." Gordon listened closely. He wanted Couhig's outrage to ring throughout the high-ceilinged courtroom, but Couhig had to be careful: Perkins had never used the word "reward," and while he did ask for "help" from Ray Liuzza Sr., they needed to convince Quinlan that "help" was understood by everyone to mean "cash."

Gordon shifted to the impact of the deception at trial. He had told Couhig to expect questioning about why Couhig had not pressed Ray Liuzza Sr. on the existence of the reward and who would be receiving it.

Couhig's answer was that since Dubelier had refused to provide any information about the reward, Couhig had no way of knowing that the older Liuzza was involved in it. "If we had known that Mr. Liuzza was involved actively in the investigation, in order to fulfill our obligation to our client, we would have had to ask him what went on. And Mr. Liuzza would have told the jury."

It was the best argument they could make on this point, but because it was a weak spot for them, Gordon quickly guided Couhig back to Funk Perkins and his conflicting statements. Gordon knew Quinlan would pick up on the real question: *Your Honor, if you can't believe Perkins, Carr, or Freeman, can you convict Thompson?* They had Perkins on the audiotape with his contradictory information. Even better, they had the never-before-revealed police report where the detective had written that Funk was "only motivated by reward." *Not only did they fail to disclose, Judge, but even the police discounted Funk's testimony. They knew all this guy wanted was cash, and they used him anyway.*

"Mr. Couhig, did you have this information available to you at trial?"

Couhig answered swiftly and definitively. "No."

Gordon put the transcripts showing Carr's trial testimony and his earlier statements to the Crimestoppers Hotline in front of Couhig. He pointed out to Couhig the differences in the two statements— Carr telling the cops that he had overheard one set of words, then telling it differently to Couhig at trial.

Gordon then read Carr's new affidavit to Judge Quinlan and the courtroom. Carr swore that after the trial, he had gone to the International Hotel and was given $3,500 in cash. His affidavit read, "I then had to sign a paper saying I got the money and was told to keep quiet. The paper was then placed in a safe at the hotel."

Gordon looked down at his notes, making sure he'd asked Couhig all of the questions he'd wanted to ask. He looked up and said, "Your Honor, I have nothing further of this witness," and sat down.

Val Solino stood up to cross-examine Couhig. Solino was largely unknown to Gordon, having taken over responsibility for the Thompson case from Jeff Bridger a few months ago. He was a "lifer" in the DA's office, a career ADA with a tremendous amount of pride in the office he worked for. Gordon had been pretty impressed with Solino so far, the ADA seeming far more reasonable and less partisan than his predecessor.

At the same time, Solino had clearly shown that he was a staunch defender of his colleagues in the Thompson murder case, and he wasn't going to give any ground to Thompson's defenders. In Solino's eyes, John Thompson was a convicted murderer, and the DA's office was going to ensure that his sentence was fairly and properly carried out.

This was the first time that the Thompson defense team had gotten the chance to see Solino on his feet before Judge Quinlan. Given his long experience as a DA, Gordon assumed he would be a talented courtroom advocate.

Solino was probably five-eleven, dark-skinned, swarthy, and the kind of guy who could make a freshly pressed suit look rumpled the second his arms went through the sleeves. He had a surprisingly high voice, but it gave him a slightly softer sound than his appearance suggested, and made him seem human and credible.

Gordon could see Solino as compelling to a jury, a guy you'd have a couple of beers with and trust to tell you the truth. Still, his appearance couldn't mask the career prosecutor underneath, and Solino's experience in cross-examination showed itself right away as he launched directly into questions for Couhig without even bothering to introduce himself, going after Couhig aggressively, if not emotionally. He held up the discovery request that Couhig had sent to Dubelier in 1985. "Mr. Couhig, could you take a minute to review your request for information to the DA's office, and could you identify for the Court where the word 'reward' appears in this four-page document?"

It was a classic closed question, giving Couhig only one possible answer if he wanted to tell the truth. "I'm not sure it does, sir." It was true, though it was the sort of semantic distinction that defense lawyers got in trouble for all the time. While Couhig had never expressly asked for documents relating to a "reward payment," he had requested "exculpatory" documents, which certainly would have included materials related to a reward payment to people testifying against John.

Solino kept going, conducting a crisp, textbook cross-examination. In contrast to Gordon's open-ended questions, Solino was the storyteller now, not Couhig. It took him only a few minutes to get to his most important question: "Mr. Couhig, were you aware of a reward?"

"I was aware that Crimestoppers had put out a reward," Couhig said.

"You were not aware of any other reward?"

"It was my understanding that either the Liuzza family or friends of the Liuzzas had offered additional rewards, yes, sir."

"Well, you used the number fifteen thousand dollars during the trial, so you must have been aware of a fifteen-thousand-dollar reward?"

Couhig answered as Gordon's stomach tied itself in knots. "I think that's a fair summary of the situation, yes, sir."

"Just as a point of fact, since you were trial counsel, did you present any evidence at trial about the existence of a reward?"

"No, sir."

Solino had laid bare their biggest weakness. At trial, Couhig had asked Perkins and Carr about the reward, even throwing out the $15,000 amount to Perkins. There was no question he had known about the reward. In four questions, Solino had undercut Couhig's testimony.

Solino continued, "Mr. Couhig, did you know before you started trial that reward money may be on the table?"

"Yes, sir," Couhig replied.

"Was it your intention during trial to impeach the credibility of these witnesses with the fact that the *possibility* may exist that they could collect a reward?"

Gordon had told Couhig this question would come. He watched tensely as Couhig responded. Couhig leaned forward and squared his shoulders and said loudly, "We asked repeatedly for the information about the reward. It was my judgment that because we did not have that information provided to us by those who had custody of it, the State, that it was impossible to cross-examine and impeach without it."

"What does that mean?" Solino asked.

That was a mistake, Gordon thought.

Couhig saw it, too. "Mr. Perkins was allowed to make a statement to the fact that he knew of no reward and was not interested in a reward. Mr. Williams and Dubelier were able to take that statement and wrap themselves in it, along with the statement of Mr. Carr that these were credible witnesses. They had in their possession information about the reward when those statements were made and, therefore, the jury was not provided with information that it needed to make a determination as to what should happen."

If Solino realized that he'd been wounded, he didn't show it. Instead, he surprised Gordon by asking another open-ended question. "What information are you referring to that the jury should have had? That a reward existed?" His skeptical tone let an unspoken conclusion hang in the air: *Because, of course, they had that information, and you, Mr. Couhig, gave it to them.*

Couhig erupted, almost leaping out of the stand. "Let me tell you what happened. The district attorneys, Mr. Dubelier and Mr. Williams, made a calculated decision to keep themselves from getting too much information about the reward. If, in fact, it turns out, as I believe it will in this hearing, that Mr. Perkins received money in advance, they had an obligation to know it." Couhig pointed at Solino, his index finger jabbing toward the prosecutor. "You, sir, as an officer of the Court, would have made it your business to know if people had received any reward. You would not put a witness on the stand and allow him not to tell the truth about something like that. As an officer of the Court, you would not do that."

Couhig had a head of steam now, and he plowed ahead: "Let me also tell you—you asked me how this case would have gone differently if I'd had that information, that they—and I think it was deliberate that they were putting these decisions off—that they had these meetings, we could have asked these people these questions. The jury could then have decided whether, in fact, these people had a motive for telling it, unlike what Mr. Williams said in his closing argument, or whether, in fact, they were motivated by money and greed."

Solino made a slight movement, pursing his lips as if to say, *Well, I guess we'll have to disagree*, and said to the judge in a completely unconcerned voice, "Just bear with me a minute."

He looked at his notes, then back up at Couhig. "You will concede that you did not ask Richard Perkins, 'Did you make a claim on a reward, or do you intend to collect on a reward at some time in the future?'"

Couhig wilted a little on the stand. Just as fast, his outrage was gone, the momentum of the argument swaying back to Solino and the DA's office. Couhig admitted that he had not asked those questions, that he had not pressed Ray Liuzza Sr. on the same topic, and that he also hadn't asked Carr those questions. Couhig's fire was still burning, but Solino's questions had absorbed all the heat. Still, Gordon knew they had scored some points themselves. *Call it even so far*, he thought.

Gordon called Frank Maselli, Ray Liuzza's landlord and close friend, to the stand. Maselli had helped the Liuzza family after Ray Jr.'s death by administering the reward fund. As such, he had key knowledge about who got paid, when, and why.

The press release announcing the reward's existence, which Gordon now showed to Maselli for confirmation, said that half the reward would be paid upon the arrest of Ray's killer and the other half upon conviction. It was a sensible structure for the distributor of the reward, ensuring that witnesses wouldn't provide information, collect, and then not appear at trial, and it also gave the witnesses both a reason to come forward and complete confidence that there would be more money if they kept playing ball. From Gordon's perspective, however, this presented some obvious concerns, since Perkins or Carr would be beholden to the DA in two ways—gratitude for payment, and wanting to please them and say what the DA needed to hear in order to get their final payment.

Frank Maselli was necessary to Gordon's argument for more than this, however. Pulling out notes that Maselli had kept about the reward, Gordon asked, "Mr. Maselli, can you read what appears under May 24, 1985?"

"The reward was paid to the two informants on May 24, 1985, right."

"Who was going to get paid?"

"Richard Perkins, as best I can recall."

"Is it also correct, looking at your notes on May 13, 1985, that it was decided Perkins was going to get eleven thousand five hundred dollars and Carr was going to get three thousand five hundred dollars?"

"I don't specifically remember that, but from my other notes that you have seen, that's what I think."

"Can we go down to the last entry in your notes, on August 24, 1989?"

"Sure. 'Read notes to Jeff Bridger,' it says."

"Who was Mr. Bridger?"

"I don't remember."

"Did Mr. Bridger inform you that he was affiliated with the district attorney's office?"

"I honestly can't recall."

Gordon shot a look at Judge Quinlan, intent on emphasizing this to him. *We'll come back to this.* He let Maselli step down.

Once Maselli had left the courtroom, Gordon said to the judge, "Your Honor, before we call our next witness, a document I'd like to bring to the Court's attention is the response from the State to our discovery request, filed and served in 1989 in response to our request for discovery post-conviction. In 1989, the State said, 'Undersigned counsel is aware of no substantial or particular information in the possession of the State regarding the payment of a reward or rewards to any persons in this case.'"

Gordon admitted the document into evidence, letting Quinlan and Solino read for themselves that the signature on the bottom of that statement was the same Jeff Bridger who had been told of the reward amounts and recipients by Frank Maselli.

Gordon sat down and Nick stood back up, preparing to examine Funk Perkins. Gordon thought it was unlikely that Funk would just admit to lying on the stand about the reward, but he thought Nick, as a local New Orleans guy and a criminal defense lawyer, was more likely to get good answers from Funk than Gordon was. He was hopeful that Nick could get to their fallback position: that Funk was an opportunist whose testimony was driven almost exclusively by the reward.

Nick set up the preliminaries well, reminding Funk of his role at the trial and talking to him about the meetings at the hotel. "Did a discussion come up about a reward?" he asked.

"They mentioned something about it."

"Do you remember what they said?"

"Said something about 'You're entitled to one.' "

"The district attorney?"

"I told them I wasn't there for the reward, but they told me I was entitled to some reward."

"Did you get the reward then?"

"No."

"What did the district attorney tell you about it?"

"They just said that you will receive a reward, you know, after trial."

After the trial, someone had called Funk, asked him to come back to the hotel, and gave him money. "How much money did you receive?" Nick asked.

"Ten-oh-five, cash," Perkins said. Ten thousand, five hundred dollars.

"Were you asked to sign any papers when you received the money?"

"Just stating that I got it."

"Do you remember if the person who gave you the money asked you not to talk about getting the money?"

Funk considered this. "It was a possibility."

Nick saw an opening and moved into it. "Do you remember the prosecution, the district attorneys, ever telling you not to talk about the money?"

"Yeah."

Stop there and move on, thought Gordon. Nick had gotten the answer they wanted. Any more questions could lead Funk to elaborate and clarify his answer in a way that would make it worse for their purposes.

But Nick didn't stop there. "One more question. At the trial, you testified that you had been working at the Hilton Hotel. Do you recall that?" Perkins nodded.

"How did you get the job at the Hilton Hotel?"

"Mr. Liuzza. He recommended me."

"He recommended you for the job?"

"Yes, sir."

It was definitely a benefit to their argument. Gordon looked over at John. *You see that? We're getting them on the run.*

The look he got back from John surprised him. What he saw in John's eyes was mainly calmness. John had been frustrated by how long the case was taking; now, he was finally seeing that Gordon and Michael weren't just sitting around doing nothing. They were fighting for him.

With Ken Carr unavailable to testify, the day was over. The lawyers spoke with Judge Quinlan about the administrative aspects of completing the hearing transcript, and the hearing came to an abrupt halt. Quinlan thanked both teams of attorneys and indicated that he would take the arguments under advisement and provide his ruling at a later date. He got up and walked out of the room, leaving it empty except for the lawyers and the bailiff, who moved swiftly to get John and return him to his cell.

The bailiff let Gordon have a few minutes with his client before taking him away.

"How do you feel, John?"

John shook his head. "Man, I don't know what to think about these things. It looked and sounded good to me, you know? What do you think? You the expert."

"You know, John, I think it went as well as it could go. We've got some problems, but we made a lot of good points, and I know the judge heard them. I thought Couhig was a good witness, and Nick did a good job with Funk. I like how today went, but I can't predict what the judge will do."

John nodded and smiled. "Yeah, we gonna see what they do. That Quinlan, he ain't gonna do nothing for me, but the Louisiana Supreme Court, they seem to like to do the right thing."

"You may be right about that, John. We're gonna keep fighting." The bailiff came up again, signaling that it was time to go. "You hang in there."

"Always do," John replied. He began to walk away with the bailiff, then turned back. "Gordon? Something I got to tell you, about what happened."

Gordon's stomach tightened, but he stayed quiet and waited.

"The gun and the ring," John said.

"What about 'em?"

"I had 'em. That part is true."

"You had the gun and the ring?"

"Yeah."

"And you sold them to J.R.? Did you use Funk to sell the gun, too? All that's true?"

John hung his head a little, but he nodded. "Yeah. All that's true."

"How'd they get in your hands?"

"Bought 'em."

"Okay, you bought them. From who?"

John looked a little uncomfortable. "Kevin Freeman."

"You bought them from Kevin Freeman?"

"Yeah." John kept talking, his cadence accelerating. "Man, I bought and sold all kind of shit, whatever I could sell and make money from. You buy and sell shit, and if you can't get money, you get things you can sell to someone else for money. I ain't never had no gun for myself. I had two young boys. Why'm I gonna keep a gun in the house? But Kevin Freeman come by one day. He wants some drugs and he offers me the gun for it. Man, a gun's as good as money where I come from. So I took the gun 'stead of the money. Then a couple days later, Richard Perkins comes by—he want some money. I do him a favor, on 'count he used to hang out a little with my sister; I tell him he can sell the gun for me, we split the money, so that's what he do. I didn't find out until later that the gun was a murder weapon, and then I guess when I told Funk, he got a little hot about it."

"Any reason you didn't tell me or Michael this before?"

"I figured if you knew I was connected to the gun, you'd think the rest of it was true, and you'd be like Couhig and Fanning. After today, I see you're the lawyer I need, you and Michael. And I didn't kill no Ray Liuzza. I had the gun, after, but I wasn't there. For all I know, someone else shot Ray Liuzza and gave the gun to Kevin Freeman. All I know is, I wasn't there."

Gordon looked at his client. He ran his fingers through his reddish hair and rubbed his eyes. "John, I appreciate what you're telling me. To tell you the truth, I'm not sure how to react. As your lawyer, I want to believe you. For the courts, for the job Michael and I have to do, it doesn't really matter whether I believe you or not. It matters what we can prove. Couhig and Fanning never argued that the ring or the gun weren't admissible, and none of our arguments focus on that. So while I appreciate your telling me the truth, it doesn't change any of our arguments. And Funk still lied about the reward, so hopefully we'll win this and get you a new trial. If we do that, then we'll talk about the ring and the gun again, see what we can do."

John nodded. He shook Gordon's hand—a first for him—saying, "A'right then."

"John? Listen. You got any other information about this that we don't have, you've gotta let us know it. We can't help you unless we know the facts."

John smiled. "Wanted to wait until I knew I had myself some lawyers, real lawyers, you know? Watchin' you in there today, I thought, yes, sir, that's what I got. So I'm tellin' you now."

Gordon patted John on the shoulder. "I appreciate the kind words. But let's not wait on any other revelations of facts, okay?"

"A'right." John turned and walked away with the bailiff.

26

MAKING A LIVING

JULY 25, 1995

JOHN WAS BACK in Angola within a week after the hearing. He didn't know if they'd win, but he was filled with excitement about his lawyers. No one had ever fought for him like that before, ever. Gordon and Nick were amazing. And Gordon had really known how to get Couhig to talk. If Couhig had talked like that during the previous trial, maybe John wouldn't have been convicted in the first place. Still, John didn't think Quinlan was on his side.

John had been amazed by the way Gordon had laid out the reward story. The way Gordon presented all the information, it would be hard for anyone to say Perkins and Carr hadn't been looking for a reward when they testified. People would *have* to see that his conviction was a frame-up.

John had never seen any lawyers do things like that. Watching Gordon get angry with Connick's men, explaining things to the judge, watching him cross-examine Funk—that was what John had always believed lawyers were supposed to do, to be there to help people who couldn't help themselves in the system.

And they were helping him outside his case as well. He had met Sarah Davies at the hearing for the first time, but felt like he knew her already from frequent telephone calls to try and get help for day-to-day, nonlegal needs. She handled all kinds of things for him that were difficult to do from prison, things like getting new sneakers and making sure they didn't get "lost" in Angola's mail system.

JOHN LOOKED OUT of his cell. Over the course of his time at Angola, his cell had changed several times, in part because death row itself had moved, from the building in the center of Angola to a different building just inside the front gate, and in part because the guards moved prisoners around from time to time for various reasons. But he had one of the better cells on the tier right now. The wall across from the cell had a window, and through it John could actually see the outside, looking across the outer fence into forest on the outside of the prison. It was a taunt, almost. Only one hundred yards out that window, John would be a free man.

One morning John had looked out that window and had seen a deer standing in the grass, eating. The deer stood there for a few minutes, then turned and ran back into the woods. John had stood there for another two hours or so, hoping it would return.

He could afford to stand and watch, to wait for it. He had all day. No one was going to make him do anything. The other inmates, the ones not on death row, they had jobs on the Farm. Some of them were "trusties," and they could roam around to different parts of the grounds. It was still prison, but it was *something*. For some of the inmates, there was actual work training. They'd teach you a skill, something you could take with you after you left Angola to earn a living. Of course, they wouldn't waste those resources on him. Why teach a skill to a dead man?

Despite all that, John tried to find ways to fill the time. He'd read, listen to music, watch the TV, write letters. He spent a lot of time praying. He'd do push-ups and sit-ups in the cell. The exercise hour was precious, so he'd plan ahead of time how he was going to use it each day. He'd take a decent shower, call Michael, Gordon, Sarah, or his family, and try to work in some time to run—outside if he could, or up and down the prison hallway if not.

Then there was the business side of death row. Get a bunch of criminals together, and eventually you'd have some guys trying to make money off the other guys. John's view was just because he was in prison didn't mean he didn't have to provide for his family. His family had no money. His grandmother had her social security and little else, and his mother, since her stroke, couldn't get a job. It was up to John to provide whatever he could to give his kids and his family what they needed, and what he needed. There was no way they could afford to take the bus or rent a car to come visit him unless he supplied the money, or got someone to donate their time or their money. Michael or Gordon or Sarah would help him out sometimes, but that got complicated, and he didn't want to be borrowing from them unless he had to. So he had to raise the money himself.

Sometimes he'd run a store for the other inmates out of his cell. The "general store" was a supply cart that came by every now and then, with things like sodas, chips, or snacks. If he got to it early, and had enough money in his prison-managed account, he could corner the market on certain items and drive the price up. The "store" would come by, and John might buy all the Cokes. Then he'd have a monopoly until the next Monday when the store was restocked. As with any monopoly, he'd raise the price and sell his wares to the other inmates.

Other times, he'd run a sports book. The white boys had run the book when John came on the Row. John looked at the system they had, and thought, *Nothing these white boys are doing I can't do for myself.* He decided to cut himself in on the action. It fit his personality. His style wasn't talking loud and proud. His style was watch and learn, observe and manipulate. He liked watching the games, but he rarely bet much, unless he thought he knew more than the book. Having that level of knowledge wasn't that hard on the tier. It wasn't exactly a center for inside information.

John ran his book from the odds in the newspapers. He'd go in half on the spread, or give one team a point or the other team a point. Sometimes, he'd have strong feelings about a team, and make some changes to the spread. It could get fairly serious, running two or three thousand dollars in a week. If the inmates lost their money, they didn't care, so lots of guys would go all in. Then they'd build it back, since it wasn't like they were going to starve in the meantime. It was like any gambling, though. One day John might get hit hard and have to dip into his bank account, and the next he'd go big, making five thousand postage stamps on one NFL Sunday.

Bringing the guards into it was all part of the business. Obviously, running a book in the prison was against the rules, but all that needed to be done was to give the guards a little something from it and they'd look the other way. Sure, every now and then a guard would shake down John's cell—that was just the cost of doing business.

Of course, there was no cash on the tier. Currency among the inmates was postage stamps or cigarettes. Once he figured out how to convert one into the other, between the store and the book, he did all right. He could sometimes send home as much as a hundred bucks in a week. The key was to get as much in stamps as he could. Once he had the stamps, he'd send them to a woman who worked in his neighborhood church at home. She'd actually buy the stamps from him, four or five hundred at a time, and give the money to his mother or put it back into his prison account. *The Lord works in mysterious ways*, he thought.

His mind came back to the present with a start, and he looked around, realizing that he was still standing, looking out the window. He rubbed his eyes and turned and grabbed the newspaper from Friday. Maybe he'd run some baseball games today, see what kind of action he could get.

27

THE CHAPLAIN

SEPTEMBER 22, 1995

Dear Nancy:

Please excuse this letter if it's not making sense. I am not thinking right, I received some bad news Friday afternoon that my grandmother died Tuesday morning. So your letter was a lift, because it came at a good time when I really needed to take my mind off what I just read.

There's a minister, a chaplain here at Angola who is the one person you do not ever want to see here. You don't want to see him no matter what else you might have got going on. He comes on the tier, everybody knows someone is dead. That's the only reason he come around, is to tell you somebody you love is dead and can he help you work it through. Only thing you don't know is who's cell is he going to stop in front of, and then who is it that's dead.

Today, the chaplain came on death row. Second his foot hits the tier, people whispering there's the chaplain, everything gets quiet. Only time it gets quiet on death row is when someone's dying, or someone's dead.

He stopped at my cell. "John Thompson?" He said, "John, I've got some bad news. Your maternal grandmother passed into the arms of the Lord today."

I didn't say anything. My grandmother raised me, as she was doing with my sister. I really feel sorry for my baby sister, now she got to go live with my father. I can't begin to know who will step forward to give the younger part of my family the leadership they will need to survive. She was the head of everything, we all look to her for guideness. I was able to keep my strength and faith through her over the years. Whenever a problem came up, I knew my grandmother would be there whenever I call. Just knowing she was there was enough to fight every second of every minute. Whenever one of us was in trouble, we could always depend on her being there for us. Me maybe more than the rest, because they would all say I was her favorite. I wasn't, only the oldest, and was always able to remember she raised me. When I was older, I went back and did alot for her. I can only wish that she have been sent to heaven. If that's a place. There is no love like that of a grandmother, I don't know how I'll ever make it here without her being apart of my life.

Just got off the phone talking with my mother. My grandmother didn't have insurance on herself, now everybody is trying to come up with the money to handle all the arrangement. But hopefully she will be laid to rest this week. Enough about it, because I am going to feel badder by the second.

Just can't understand the Saints. I gave up on this year already. I can't see nothing coming out of this year but maybe a high first round draft pick. They look real bad, every since Jim Fink been away nothing seem to be going right. We need Jimmy Johnson and let him do whatever he want to bring a winning team.

Well I'll end for now, take care of yourself.
Love Always,
John

28

PETITION DENIED

Judge Quinlan's judgment was five pages long, double-spaced on long legal paper. Michael flipped to the last word, which was in bold: **denied**.

He turned to the front page, started reading, and scanned to get to the important sentences. Before he called Gordon, or Andy, or Thompson, he wanted to understand Quinlan's logic, figure out what the next appeal should look like.

It was a pretty short opinion, and Quinlan set out his conclusion at the end:

> From the evidence presented at the hearing, this Court is unconvinced that Perkins or Carr lied at trial about their knowledge of, or the benefit they hoped to derive from, the reward offered by the victim's family. Neither the trial transcript nor the testimony presented at the hearing bear out this fact. . . . [T]he State was never a participant in the reward process. Further rewards were distributed by the family after the trial was over. Finally, it is the finding of this court that given the overwhelming evidence of the guilt of this defendant, there is not a reasonable probability that the outcome of the trial would have been different had the

defense effectively cross-examined the witnesses regarding their anticipation of a reward.

It was a tough verdict. First, it made clear that Quinlan simply didn't believe that Perkins and Carr had lied about the reward, and didn't agree that Dubelier and Williams should have revealed that information.

More troubling, though, was the fact that Quinlan was now on record stating that even if the reward had been known to the jury, the jury would not have ruled any differently, because they had seen "overwhelming evidence of guilt." That would be hard to overcome on an appeal, as Quinlan's closeness to the case would have some sway with higher court judges.

The decision was a little self-serving—the judge not wanting to be reversed on appeal, and laying out a record of why he shouldn't be. Quinlan patted himself on the back, pointing out his largesse in letting Gordon and Nick present testimony on Carr, which was beyond a strict wording of what was required by the Court of Appeals.

Michael picked up the phone and dialed Gordon's number. Gordon had read the opinion, too. He was astonished that Quinlan had found nothing persuasive in their arguments. Quinlan even mentioned that he thought that some "friend" of Funk's had actually received the money and never gave it to Funk, so that part of the reward was null and void, as if it was the actual receipt of money, rather than the expectation of the money, that controlled the credibility of Funk's testimony.

Michael could hear the tone in his friend's voice and decided that he needed to boost Gordon's morale. He reminded Gordon that they had given this argument a less than fifty-fifty shot of succeeding from the very beginning. Gordon agreed, but he was still upset that after all of their work and their step-by-step description of the reward, Quinlan's opinion totally ignored the Liuzzas' reward money and continued to view Ken Carr as a good samaritan. According to Quinlan, Ken Carr had never wanted a reward and never asked for one, even though his first move was to call Crimestoppers, which advertised rewards, and even though he ultimately received $3,500 from the Liuzzas.

Michael tried to be philosophical about the defeat. They had had good arguments and had written a good brief, good enough to get a hearing on the issue. This time, they lost. Quinlan was obviously convinced that John was the killer. The facts surrounding the reward weren't enough now; they needed to get into a higher court to have a shot at winning.

Unfortunately, they would have to tell John. Michael felt a little sick about it, knowing that it would only be a few days until John received his fourth death warrant in the mail.

In some sense, the ruling was a blessing. Now that they were done with the Louisiana Supreme Court, they'd have to take John's appeals higher, into the federal courts—first the United States District Court for the Eastern District of Louisiana, and then the 5th Circuit Court of Appeals for the United States, and ultimately, the U.S. Supreme Court. Prevailing wisdom was that federal judges, who were appointed, were both smarter and less biased by local politics then state court judges, who were elected in local elections. Morgan, Lewis lawyers had far more practice in the federal courts than they did in Louisiana, and the federal rules were standardized. It would be a lot easier for them to research, brief, and argue issues in the federal courts.

It wasn't much to place their hopes on, but it was something. This would be a war of attrition. They had to keep taking these hits and keep getting up. *Lots of battles left to fight,* Michael thought.

29

5TH CIRCUIT APPEAL

OCTOBER 27, 1998

MICHAEL PEDALED HIS mountain bike up the single-track trail that rose from the Wissahickon Creek, an extension of Philadelphia's Fairmount Park not far from his home. He shifted into his small chain ring and leaned forward, pushing himself out of the saddle to make his front tire bite into the dirt and continue up the incline. Mountain biking had become Michael's favorite form of exercise in the past few years. Biking in the woods was a great way to relieve stress and clear his head, and that was exactly what he needed to do today.

He needed to figure out how to make the American judicial system pay attention to John Thompson. His client was going to die, and Michael was running out of options to save him. In fact, he was starting to wonder if their efforts weren't doing more harm than good. How many times could he raise John's hopes, only to dash them again?

As his legs churned the pedals, Michael counted the failures they had had so far. He and Gordon had been at this for almost ten years, and they had accomplished practically nothing. All of the Kitchen Sink arguments had been dismissed. The Louisiana Supreme Court had given them a ray of hope on the reward money, but Quinlan had shot that down as well. They had moved into the federal courts and resubmitted all of their arguments, now made stronger with the audiotapes and other information they had gotten from the NOPD case file. It didn't change the result: Judge Marcel Livaudais in the U.S. District Court had rejected all of their arguments.

Michael wasn't accustomed to losing in general, but losing in this way, with so much at stake, was torture. He'd had a dream the night before: He'd been at the beach with his family and John. In the dream, he knew he had to keep the waves away from his family, and all he had was the sand. He kept building these sand castles and moats to protect them, but then a wave would come in and wash it all away. He was running out of time.

Each loss made all of them more desperate. Michael, Gordon, and, perhaps most of all, John all knew that their options were dwindling. Michael wasn't sure how to discuss it with John, either. He wanted to be realistic, but then John would tell him that he was saving money so that his sons could go on school trips. How could Michael tell a man who set aside being on death row to put his kids' well-being first that he was getting closer to a lethal injection?

He couldn't. So he shaded the truth, always sure to leave a glimmer of hope: *Well, John, it's a long shot, but . . .* or *Now, John, I wouldn't bet on it, but you never know . . .*

Michael did it partly for John, and partly for himself. But he hated feeling like he was creating false hope, and he hated the circumstances that made the hope false. John Thompson was going to die because Michael couldn't save him. He tried to swallow his own self-disgust as he crested the rise and watched the trail snake downward and bend left. He pushed the pedals into the descent. Every new court, every new judge had been a ray of hope, and each had dashed those dreams of getting a retrial.

And once a higher court had ruled against them, Quinlan jumped to reissue a new writ of execution. Michael thought, *He can sit on our motions for years, but give him a ruling from a higher court that he's been upheld, and he'll come in to work on a weekend to issue a new writ of execution.* The new writ created a new date, and forced

John to think about his life as a timeline, a constant countdown to lethal injection, 24 hours a day, 365 days a year. Right now, John was on his fifth date. As long as he had appeals, he couldn't be executed, but each new writ of execution was harder to get than the last; at some point, his stays would be up. The pressure only became more crushing.

Judge Livaudais had ordered a stay of John's execution, too, as long as John continued to appeal his sentence in federal court, but he had waited until twelve days before John's last date to issue it, causing no small degree of stress for both John and his lawyers. Michael thought that this was unnecessarily insensitive; it wasn't Livaudais who had to field the increasingly frequent calls from John about the hair on his head falling out in his hands as his date neared. Plus, when Livaudais did finally issue the stay, it wasn't because he thought it was the right thing to do to protect John. It was because he hadn't even bothered to look at the brief that Michael and Gordon had filed months before.

Michael and Gordon had hoped the federal judges might be more open in their review. It was a misplaced hope. With no evidence of any actual analysis, Livaudais shot them down across the board. He adopted the views of Quinlan and the Louisiana Supreme Court, and rejected every argument in the Kitchen Sink brief.

Michael could see John's resolve straining. On one call to Michael, John said that he understood why some inmates waived their appeals and just accepted their sentences.

This rising and falling rhythm of hope reminded Michael of a pheasant flapping furiously for the sky until a shotgun blast dropped it to earth. It was all the more painful to Michael because in spite of it all, he could see John becoming a more serene, more contemplative, more graceful, and more articulate person. Even as he got more desperate and stressed, his way of coping with it was becoming less angry and violent. Wasn't that what prison was supposed to do—reform people? And with every step John took forward, the system held him back, unwilling or unable to acknowledge who John Thompson was becoming.

John had never said anything other than that he was innocent. He sometimes got frustrated if Michael didn't think one of his "jailhouse lawyer" arguments would hold water, but even those were getting more sophisticated. Michael was surprised and amazed at that, at the thought that someone on death row could find ways of improving himself. There were lawyers at Morgan, Lewis who weren't growing the way this high-school dropout in Angola was. *Shouldn't that alone be worth a reprieve?* Michael thought.

Michael wanted to support John's growth. He would tell himself, *Even if John dies, improving oneself is the point of life.*

Somewhere along the line, things had shifted: As things got worse in the courts, it was John who started keeping Michael's spirits up, telling Michael he thought there were other chances, to keep pressing, to not give up.

Michael wasn't giving up, but he wasn't sure what else he could do, either.

He and Gordon had thought they really had a shot once they got past Judge Livaudais to the federal 5th Circuit Court of Appeals. Gordon wrote a brilliant brief arguing that Dubelier and Williams had used racial bias to exclude black jurors from John's murder trial, and they had been granted an oral argument to discuss it in person with a panel of three judges. The panel included Judge Carl E. Stewart, the first African-American ever named to the 5th Circuit. If anyone would give them a sympathetic ear in a racial-bias argument, it would be Stewart.

The ray of hope had gotten brighter at the oral argument, Gordon flying down to New Orleans to match wits again with Val Solino. Michael replayed the call from Gordon in his mind as he came down off the ridge, picking his way between tree stumps and roots as the trail veered steeply downward.

Gordon was typically a pretty buttoned-down person. He knew that someone won and someone lost every argument, and he typically didn't get effusive until after a win was declared. So his enthusiasm after the argument was particularly notable.

Gordon described how the judges had listened to him present John's case and waited for Solino to rise. He described Judge Stewart greeting Solino: "Mr. Solino, if this isn't a prima facie case of discrimination, I can't imagine what one would be."

John, we won't know until we get the ruling, but . . .

Once again, they had waited for the wheels of justice to turn, this time with a little more anticipation. A favorable ruling would bring a guaranteed new trial, one without the DA's star witness—one where the defense had a lot more evidence that Perkins and Carr were lying. All they needed was for Judge Stewart to write the opinion.

Michael pedaled on down the trail. He wasn't ready to go home yet. His mind brought him to the 5th Circuit's decision, released to them this morning. Once again, the key word was in bold caps, this time on the first page of the decision: **DENIED**. Their ray of hope, their pheasant fluttering for freedom and safety, had been shot down by Judge Stewart himself, and the action agreed to unanimously by the other two judges.

The judge began his opinion by summarily rejecting the claim that Leola Chaney had been pressured into voting for the death penalty: "The trial judge exerted no deliberative pressure, but only attempted to assess the state of the deliberation process," he said. "Any treatment by jurors, whether incidental or consciously designed to bring about such a reaction by Ms. Chaney is unfortunate and regrettable, but it in no way stemmed from the court's actions."

Michael knew that was the last gasp for the Leola Chaney argument. There was no way they would convince the U.S. Supreme Court to revisit the factual issue of whether Leola Chaney had been coerced. That was disappointing, but it wasn't the crushing defeat that Stewart delivered next. After all of the outrage he had directed at Solino during the oral argument on the *Batson* issue, after showing his grasp of the legal standards and the shifting burdens of proof that *Batson* required, the judge had somehow managed to write an opinion that correctly stated the legal standard and at the same time failed to apply it.

They'd presented facts that were persuasive on Leola Chaney, and Stewart had strictly interpreted the law to say that because the coercion didn't come from Quinlan, it wasn't valid. They'd presented a legal argument that was persuasive on *Batson*, and Stewart had ignored that and looked at the self-serving facts stated by Dubelier on why they struck those black jurors. *It wasn't the arguments,* thought Michael. *It's that no one wants to let a guilty man go free, and they all believe the jury got it right.*

Michael turned his bike back toward home. He stayed on the trail, but all he could focus on was John in his cell and the image of Gordon, as upset as Michael had ever seen him, pacing back and forth in Michael's office, his blue eyes flashing, his face flushed with anger.

We're not going to save John's life, are we? he thought as he raced down the trail.

All they had left was the United States Supreme Court, and maybe a clemency petition to the governor, who had never approved a clemency petition and was probably the recipient of huge campaign contributions from the Liuzza family and their friends. And they'd be using the same arguments that had just been blown out of the water by an African-American judge from Louisiana who knew how things were really done in New Orleans.

John had been sitting in prison for thirteen years. Michael and Gordon had been hammering away at this for ten years, beating their heads against a wall, and now they were back around to the same fundamental question they had discussed when they took the case: Was John Thompson guilty of killing Ray Liuzza?

Michael turned his bike off the trail and onto the street, pedaling the last few miles back home. The last ten years had been a preordained waste of time, a torture device to break John into a million pieces, to make his execution merciful, to literally put him out of his misery.

There was nothing more to be done, Michael knew that. The arguments they had were losers, and they weren't going to convince the Supreme Court any more than they had convinced anyone else. What they needed was a way to make John look *innocent*.

Michael turned into his driveway and pushed the bike into his garage. He took off his helmet, hung it on the handlebars, and stood there for a second with his hands on his hips. Then he reached into the bag under his bike seat, took out his cell phone, and dialed Gordon's number.

30

SCRAMBLING

DECEMBER 17, 1998

THEY ONLY HAD ninety days to prepare their writ of certiorari to the Supreme Court after Judge Stewart and the 5th Circuit rejected their appeal. It wasn't a lot of time, and the arguments could not simply be scribbled down and mailed to Washington. One might not agree with the views of any individual justice, but there was no denying that each justice was brilliant, and any weak or simplistic argument would be quickly discarded.

Michael and Gordon both thought that their argument on racial discrimination in jury selection was worthy of the Supreme Court. They had a defensible argument that the 5th Circuit had misinterpreted the requirements of the key case on the issue, *Batson v. Kentucky*. Briefing it properly would take careful analysis of the appeals court's opinion, as well as researching similar law throughout the federal court system. And they had to do this work without Andy Leipold, who had decided to leave Morgan, Lewis for a coveted law professorship at the University of Illinois. Andy was devastated to leave the Thompson case, after putting in such effort for years, but he had complete confidence that Michael and Gordon would see it through to the very end.

What with the tight deadlines, the complex legal arguments, and the sudden reduction in the number of people on their team, what Michael emphatically did *not* need was Judge Quinlan jumping the gun and filing a new warrant of execution based on the 5th Circuit Appeal, setting up a second front in the war to keep John alive. But that was what Michael had just received.

It wasn't entirely surprising that Quinlan had filed another writ of execution. He had done so after most of the other decisions against them in the appeal, and this warrant was his eighth in the case, if Michael was counting right. But this writ was bogus, clearly improper given the current appeal. It would take time and energy to fight at a time when they had none to spare, and it was hard for him to create a reasonable judicial purpose other than harassment of the defense to support its existence. It spoke volumes about Quinlan's mind-set that John ought to be executed sooner rather than later.

What made Quinlan's writ clearly out of line was the stay of execution issued months ago by Judge Livaudais, in the U.S. District Court, "pending the disposition of the pending Motion . . . and any appeal that may be taken to the United States Court of Appeals for the 5th Circuit and/or application for writ of certiorari to the United States Supreme Court." In other words, as long as John had a federal appeal pending, Louisiana couldn't execute him.

The deadline for the writ of certiorari was March 1, 1999. Quinlan and his clerk knew the ruling, and Judge Livaudais's order was perfectly clear. And yet, Quinlan's signature was on the warrant ordering the Louisiana Department of Public Safety and Corrections to execute John by lethal injection on January 26, 1999.

Beyond the procedural point, Michael was annoyed at the bush-league manner of it all. He had been representing John for more than a decade now, and felt like he had gotten to know Quinlan's chief clerk fairly well. Quinlan had worked with her for quite some time, and he gave her quite a bit of independence in making decisions on his behalf. Michael thought that he understood the dynamic there, and that his relationship with the clerk was strong, but there had been some ominous signs that Michael was misreading her—that what he thought was a good relationship had been standard Southern charm, and that the clerk's true thoughts of him and of John Thompson were kept beneath the surface.

There were two possible reasons why Quinlan had chosen this moment to file the new death warrant. One was to send a message to the U.S. Supreme Court that the trial court believed that no further legal analysis was needed. The other was to distract John's legal team from its cert petition.

He couldn't do anything about the former reason, but he had to move quickly to minimize the latter. Michael banged out a quick letter to Judge Quinlan putting John's defense on the record, in writing. He enclosed a copy of the federal court order staying the execution until after the Supreme Court ruling, and noting that they fully intended to file a timely petition for appeal to the Supreme Court.

Michael then phoned Quinlan's clerk but did not get much help from her. She told him quite directly that Judge Quinlan was unwilling to withdraw the warrant for execution, forcing Michael to take the matter up with the Louisiana 4th Circuit Court of Appeals.

While Michael was infuriated, his feelings were softened somewhat by Gordon's relative serenity regarding the problem. Gordon was confident that no federal judge would let a state court judge tell him that he couldn't issue a stay on an execution while a federal habeas petition was pending.

As he calmed down, Michael admitted to himself that Gordon was right. They'd win on this point. But how much energy would it take while they were preparing for the Supreme Court? They needed unobstructed access to John for that. His participation was essential to any number of administrative and procedural details. John's status was known at Angola, and Michael had called the warden's office to ensure cooperation. The prison allowed John his constitutional rights, but only grudgingly, when Michael or Gordon was actually on the phone demanding them. Even then, it happened in fits and starts, with the rules constantly changing. One day, John would be allowed to call them, and the next he wouldn't. Even when he could call them, his ability to participate would be limited because the guards would take his legal papers away for an "inventory," so he wouldn't have access to his files. It made everything that much harder.

The current warden seemed to Michael and Gordon like an aggressive, Bible-thumping self-promoter, though according to John, he wasn't that bad a guy. He was no pushover, certainly, but John had always said that the warden shot straight with the inmates. Still, it was odd that these administrative hurdles were being thrown in their way as they prepared for their last legal challenge.

Probably coincidence, Michael thought again, and opened the file on his computer to take another run at the *Batson* argument.

JANUARY 9, 1999

MICHAEL HELD THE *Times-Picayune* article in his hand, a fax from Nick Trenticosta. *I'll be damned,* he thought. Harry Connick had finally decided to release Shareef Cousin.

Shareef was another inmate on Angola's death row, one Michael had been following closely for a number of reasons. Sentenced to death when he was only sixteen, Shareef's case had some striking similarities to John's case. First, it was an Orleans Parish case, tried by Connick's office. Second, like John's case, there was no physical evidence linking Shareef to the murder, just an eyewitness ID. Third, the case had some allegations of prosecutorial misconduct—both witness tampering and failure of the prosecutors to turn over exculpatory evidence that would have suggested Shareef's innocence. Since they had made some similar claims in John's case, they were watching to see how the courts handled the issue.

Perhaps the most interesting thing about Shareef, to Michael, though, was the relationship he had built with John.

John had reached out to Shareef from the very beginning, the older man taking the teenager under his wing in much the same way that he himself had been cared for by Thomas Lee Ward. He understood, perhaps better than anyone else in the world, both what Shareef was feeling and how this had happened to him, and he worked hard to keep the boy's spirits up. He also displayed an impressive amount of savvy in helping Shareef tell his story. Because Shareef was a minor, and the youngest person on death row in the United States, his case had become a cause célèbre for the media, with profiles in *Time* magazine and in an Amnesty International report on the death penalty. John helped Shareef prepare for his interviews and express his plight in plain, powerful language.

John was willing to talk about Shareef and his emotions in a way that he would never have spoken about himself, but for Michael and Gordon, it was an invaluable window into the inner workings of their client. When Shareef had said to Amnesty International, "To sit here in the shadows of death, surrounded by death on each side of me is very hard to deal with. Almost every day I think of killing myself, but I'm too scared to die," Michael heard John's voice.

Shareef's lawyers had scored a surprise victory the previous April, when the Louisiana Supreme Court overturned Shareef's conviction. Both Shareef and John were ecstatic, Shareef believing he'd be released soon, and John believing that once one court saw how Connick's DAs had framed up a case, they would see that the same had been done to him.

At the time, Michael had told John what a great development this was, but after reading the opinion, he was no longer quite so optimistic that what was good for Shareef would be good for John. John pinned many of his hopes on their *Brady* arguments, despite their lack of success to date. Shareef's case had *Brady* arguments as well, arguments that in Michael's opinion were even stronger than John's. Even so, the court, while noting the *Brady* violation in a footnote of its opinion, had not specifically used that to overturn the conviction, choosing instead to focus on improper hearsay testimony. To Michael, the fact that the court had seen the

Brady issues and had actively resisted ruling on them was further proof that no appeals court would ever actually call out the DA's office for its misdeeds.

Even worse, Connick was apparently unfazed by the Louisiana Supreme Court's ruling. He had taken a few potshots in the local media when the opinion was released, but only now, nine months later, was Connick reluctantly deciding not to retry the case. The fact that Connick would hold so tightly to a conviction in the face of a Supreme Court reversal and widespread negative public opinion did not bode well for how he would respond in the highly unlikely event that they were able to get John's conviction overturned.

Still, Michael and Gordon had a more immediate situation to address. Shareef's improbable legal success had inspired John to want to assert more control over the case strategy. John had called him that morning and said, "Michael, look, I been thinking. Shareef had an investigator working on his case. Why I don't have no investigator looking into my case?"

Michael groaned inside. John was smart and creative, but he didn't always see the strategic details of how Michael and Gordon were working. Michael knew that John had every right to push him to do more, or to do things differently, but it was one more energy drain away from his preparing the petition for cert for the Supreme Court.

"We do have an investigator on your case, John," he said. "We have Garry Eldredge working on your case. Nick says he's the best in New Orleans. We told him to go digging for anything he could find."

"Well, what's he doing? You got any reports from him?"

"I can get one. What do you have in mind? I'd rather he spend his time looking for people and facts that we can use in the petition, rather than writing me reports."

"Shareef had this investigator. Her name's Elisa or something. She was sending him these reports, showing all the stuff she's doing, all the people she's meeting with. I'm just saying, you say we got this investigator, you know—how you know he's doing what all he's supposed to be doing if he's not sending you no reports?"

"John, I'm really not sure what an investigator's going to do for you at this point in the case. And paying for two investigators to do the same work isn't going to help you any."

John was quiet, a strategy for dealing with Michael that he had honed to perfection over the years. From John's perspective, Michael was a smart guy, and he knew a lot of things that John didn't know. But like anyone else, Michael might think he knew what it was like on death row, but he didn't know. It didn't make him a bad guy; it just meant that he didn't always listen when John had ideas. Gordon would listen, and if he disagreed, he'd tell John why. Michael would just interrupt, tell John that he already knew what John was asking for, and tell him why it was already being done or why it was a bad idea. John's reaction, when he was sure he didn't want to back down, was to become really quiet. If he challenged Michael, the two of them would dig in and have an argument. Better to let Michael think it through a little bit more himself, and he'd usually figure out a way to help.

After an uncomfortably long silence, John said, "Look, I don't know who you got on it, and I sure as hell don't have any money to pay any new investigator. But this woman Shareef got, at least he knows that she's out there, you know? Working on his case, talking to people, all that. I want that on my case. Just think about it, talk about it with Gordon. You do that for me, I'm fine."

Michael sighed. *It can't hurt the case any,* he thought. "Okay, John, I'll look into it. Anything else I can do for you in there?"

"Yeah. You can get me out of here."

John hung up the phone. He looked at the clock near the door. He had another thirty-four minutes of his hour out of solitary. He turned from the phone and started jogging, back and forth, up and down the tier. He needed to run off some stress.

31

OUT OF APPEALS

APRIL 5, 1999

DEEP DOWN, MICHAEL had known it was coming, but that didn't soften it any. More than anything else, it was just that he *wanted* a different result. He wanted to believe that a different outcome was possible, that the Supreme Court would read the petition and see what a person of worth John had become and how wrong this all was. He wanted to believe that somehow, somewhere, the system would get this right.

Instead, the Court had denied their petition for certiorari without fanfare. The order said, "Certiorari denied," and nothing more.

Michael felt as if he would be the one killing John. He felt like a total, unmitigated failure. He couldn't keep John alive. He couldn't improve his life. He'd taken on John's case, naively, in an unfamiliar area of law with the highest of stakes. He had failed, and because of it, a good man was going to die.

There was no way to make this right. Quinlan would probably refile the writ of execution by the end of the day.

As sure as if he were the one putting the poison in John's veins, Michael had sealed John's fate. The arguments he thought had been so intelligently crafted seemed now to be laughably inadequate in the face of the Supreme Court's terse rejection. He felt like an impostor in a suit, a fraud with a degree.

He got up, closed the door to his office, and went back to his chair. He looked out the window, up the parkway to the Art Museum, to the river barely visible beyond it, and to Fairmount Park extending to meet the horizon. Farther north was the Fairmount Prison, a pioneer of solitary confinement until the prison was shut down because all the inmates were going crazy. Fairmount seemed to stand for the proposition that even death was better than protracted solitary confinement.

Michael wasn't feeling that way at the moment.

He didn't know how long he sat there, or when he decided to get up and leave. Later, when friends would ask how it was at the darkest moment, Michael would not remember the drive home or what he said to Lori and the kids when he got there or what words of encouragement or sympathy they offered back. What he remembered was knowing, for the first time, that no matter what he or anyone else did, it didn't matter at all.

APRIL 10, 1999

MICHAEL PEDALED UP the rocky trail winding up the Wissahickon Ridge. It felt good—his ability to control the bike a welcome feeling given how out-of-control everything else seemed. He reached the top of the hill and pulled up at a scenic overlook, gazing out over the valley that was struggling to be green in the early spring chill.

Michael dismounted and walked to the edge of the overlook with his water bottle. He tipped the bottle back, feeling the water infuse his mouth and throat, and thought, *It's done. John's gonna get executed May 20th. It's over, and I have to go tell John that he's going to die.*

Michael thought of himself as a fairly stoic guy, but he was pretty emotional at this moment. He looked out over the valley and let the tears come. The voices inside his head continued, saying, *John already knows, and he's known for a long time.*

Michael thought, *What have I done? Nothing. Have I saved him? Have I won one goddamn argument, one point of law? Maybe I've prolonged a condemned man's life. Big deal. I've done nothing.*

Another voice inside his head chimed in: *You know why you did this, and you know what you've done. It makes John's life better, the system better, and you better.*

Michael looked out across the park. Yeah, he knew all that. Maybe someday he'd write a memoir: *John and Me: My Life Not Saving a Death Row Inmate.* He'd failed to stop the execution of his wrongfully convicted client—but not until the reader came to admire and respect him. Only then would the inmate be executed. It was the perfect made-for-TV movie.

How do you tell a guy that he's going to die because you weren't good enough at your job? Michael wondered.

Of course, John wasn't at death's door because of Michael, any more than someone hurt in a car crash was injured when their personal injury lawyer failed to secure a million-dollar settlement. Instead, John was to be executed because a dozen random people from the New Orleans community decided that he'd killed a man, and the jurors felt that death was the appropriate punishment.

Still, Michael and Gordon had not been able to turn that decision around, and that had been their job. And what was worse, far worse, was Michael's firm belief that John Thompson, whatever else he was, was a good human being. He was so different now, so thoughtful and gracious and giving.

Michael stood there, thoughts flowing through his head: *You've given this dead-end, no-win shit show a decade of blood, sweat, and tears. You've given the New Orleans DA a run for his money in his own backyard.* They had represented John with honor, dignity, and dedication, and had done everything they knew how to do. There wasn't anything else Michael could think of that he could have, or would have, done differently—except win.

Michael knew he had to go down there, look John in the eye, and tell him he was sorry. He stared out from the ridge for another few seconds, got back on his bike, and pedaled down the trail as fast as he could.

APRIL 12, 1999

GORDON AGREED COMPLETELY that John deserved to hear the news that his appeals had run their course from his lawyers and not from anyone else, and he deserved to hear it face-to-face.

But even now, both Michael and Gordon refused to simply give up. While making travel plans to give John the bad news, the Morgan, Lewis team organized last-ditch efforts to get another stay or a change in the case. Nick's grassroots anti–death penalty crusaders were writing all kinds of letters, to see if they could get someone influential to intervene on their behalf. There were letters going to Jesse Jackson, known advisors of President Clinton, and even the president himself. Of course, they didn't expect any of it to work, or even to delay the proceedings, but Michael knew they had to try.

John's new private investigator, Elisa Abolafiya, fell into that same category of last-ditch efforts, an expense worth paying mainly so that Michael might someday have a prayer of sleeping again, and wouldn't be forever haunted that he hadn't done the one thing that might have saved his client's life. They had given Elisa the basic facts surrounding both the murder and the armed robbery cases, and had sent her off to learn whatever she could.

They would also try petitioning the Pardon Board, since John had exemplary conduct in prison, even though they knew this, too, was a long shot. It was a catch-22: If they'd had the evidence they needed to get the clemency petition, they wouldn't have needed a clemency petition in the first place. Only one clemency petition had been granted by Louisiana in the last thirty years, and that one wasn't by the current governor. The fact that John had become a

thoughtful, decent, sensitive, caring human being in prison probably wouldn't excuse his crimes in the minds of those on the Pardon
Board. It hadn't worked for Thomas Lee Ward, and there was no
reason to think that John's case would be any different.

They would also try to approach Ray Liuzza Sr. Perhaps if the
victim's father were to ask for clemency on John's behalf, the governor would revisit the case. Michael and Gordon had explored
this route a decade ago, writing a letter to Mr. Liuzza and asking to
meet with him, to no avail. Still, maybe Liuzza Sr. had softened and
gained a new perspective over the years. As with the new private
investigator, the time to take risks was at hand. What more did they
have to lose?

32

THE VAULT

ELISA TOOK THE elevator down to the NOPD Central Evidence locker. She walked up to the counter, staffed by a middle-aged man in a lumpy police uniform. Behind him were rows and rows of iron utility shelving. It reminded Elisa of Home Depot garage shelving— giant erector sets enclosed in a floor-to-ceiling chain-link fence with a lock and key. In theory, every case number had a shelf location, and every piece of evidence was kept on a card. When the evidence was needed for a hearing or a trial, the man behind the counter would check it out to the police or the DA. The officer would sign the card for the pieces of evidence being removed, and when the evidence was brought back, the officer would sign the card again to show the date and time each item was returned.

Of course, the evidence locker was supposed to have limited access—it wasn't available to just anyone. The locker housed a wide variety of seized material in the possession of the State. It was a crapshoot, really—whether the "good ole boys" behind the counter would let her look for anything related to John's case, and then, an even bigger question, whether she could find anything in there even if they did.

Elisa tugged her shirt down and adjusted her push-up bra. It wasn't "rocket surgery," as one of her friends said—put on a low scoop-neck shirt and a short skirt, get made up, look those boys in the eye, smile and laugh at everything they said. It was amazing what a girl could do with a giggle and a walk.

She walked up to the counter. She was in luck—it was a guy she had dealt with before. She gave him a big, flirtatious hello and told him that she needed his help. She explained John's situation and asked him if he could help her find any evidence they had on the case numbers she provided. The man looked at the date—1985—and told her there was no point in looking for those cases. Nothing would be back there.

Elisa persisted. The cases were still on appeal, meaning that the police had a continuing obligation to hold the evidence. If the evidence had been destroyed, that would mean there was a bigger problem. The man bristled a little, so Elisa smiled and said she was just trying to make sure nothing was in either of the two case number files. If not, no harm done.

The man looked at her, his lips pursed while he considered her request. He said he'd take a look and that she should come back on Thursday. He wasn't going to promise anything.

Elisa smiled and patted the man's arm, keeping her hand on it as she cooed a thank-you. She turned and left the building for her next stop: the Crime Lab.

ELISA DID THE same song and dance with the NOPD Crime Lab, except the push-up bra wasn't the thing that got her in the door. The men working at the lab were cops, but they were also scientists. They were less likely to deny her access to scientific data, regardless of who she was representing. She told them the situation and they walked her back into a room with mountains of files and told her to have a good time. Then they went back to work.

She came out of the room once, two and a half hours later, to get a cup of pseudo-coffee from the coffeepot, and then she went back in. Ten minutes later, she found what she was looking for. She made a copy, tucked it in her purse, and walked out of the office before anyone could ask her how it was going.

33

GRADUATION

APRIL 20, 1999

MICHAEL AND GORDON drove from New Orleans to Angola in a rental car, each man feeling tense and awkward. For the first few miles, Gordon tried to make conversation, commenting on whatever he was looking at out the window, anything to try to break the tension building in the car. Michael responded with polite but distracted indifference. After about forty-five minutes of this, Gordon simply stopped talking and the two men drove in silence.

When they saw the gates of Angola, the barbed wire and guards, Michael felt none of the tension or anxiety he remembered from previous trips. Instead, he felt stifled, the Louisiana air turning heavy and wet, making him sweat through his suit as he walked toward the death row building.

They produced their IDs, went through a metal detector and a hand patdown, and were taken to a partitioned interview room on the second floor. They waited for a few minutes while the guards went to get John.

Before they had left Philadelphia, some of Michael's colleagues had told him what a stand-up guy he was, how classy he and Gordon were for flying down to Angola to deliver the news personally. Michael wasn't impressed. He took no pride in the truth this time. The truth, as he saw it, was that his arrogance had finally gotten him into trouble. He should never have taken this case, should never have thought that he could handle a death penalty representation. He wasn't qualified for it, hadn't known what to do with it, couldn't manipulate the system and make it do what he wanted. He wasn't proud of himself. He was ashamed and embarrassed.

A door opened and John walked in. Unlike previous visits, there was no mesh curtain. The warden had relaxed the rules, and let the death row inmates have supervised visits that permitted personal contact. John hugged them both, then sat down in front of them. His tone was soft, but his words were direct.

"What's the date?"

Michael had thought a lot about how he was going to say to John what needed to be said. He'd rehearsed it a thousand times. Now he ignored all of that. He looked away for a long moment, composing himself, then looked back at John. "The 20th of May."

Both men watched John, expecting his head to drop. It did, just for a moment. Then it came back up, nodding. John kept his voice quiet as he asked, "Think we can push it back for, like, four days?"

Michael hesitated, considering the unexpected question. They were going to file the clemency petition, and he'd have a final hearing before the Pardon Board, but neither of those procedures were ones that would push the execution date back for only a few days. "John, I don't know. I doubt it, to tell you the truth, but I don't know. Why?"

John looked at the ground and then glanced up at the ceiling before bringing his focus back to Michael. "Tiger's graduatin'. Graduation day is May 21st. Be the first in our family to graduate from high school. They give me May 20th as a date, I don't know what he'll do with that, you know? Might make him do something stupid, or I don't know what. I don't want my situation in here to get in the way of celebratin' that out there."

Michael looked at Gordon, trying to find some words to convey how selfless and graceful he thought John's reaction to their news was, and how inadequate and impotent he felt.

Gordon said, "John, we understand completely. I don't think they're going to be willing to change the date, but we'll certainly get in touch with Judge Quinlan's office and see if we can get it moved. And we're going to keep doing everything we can, right up until . . ."

John gave a rueful smile as Gordon stopped himself. He knew how the system worked. "I'm not worried about that none," John said. "If this is how I'm gonna go, then that's how God wants it, and I gotta deal with that. I've had a lot of time to get ready. I'm just sorry y'all gotta feel like you failed, and I'm sorry my sons and my family gotta deal with this. But it's cool; it's gonna be what it's gonna be. I just gotta see my mom, see my boys, before it's all done."

The three men sat for a few moments in silence, until John said, "You both will be there, right, when they do it?"

Michael and Gordon had known this question would come, and they had dreaded it. They had thought about it for years, discussing it in quiet moments when their optimism was low or their stress levels were high. Each time, they had reached the same conclusion. There was really only one answer, and they gave it reflexively.

"We'll be there, John," Gordon said.

"A'right," John said. He looked at both men seriously. "Look, I know you both done everything you could do. I don't want you feeling bad about yourself, now. I was the one put myself in here. I need you to help take care of my boys, though, now that I can't be there myself. You do that for me?"

"You know we will, John."

"A'right, then. Guess I gotta go back." John smiled a little. "Guess I'll see you two in a few weeks."

The men hugged, and the lawyers left the room. Michael was thankful that he'd managed to keep his eyes from tearing up until after they had left the meeting room.

THEY DROVE DOWN the Snake Road in silence. It wasn't until they were outside Baton Rouge that Gordon broke the silence: "The only thing John was worried about was his son's graduation."

Michael nodded. He couldn't bear to talk, even to Gordon, the one person who could possibly understand how he felt. Instead, he drove in silence as the green trees and undergrowth passed them by.

Wanting to distract himself, Gordon pulled out his cell phone and called his office voice mail. He skipped through a couple of messages, then listened the last one: "Gordon, it's Elisa. You need to call me. It's urgent."

34

THE BLOOD TEST

WITHOUT A WORD, Gordon hung up on his voice mail and immediately called Elisa back. Michael heard him talking into the phone, and got more and more interested as the conversation went on: "Addressed to the DA's office? Before the carjacking trial? B? You're sure? We're on our way to New Orleans now; we've left Angola and we'll be there in about two hours. I'll call you when we get there, and we'll figure out what to do with this. Thanks." He hung up and turned to Michael.

"You're not going to believe this."

Michael turned his head from the window. Gordon said that Elisa was holding a piece of microfiche dated April 1985. It was a blood test from the carjacking, taken before John's armed robbery trial. No one had been told about the test—until Elisa found it. The blood tested was type B.

Michael looked at Gordon, each knowing what the other was thinking: Neither one of them knew John's blood type.

MICHAEL THREW THE keys at the hotel valet and ran into the lobby where Elisa was waiting. She stood up, expectantly, a big grin on her face, holding out a single sheet of white printer paper. Michael scrutinized it as Gordon walked up behind him.

The blood test results were dated April 9, 1985—two days before the armed robbery trial, and well after discovery requests made by Couhig and Fanning that should have revealed the existence of this test. They were in a report that was addressed to Bruce Whittaker, the screener in the Lagarde armed robbery case.

Michael couldn't believe what he was looking at. He kept repeating it to himself, as if the repetition would make it more believable. *Dubelier and Williams tested the blood samples from Jay Lagarde's shoe and pant leg. In 1985. Before the armed robbery trial*. He turned to Gordon. "How many times did we ask for this?"

Gordon couldn't take his eyes off the report, or the excitement out of his voice. "Several."

"Did Numa Bertel ask for this?"

"Definitely."

"Did Couhig and Fanning?"

"Definitely."

Michael turned to Elisa. "How'd you get this? You didn't do anything illegal, did you?"

Elisa shook her head. "Of course not. It was right there in the file. I copied it and brought it to you."

"How could it have been there all this time? Haven't we looked at these files?"

"I don't know, Michael. Maybe this was a different file. But the original is there, and it's real, and this copy is accurate."

How had this happened? Gordon thought. *Could it have been Whittaker acting behind the scenes during the screening?* Probably not, he decided. The screener wouldn't order a blood test that late without telling the lead prosecutor, because if it had turned up bad information, it would have had to be given to the defense. *No, this wasn't a lone gunman*, he decided. *There was a second shooter. This was a full-blown conspiracy.*

Michael asked Elisa if she could track down Bruce Whittaker. He also asked whether she had found the actual pant leg and shoe that were tested. Elisa shook her head, her earrings rattling in her thick black hair. The evidence itself had been separated from the test results, and there was no telling where it was, or if it even still existed.

Without the actual blood sample, they couldn't do a DNA test, so they'd have to hope that the blood types didn't match. If John was type B, the report couldn't prove his innocence. Given that only 10 percent of the population had type-B blood, Solino would argue that it worked to John's benefit that the DAs didn't use the report, since a jury would be more likely to assume that John was the robber with the report in hand. They'd need to know Jay Lagarde's blood type as well, to eliminate him as the source. Michael didn't remember Lagarde's testimony exactly, though he seemed to recall that the boy had not been hurt and hadn't bled during or after the attack, so it was most likely the perpetrator's blood.

Michael turned back to Elisa. He wanted her to try to get John's blood type. She agreed to see if hospitals near his home had such records, and walked out of the hotel.

Michael shook his head, feeling giddy with relief and flushed with a renewed hope. He and Gordon walked into the hotel bar and ordered drinks, talking excitedly to each other.

Finding out John's blood type was the key. If both John and Jay Lagarde came back with blood types other than B . . . Michael didn't want to jinx it. But if they did, then the blood test would be scientific proof that John Thompson could *not* have been the man that carjacked the Lagarde kids. Moreover, the fact that the report, with an ADA's request and receipt on it, had never been revealed to John's lawyers was a smoking gun pointing to prosecutorial misconduct on the part of Dubelier, Williams, and Whittaker.

Michael thought, *Dubelier and Williams must have known about this test and the results, and they didn't use them. Why not?* The only answer that made sense was that the results were not good for the prosecution.

It was one piece of microfiche, on an unrelated felony, but it changed everything. Without a charge of guilty for the armed robbery, the murder trial would have been completely different. John would most likely have taken the stand in his own defense, and Dubelier and Williams would not have had a prior violent crime to use as their foundation for seeking the death penalty. It was clear grounds for a new murder trial.

The two of them thought about telling John, but they didn't want to get his hopes up. John had been calm during their meeting, but both men thought he'd looked frail. The pressure he was under was crushing, and only intensified with each new piece of bad news. They couldn't tell him this until they knew, for certain, that it might change his date forever.

They also had to be sneaky about getting John's blood type to avoid tipping off the DA's office as to what they had learned until they were sure of its accuracy. Gordon picked up the phone, dialed Angola, and got patched through to John. He asked John for his blood type, but John didn't know. Gordon then revealed a plan: He told John to expect a FedEx envelope tomorrow. They would put a two-page letter in it, the pages stapled together, and a return envelope. They'd write a legitimate letter, but Gordon told John to ignore it altogether. Instead, he told John to take the staple out of the letter and use it to prick his finger, allowing the blood to soak into the second page.

With that done, John was to return the FedEx envelope with the paper and blood in it, quietly and with no questions asked.

"Gordon? What you got goin' on over there?"

"I don't know yet, John. Probably nothing. Let's do this, and we'll tell you as soon as we can."

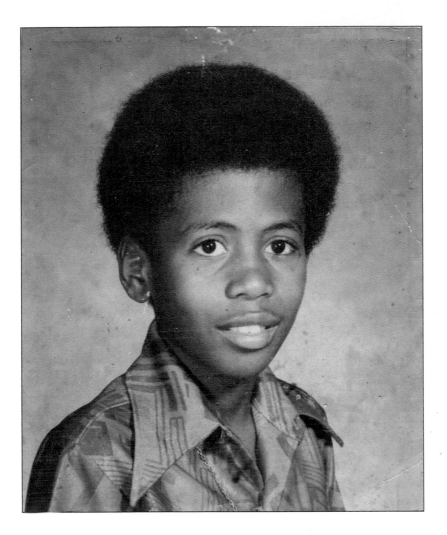

John Thompson, age 10

John Thompson with his
mother, Josephine Casby,
and his son, John Jr.

John Thompson's mug shot, taken on the day he was arrested in 1984. Photo courtesy of Michael Banks and Morgan, Lewis.

Kevin Freeman's mug shot, taken in 1985. Photo courtesy of Michael Banks and Morgan, Lewis.

Orleans Parish Prison (OPP), where John Thompson was held for four of his eighteen years in jail, is seen behind the Louisiana courthouse.

The entrance to the Louisiana State Penitentiary, aka Angola or "The Farm." Photo copyright Matt Shirkey/MrChrisCornwell.

A photograph of the actual death chamber at Angola, which now administers lethal injections. This photograph was taken at the Angola Museum. Photo copyright Matt Shirkey/MrChrisCornwall.

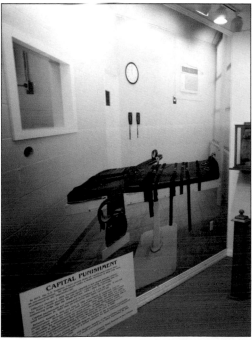

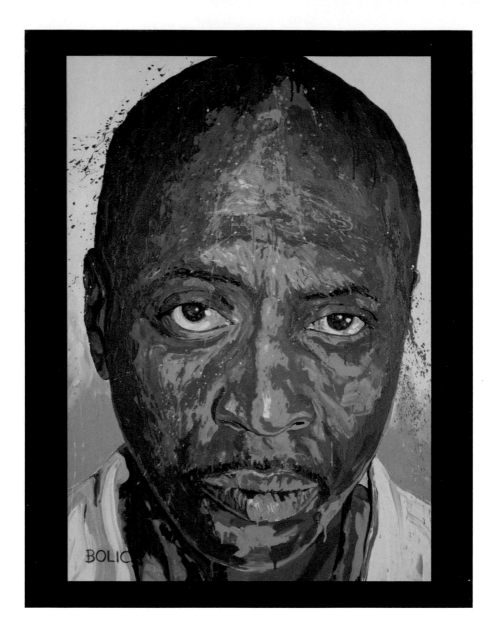

Artwork titled: *John Thompson—Sentenced to Death for a Murder He Did Not Commit. Exonerated after 18 Years. 14 Years on Death Row.* Copyright Daniel Bolick.

The Criminal Justice System doesn't work!
It doesn't recognize that poor people are human.

The prisons are full of the poor.

My family couldn't afford $80,000 for a capital lawyer. I was at a disadvantage, but I was human before I went to jail. I didn't lose my right to be a human when I came home but society does not welcome people coming out of prison.

Where is the second chance?

I have problems finding a job, getting a home, getting healthcare, Reconnecting with my family.

If being innocent is this hard I can only imagine how hard it is being guilty and Returning.

Who is the victim here?

Me, my family, the jury, society?

They were all deceived.

Who are the criminals here?

The DA, my trial lawyer, other Attorneys, the judge?

I am a victim of a state crime and have experienced severe trauma!

Bolick

Sketch titled:
John Thompson.
Copyright Daniel Bolick.

A photo taken while John was incarcerated, sent home to his mother, Josephine Casby.

I Love You Mother !! "John"

John on one of his first contact visits while on death row. From left to right: Gayle Jackson (John's stepmother), Josephine Casby, John, Nancy Wohl (John's spiritual advisor), and Sermaine Jackson (John's younger sister).

John, his good friend Lawson, and Norman at a death row seminar. All were inmates together. Norman is now free of his death conviction.

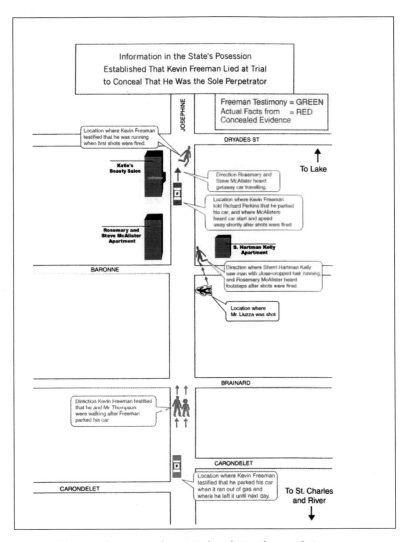

This is the map that Michael Banks and Gordon Cooney used in John's new trial in order to illustrate for the jury Kevin Freeman's original testimony and the new evidence that was concealed and subsequently used in the retrial. The images in green represent the information from the original trial, and the images in red indicate new evidence in the retrial. Note particularly the position of Kevin Freeman's car and the new evidence—the placement of the car, the McAllister's testimony, and Ms. Kelly's eye contact with Freeman. Map courtesy of Michael Banks and Morgan, Lewis.

John with his Philadelphia attorneys Michael Banks (left) and Gordon
Cooney (right) after his trial.

The Resurrection After Exoneration (RAE) staff, from left to right:
John Thompson, Christopher Raines, Ora Nitkin-Kaner, and Tina
Wexler.

35

JAY LAGARDE

APRIL 23, 1999

MICHAEL HAD MADE five calls to Jay Lagarde in the past two days. On the sixth attempt, Lagarde answered. Michael introduced himself as John Thompson's lawyer, explained the connection between the armed robbery case and John's death sentence, and the fact that John was scheduled to be executed in three weeks. "Mr. Lagarde, we recently learned that a blood test was conducted in the armed robbery case—your armed robbery case—before the trial. That blood test was not used at the trial, and was not turned over to Mr. Thompson's lawyers at the time, or any time since then by the DA's office. We need to know whether it has any relevance to Mr. Thompson's appeal. To do that, I need to know your blood type. Is that information you're willing to share with me?"

"I'm type O."

Michael stood in his office holding the phone to his ear and pumping his fist in the air, like a corporate Kirk Gibson rounding first after hitting that game-winner in the World Series.

Michael explained that the blood type in the test had been type B: "That means the blood on the pants and shoes could not have been yours."

Jay was extremely helpful; he agreed to fax a copy of his blood donor card to Michael, and even agreed to retestify in any new trial if need be. He seemed a little embarrassed and asked Michael if they had been wrong, if Mr. Thompson was not the man who carjacked him and his siblings. Michael said, "I don't know that yet, Mr. Lagarde, and I don't want to make judgments too quickly here, but it's certainly beginning to appear that way."

Lagarde said, "You know, Mr. Banks, after the trial, I went up to the DA—I don't remember his name—the DA that tried the case."

"Jim Williams?"

"I don't remember his name, but that sounds right. I went up to the DA and I asked him if they'd ever tested the blood from the samples they took from me that night."

"What did he say?"

"He told me that they had, and that the blood test had been inconclusive."

Michael thanked Mr. Lagarde for his time and assistance, and hung up the phone.

Inconclusive, he thought bitterly.

36

CONSPIRACY

AS HE SAT in the back of the courtroom in Orleans Parish Court-house waiting for Bruce Whittaker, Michael read the motion he had drafted and sent to the court six years earlier: *Petitioner's Motion for Scientific Testing of Evidence and for Production of Physical Evidence.* In it, he and Gordon had asked for the production of "any and all blood tests performed by or on behalf of the New Orleans Police Department or agents of the State of Louisiana regarding the blood found on the pant leg and tennis shoe taken from Jay Lagarde at the scene of the armed robbery." They had filed the motion in 1993, after ADA Jeff Bridger had refused to provide the materials.

In Michael's opinion, the documents painted a pretty grim picture for the DAs. They were handwritten notes from the carjacking crime scene listing the collection of the blood-stained pants and shoe. There were typed versions of the handwritten notes, listing the same evidence. And they had the evidence locker's card for the armed robbery, which showed a single left-footed FootJoy tennis shoe with blood on it and a piece of "victim's right pant leg, w/ blood."

Moreover, Michael and Gordon had gone back through their files on the armed robbery case, and had found Bruce Whittaker's screening report on the Lagarde carjacking, on which Whittaker (or

253

someone) had written at the bottom, "May wish to do blood test." And the transcripts of the armed robbery case included an evidentiary hearing in open court during which Jim Williams informed Judge Quinlan, "Your Honor, it is the State's intention to file a motion to take a blood sample from the defendant, and we will file that motion—have a criminalist here on the 27th." Williams had clearly chosen his words carefully—no such motion was ever filed.

It was all making sense to Michael, who had been playing and replaying it in his head all morning. Williams wanted to test the blood sample because if it matched John's blood type and not Jay Lagarde's, it would be ironclad proof of John's guilt. But to get John's blood type he would have had to test John, which he couldn't do without informing Numa Bertel, which would mean he'd have to share the results—and if the results came back as anything other than matching John's blood type but not matching Jay's, Bertel would use it against him in the defense case. So, *Williams decides to test the sample first*, Michael thought. *If it came back with a common blood type, he would have tested John. But it came back "B," and Williams knew there was a good chance John wasn't "B," so he just buried the test.*

Of course, Michael wanted more proof before he made any accusations. He pulled out the evidence custody card and looked at it again. According to the card, all of the physical evidence in the armed robbery case had been checked out on April 4 by Gerry Deegan, a junior ADA who had assisted Jim Williams on the armed robbery case. It made sense that Deegan would check the evidence out a few days before trial. It appeared that Deegan brought it back on April 11, after the trial. However, according to the card, the shoe and pant leg were never returned.

Unfortunately, according to Elisa, Deegan was dead. That made Bruce Whittaker the key to understanding what really happened, before they alerted Connick to the misconduct of his office and he started covering whatever tracks were still out there. The blood test results had been addressed to Whittaker by the police labs. That, coupled with Whittaker's "May want to do blood test" on the screening form, suggested that he knew what the strategy had been and had participated in it.

Elisa had easily tracked down Whittaker. He was still practicing law in New Orleans, in private practice, focusing mostly on criminal defense work and supplementing his caseload with work as a public defender.

Michael glanced up. Whittaker had finished his business before the court and was walking down the middle aisle to leave. Michael stepped in front of him and introduced himself as John Thompson's lawyer. Whittaker's face was full of confusion as he shook Michael's hand.

Whittaker said right away that he remembered the Thompson cases, which Michael took as a good sign. There was nothing defensive in the man's tone. As he had done with Jay Lagarde, Michael started with the fact that John was scheduled to be executed in less than three weeks, and then moved into their recent discovery of blood test results.

Whittaker seemed genuinely surprised but said nothing, allowing Michael to continue. Michael kept his voice calm and explained that the document could very likely exonerate Mr. Thompson of the armed robbery, and that his murder conviction most likely could not stand without the armed robbery conviction as a predicate offense.

"Mr. Whittaker, it appears from our documentation that you requested the test, or at least that the Crime Lab report was addressed to your attention. We are trying to connect the dots here and figure out where the report went after it left the Crime Lab."

Whittaker was clearly taken aback. Michael decided to soft-pedal a bit; Whittaker seemed like a decent guy and was not responding aggressively. He reassured Whittaker that he was not suggesting that he had done anything wrong, and that their sole motive here was to make sure their client was not unfairly put to death.

Whittaker tried to remember a single blood test of the thousands he had requested while serving as an assistant DA. He claimed not to remember ordering a blood test in John's case, though he said he certainly could have. As part of the standard procedure, had he done so, he would have given it to Jim Williams as the lawyer in charge of the case.

Michael didn't know Whittaker at all, but he didn't sound like a guy who was trying to cover anything up. He sounded sincere, like he was actually trying to remember.

"One more thing, Mr. Whittaker. The evidence was checked out for trial by a Gerry Deegan, and when it was checked back in, the pants and shoe that were the subject of the blood test were not with the rest of the evidence. We're trying to locate Mr. Deegan to see what he remembers; do you happen to keep in touch with him?"

Whittaker shook his head sadly. Elisa had been right. Deegan was dead, a victim of cancer.

Michael thanked Whittaker for his time, and gave him his phone number and Gordon's in case he remembered anything more. Then he walked out of the courthouse. Whatever was going on, it didn't feel like Whittaker was part of it.

APRIL 27, 1999

GORDON GLANCED DOWN at his cell phone and excused himself from the deposition he was observing. He answered the call as he closed the conference room door softly behind him. His assistant knew where he was and wouldn't have called if it weren't important.

She informed Gordon that Bruce Whittaker had just called from New Orleans. He said it was about the Thompson case. Gordon hung up and dialed Whittaker's number.

Whittaker answered the phone and told Gordon that he had tried to call Michael, but got no answer. He said his conversation with Michael the day before had gotten him thinking, and he discussed the case with one of his partners, Mike Riehlmann—another lawyer who had been an assistant DA during the time of John's trials.

Whittaker had specifically gone to Riehlmann because Riehlmann had been a close friend of Deegan's. Riehlmann told Whittaker that he wasn't surprised to hear this accusation against Deegan. According to Riehlmann, Deegan had known he was dying, and Riehlmann had visited him often during the last stages of Deegan's illness. On one of those visits, Deegan had said that one of his life's regrets was that he had taken a blood test on a case and he had sat on it—basically made it disappear. He said that he'd never been sure, that it wasn't conclusive evidence of guilt, but that it might have shown that the person was innocent. At the time, Deegan had thought the greater good was for the guy to get convicted, and so he'd buried the evidence.

Gordon paced back and forth outside the conference room, thinking frantically. No court would accept Gordon's rendition of Whittaker's story of Riehlmann's recollection of his years-old conversation with Gerry Deegan, so Gordon asked Whittaker whether Riehlmann would be willing to sign an affidavit and testify, if necessary. Whittaker said that he would.

That was what they needed. Gordon thanked Whittaker profusely. "Mr. Whittaker, you have no idea what this means to Mr. Thompson."

"Actually, Mr. Cooney, I think I have a pretty good idea."

37

CONNICK'S RESPONSE

APRIL 28, 1999

MICHAEL AND GORDON walked into the District Attorney's office and asked the receptionist to let Harry Connick know they were there.

Elisa had called Gordon that morning. She had gotten Charity Hospital to let her see John's medical records—unofficially, of course. John Thompson was blood type O. He could not have been the man who carjacked the Lagarde family.

This piece of information, coupled with Mike Riehlmann's affidavit and willingness to testify, convinced Michael and Gordon that it was time to notify the district attorney himself. Michael had called the office earlier that morning and had spoken to Tim McElroy, Connick's first assistant and second in command. The conversation was brief, McElroy explaining that Connick was simply unavailable. Michael explained about the blood test, the hidden evidence, and Deegan's confession on his deathbed.

Before McElroy could respond, Michael told him that he and Gordon thought it appropriate to bring this information to the DA himself before bringing it to Judge Quinlan or the media, so that they could discuss the best way to handle this information. Michael told McElroy that he was aware that this information was explosive and had the potential to create a media frenzy. Still, their goal was to get John the best result, not to create a media firestorm. Dealing quietly with Connick gave him a reason to play ball; if he chose not to, they could always disclose the information to the media. Plus, with Deegan dead and Dubelier and Williams no longer working for the DA, Connick could easily wave this off publicly as actions by rogue prosecutors no longer with the office.

Michael apologized for the urgency of their request, but given John's impending execution date, he asked for a meeting with Mr. Connick for later that day.

If he was flustered, McElroy didn't show it. He said he'd let them know if Connick could meet with them or not. Michael hung up the phone and smiled. This was going to be fun.

McELROY HAD CALLED back ten minutes later, and soon Michael and Gordon were in the DA's office. Tim McElroy came through the door, a man with a macho bushy mustache and fake Southern charm. He led them into Connick's office. Connick was the picture of a Southern politician, distinguished-looking in a well-tailored, light blue summer suit with a striped button-down shirt and dark tie. He looked much younger than his sixty-some years.

Connick had considerable bearing, and his office augmented that. It was full of dark wood furniture, with awards and pictures of visiting dignitaries placed about. Connick stepped out from behind a huge mahogany desk and walked over to greet them. He thanked them profusely for coming in and motioned for them to sit down.

Michael got right to the point, keeping his explanation short and on topic. He showed Connick and McElroy the initial blood test results, Jay Lagarde's donor card, the evidence of John's blood type, and an affidavit they had recently drawn up from Mike Riehlmann, identifying Gerry Deegan as the one who had hidden the evidence.

Connick took in all of this without a word, nodding calmly at each piece of paper that Michael put in front of him. When Michael finished, Connick flipped through the pages again, put them down, and finally looked up at Michael and Gordon, smiling. He said that his office would need to review this and get back to them in a day or two. He smiled and stacked the papers, a gesture clearly indicating that the meeting was over.

Gordon, who had been quiet thus far, spoke up. He told Connick that he understood it was a lot of information to process, but that John was now three weeks away from execution, and they had no time to waste. "Mr. Connick, this evidence shows incontrovertibly not only that John Thompson did not commit the armed robbery for which he was convicted in 1985, but also that at least one prosecutor from this office actively framed him for the crime. Furthermore, the armed robbery was *the* key component in Mr. Thompson's capital sentencing phase. Without the armed robbery, there would have been no death sentence. We simply cannot wait any longer before bringing this to Judge Quinlan's attention. We're not interested in a media circus. We came here as a courtesy to allow you to participate with us in doing the right thing by overturning John's armed robbery conviction and death sentence. We'd like your agreement to do that so we can approach the Court together rather than as opponents."

Connick looked at Gordon and nodded again. He asked for twenty-four hours to confirm the information he had just been given. He said that if things appeared to be as Michael and Gordon had said, his office would join them in filing a motion with Quinlan to overturn the armed robbery conviction.

Connick's expression then hardened: "But let's be clear on something. I'm not going to do anything about the murder other than stay your client's execution until this gets sorted out. As far as I'm concerned, there's nothing here that implicates the murder case, no allegations of impropriety. You're not saying you have any evidence that anything was hidden in the murder case, are you?"

Michael replied, "At this point, no, we don't have anything to suggest that the same prosecutors who framed Mr. Thompson in the armed robbery also framed him in the murder, although Eric Dube-lier and Jim Williams were involved in both cases, and that certainly raises serious questions that will need to be addressed."

Connick said, "The murder case stands alone. I don't see any connection between this armed robbery and the murder. But if someone in this office failed to turn over a blood test that they should have turned over, we will look at that, and we have no objection to a stay of the execution while this is evaluated."

Michael looked over at Gordon, who cocked his head briefly, indicating his agreement with Connick's offer. It was what they'd expected. Michael stood and shook hands with Connick. McElroy escorted them out of the office and into the elevator.

Both men waited until they were outside the building to breathe their sighs of relief. They had a stay, and for the first time, they had some leverage against the DA. Gordon extended his hand word-lessly to his friend, and Michael shook it with a big smile.

38

GRAND JURY INVESTIGATION

APRIL 29, 1999

Val Solino walked through the crowded cubicle farm in the DA's office, nodding politely to various folks as he scanned the cube tops for his colleague Jerry Glas.

Jerry looked up at Val, smiled, and gave him a sincere hello. From anyone else, it would have been laced with sarcasm, the standard DA response to stress and overwork. From Jerry, though, it meant that he was honestly happy to see Val. Jerry was the Eagle Scout or Beaver Cleaver of the office—Mr. Sincerity. Behind that earnestness, however, Jerry had a sharp mind, good street smarts, and a terrific work ethic. He was a talented lawyer, and since joining the DA's office two years ago, Val had worked often and effectively with him.

Val told Jerry they had a meeting with Harry Connick. Jerry's expression showed curiosity and some concern. Was he going to be disciplined for something? Solino, amused, just smiled and said Connick needed some research done. Jerry grabbed paper and pen and followed Val, his mind moving at high speed to figure out what was happening so he didn't look like such a rookie. Val asked him, as they walked, if he knew anything about the John Thompson case. Jerry sped up a half step, listening as Val filled him in.

Part of the reason Jerry and Val got along so well was that the only thing either of them ever really wanted to be was an ADA in

New Orleans. Jerry was born and bred in New Orleans, leaving only to get a philosophy degree up North. His mother was a little disappointed when he didn't become a priest, but Jerry thought this was a more honest way for him to do God's work.

Jerry's philosophy classes had prepped him well for criminal law, and he took to it from the get-go. Why do we have the criminal code? Why do we imprison people? Does it meet its stated purposes? Studying for his criminal law classes never felt like studying. So, in 1996, he took the Louisiana bar, passed it, and went to work for Harry Connick in the appellate group along with Val.

Jerry enjoyed working for Val, who didn't cut corners and didn't pretend the DA's office always made the right decisions. As Jerry saw it, there were three kinds of ADAs: First, there were the guys who really weren't that good at the work. They generally washed out pretty early on. Next, there were the true believers, guys who thought they were better than the scumbags they prosecuted and were driven by their own moral superiority. These ADAs thought that the righteousness of their path justified a fair amount of manipulative activity, and they might do some pretty questionable things if the third kind of ADA wasn't around to help prevent it. The third kind of DA, the kind Jerry wanted to be and the kind he thought Val was, believed in the work, but even more, they believed in the ideals behind the system. They wanted to ensure that the checks and balances were in place for the rules of evidence, procedure, and the rights of the accused. It was important that they not abuse the power they had been given to decide who was imprisoned, and who walked the streets as a free man. Better that a guilty man go free than an innocent man be imprisoned.

Jerry followed Val into Connick's office, where Connick and McElroy were waiting for them. McElroy nodded and got right to business, explaining the visit they had received from the Philadelphia lawyers representing John Thompson, and showing Jerry the blood test that had been recovered from the evidence locker.

Jerry listened intently as McElroy laid out the facts. *This is bullshit,* he thought to himself. *It has to be a ruse by the defense lawyers to just buy time, any time, no matter the risk. Why else would these guys not try to crucify us in the media? Why come to us first? No, it has to be a stall tactic. They forged the test and came quietly to Connick, wanting to see if they could make something good happen before putting it up to media scrutiny.*

Solino handed him the copy of the blood test, and Jerry scanned it. *Probably changed the blood type on the report and then copied it,* he thought. *Fake ID sort of stuff.* That was just the sort of thing a capital case could do to a defense lawyer. He looked at the paper again. Yeah, he'd bet money this was fraud.

There would be time to prove that assumption. For now, he'd just keep his mouth shut and listen. He let McElroy explain things and bring him up to speed. From McElroy's story, it seemed like there were a lot of coincidences and unprovable things going on here, not the least of which was blaming the dead guy, Deegan. Plus, the timing was suspicious, to say the least.

Connick told Jerry and Val that they needed to find out what was real and what was bullshit, and to stay out ahead of the media. Connick was getting ready to announce an official grand jury investigation into the matter, he said, but because he and McElroy had talked to Whittaker before any official investigation had been set up, they had made themselves potential witnesses. They needed someone else to organize the investigation and question witnesses on behalf of the DA's office.

Jerry was eager to accept the task. Connick and McElroy told him to do some digging, but gave specific instructions that he not contact any of the DAs involved. Jerry looked over at Val, who nodded, and Jerry knew he had his orders.

THAT AFTERNOON, JUDGE Quinlan's clerk escorted Gordon and Michael into the judge's chambers. Connick was already there.

The Big Easy way of doing things still surprised and amazed Gordon. If a lawyer went over to see a judge without telling the other side in Philadelphia, he'd be close to getting disbarred. Not in New Orleans. No, in these parts, the DA could waltz into a criminal judge's office all by himself and have an ex parte discussion with the judge. It didn't mean that anything inappropriate was happening, but the *potential* for impropriety was certainly in the air, and Gordon suspected that it happened more often than not.

The men exchanged the usual pleasantries, and Judge Quinlan said to Michael and Gordon, "Mr. Connick has explained to me the situation, I suspect fairly, but I would like to hear your side of it."

Michael told their story again. Connick and Judge Quinlan listened until he was finished. Connick acknowledged to Judge Quinlan that what Michael said appeared to be true, that based on this newly discovered scientific evidence, which had been in the DA's possession and should have been turned over to the defense, John Thompson should not have been convicted of armed robbery.

For Judge Quinlan, this was a very serious matter. He had read Mike Riehlmann's affidavit and was clearly upset. He reminded Connick that he had spoken many, many times with assistant DAs in this case about their obligation to turn over *Brady* material that could be used by the defense to show John Thompson's innocence, and the DAs had repeated over and over again that no *Brady* evidence existed.

"Now, on the eve of Mr. Thompson's execution, we find out we do have a problem," said the judge.

"This Court is not going to dispense justice in this case in some back-room fashion. I'm going to stay Mr. Thompson's execution pending a full review of these facts and their implications to the armed robbery. We're going to have a public hearing, on the record, in open court, where both State and Defense will have the ability to call and examine witnesses. We are going to learn what happened here, and who did what, when."

Connick protested, arguing that because the motion to vacate Thompson's armed robbery conviction was unopposed by either party, such a public hearing was unnecessary, but Quinlan was having none of it. The judge wanted the actions of the DA's office on the record, in open court.

The judge scheduled a hearing in sixty days to allow both sides to explain what had happened and its impact on John Thompson's guilt and sentencing. Michael asked the judge whether the hearing would also encompass their request for a new trial in the murder case, which Connick opposed. The judge left that possibility open, saying that if the armed robbery was vacated as both parties were currently seeking, he would entertain arguments from each side about the impact of the armed robbery case on the murder case, both on guilt and on sentencing issues.

It was a good outcome for Michael and Gordon. First and foremost, against all odds, John was back "off the clock," his execution postponed indefinitely. He would get to live knowing that his son had graduated from high school, and knowing that whatever his faults as a father, he had not ruined such a momentous day for his son.

What really made this different, though, was having the DA's office on the run. Quinlan had made his displeasure with Connick quite clear, and for the first time, they had a client who was *innocent* of something. The blood test was a string, and as they pulled on it, more and more of the legal straitjacket that had restricted them was coming apart. It was too soon to see if they could escape it altogether, but Michael allowed himself some hope for what felt like the first time in a long while.

APRIL 30, 1999

JERRY'S FIRST MOVE in his investigation was to go down to the evidence room and get a clean copy of both the lab report and the hand-written notes from the lab tech who had conducted the test. To his great surprise, Thompson's lawyers weren't forging anything. The blood test was legitimate, and the type B result was confirmed by the handwritten notes from the tech.

Next, he pulled the police report on the armed robbery. No mention of blood evidence in the police file, so nothing there to alert the defense attorney trying the case. Who was the public defender? He leafed through the file—ah, Numa Bertel. Glas knew Numa. Everyone knew Numa. And a guy with his experience would have asked for this kind of information.

Jerry kept skimming through the file. Yes, there it was—Bertel's discovery request to Dubelier looking for "all scientific evidence." Dubelier had responded, saying that any evidence the DA had would be made available.

Interesting, Jerry thought. *The response predates the blood test.* He thought for a second, then reopened the trial transcript. The samples of the bloody shoes and pant leg had been collected by the crime scene tech on the scene, a guy named Cusimano. Cusimano's examination, according to the transcript, had been conducted by Gerry Deegan, rather than by Williams. Deegan had asked about the photos but not about the blood samples.

That wouldn't have raised any questions during the trial, but looking back on it now, it seemed a conspicuous absence. What had happened to the shoe and the pant leg? They'd want to get them retested.

Jerry walked down to Central Evidence and Property. He was told that it was official procedure to destroy all physical evidence after five years. The blood samples were long gone. But CEP still had the property card that showed the chain of custody, the list of everyone who had had the physical evidence in their possession since it was first checked in by the cops. The last entry showed the materials being checked out by Deegan.

Jerry scanned the property card. Seven pieces of evidence had been checked out. Five were checked back in. The pant leg and shoe were missing.

Jerry called Val and briefed him. Val took it all in, and told Jerry he'd report it to Connick and McElroy.

SEVERAL HOURS LATER, Val and Jerry walked into Connick's office. There was one new person in the room—a reporter from the *Times-Picayune*. Jerry hadn't met her before, but he'd seen her around the courthouse, and he recognized her name from the paper. He wasn't entirely surprised to see her—this was going to be a big story. In fact, he was surprised it wasn't already a big story. Staying in front of it was smart.

Connick asked the reporter what she knew about the story. The reporter had spoken to Thompson's lawyers, who seemed to be taking the high road. Certainly, they were arguing that Thompson should get a new trial because this altered the outcome not only of the armed robbery trial, but also of the murder trial. But they weren't yet holding press conferences to complain about deliberate misconduct by the DA's office. The reporter also had a quote from Nick Trenticosta: "We are not clear yet on what happened, whether something fell through the cracks or whether a prosecutor knew about it." They were still playing ball, not trying to embarrass Connick. And Whittaker hadn't named any names. So far, so good.

Connick was in campaign mode: "This is a first for us. I've been DA for twenty-five years, and I did something today that I've never done before. I went and joined with defense lawyers in a motion suggesting that a convicted felon's writ of execution should be stayed until we really know what went on here. These are serious matters that were brought to our attention. This is not a question of whether Mr. Thompson is guilty, but whether the process was infected by these matters—whether there was an absence of turning over evidence."

McElroy chimed in, pointing out that the lab report in question had not been in the DA's file on the Thompson case at all. Certainly, it wasn't supposed to be that way, and neither McElroy nor

Connick could say for sure why the evidence had not been in their files, but since none of the DAs involved were still with the DA's office, it would take them a little time to understand what had happened, how, and why.

The reporter nodded as she wrote in her notebook, and Connick took over the conversation again. He handed her a copy of the lab report. It was dated April 9, 1985, two days before Thompson's armed robbery conviction, and a month before the murder trial. "Standard procedure in the office," Connick said, "would have been to compare Thompson's blood type to the type B blood found on the pants. We're going to do now what should have been done then, and we're going to authorize the testing of the pant leg, including using DNA, which they didn't have the ability to do in 1985."

Jerry looked up. Didn't Connick know that the pant leg and shoe had been destroyed? He looked at Solino, but Val didn't give any signal.

Connick was still talking, getting to the main point he wanted to deliver. "Whether or not John Thompson committed this armed robbery, the murder conviction is something we're quite comfortable with. But we felt we had to do this now. John Thompson can rest a little easier—for now."

With that, the reporter departed, but the prosecutors stayed in the room.

Connick and McElroy had been briefed by Val already. Connick waited for the door to close, then said, "Look, my concern is this: Let's say we go investigate this. Is it worth our while? This happened in 1985, for God's sake. Aren't we prescribed? The statute of limitations? Hasn't the clock run out on our prosecuting anyone for this? I mean, we couldn't prosecute Thompson for the armed robbery now—it's too late. How can we prosecute our own guys for something bad they may have done then?"

Jerry was a little surprised that Connick didn't already know this, but he had researched that issue: "Mr. Connick, the doctrine on the statute of limitations in civil court is called *contra non valentem*. It's used in civil court, negligence cases. Say you've got a doctor who leaves a sponge in a body after a surgery, something like that. In civil court, the clock starts ticking when the sponge is discovered, not when the surgery occurs. So in civil court, I'd say no, you're not prescribed. But there's no direct case law that extends to a criminal case.

"So we know that Deegan checked out the pants and shoes, and they never got checked back in. Does the clock start ticking when Deegan hides the evidence, or when people find out about it? I think it has to be when the discovery of malfeasance occurs, so we're not prescribed. But I can't guarantee that a court will feel the same way."

Val spoke up. "Mr. Connick, you mentioned a grand jury yesterday. I think that should still be the plan. We should convene a grand jury to see whether any of the former prosecutors involved here should be charged. We've got Deegan checking out seven pieces of evidence, and only checking in five. With Riehlmann's affidavit, we've got a pretty clear case against Deegan. But Deegan didn't try the case alone. I don't know what Jim Williams did or didn't do, but it's not going to surprise anyone that he was first chair on this case. And Dubelier had his share of *Brady* issues while he was here. You want to stay out ahead of this, say that this is the sort of thing we won't stand for at all, we won't tolerate this, and we're conducting an investigation into it. I think the grand jury is the way to go."

Jerry watched Connick. Grand juries met on Thursdays, so if they went forward, he'd have five days to put together their first list of witnesses and examinations. Connick turned to McElroy. "Tim?"

McElroy considered. "I'm not a fan of investigating ourselves, and I'm not sure I agree that we aren't prescribed. I wouldn't do the grand jury. Once you go there, you lose control of what's going on."

Connick looked at Val and Jerry and said, "I'm going to announce a grand jury investigation into this on Monday. You boys keep digging, but don't talk to any of the prosecutors. Tim here will continue to handle that."

"Yes, sir," responded all three men. Val and Jerry left, leaving the district attorney and his first assistant alone in the office.

MAY 1, 1999

JERRY WAS LOOKING through the armed robbery file again. The timeline was telling. Bertel had asked for any and all scientific evidence related to the case. Dubelier's response was that it would be provided, but he hadn't mentioned the blood evidence. It was the day *after* Dubelier had filed that response that Deegan had checked out the evidence, including the shoe and pant leg. Jerry didn't know whether Bertel had gone looking for the evidence Dubelier had said he would provide, but if he had, it wouldn't have been there.

The Crime Lab conducted the test on the following Monday. That took a day, and then the results were typed and sent to Whittaker on Tuesday. The report was a rush job, because the trial had been scheduled for a Wednesday, but that was even pushed back a day due to other trials Williams and Deegan were handling.

Jerry thought about that. *It was a rush job.* That meant that even after writing "may want to do blood test" on the screening intake form months before, Whittaker had not made the actual request to conduct the test at that time. And that meant that it was one of the prosecutors, not the screener, who had ordered the blood test just before trial. They wanted more than the Lagarde eyewitness IDs, and they wanted to see what the blood test might show. They rushed it to get it done before the trial began, so Deegan had to run over Friday afternoon to get it to the Crime Lab so they could start on it Monday morning.

But would Deegan, as the junior ADA working with two of the more senior ADAs in the office, make that call himself?

No, thought Jerry. *Williams or Dubelier ordered this. They had to.*

The scary question, the one he wasn't really ready to ask himself yet, was whether this plan went higher than Dubelier or Williams. *What will you do then, Jerry?* he thought.

LATER THAT DAY, Jerry walked into the conference room and poured himself a Styrofoam cup of virtually undrinkable coffee. He sat at a table with Connick, Val, and McElroy to hear what Bruce Whittaker had to say.

Whittaker admitted that he had requested the test from the lab and that he had received the report. Given that his name was on the report, it would have been hard to argue otherwise. As for what he did with the report once he received it, Whittaker screwed up his face, like he wasn't sure, or didn't like what he was about to say. He was clearly uncomfortable, tense and squirming. "I've been trying to remember that. Best I can remember is, I took the report when it came in and put it on Jim Williams's desk. I was trying the *Norris Vessel* case on that day, so I wouldn't have spent a lot of time on it, but I would have known that Jim would have wanted it for his case, so I got it to him as quick as I could."

"Did Williams ever get the report?"

"I don't know. I assume so, since I left it on his desk."

"What did he do with it?"

"I don't know."

Jerry thought, *We've got to get Jim Williams in front of that grand jury and hear his story.*

MAY 6, 1999

THE NEWSPAPER HEADLINE really didn't surprise Michael any. Connick had declared a grand jury investigation into his own office. He was getting a lot of phone calls from well-wishers, folks from New

Orleans who told him what an amazing achievement this was, that Harry Connick had never done this before. Michael knew better. It was a publicity stunt. Connick had Deegan and Riehlmann as fall guys if anything got too serious.

Michael also knew that it would never come to that. The grand jury was investigating the DA's office, but who empaneled the grand jury? The DA. Who would conduct the investigation? Other assistant DAs. Who had the power to call off the investigation? Harry Connick. And best of all, Connick was prohibited by law from ever telling anyone about what was told to the grand jury.

Michael was impressed with the plan's elegance. Connick called a press conference, got all the flashbulbs to pop while announcing that he'd convene a blue-ribbon grand jury investigation. He would have his own guys go through the motions for a couple of weeks, and when the flashbulbs moved on to the next story, he would slip onto page eight below the fold in the *Times-Picayune* with some technical reason to explain why the investigation didn't find anything. The grand jury would be dissolved, and that would be that. Connick would get all the benefit without ever having to find anyone who would really address whether it was Dubelier and Williams, or whether they were following orders from Connick or McElroy—or worse, whether this was a pattern and practice of the way the DA's office goes about its business.

WEDNESDAY, MAY 12, 1999

JERRY WALKED INTO Connick's office and looked around. He wasn't surprised at the group he saw assembled there: Connick, McElroy, Solino, and Connick's personal lawyer.

Jerry originally thought that this assignment was a reward for his loyalty. He knew now it was a test of it, and he was going to fail.

The past six days with the grand jury had convinced Jerry that the right thing for the DA's office to do was to indict Jim Williams and Bruce Whittaker for prosecutorial misconduct and conspiracy.

Unfortunately, he hadn't been able to convince Harry Connick of that course of action.

Indicting ex-ADAs wouldn't make Connick or the office look good, to be sure, but wasn't it better to go public with the acknowledgment—*the truth*—and the fact that it was finally being dealt with? He was sure that was the way they had to go. It was the law, it was the professional code of conduct, and it was the right thing to do.

Connick nodded when he came in, the expression on his face looking like he'd just taken a big swig of sour milk. Jerry sat down at the table and looked around at the men. No one else spoke, so he took a deep breath and started on the same argument he'd been making for the past week, hoping that this time, Connick might see the light.

"Sir, our investigation has revealed that this was, in fact, a criminal enterprise designed to hide evidence that could have exonerated Mr. Thompson. The leader of the enterprise, the real bad guy here, is Jim Williams. He was in charge of the armed robbery case. He knew about the existence of the blood samples on the shoe and pant leg. We know this because at a pretrial discovery motion, he told the Court, in front of defense counsel, that the prosecution might want to take a blood sample from the defendant. We haven't been able to find any instance where he, or anyone else, actually told Mr. Bertel or other defense counsel about the existence of the blood samples. We have a written discovery request from Mr. Bertel asking for scientific evidence, and we have Mr. Dubelier's response that such evidence 'would be made available,' but no one specifically said, 'We've done a blood test.' We also have Williams, in his trial report given to Bertel and to Judge Quinlan, saying that there is no corroboration for the identifications of Mr. Thompson by the Lagardes.

"I checked the DA files, to see if the blood report was in the DA's case file," Jerry continued, "and it wasn't. So the report goes from the Crime Lab to Whittaker's in-box, and then Whittaker says he puts it on Williams's desk, but the report stops there. It doesn't make it into the file. The file now has Williams's signature on it on the inside front cover showing that he closed it out. He's an experienced prosecutor at this point; he knows the file is supposed to be complete and have everything in it before he closes it out, but there it is, signed and complete, without a blood test he had received.

"So what you've got is some sort of conspiracy," said Jerry. "Williams and Deegan, certainly; Whittaker, almost certainly; Dubelier, maybe. Williams's story is that he didn't know anything at the time. What he does say, though, is that sometime after all of this, months, maybe years after, he's with Deegan in a bar, and Deegan is drunk and starts to tell him about withholding some evidence. Williams says—and I can't believe this; if it's true, it's bad, but if it's a lie, it's the dumbest lie I've ever heard—but Williams says he told Deegan to stop talking, that he stopped Deegan before he could say anything more.

"So, Mr. Connick, what we have, the recommendation that Val and I are going to make, is, I've got two typed-up indictments here for Bruce Whittaker and Jim Williams for obstruction of justice and malfeasance in office."

"Nothing on Dubelier?" Connick asked.

"No, sir, not yet. We don't have enough evidence to charge Mr. Dubelier with anything at this point. But we hand down indictments on Whittaker and Williams, I think that we might get one of them to start telling us what really happened, and we might learn enough to know how high this went, whether Dubelier was involved. Plus, I've got a list of additional witnesses—"

"No." Connick interrupted. He was speaking calmly, but there was a tone of seriousness in his voice. "We're not charging anyone with anything. You're not giving anyone those indictments. I'm not ruining the careers of good prosecutors because of some rogue DA with a drinking problem who drank himself to death in the meantime. Deegan did this, the man suffered, now he's dead. That's it. That's as far as this case goes."

Jerry looked around the table. He hadn't really expected any support, but he looked around anyway. No one said a word. Val was looking at him, the look not encouraging. Val thought the same way Jerry did, Jerry knew that. He had helped Jerry type up the indictments. But he wasn't going to cross a direct order from the DA himself.

Jerry put his head down and took a deep breath. He looked up at Connick, and said, "Sir, you asked me to manage this investigation. I was in that room with the grand jury when we empaneled them last week. They didn't believe that the DA's office would investigate itself, that we'd turn the light on our own people. I gave those people my word; I made them a promise that I'd show them every piece of evidence that we found. I told them I'd call every witness to help them understand the truth here."

"What do you have here?" Connick asked. "This isn't an investigation. This is a witch hunt. We can't charge people here. We can't charge anyone with this. You've got no proof. All this evidence is circumstantial."

Val spoke up. "Sir, you're right, all of this is circumstantial, but of course, we charge people on circumstantial evidence all the time here." Jerry took note of Val's tone. He was being careful, not raising his voice, not taking on the DA directly. "Jerry's investigation is excluding every reasonable reason for the actions, and you're left with obstruction of justice and malfeasance."

Jerry jumped in, ignoring Val's look that said *Shut up*. "Mr. Connick, I think it's quite possible that a jury *would* convict based on what we have today." He could hear the emotion in his voice, knew that it wasn't helping his argument, but he couldn't stop himself. "If I need to, Mr. Connick, I can try this case myself and get a conviction with this evidence, circumstantial or not."

He knew he had gone too far, even before receiving the DA's withering stare, a mix of fury and shock at this junior assistant who had the balls to talk to him like this.

Connick held that stare on Jerry as the room got quiet, but Jerry glared right back. *I'm right. Hell if I'm going to back down from this,* he thought. Finally, Connick broke off the eye contact, turned to McElroy and the others, and said, "Let's go around the room. What have we got here? I mean, I don't care if there *is* enough evidence or not, it's prescribed."

Jerry snapped. He threw his arms out, yelling, "We've talked about this. We've been *through* this. The Supreme Court says the standard for prescription is that the clock starts ticking when the wrong is discovered. They wouldn't say if you keep it hidden for five years, it's a crime, but if you keep it hidden for six years, it's not a crime.

"And besides, Mr. Connick, even if you believe it's prescribed, that isn't the DA's call to make. It's an affirmative defense." He realized he was yelling, swallowed, took a breath, and lowered his voice. "Sir, the DA's job—our *obligation*—is to charge these men for the crimes they've done. We need to make these charges and let Williams and Whittaker defend themselves, let the courts decide the legal issue."

Connick looked at him, that same stare, mixed now with amazement, almost pity. "No. We're done here. We're finished."

McElroy jumped in, talking over Connick. Connick held up his hand, silencing McElroy and saying, "Is there even a duty to turn over the blood test anyway? The blood test doesn't prove that Thompson did or didn't commit the murder at that point. Williams, Deegan, they don't know anything. If you don't intend to use that piece of paper and you don't actually know what John Thompson's blood type is, then you don't have a duty to turn it over, do you?"

McElroy was nodding now. "That's right. That's right."

Jerry looked back and forth from McElroy to Connick, incredulous. "That's not right. That's ridiculous. That's the most ridiculous thing I've ever heard in my life. If you don't use it, it's not *Brady* and you have no obligation to turn it over? That's what we're going to go with?"

Jerry continued: "Sir, please . . . just let me go in and tell them the evidence. Let me show it to the grand jury, and let's see what they say. I gave them my word I'd show them the evidence. Let me do that, and then after that you can tell them whatever you want."

Connick was yelling now. "No! Goddammit, we're not—*you're not*—showing them another piece of paper!"

"Why?" Jerry was shocked at himself, at his insubordination. But what else was there to do?

Connick looked at him like he was talking to a child, speaking slowly and definitively: "Because that will make my job more difficult."

The room got quiet again. Jerry thought, *I'm twenty-nine years old, and this is all I've ever wanted to do.* He was good at it, too. That was the most difficult part of all of this. It was maybe the first thing he'd ever been really good at in his entire life. *I'm good with the victims, I'm good with the witnesses, and I'm a good trial lawyer.* He looked down at his shoes, the soles worn down because he couldn't afford to get them resoled yet, thought about his wife, the baby on the way. He looked up, and said, "Well, then, your job just got more difficult."

JERRY STOOD IN front of a cardboard box balanced on his desk chair. He was looking at a Certificate of Merit, given to him last year by Tim McElroy. McElroy had written *Congratulations, and a great result from a rising star* across the bottom. Jerry fingered the corner of the thick paper, looked at the seal of the District Attorney for the Parish of Orleans, State of Louisiana. The room was empty except for him, the lights off except for the cube underlight shining on his desk and hands.

After his outburst, Connick had just looked at him. Finally, the DA said, "Why are you being a pain in my ass?"

Jerry knew it was done, but he tried to pull it back anyway. He asked Connick to think about what he was telling Jerry to do. Connick was asking him to withhold evidence from a grand jury probe into rogue DAs hiding evidence. He tried to make Connick see that he, Jerry, was trying to *protect* the office, not smear its image.

All he had wanted to do was to live up to his promise to the grand jury, to show them everything. *Stupid,* he thought. He sat down at his computer and typed the letter he knew he'd need in the morning. He put a few things in a box, walked them out to his car, and drove home to tell his wife that he'd lost his job.

THURSDAY, MAY 13, 1999

THE NEXT DAY, Jerry went right to McElroy's office, not even stopping at his own desk. He knocked on the open door and walked in. He asked, one last time, to be able to show the evidence to the grand jury.

McElroy looked up and shook his head in disbelief. "Jerry, you know and I know that's not going to happen."

Jerry held up the resignation letter he was holding in his left hand and put it on McElroy's desk.

By the time Jerry walked back to his cube, the office pager blared, asking Solino to call McElroy. Jerry pulled up a chair, opened the first file on his desk, and started to write up a transfer memo for one of his cases.

It was only about five minutes later that Solino came over to escort Jerry out of the building. There were a couple of NOPD officers coming. He told Jerry not to take anything.

Jerry smiled, shaking his head. He extended his hand, thanking Val for all the opportunities he had given him. Over a hundred trials, several years of his life, and here he was getting thrown out of the building like a messy drunk.

Fifteen minutes later, Harry Connick ended the grand jury probe into the misuse of evidence in John Thompson's armed robbery trial.

39

A NEW TRIAL?

JUNE 29, 1999

GORDON AND **M**ICHAEL got out of their taxicab at the corner of Tulane and Broad. As Gordon paid the cabbie, Michael looked up at the dirty, gray-stone gothic edifice with its cast-iron moldings around the windows.

They were at the courthouse for the public hearing demanded by Quinlan in April to evaluate the blood evidence and its impact on the case. Whatever Quinlan's view of John, it was clear he was unhappy with Connick, and that he expected to give the DA a public tongue-lashing. While that would be enjoyable, Michael and Gordon wanted more. They would be satisfied with nothing less than a new trial on John's murder conviction.

To do that, they had engaged Robert Glass, a well-respected criminal defense lawyer from New Orleans, to help them. They wanted Robert to help them prepare and describe the case the way a New Orleans judge and jury were used to seeing it, and someone whose reputation in the community would give their case credibility with the DAs and Judge Quinlan.

They walked into the courtroom and saw Robert standing at the defense table. He was a thin man with a shock of gray hair and a manner that was so unassuming and quiet that Gordon wondered whether a jury would even be able to hear him in the courtroom. Still, his résumé was impressive, including a string of improbable victories in criminal defense cases in New Orleans dating back to his landmark defense of several Black Panthers in murder trials in the 1960s.

The three men had agreed that Robert would do most of today's talking, as a sort of dress rehearsal for the new trial they wanted, and to see if their new "strategy" would get them where they wanted to go.

Harry Connick and Tim McElroy walked in and put their brief-cases down. It was a rare day indeed when the top two lawyers in the DA's office came in themselves to conduct a hearing. Michael would have expected a crowd based on the subject matter alone, but with Connick and McElroy both stepping into the ring together, the courtroom would have a rotating audience of ADAs and press taking advantage of a rare chance to see how the big chiefs conducted themselves in court. Connick would have been the first to tell anyone that he didn't really practice law after he became the DA. He was a politician and a manager more than a lawyer. The Orleans Parish DA's office handled 13,000 criminal prosecutions every year, and managing the number of lawyers needed to handle that volume ensured that the DA himself was almost never in court. Today, though, Quinlan had the DA under his thumb. The integrity of Connick's office was at stake, and that meant he had to face the music.

Michael was certain that by the end of the day, John's armed robbery conviction would be thrown out. Connick had asked for that already, and Quinlan would grant it once he was finished with this hearing. The question was, what would Quinlan do to John's murder conviction once the armed robbery was thrown out? It seemed obvious to Michael that once the armed robbery was thrown out, there was no way that John's death penalty could stand, and the fact that Quinlan had scheduled this hearing seemed to suggest that the judge felt the same way. Still, even though it seemed that Quinlan agreed with them time and time again, the reality was that in the past fifteen years, he had never once ruled in John's favor.

Plus, for all of the Sturm und Drang they could generate on the blood test and cover-up, for all of the righteousness and accusations they would throw at the DA's office, what they really had evidence of was Deegan doing a cover-up in 1985 and Riehlmann not disclosing what he learned several years later. They had no hard evidence suggesting the cover-up went any higher than Jim Williams, and even that was flimsy. There was no evidence at all connecting it to Eric Dubelier, although Michael believed that a prosecutor as smart and aggressive as Dubelier would have known what was going on. Nor was there evidence connecting this to Connick. Barring some surprising revelation in today's testimony, Michael assumed they would never get such evidence. Even if Connick had been involved, he was too smooth to get tripped up on something like this.

There was one other troubling but unavoidable fact: They still had no new evidence suggesting that John Thompson was innocent of the murder of Ray Liuzza Jr. Today, for the first time in open court, Robert, Michael, and Gordon would disclose the cover-up of the blood evidence. They would be able to give voice to their belief that Dubelier, Williams, and Deegan deliberately hid the blood evidence to guarantee an armed robbery conviction, and that they used the armed robbery conviction to ensure that John's guilty verdict in the Liuzza murder trial would lead to a death sentence. But none of that would change the fact that the Liuzza jury's verdict of guilt had been reached without any information about the armed robbery case at all, from a jury that knew nothing of the Lagarde carjacking.

So really, the questions were whether Quinlan would agree with their argument that a new trial was needed because the armed robbery conviction had kept John from testifying in his own defense in the murder trial, and whether Quinlan would decide that the corrupt conduct of the DA's office was egregious enough to justify punishing the DA by revoking not only the armed robbery conviction, but the murder conviction as well.

Connick had played it smart so far. By filing the motion for a new armed robbery trial himself, he was positioning today's DA's office as honorable and respectable, its reputation besmirched solely by a rogue prosecutor. His personal appearance here with McElroy underscored how seriously he was taking the matter. And Quinlan, as an ex-ADA himself, was likely to be sympathetic to this position.

John Thompson was led over to the defense table, shaking the hands of Michael and Gordon, and meeting Robert for the first time. He looked quite different from their recent visit to Angola, walking with some spring in his step and a smile on his lips.

"You ready?" Michael asked.

John smiled. "Always ready to take the fight to Connie and Williams and Dubelier."

A voice boomed, "All rise."

Michael stood as Quinlan walked in from his door in the front of the courtroom. The sound of many other people standing in unison surprised Michael. He glanced around the courtroom, which had filled considerably during the past ten minutes, in which he'd been lost in thought.

Quinlan walked up to his seat, sat down, and brought the case to order. Connick stood to begin. If the district attorney was concerned by the predicted arc of the day, it didn't show. He looked distinguished and classy, and he spoke confidently to the judge.

"May it please the Court," Connick began. "The State has asked the Court to set aside the attempted armed robbery conviction and sentence in the case against John Thompson. This request is made because the State has failed to turn over a report, a report that the defense requested, and to which the defense was entitled. Even if this report had *not* been requested by the defense, it should have been given to them anyway. Had the report in question, the Crime

Lab report, been furnished to the defense, the outcome of the case would have been altered significantly.

"What will be shown at this hearing, therefore, will be that such a report existed, that the defense requested a copy of the report, that the State had the report and did not give it to the defense. Once the Court is satisfied that these are the facts upon which this motion is based, it should grant the State's request and set aside the conviction of the defendant, John Thompson. Once the Court does this, the State will immediately dismiss the armed robbery case against the defendant."

Quinlan showed no reaction to this. He simply said, "Call your first witness."

Connick called Bruce Whittaker. He showed Whittaker the screening report form that Whittaker had written back in early 1985. Whittaker read from it: "Gun same make and model as Liuzza weapon. The victim made photo ID, will be in town 3-11-85, if physical [lineup] desired. *May wish to do blood test*."

Next, Connick handed Whittaker the Crime Lab results and asked him to explain them. Whittaker said, "Well, in a nutshell, it indicates that a couple of items of evidence in the armed robbery, involving the victim, Jay Lagarde, were tested by the New Orleans Police Department Crime Lab for evidence. And one of the things was, apparently, Mr. Lagarde's pant leg. It was tested and found to be positive for Group B human blood. The other item was a tennis shoe. It, too, was tested and showed the presence of human blood, but they could not type it."

"And how did you come into possession of this document?" Connick's tone was serious and probing.

"I don't know. I know—I don't recall; it probably turned up on my desk or in-box, when I was in screening."

"So, what did you do with it when you received it?"

"My best recollection is that I passed it on to the trial attorneys, and I put it on Jim Williams's desk."

"Do you know if he ever saw this document?"

"I do not know."

"At the time that you received this document, did you talk to anyone else at all about the document?"

"Not that I recall."

"Thank you, Mr. Whittaker." With that, Connick sat down, and Robert Glass stood up, introducing himself to Whittaker in a voice so quiet Michael had to strain to hear it.

Their plan was to expand this hearing as much as possible. Quinlan may have limited his review to the armed robbery case, but to understand how this had happened, Michael and Gordon wanted Robert to get into the standard policies and procedures of the office. If they could show that Connick's management of the office was flawed, that would then lead to a question of whether there was anything left to learn in the murder case. What didn't they know there? Once that question was asked, Michael thought, Quinlan would have no choice but to grant John a new trial and authorize new discovery on the murder.

The strategy was no surprise to Connick, who quickly rose to interrupt Robert's questioning. "Your Honor, we are prepared to admit that this is a report, a blood type report that was not given to the defense, and as I understand the Court's interest in this, that we were going to limit the hearing today to what happened in this case and not go into the operations of the office and procedures of the officers and all of that."

Quinlan locked his eyes on Connick. "Mr. Connick, we are going to get into this case and what happened with this case. And what might have happened with other cases in your office, I'm not concerned about, but anything that did happen with this case, the Court is going to allow the defense. As I told you previously, I want on public record what happened with this case, and I'm going to allow Mr. Glass to ask about the history of this case." He turned to Robert and said, briskly, "You can proceed."

Gordon looked at Michael and raised his eyebrows. Quinlan was *pissed*. It was a good sign.

Robert conducted a thorough and methodical examination of Whittaker. Robert wasn't a particularly fast examiner, and his questioning style was unemotional, but both of those were good things in their current situation. His questioning pace kept the DA's wrongdoing in the spotlight, and his calmness conveyed a valuable objectivity and solemnity.

Robert spent a lot of time tracking the movements of the bloody pants and shoe, as crucial to their argument as the blood test itself. They had to prove that Numa Bertel had made reasonable efforts to learn about the existence of the blood evidence, and that the actions of the DA's office had prevented him from that, in order to show that the effect on John's armed robbery trial was "material."

For his part, Whittaker was a willing witness. He readily admitted that it was standard practice in the office to link cases together that involved the same defendant, and that the lesser offense—in this case, the armed robbery—would be transferred to the courtroom with the more serious offense—the murder. Robert asked Whittaker whether the murder case was being specially handled, and Whittaker pointed out in his screening report that Eric Dubelier was the Special Prosecutor. Michael was pleased—they had linked the robbery to the murder and shown that the same lawyers were involved. It wasn't proof, but it was certainly persuasive evidence that Dubelier and Williams should have known what was going on, and that this could all be part of a larger plan to frame John for the murder.

Robert had Whittaker explain the evidence custody card to Judge Quinlan, tracing the dates and locations of the blood samples as a way to address this argument. Looking deeper, they realized that the pants and shoe had been delivered the day before the three-day Easter weekend, so no work had been done until Monday, April 8, and the lab tech wrote his report on Tuesday, April 9. It gave the custody card credibility and implied (if one wanted to read it this way) that the DAs had waited until the last possible minute to test the blood, taking advantage of the holiday to maximize the time that the evidence was out of the vault and thus unavailable to John's defense.

With this done, Bruce Whittaker stepped down. Robert moved on to Numa Bertel. In particular, Robert wanted to hear about a statement made by Jim Williams at a pretrial motions hearing one month before the armed robbery case, a hearing attended by Bertel to discuss what evidence would be allowed.

Williams had stood up and told the Court, "It is the State's intention to file a motion to take a blood sample from the defendant, and we'll file that motion and have a criminalist here on the 27th."

This statement was crucial to both sides. To Michael, it was proof positive that Williams and Dubelier knew that they had blood evidence and intended to take a blood test. Connick and the DAs, of course, took the opposite view. To them, Williams's statement to the Court at the motions hearing showed that the fault here rested with Numa Bertel. Williams had publicly stated that he intended to take blood from John Thompson. To Connick's way of thinking, the burden of reacting then rested on Numa Bertel to see why the DA wanted to conduct this test. Connick thought Bertel should have known there was blood evidence—and if he had gone to the evidence locker, he could have had it tested himself. The fact that he didn't, to Connick, meant that his office was relieved of any further obligations.

As Connick rose to examine Bertel, the energy level in the courtroom rose noticeably, people leaning forward in their seats and whispers filling the air as Connick's legal nemesis walked to the stand to be interrogated by the DA himself. Bertel had been first assistant DA for Jim Garrison, Connick's predecessor, and had left the DA's office when Garrison lost the position to Connick.

Connick started by asking Bertel about the written request he had made to Dubelier for scientific evidence against Thompson in the armed robbery case. It was a standard form typically filed by the New Orleans Indigent Defender Program to obtain whatever evidence the DA's office might have that was related to the case.

The two men shadowboxed for the packed courtroom, Connick's questions rapid and precise, Bertel's answers the same. It was clear that Connick was on the attack—and equally clear that Bertel wasn't going to give any ground.

Connick pointed to Dubelier's answer to the motion for discovery of evidence that Bertel had submitted in April, 1984. "It says on here 'inspection to be permitted.'"

"Correct."

"Well, what did you do after you got this document? Did you try to find out what the State had that would have helped your client?"

"Yes, of course."

"Tell us what you did."

Bertel spoke calmly, plainly, and disdainfully. "Went down to the evidence room and checked all of the evidence, asked them for any reports, and we didn't get it."

"Tell me, where did you go to look at this to inspect the evidence?"

"To the clerk's office."

"And they didn't have anything over there?"

"They didn't have any blood evidence."

"Well, did you go anywhere else?"

"No place in this building, no."

"I didn't ask you if there was any other place in this building that you had gone into," Connick snapped. "What about another building somewhere else that you had access to?"

"There was no other building that I had access to."

Connick spoke more slowly, like Bertel was a child. "The gentleman on the bench up there wearing the black robe is the judge who can order the production of documents; you're familiar with that, are you not? It's in the code that you said you're familiar with. Why didn't you ask him to inspect this, to go look at this documentation, go look at the evidence?"

"Because there was nothing over there to inspect." Bertel gave Connick's tone right back to him.

"So, as a defense lawyer, it is not your procedure to find out what the State is going to use against your client at trial?"

"No, the State is supposed to advise me what evidence they have and where it is."

"So, the State is supposed to make your case—in other words, tell you 'This is all the evidence we have, Mr. Bertel.'" Connick was triumphant. "You don't have to do anything . . . just sit there in your defense chair and not do anything?"

It was the opening Bertel had wanted, and he didn't let it pass. He leaned forward slowly, expectantly, and spoke aggressively into the microphone, his words echoing through the courtroom. "You know what, Mr. Connick? That's exactly the way it works. That's *exactly* the way it works. We rest on a presumption of *innocence,* and it's your office's obligation to prove the case. That is correct. That was my obligation, and it didn't go any further."

That stung, thought Michael. But Connick moved on as if nothing had happened, asking Bertel why he hadn't examined the evidence in the courtroom on the day of trial. Bertel, of course, had inspected any physical evidence brought to court, but the box of physical evidence had not contained a bloody pant leg or shoe.

Next, Connick asked Bertel about the crime scene technician's report, which listed the pant leg and shoe as pieces of evidence collected from the scene. Bertel had never seen it before John's trial. Connick was indignant. "You mean to tell me that you are representing a man in an armed robbery case, and there is a crime scene report that lists the evidence from the crime, and you didn't look at this?"

"They didn't give it to me, Mr. Connick."

"Again, are you aware of the codal article which allows you to ask the judge to mandate the State to produce this to you?"

"Can't produce something if you don't know it exists."

"Never mind," Connick said, dismissing Bertel with a wave of his hand. "I have no further questions."

Robert Glass knew better than to disturb a good examination by digging too far. "No questions by the defense."

With Bertel's testimony done, Tim McElroy stood up and stipulated that John Thompson's blood type was O, not B. Connick tried again to end the hearing at this point. "The question that the Court wanted answered, I think we can address that now. John Thompson's blood type is type O. You have the document showing that the blood type that the policemen took of the perpetrator, whoever that is, is Type B. You have evidence that the document was never given to the defense. Therefore, they didn't get it, and I don't know beyond that what the Court would be interested in."

Quinlan was having none of it. "The Court, as I said, Mr. Connick, is interested in having the State prove up the allegations that they made in the motion for a new trial. So, we will proceed."

Connick just nodded. He had to be furious, thought Michael, but he was doing the dance required of him. "Your Honor, we would call Mike Riehlmann."

Riehlmann was a big guy, easily over six feet, with dark hair and a beard. He sat in the witness chair with his body turned in on himself, answering questions quietly, contritely. *He's ashamed*, thought Michael. It was too bad. Mike Riehlmann had done the right thing, even if it had been ten years too late. And his reward was that he was about to be the grand marshal of Harry Connick's scapegoat parade.

Connick started by asking Riehlmann if he was familiar with *United States v. Brady*. He established Riehlmann's close friendship with Gerry Deegan. And then he moved in for the body blows, asking why Riehlmann hadn't made Deegan turn himself in when Deegan confessed that he had withheld exculpatory information. "How do you view what he did?"

"Terrible. I think it was terrible."

"Did you tell him that?"

"Yes. I viewed it as terrible then, as I do now. And I told him that he should do something to remedy the situation."

Connick slipped easily into his role as a crusader for justice, distancing himself from his former employee and the other lawyers involved in John's case. "How do you regard your responsibility since you were the recipient of this information, which clearly was a violation of *Brady;* how do you view your responsibility in that regard?"

Riehlmann answered the only way he could. "I should have reported it. Ultimately, I did. But, I should have reported it sooner, I guess."

As Riehlmann talked, Michael began to think that maybe it had happened just like Riehlmann said, with neither Whittaker nor Riehlmann knowing anything at the time, and Deegan confessing to Riehlmann, who stayed quiet, not wanting to ruin his dead friend's legacy.

But there was another possibility, one Michael found more believable. Maybe Riehlmann was making up his own role now, to protect his law partner Whittaker. *Maybe Deegan did this, maybe it was Williams or Dubelier. Probably Williams. Whittaker gets the blood tested, shows it to Williams, maybe to Dubelier. They know it's B; they figure the odds are long that it's Thompson. Do they talk to Dubelier? Probably. They need the robbery conviction to get death because Thompson has no priors, nothing violent. They need the similarities in the Lagarde case so that if John takes the stand, they can hammer him.*

But now, the blood test surfaces, and Gordon and I show up. Now Whittaker is going to get tagged for being involved, since his name is on the report. Plus, Whittaker genuinely feels regret, and doesn't want John's death on his conscience. If he comes forward, though, he's exposed. So he goes to his buddy, Riehlmann, and they decide that Riehlmann will write the affidavit and blame Deegan, who's dead. They figure no one punishes Riehlmann for coming forward, and Whittaker is off the hook.

Connick's next question to Riehlmann snapped Michael back to the courtroom: "Did Mr. Deegan express his conviction to you that John Thompson committed a murder in which Mr. Liuzza was the victim?"

The old man still has some tricks left, Michael thought. With one question, Connick had given Deegan a motive that made him seem flawed, to be sure, but pragmatic and motivated by the greater good. At the same time, he reminded Quinlan that whatever John Thompson was or was not, he was still a convicted murderer in an as-yet-unchallenged first-degree murder case.

They broke for lunch, and Michael, Gordon, and Robert walked across the street to the requisite courthouse greasy spoon. They pulled up chairs, huddled closely, and assessed the morning, strategizing for the afternoon session. Robert would be cross-examining Eric Dubelier in the afternoon, and they needed to figure out the best approach. There was no way, in anyone's view, that Deegan had acted alone. Williams was the most logical driver, with his mini electric chair and all. Robert believed strongly that Dubelier had to be in on it as well. After all, according to Nick Trenticosta, Dubelier was known for saying, "It's not *Brady* if the defense never finds out about it."

ERIC DUBELIER WAS the first witness after lunch. *He must be pretty worried,* thought Michael, *if he flew all the way down to New Orleans to testify.* Though he was sure Dubelier would simply claim that he was doing his duty and didn't know anything about this, he had to be worried about what this would do to his reputation.

Dubelier looked just about the way Michael had pictured him. He was a bulldog of a guy, with a receding hairline and light hair that was slowly graying. His forehead sloped pugnaciously toward two gleaming, inset eyes, and his voice, while higher than you expected when you looked at him, was powerful and clear and conveyed a lot of emotion. He spoke quickly and intelligently, and answered Harry Connick's questions with vigor.

"Mr. Dubelier, what does your response to Mr. Bertel's discovery request say?" Connick asked.

"Inspection to be permitted," Dubelier said. He looked up at Connick. "Means they can inspect it, they can do whatever they want with it, other than destroy it."

Connick, in mock surprise, said, "So, no obstruction was placed in the way if defense lawyers wanted to see what evidence the police had, whether that evidence was in the property room of the Clerk of Court or in the custody of the Police Department?"

"That is correct."

Connick became fatherly and gracious. "I know you weren't involved in the armed robbery case," he began, "but I'm going to show you a document . . ."

Connick's questions continued in this theatrical, self-serving style. Michael wasn't surprised. Given Dubelier's high rank in the DA's office at the time, any suggestion that Dubelier was involved would bring the blame closer to Connick himself. No serious questioning would happen while Connick was asking the questions.

When Connick was done, Robert stood up, buttoning his blue suit jacket over his dark plaid shirt and his even darker tie and smoothing his wild, wiry hair. He knew about Dubelier's reputation for being ferocious and personal in the courtroom. In fact, he was counting on it.

"The Liuzza case was a very high-profile case," Robert stated.

"It was, yes, it was."

"A lot of publicity."

"I assume. I just don't remember."

"Substantial reward."

"I don't know what you mean by that."

"A reward put out, a $15,000 reward for information leading to the arrest and conviction in the Liuzza case," Robert clarified.

"My review last night of the appellate record of this case suggested that there was a reward involved, yes. If you had asked me about that before I had looked at those materials, I wouldn't have been able to tell you that."

"Now, once John Thompson was arrested and indicted, he was indicted for first-degree murder."

"Yes."

"You were seeking the death penalty."

"The State was seeking the death penalty. This wasn't me seeking the death penalty."

"Sure," said Robert, calmly. "You, as a representative of the State, were seeking the death penalty."

"That is correct."

"You, as the representative of the State, wanted to get the death penalty."

Dubelier's answer was careful. "It was the policy of the DA's office at the time that the death penalty would be pursued in all first-degree murder cases, and we were pursuing that in this case as we did in every other capital case that I handled."

"I see," Robert said, with a wry smile. "This capital case was handled no differently than any other capital case?"

"In this respect, that is correct." Neither Dubelier nor Quinlan were morons. They both heard the trap in Robert's question.

Robert changed direction, asking Dubelier about the armed robbery conviction. "You don't deny the fact that the robbery conviction was important to your presentation in the capital case?"

Dubelier leaned forward and spoke sharply. "It was one of several factors in the sentencing phase of the capital case. I believe there were other factors in the penalty phase of this trial that caused the penalty to be imposed that was imposed, and not the armed robbery conviction. What I remember about the penalty phase of this case—the most compelling evidence in the penalty phase was put on by Mr. Thompson's lawyers, who put on some nutty sociologist who testified, essentially, that Mr. Thompson wakes up every morning and commits crimes. I remember sitting next to Jim Williams at the table and we looked at each other, saying, Can you believe that this is their witness that they have called to testify in this penalty hearing? I believe it was that sociologist more than anything that caused the jury to impose the death penalty."

Michael hoped Quinlan noticed how much more detail Dubelier suddenly seemed to recall about the case once there were some facts in his favor.

Robert took another tack. "You wanted him convicted in the armed robbery case?"

Dubelier's temper, what Robert had been waiting for, made its first official appearance, his voice rising and his speech intensifying. "I had a responsibility as an assistant district attorney in any case that I prosecuted to do the best job that I could if I believed the person had committed the crime based on the evidence, to ensure that the people of the State of Louisiana were represented fairly, and that if a conviction was proper in the case, there would be a conviction.

"Mr. Glass, let me say something to you," Dubelier continued, "and then I'll be happy to sit here all day and answer your questions. I didn't do anything unethical. I didn't do anything illegal. I didn't do anything immoral in connection with any case I have ever prosecuted, period. I know that to a moral certainty. That is a fact. And if the purpose of your questions are to suggest to the contrary, my answer to you is that it didn't happen. Nor did it happen under my supervision, under any circumstances where I knew about it, period. Now, given that answer, I'll sit here and answer any questions you want to ask me."

Robert smiled his little smile again, his quiet voice keeping its cadence, slowing the courtroom back down again. "Now, of course, and I don't mean to be coy, given your little speech, but it's a fact, isn't it, that if you had hidden the exculpatory evidence that almost caused or allowed the execution of Mr. Thompson to go forward, you would not admit it on the witness stand?"

Connick almost jumped out of his chair. "We object! The question is absolutely uncalled for!"

Quinlan dismissed him. "Overruled. It's cross-examination."

Quinlan wants to hear the answer, Michael thought.

Robert continued: "You would not admit it if it happened?"

Dubelier was almost vibrating with anger now, his jaw clenched as he tried to control himself. "It didn't happen. You're asking me, Did I stop beating my wife? That's the type of question you're asking me. It didn't happen, period."

"And without quarreling over the value of your word, what we have is your word for that?" Robert didn't wait for an answer, asking instead, "Did you ever adhere to a policy that it's not *Brady* if the defense doesn't know about it?"

"Absolutely not."

"Did you ever say to anybody, 'We don't need to turn that over; if they don't know about it, it's not *Brady*'?"

"I don't know what you're talking about."

Robert slowed down and spoke even more quietly, forcing the courtroom to strain to hear him, and in so doing giving each word extra power. "Did you ever sit down with a lawyer who said evidence needed to be turned over to the defense, and you responded that if they don't know about it, it's not *Brady*?"

Dubelier went off like a Roman candle. "The answer to that is no. And if you have a legitimate basis by which to ask me that question, I ask that you state it right now and tell me who said I said that. Because that person's a liar."

Robert was surprised. "Are you examining me?"

"No, Mr. Glass, but you have an ethical obligation before asking me a question like that—"

"*You're* telling *me* that *I* have an ethical obligation?"

"Mr. Glass, you're making accusations against me, and you better have a reasonable basis for it."

"I better?"

"That's right." Dubelier was spitting his words out, hunched forward, almost shaking with anger.

Quinlan stepped in. "Your argument has gone on long enough."

Robert sighed. "I'll be happy to tell you where it came from in another setting. But the fact is, it has been said."

"It is a *lie*."

Michael was pleased. *This is the rush that makes these DAs go overboard,* he thought, *catching someone doing something wrong, and showing them in public for what they really are.* They had never expected to break Dubelier on the stand, but they had hoped to reveal his righteous indignation to the Court. Dubelier, for his part, was clearly upset, answering a few more questions from Connick in a curt, red-faced fashion, and practically leaping off the witness stand. He walked between the counsel tables, pausing next to Robert as if he had something more to say before walking on, out of the courtroom, to the street and the airport beyond.

IT WAS TIME for the defense witnesses. First up was the one Michael and Gordon had wanted all day—Jim Williams.

Michael's scenario for the conspiracy—Dubelier being more involved than he let on, Riehlmann taking a fall for Whittaker—all of that was conjecture. But Williams was different. No matter how you cut it, Jim Williams needed to be punished for what he'd done to John Thompson. Williams was a schoolyard bully, and this was a sanctioned rumble, with the whole school gathered around to watch.

While John sat in prison, Williams had given an interview to a reporter for *Esquire* magazine who was researching the death penalty. He reveled in his role as a weapon of vengeance and justice, and bragged about how tough he was in court, how he and his prosecutor buddies would walk past defendants charged with murder and make buzzing noises to sound like the electric chair. He had crowed then about his coldness—how he could get someone sentenced to death and then order a big meal without a care in the world. The reporter had taken photographs of Williams in his office, sleeves rolled up, knuckles on his desk, posing sternly over his miniature electric chair, with John Thompson's photo front and center.

Williams's self-congratulatory machismo wasn't limited to Thompson, either. Not by a long shot. Once Louisiana became a lethal injection state, he and his colleagues started giving each other plaques to celebrate death penalty convictions. They called them the "Big Prick" awards—giant hypodermic needles mounted on pieces of wood. And, more recently, his mockery of prosecutorial objectivity had included working with colleagues who wore neckties with nooses on them to court in capital punishment cases in nearby Jefferson Parish, where the DA was none other than Paul Connick, Harry's nephew.

Michael had to admit that he was looking forward to taking Williams down a peg or two in the public eye. He wanted Williams to know that he had disgraced the job of the prosecutor, that he had been corrupted by the power invested in him, and that he had cheapened the criminal justice system with his bravado and his insensitivity. He wanted to embarrass Williams for deliberately ruining John's life.

It was clear as Williams walked to the witness stand that he knew he was in trouble. The "cock of the walk" profiled in *Esquire* magazine was nowhere to be seen as Williams shuffled uncertainly to the stand, casting furtive glances at the judge and Harry Connick. Williams was a pretty big guy, maybe six-foot-two, 220 pounds, his eyes mere slits behind his glasses but his posture suggesting contrition and fear. His narrow lips pursed nervously and his gait was clipped, his shoulders sloped a little forward. For a guy who talked so tough and laughed so hard about how his victims would fare poorly in prison, Williams looked like a guy who was not at all sure he'd do any better.

Even more than Dubelier, Williams suffered from "Thompson Alzheimer's," unable to remember even the most basic details of the case. To the extent he remembered anything, he recalled that the armed robbery had really been Eric Dubelier's case, because it was connected with the capital murder case that Williams said Dubelier was in charge of. (Of course, in Dubelier's testimony, Williams had been the one calling the shots in the armed robbery case.) Even more important, at the time of the discovery hearing, Williams explained in a subdued voice that he had not expected to have any further role in the case; he'd only handled the discovery motions as a favor to Dubelier.

Robert had been speaking calmly from behind the podium, but now he casually walked out toward the jury box. Michael and Gordon had come to recognize this as his signal that a loaded question was coming. It came, in the same tone as all of his previous questions: "If the DA's office has evidence and says we want to withdraw blood and then does nothing about it, why is that a problem for the defense?"

Williams dissembled for a moment about the trial being fourteen years ago, and then collected himself. "My opinion is that the defense was aware that blood was an issue and chose not to follow up on it."

Robert pounced. "You had a conversation with Mr. Bertel about that?"

"I do not recall. I may have. I do not recall."

"You're speculating that Mr. Bertel had a conversation with his client, and that you may have had a conversation with him, and you have *nothing* to back either of those things up, do you?"

"Mr. Glass, I don't want to spar with you or be disrespectful to you because I understand the job you have today, but my best reconstruction of these events is the fact that the defense never objected to our proceeding with this case. The only thing, the *only* thing that I can presume from this is that they weren't interested in the blood evidence either. And perhaps Mr. Bertel felt that this was the best defense of the case, to defend it on the ID rather than to risk the fact that if blood was taken back in 1984—which certainly he had the right to do—he could have filed a motion on behalf of Mr. Thompson to withdraw blood. The discovery answer was 'inspection to be permitted.' I can only assume that Mr. Bertel availed himself of that opportunity that was given by Mr. Dubelier, or he ignored it."

Robert wasn't satisfied. "Are you telling us that prior to trial on April 11th of 1985, that you didn't know that the blood evidence had been sent from Central Evidence and Property to the Crime Lab for typing?"

Williams backpedaled. "I'm saying I don't recall if I knew it or not."

"You're saying you *could* have known it?"

"I'm saying that, Mr. Glass. I do not recall whether or not I knew the blood was being tested."

Robert, without changing his volume, nevertheless managed to convey his outrage at Williams's lack of knowledge on such a key point. Did Williams ask Deegan? He didn't recall. Did he ask Whittaker? He didn't recall. Did he ask Dubelier?

At that question, Williams changed his answer. No surprise, thought Michael, since Dubelier was Williams's fall guy. "I'm sure that we had a discussion."

Robert waded in again. "So that a decision not to use blood evidence was a conscious decision—you're certain of that—a conscious decision before the trial began?"

"Yes, sir." Williams paused. "Uh, I mean, I'm speculating that is true."

Having pinned Williams's testimony down, and having established his alibi as a string of *I don't remember*'s, Robert sat down. The respite for Williams was brief, however; Connick was clearly in no mood to coddle Williams. Now that Williams was out of Orleans Parish, Connick could hang him out to dry. Williams had become a rogue that Connick had already dealt with by firing him, and now he became a convenient fall guy.

"You have talked about the opportunity of the defense lawyer to check these things out because they were on the table in front of you when the case was being tried, as I understand it?" Connick asked.

"Down in the basement, yes, sir, they were," said Williams.

"But then again, as Mr. Glass said, while they have an obligation to represent their client very fully, the primary obligation is upon the State to make these things known to the defense; am I correct?"

Robert stood up. "Judge, may I enter an objection? This isn't an examination of Mr. Williams—it's a statement by Mr. Connick."

Judge Quinlan swiveled in his chair and fixed Connick with a stare. "What he is saying is you should have had this conversation with Jim Williams fourteen years ago."

The courtroom gasped. Quinlan had just given every news outlet in the city its headline for the next edition. Pencils started scribbling in reporters' notebooks throughout the courtroom. Almost everyone missed Quinlan's punch line, though: "The objection is overruled."

The district attorney was not accustomed to being slapped like that, let alone in public. Still, he was smart enough to push through and not show the red mark on his face. He moved on to the more recent dialogue between Williams and Whittaker, when Williams told Whittaker about Deegan trying to confess to him, and Williams's curt reply, "I don't want to know" before he walked away.

Williams's recollection was somewhat different: "I told Mr. Whittaker that I recall there being a time in the past where Gerry was very sick and not taking care of himself and was pretty much out of control when he approached me, boasting about something, and I walked away from him."

"Why did you walk away?" Connick continued.

"Because I didn't want to hear it."

"How did you know what he was going to say?"

"I just anticipated that he may have been wanting to say something that I didn't want to hear."

If Connick wasn't truly disgusted with Williams, Michael thought, his tone and expression were pretty convincing. "No further questions."

It was close to 5:00 PM. Quinlan called a recess before closing statements.

Gordon grabbed Michael's shoulder, and whispered, "Believe Williams or not, did you hear what he just said? Sometime in the late 1980s, Deegan approached Williams and *tried to confess*. Williams must have known that he was referencing Thompson, or why would it come up now? So his story is, he didn't know about the blood test, but he *did* deliberately avoid learning the truth, turned his back on it, and left John in the hell pit of death row for another ten years and counting. And now Riehlmann's gonna take the hit with the Bar Association for an ethics violation? Unbelievable."

The judge returned and called them to order as Gordon was speaking. Robert stood, buttoning his jacket. "Judge, the State basically concedes that because of its actions and their failure to turn over evidence, to pursue evidence, that an innocent man was convicted of a crime he didn't do. The evidence proves that he was not the robber. No question: He was not guilty. The efforts by which these witnesses, former prosecutors from the DA's office, describe what must have occurred to justify their actions in this case is just beyond belief. To hear Mr. Dubelier talk, he had nothing whatsoever to do with the prosecution of John Thompson. To hear Mr. Williams talk, Mr. Dubelier had everything to do with the prosecution of John Thompson. They're blaming each other. It wasn't me—it was him.

"Nobody in this courtroom except Mr. Riehlmann made any statements that would in any way suggest they were really forthcoming about what must have happened. I wouldn't expect Mr. Dubelier or Mr. Williams, if they were just deep-sixing the evidence, to admit in this courtroom that they had done so. They needed a conviction of an innocent man to get the death penalty. To admit that kind of thing is to concede the loss of the license to practice law. So, we will never know, because the stakes are so high for these individuals.

"The evidence in this case, the blood evidence in the case, either would have strengthened an eyewitness case to the point that it could not have gone for the defense, or would have exonerated the defendant. It was an either/or. It matters not, ultimately. We know that an innocent man has served time for this crime because of the hiding of exculpatory evidence. And the armed robbery case became the banner for death in the murder case."

Harry Connick stood. "May I have time to rebut?"

Quinlan's eyebrow went up slightly, but that was his only signal. "Sure."

Connick was in full-on aggrieved mode. "It was my impression when we started that we were going to talk about the armed robbery case and save the contingents about the homicide case for another day. Well, that didn't happen. The Court let everything in that the defense wanted to get in just about this case, and so what I think it boils down to is that there is some allegation of bad faith by the DA's office regarding the homicide case. The record speaks for itself, and it speaks very clearly. Mr. Dubelier brought that case to the grand jury before this defendant was even arrested, so there was nothing sinister about the charging of this defendant with the armed robbery to bolster the case. John Thompson was convicted, by evidence, by a jury, who obviously concluded that he was guilty beyond a reasonable doubt. And your testimony about the penalty phase of the case didn't rely exclusively on this.

"So, if there's some sinister motive attributed to the DA's office regarding the prosecution of this defendant, we shouldn't have prosecuted him. No question about it. That was a mischaracterization of justice, and we told you that from the beginning, from the very day it was brought to my attention. Thank God they found that document, this document that had been secreted from my office after this thing was over with."

Connick was still going. The man was wound up. "They were going to ask for the death penalty, regardless of what happened in this case. They were going to do that anyway. It's a matter of office policy, and the Court is well aware of that fact. All I can tell you, again, is that it was wrong, but there was no evidence whatsoever that there was some design to put this particular defendant in some kind of a box to see fit that he got the death penalty. There's nothing to support that. So we would like the Court to grant our motion and get this behind us."

"You'll get your chance to do that in a second, Mr. Connick." At the sound of the judge's voice, the energy in the courtroom shifted to rapt engagement. "You have asked all day why we are here. We're here because this Court, given the history of this case, was not willing to accept the representations that you and your office made on this piece of paper. That's a sad commentary. Even when the defense says they will stipulate to this, this Court is now at the point where I want the testimony and evidence to come from this witness stand so that I know what people said under oath, and so that everybody knows what people said under oath. Of course, there was a lot of finger pointing one way or the other. We didn't get any real conclusive evidence, and the Court never thought that we would."

Quinlan continued: "The other reason the Court had this hearing is because all day long, there have been a number of young assistant DAs—most of them are not here right now, but they were sitting in the courtroom, watching this—and I hope that they take to heart the message that this kind of conduct cannot go on in this parish if the criminal justice system is going to work. Those are the reasons, Mr. Connick, that we had this hearing."

Then Quinlan spoke the words Michael had been waiting for. "This Court will grant both the application for post-conviction relief, and, since they were consolidated, the motion for a new trial."

Connick stood and simply said, "Thank you, Judge."

Without another word, Quinlan rose from the bench and disappeared into his chambers. The hearing was over.

Michael turned and looked at John, the wardens approaching as the courtroom emptied. They wouldn't get any privacy in this courtroom, but he desperately wanted to talk to John, to reassure him that things were finally turning their way. Quinlan had granted a new trial on the armed robbery, but Connick would drop that charge now, so the Lagarde carjacking was officially a thing of the past, and expunged from John's record. With the armed robbery charge gone, their argument for a new sentence—if not a new trial—in the murder case had serious momentum.

Michael walked over, motioning to the cops to give them a second, and put his arms around John. For what seemed like the thousandth time, he was surprised at how small and frail John felt in his embrace.

John was smiling, but his grasp on Michael was fierce. "We got the Big Mo, John," Michael said into his friend's ear. "This is the first step. We're going to get there."

"I know, bro. I have faith in you."

They released from their embrace, John turning and hugging Gordon as Connick approached to shake their hands.

Michael congratulated Robert, both men putting their notes in their briefcases. He could tell, in the glances from the judge's clerks, how big a home run they had hit today. Michael felt as good as he had felt in a long time. How could the judge not grant them a new trial in the murder case?

Connick packed up his bags briskly and left as well, and most of the reporters ran after him. Michael, Gordon, and Robert stayed, speaking briefly about the next steps. After the door had closed, Connick's clerk walked over to them, a small piece of paper in her hand.

"You boys will enjoy this," she said, smiling, and handed the note to Gordon. He unfolded the piece of paper and looked at it as the clerk said, "The judge passed me this note while Dubelier was saying that if anyone said that his stated position on *Brady* was 'If the defense doesn't know about it, it's not *Brady*,' then that person was a liar."

The note read, *I guess that makes me a liar, then.*

Gordon looked at the clerk, a wry smile crossing his face.

Without a word, the clerk took the note, folded it back up, and walked out of the courtroom.

40

THE ILLUSION OF HOPE

NOVEMBER 4, 1999

J OHN HAD HEARD them while it was happening—three days ago, four inmates gently scraping the bars of their cell doors. They had spent the past few weeks cutting through the bars with mini hacksaws, supplied to them by freemen they had bribed. This was the night they were getting out.

Eight months ago, if they had asked, John would have gone with them. He used to have conversations with other inmates about whether they should just drop their appeals and go to the Death House. They read *The Art of War* and passed it around on the tier. *Go out like a warrior*, they thought.

They'd say to each other, "This ain't no kind of life." They would talk, each of them leaning on opposite sides of the same wall, with their faces pressed up to the corner of their cells to penetrate the din. "Caged like this, our cases not movin' along none, man, for years, and what we got? Sittin' here, waitin' to have them kill us, only we all believe that somehow, some way, we gonna get out first. We gonna get paroled, or overturned, and we gonna beat the system and the man? Ain't no kind of life."

John believed this, and these four men had tried to do something about it. Die free, die in prison, but don't die inside and keep on living.

John could have gone with them. He got on well enough with those guys, and they would have let him come. They had asked him, saying, "You know, John, you can come with us, you want to." He'd thought about it. It had been a pretty good plan, and John wouldn't have been surprised if they had made it.

But then he thought that maybe he could get out of Angola the right way—win his case, get out, and not get chased the rest of his life. He'd thought about whether true freedom was an irrational hope, more damaging than sustaining in the long run, but as he lay rigid and still in his cot, as he listened to the four men remove the bars from their cell doors and then turn their hacksaws to the bars across one of the windows on the far wall—bars already sawed almost all the way through in the preceding weeks—he had stayed still and silent.

The next day, when the four men had been captured and returned to death row, and when the new punishments on all the prisoners had been ordered—punishments that would have come whether they had made it or not—and contact visits had been revoked, he would hear the story from the men who had escaped.

John wondered how the men had felt as they wriggled through the space they'd cut in the bars over the window and out the second-story window toward the building's roof. He wondered whether they'd thought about the crimes they had committed that got them sent here—whether they were taking responsibility for their lives or fleeing from it.

He thought about the men walking quietly across the roof of death row, bringing the rope they'd made by stringing their sheets together. They tied one end to a ventilation pipe on the roof and let the other end fall down, where it just about reached the ground. Then they climbed down the homemade rope onto the ground.

They'd gotten the two hacksaws from freemen—another word for "guards"—at a cost of fifty bucks apiece. They were small enough to keep hidden in a book cover, but strong enough to file down the bars in their cells. The hard part was cutting away just enough so that the bars stayed together and fooled the eye, but were still movable by the prisoners.

The window across the hall, which also had bars on it, had been a tougher challenge. For that, they had shared the saw as they walked up and down the hall, talking to people and getting their hour of exercise at night or on a rainy day. One of the other prisoners would distract the guard, or would be watching and give a hand signal, and the other would take a few quick cuts at the bars on the window. If they were lucky, they'd also have time to wipe the metal filings away from the window before putting the hacksaw back into hiding.

It took several weeks of this to weaken the bars on the window, and as they worked on it, they put their other plans into place. They made *Escape from Alcatraz* papier-mâché busts of themselves that they would put in their beds to pass a lights-out bed check. They knew the heads wouldn't pass the morning inspection, but by that time, if their plan had worked, they'd be long gone. One of the men had an uncle who had grown up hunting and fishing in the land to the west, in the curve of the Mississippi. He'd agreed to leave them some Jet Skis in a secluded spot. Death row was right by the front gate, on the far eastern side of the Farm, but they'd fool their captors by heading farther into Angola's compound instead of cutting through the fences and getting out that way.

After they'd left, John had lain on his back in the dark, listening to the silence. It was half an hour before the next check, but the escapees had figured that with the bars back in place and the plaster heads placed in their beds, they would not be missed for at least six hours—until morning broke.

John had stood outside during his exercise time in the days before the escape, imagining it in his mind: the feeling of pushing himself up off the window ledge and pulling his body up on the roof; rappelling down the side of the building in the cool night air; seeing the lights over at the front gate that could be trained their way at any moment, knowing the risk but also knowing that he was out. Then, he was running through the grass, shuffling, the ground whizzing beneath his feet as he charged out to the lake and the Jet Skis and the river and the life out past that.

Whatever was out past that, the men didn't find it. They ran into an unmarked lake that slowed them down, couldn't find the Jet Skis, and got run down by the police dogs. They were back in their cells by dawn.

Still, John wondered if it had been worth it—just to feel that freedom, even just to be able to turn right or left by one's own choosing, to take action of one's own accord. He put one arm behind his head, still lying on his back, and rubbed his face with the other, wondering if he was smart to stay behind or stupid for not trying to get out.

41

MOVEMENT

IT **HAD BEEN** a while since he'd gotten a letter from Nancy, so John decided to make a little fun of her.

Dear Nancy:

Since you have just completely forgot about poor John, I suppose to be your brother. This is getting very scary here. I feel like I'm about to lose my mind. This new environment, Camp J. This is a new experience; if I could survive this here, I'll never be the same!

This is a mental health camp, got to be. Because I can't believe these dudes back here is from the same planet I came here in 1962. They do it all here—throw shit-piss and anything else on each other. I only could hope that I don't fall to this level. But I can't set there and let someone throw anything on me without fighting back. It's a sign of weakness, and it would mean I would be forced to entertain them on this level or be entertained daily. Sick, huh?

You wouldn't believe the level of noise here. It start at 5:00 AM and end at 5:00 AM. There is no control here; this is the bottom of the prison. Inmates they can't control, this camp is for them. They leave them here until they could go six months without a writeup. I tell you, most of them been back here for years. I hope I don't be here but the six months I am show to be here. One writeup set you all the way back to level 1. I am on level 2; every 90 days you move up a level. On level 3, I could get most of my things back. The only thing that will be missing is the TV, which isn't shit.

Well, that's life in my new city; hopefully it's only six months. But life goes on, and I can handle it. Hopefully you help me stay out or keep my sanity. I need some more books to read. Look for something on the top ten or twenty list. I liked both of them, but wasn't nothing like some of the others. Look like the cheaper the better. At lease, send me Ted Turner book about his life. I want to read some real things!

I just read where Shareef lawyers just filed a lawsuit against Harry Connick and the police department. I will go next month, and file my suit right after I come out of court! My year to do so will be up in April. You only have a year to do so.

Well, hopefully, the New Year was good for you and the girls. Everything here is so crazy as I mention, and more. Every day it's a new experience here, so books will be my way out. I never read this much in my life. While I need the books, I can't get any. Crazy, huh?

Well, take care of yourself. I'll try to do like-wise on this end.

Love ya!
John

John read the letter again. There were some mistakes, mistakes that he would have corrected if he still had his typewriter, but it was so loud that he couldn't hear himself think, so he decided the letter was good enough. He got the guard to give him an envelope. When he got a stamp he could mail it, and then he would wait for

Nancy to send him some books to help him forget everything going on around him.

FEBRUARY 15, 2000

HE WAS FINALLY out of Camp J. He didn't know why they had put him there in the first place, or why they had finally returned him to the Row. It happened the same way it always did, the way everything happened. He was in his cell with nothing happening for weeks, months, years, and then one day for some reason something happened. This time, a guard had come and taken John from Camp J to death row again, telling him to get ready because he was leaving Angola for OPP. Just like that.

Since the DA had moved to drop the armed robbery charge, Nick Trenticosta had been pestering both Angola and Judge Quinlan to move John off death row and into OPP, where he could have better visitation with his family—and where he would cost Louisiana less money. Someone apparently agreed, and had approved John's transfer off death row, even though Quinlan had not officially ruled on the motion.

John was excited for the change of scenery. It would make seeing his family a lot easier, since OPP was right there in the city. At the same time, conditions in OPP had been pretty bad, and the overcrowding and violence and filth was at least as bad now as it had been in the '80s. It was a "pick your poison" kind of deal.

One new thing at OPP was that visitation rights had changed. With all the people coming into and out of OPP from the neighborhood, he would be tied to the community. There was bound to be someone who could pass on news or messages to and about his family.

Nick had told him that he got the prison to move up his transfer date, so John could be in OPP by the end of the month. John was excited to start getting family members' names on the visitors list. Trying to figure out the logistics of the move was complicated, however. Even more frustrating, the warden had restricted phone use on the Row, so he hadn't been able to use the phone and had no idea how his case was progressing. All he could do was try to keep reminding himself that his lawyers knew what they were doing.

Quinlan had agreed to let Michael and Gordon strengthen their motion for a new trial by renewing their investigation into the case, and they were finally doing things John had been telling them to do since they'd first taken the case. At the time, Michael had said there was no point in investigating the facts around the murder because they couldn't appeal the facts. They said that whatever the jury had decided, those were the facts, and that was that.

But things were different now. Michael and Gordon were investigating everything in the police file again, and they had a new investigator, Maureen Kelleher, who seemed to be digging up some good new information.

John didn't like not knowing what was going on in his case every day, but Michael and Gordon had told him that they needed to be careful how they communicated updates to him; their communications might be monitored, and they didn't want to tell him anything sensitive that could be read or found out by the DA. John accepted that. This was a serious fight, and they had gotten him this far. For now, he'd follow their lead and trust them to do what was right by him.

42

THE DAILIES

THERE WAS A manila envelope on Michael's chair when he walked into his office. He picked it up and looked at the label. It was from Val Solino. He ripped it open and poured the contents out onto his desk.

Inside were about fifty pages of paper, with a cover letter: "Materials newly discovered in the NOPD's files." Michael chuckled at that. *Eleven years, and we're still finding new materials,* he thought.

Michael looked at the first page. Its header read CRIMINAL INVESTIGATION BUREAU. These looked like police reports, but he'd read the police reports for the carjacking and murder cases thousands of times, and that wasn't what he was holding now.

He found the date in the bottom right-hand corner of each page. The first was dated December 6, 1984, but the next was dated December 8. There were others: December 13, 21, 29, and January 5, 1985.

It's the dailies, he thought. After years of asking, here they were.

Without taking his eyes off the page in front of him, Michael walked over to his office door, called out into the hall, asking his secretary to hold all calls, and shut the door. The first page—*the first page*—had information that he had never seen before, some new witness who lived in Liuzza's apartment building named Nora Mestayer. Why wasn't she used at the trial? Did Couhig and Fanning know about her? What would she have testified to? Would she agree or disagree with the key witnesses?

He kept reading, mentally comparing these reports with the summary police report they had used since 1989. If the report used at trial was the memoir of Curole's investigation, these reports, filed in real time throughout the police investigation, were the diary. They represented all the evidence the police had to take to the grand jury. Of course, the summary had focused exclusively on Thompson; by that time, the Freeman plea bargain had been accepted, and Curole knew whom he had to focus on for the conviction.

Michael pulled out a yellow legal pad and a pen and started taking notes.

DECEMBER 6, 1984
1:30 AM

DETECTIVE DONALD JAMES Curole was notified about the case by Sixth District officers. The initial scene investigation was complete. Victim Ray T. Liuzza (WM 12-3-50), vice president of the International Hotel. Shot in front of 1745 Josephine Street. Robbed of a Cartier watch, a gold ring with the initial "R," a silver chain, and a wallet with credit cards from Saks and AmEx.

Michael circled the description of the ring. For eleven years he had heard the ring had an "L" on it, but this report said "R." Probably nothing, but you never knew.

Three witnesses: Paul Schliffka, Pam Staab, and Nora Mestayer. Wanted subject: Unknown Negro male, six feet tall, black jacket, blue jeans, close-cut hair, with blue steel revolver. Two pellets recovered from the scene, one from interior hallway of 1745 Josephine, one from exterior wall.

2:15 AM

AFTER GOING TO the hospital and learning that Liuzza was in surgery, Curole met with the initial scene investigation officers. Liuzza had told them he'd been robbed, but didn't give any other details. Initial statements had been taken from witnesses.

Paul Schliffka (WM 4-27-62) residing 2026 Baronne Street, Apt. 4, told Curole he saw a Negro male running from the scene, up Josephine toward Dryades, with a pistol in his right hand. Pamela Staab (WF 4-27-62) residing 1745 Josephine Street had been inside her apartment. She heard victim saying "Take my watch" and the robber saying "I'm'a shoot you," but didn't see anything. Nora Mestayer (WF 6-4-61) residing 1745 Josephine Street was Pam Staab's roommate, and told Curole that she heard and saw even less than Pam Staab.

Curole interviewed Gerald Schreiber (WM 8-24-49), a close friend of the victim. Schreiber and Curole went into the victim's apartment and located his Rolex watch, leading Schreiber to speculate that the victim's Cartier watch was the one stolen.

Back downstairs, Curole spoke to Lt. Antoine Saacks of the NOPD. Responding to the initial call at 12:49 AM, Saacks observed a Negro male subject walking on the 1800 block of Carondelet and fitting the description of the perpetrator in the shooting. He stopped the subject, Ronald Robertson, and transported him to the scene of the killing. Paul Schliffka advised the officers he was unable to identify anyone as the perpetrator. Robertson was later booked at Central Lockup on an outstanding warrant for attempted murder. At the time of his arrest, Robertson was clad in a black jacket and blue jean pants.

2:17 AM

DR. MARK VALENTINE of Charity Hospital pronounced the victim dead.

9:00 AM

Coroner's Pathologist Dr. Monroe Samuels began the autopsy of Ray Liuzza. Dr. Samuels provided the following information:

1) 1-gunshot entrance wound to the right upper anterior chest, just above and to the left of the nipple, with a corresponding exit wound to the right upper posterior back. This wound is superficial and did not penetrate the chest cavity.

2) 1-gunshot entrance wound to the left lateral abdomen at the waist, penetrating the large and small intestine, and the liver, with a corresponding exit wound to the center anterior chest.

3) 1-gunshot entrance wound to the lower right posterior chest penetrating the spine, right kidney, and liver, with a corresponding exit wound to the upper right lateral chest.

4) 1-superficial gunshot wound to the lower center posterior back, with a corresponding exit wound to the right lateral chest.

5) 1-gunshot wound to the right inner buttocks, with a corresponding exit wound to the right lateral thigh.

DECEMBER 6, 1984
8:00 AM

DETS. BERARD, R. Miller, J. Miller, Saucier, and Sgt. Eaton were assigned to assist Det. Donald Curole by canvassing the area around Josephine and Baronne. Detectives checked the below listed addresses as follows:

2031 Baronne: No response.

2103 Baronne: Stephen McAllister (WM 33) was awakened by gunfire. Heard six shots and ran to front window but could only see victim laying on the corner. Did not see the perpetrator. Rosemary Cash (WF 24) was awakened by gunfire, heard six shots, heard someone saying "No, no." Did not see the perpetrator.

2105 Baronne: No response.

2030 Baronne: John Branella (WM 25) and James Glade (WM 28) were not home at the time, and saw nothing.

2032 Baronne: No response.

2022 Baronne: No response.

2026 Baronne: Evangelina Poisson (WM 74), manager of building, was awakened by Pam Staab, but did not see anything.

1734 Josephine: Sharon Robinson (NF 39) heard four or five shots but did not see anyone.

1737 Josephine: Theresa Hollins (NF 37) heard one shot, did not see anyone.

1733 Josephine: Mary Wilson (NF 68) heard four shots, did not see anyone.

2021 Brainard: Joseph Mizelle (WM 55), sleeping and did not hear or see anything.

1747 Josephine: No response.

Dets. summoned the S. & W. B. for the purpose of lifting the covers on the storm drains in the area, from the scene on Josephine and Brainard to St. Andrew, to the 1800 block of Carondelet. No evidence recovered.

DECEMBER 7, 1984
10:30 AM

CUROLE BEGAN REINTERVIEWING the witnesses located during the initial scene investigation.

Miss Pamela Staab (WF 6-5-62) and Miss Nora Mestayer (WF 6-4-61) repeated their original descriptions of events, as did Mr. Paul Schliffka (WM 4-27-62). Mr. Schliffka did state that he was positive that the man the police returned to the scene, Ronald Robinson, was not the man he observed running from the scene of the shooting.

Miss Susan Crane (WF 10-31-58), residing 2032 Baronne Street, reported that she and her husband were sitting in their living room when they heard the sound of gunshots. She did not hear any conversation prior to the gunshots, and she did not look outside following the gunshots.

3:00 PM

DETECTIVE DONALD CUROLE met with Mr. Bill Brown, chief of security for the International Hotel, at his office. Mr. Brown provided information about the victim's credit cards, and about the victim.

Mr. Liuzza had been with the hotel since 1976 and had recently been promoted to vice president. He had very little contact with its employees and had no power to hire or fire anyone there. Mr. Brown advised Det. Curole that he had received information that Liuzza was possibly homosexual, and had strong evidence to suggest that he regularly used cocaine. Mr. Brown suggested Det. Curole interview Mr. Chris Braiwick, victim's closest friend, and Miss Jody Beauregard, his longtime girlfriend.

4:00 PM

DET. CUROLE MET with Mr. Ray A. Liuzza, father of the victim. Mr. Liuzza described the watch as a Cartier Tank watch, with a small square white face, blank numerals, and a black leather band. The articles of jewelry were probably purchased at Adler's Jewelry on Canal Street. Due to his emotional state, Mr. Liuzza was unable to continue with the interview.

4:20 PM

DET. CUROLE SPOKE to Mr. Schiffer Michaels at Adler's Jewelry. Mr. Michaels kept a file of the articles purchased at Adler's by victim and would provide the contents of that file to Det. Curole.

DECEMBER 8, 1984
2:00 PM

DET. CUROLE MET and interviewed Miss Sheri Hartman (WF 9-29-49), residing 2031 Baronne Street, Apt. 2. While in her apartment, Miss Hartman heard six gunshots fired outside her side window, which faces Josephine Street, but upon seeing nothing ran to the front of her apartment. She walked out onto her balcony and observed a blond-haired man, who lives across the street, kneeling over a body on the side of the house at 2032 Baronne. Miss Hartman then ran downstairs to the scene and realized that the victim was Mr. Liuzza. She stated that she never saw anyone else near the scene, or fleeing the scene after hearing the shots fired.

2:30 PM

DETS. CUROLE AND Demma interviewed Miss Angie Poisson (WF 8-4-10), manager of the apartment complex in which Mr. Liuzza resided. She had no knowledge of the shooting incident.

3:00 PM

DETS. CUROLE AND Demma interviewed Mr. Logan Faust (WM 8-29-62), residence 2022 Baronne Street, in the apartment downstairs from victim. He heard six shots fired at 12:30 AM, but saw nothing.

5:00 PM

DETS. CUROLE AND Demma reinterviewed Susan Steiner in the offices of the Homicide Division. She indicated that she only knew the victim for a short time and had not had sexual relations with him. She had heard rumors that the victim was gay, but had no personal knowledge to that effect. She had no knowledge of Mr. Liuzza's cocaine use but would not be surprised by it. She recommended Dets. speak to Chris Braiwick for additional information.

SUNDAY, DECEMBER 9, 1984
4:30 PM

DET. CUROLE INTERVIEWED Miss Patti Pulitzer (WF 9-13-43) residing 1002 Webster Street, a close friend of the victim. She was with Pierre Villere, Ray Liuzza, and his girlfriend Susan Steiner at Lenfant's prior to the murder. Mr. Liuzza left Lenfant's with Miss Steiner at 12 midnight. He mentioned he was fatigued, and intended to proceed straight home. Miss Pulitzer has known Liuzza for about ten years, and had never known him to use narcotics. She lent credence to the rumor that he may have been a homosexual.

5:30 PM

DET. CUROLE INTERVIEWED Chris Braiwick (WM 12-11-55) residing 813 Hidalgo Street. Mr. Braiwick told Det. Curole that Liuzza was not a homosexual. He did use cocaine recreationally but never purchased the narcotic and had no regular connection for purchase of the drug. He described Mr. Liuzza's possessions: Yellow gold block-type ring with the initial "L" in gothic script. Cartier Tank watch, square white face, black leather band. Sterling silver chain with a religious medal, worn always around his neck. Black calfskin billfold with an American Express Card.

MONDAY, DECEMBER 10, 1984
3:00 PM

CUROLE SPOKE WITH Schiffer Michaels. Liuzza had purchased a Cartier Tank wristwatch for $1,800.

4:00 PM

DET. CUROLE INTERVIEWED Miss Jody Beauregard (WF 3-9-56) residing 546 Jefferson Avenue. She had dated victim for a number of years. She said Liuzza not a homosexual, but did use cocaine occasionally, only when offered it by friends. She was able to render an artist's conception of the ring.

9:00 PM

DET. GEBBIA MET with Jody Beauregard and prepared a sketch of the ring, now contained in the police file.

WEDNESDAY, DECEMBER 12, 1984
5:30 PM

DET. CUROLE INTERVIEWED Miss Charon Kiehl (WF 6-4-54) residing 2103 Baronne Street, Apt. 5. Miss Kiehl was in her kitchen and heard five gunshots. She ran to her bedroom window, observing a tall slim black man with a hair net on, bending over the body. Miss Kiehl went to a phone and notified the police. Since then Miss Kiehl spoke to the witness Paul Schliffka and now believes that the man she observed kneeling over the body of Mr. Liuzza was the witness.

6:00 PM

MISS ROSEMARY CASH (WF 6-5-60), residing 4500 Elysian Fields Avenue, stated she was in bed with Steve McAllister when she heard someone yell "No, no" followed by gunshots. She telephoned police but never left her bed to investigate.

THURSDAY, DECEMBER 13, 1984
3:00 PM

DETS. DEMMA AND Curole met Mr. James Skelly at Investment Diamond Exchange, 3300 West Esplanade. Two white males attempted to pawn a white Cartier Tank wristwatch on 12-11-84. They were referred to Gulf States Pawn Shop. Detectives made inquiries at Gulf States but the men never returned.

7:00 PM

DETS. CUROLE AND Demma secured release of Ronald Robinson (NM 5-5-56) from Orleans Parish Prison. Robinson told Dets. he had been at the house of Olivia Ford from early the evening of December 5th until about midnight. The house in question is near the intersection of Martin Luther King and Baronne Street. Robinson left Ford's house and walked to 1500 block of Baronne where a police car pulled over and shone a spotlight on him, then took him to Josephine and Baronne where a young white man and old white lady looked at him. Both witnesses told the police he was not the man they were looking for because he was too short. The police then booked him for an old charge he had for shooting a man.

Robinson admitted shooting a man in the 1800 block of Euterpe Street in September. He owed the man money and the man had been shooting at him. Robinson denied any knowledge of the shooting of Ray Liuzza.

9:00 PM

Curole and Demma placed Robinson in the rear of their vehicle. Robinson directed them to 1724 Melpomene, where Curole and Demma met and interviewed Olivia Ford (NF 9-9-47). Miss Ford told Demma that Robinson came to her house about 6:00 PM on 12-5-84 and remained there until midnight or 12:30. Robinson had spent the entire night smoking marijuana with her, and she was sure he was not involved in the murder of Ray Liuzza.

10:30 PM

Curole and Demma met Miss Aline Stingeon (NF 12-29-59), 219 Crozat Street. Dets. had received information via Crimestoppers that Harold Cooper (NM 30) was responsible for killing Mr. Liuzza, and that information had been provided by Miss Stingeon. Miss Stingeon indicated this was a domestic dispute and denied possessing any knowledge of Cooper's involvement in the shooting of Mr. Liuzza.

DECEMBER 14, 1984
4:00 PM

Curole prepared an application for a search warrant for residence of Charles Patterson, 457 Jackson Avenue, Apt. 5, based on information received during interviews of Michael Vance by Officer James Keen concerning the weapon used in the Liuzza killing.

5:08 PM

Curole and Demma met with Criminal Court Magistrate Andrew Schambra in his chambers. Judge Schambra issued a warrant for the search of 457 Jackson Avenue, Apt. 5. Application and search warrant are contained in case file.

7:00 PM

DETS. CUROLE AND Demma executed the search warrant on 457 Jackson Avenue, Apt. 5. The search turned up nothing related to Ray Liuzza.

7:40 PM

DETS. CUROLE AND Demma interviewed Charles Patterson (NM 8-10-50), residing 457 Jackson Avenue, Apt. 5. Patterson admitted he knew a Michael Vance, aka "Black," and that he had heard that Black was talking to police, trying to set him up for a murder charge. Patterson knew only scant details about the Liuzza crime, which he had heard from news media.

DECEMBER 18, 1984

THE FOLLOWING INFORMATION has been received by the New Orleans police Homicide Division relative to the armed robbery/murder of Ray T. Liuzza:

DECEMBER 11, 1984
10:15 PM

DET. JOHN REYNOLDS received a phone call from a man affiliated with the Home Improvement Center in Metairie. He overheard a subject named "Gayskin" mention the day before the homicide he was desperate for money. Gayskin disappeared the day after the homicide and has not been heard from since. UNDER INVESTIGATION.

DECEMBER 12, 1984
9:00 AM

MR. JOHN POPE of the *Times-Picayune* newspaper received a phone call from a while female who stated that Michael Monroe (NM) has been bragging about the murder, saying, "I got that white honky." UNDER INVESTGATION.

DECEMBER 12, 1984
3:30 PM

ANONYMOUS CALL TO Crimestoppers. Henry Smith, who lives in the St. Thomas Project, shot and killed Liuzza. UNDER INVESTIGATION.

DECEMBER 13, 1984
4:20 PM

ANONYMOUS CALL TO Crimestoppers. Harold Cooper (NM 30) residing 219 Crozat Street obtained a large sum of money from a man who begged him not to kill him. Curole and Demma later spoke to Adele Sturgis, who resides at 219 Crozat Street. She was involved in a domestic dispute with Cooper, but knew nothing about Cooper being involved in any murder.

DECEMBER 14, 1984
9:50 AM

ANONYMOUS CALL TO Crimestoppers. Charles Bradford (NM 32), St. Thomas Project, killed Liuzza. Bradford was also involved in the murder of Bobby Caesar in the 1700 block of Dryades in November 1983. UNDER INVESTIGATION.

DECEMBER 14, 1984
4:00 PM

PHONE CALL TO Det. Curole from Mr. Albert Leonard, elderly NM at 3120 Gravier Street. Mr. Leonard was told by a man named Stanley that the man who killed Liuzza lives in an apartment complex between Thalia and Clio on Clara Street. The perpetrator said he had to kill the victim because the victim would have recognized him. The perpetrator is very scared and ducks into his apartment every time a police car passes. Dets. obtained a printout of suspects who reside in that complex. UNDER INVESTIGATION.

DECEMBER 14, 1984
6:00 PM

ANONYMOUS CALL TO Homicide Office received by Miss Johnson. NF caller stating that Gerald Lewis, 2520 Mistletoe, has been bragging about killing Ray Liuzza.

DECEMBER 14, 1984
2:30 AM

TELEPHONE CALL TO Det. Robert Lambert from Doris Smith (NF 29), 948 Felicity Street. A male friend told her that Gene Quinn (NM 30) residing 2217 Amelia Street killed Ray Liuzza.

DECEMBER 15, 1984
4:40 AM

ANONYMOUS CALL TO Det. Donald Hoyt from a man who stated that "Tyronne" in the Iberville Project killed Liuzza.

DECEMBER 16, 1984
12:05 AM

ANONYMOUS CALL TO Det. Saladino from a NM who stated that Anthony Morgan (NM 28), Martin Luther King and S. Robertson, and drives a two-toned 1975 Cordoba, killed Ray Liuzza. Liuzza was killed as the result of a hit, and Morgan made the incident appear to be an armed robbery. UNDER INVESTIGATION.

DECEMBER 21, 1984
10:00 AM

DET. CUROLE RECEIVED information from Det. McDonald of the Intelligence Division. Det. McDonald had received information from an informant that a NF named Mary, age 26, 3208 Lasalle Street, witnessed the murder and knows the perpetrator's identity. Det. Curole checked the address and found utilities registered to Miss

Mary E. Wells as of August 1984. Det. Curole proceeded to 3208 Lasalle Street and found no one at home.

DECEMBER 23, 1984
12:30 AM

DET. DEMMA MET and interviewed Miss Mary E. Wells (NF 10-14-51). Miss Wells admitted to Det. Demma that she in fact witnessed the armed robbery/murder on Baronne Street and identified the perpetrator as Charles Bradford. Miss Wells provided Det. Demma with a brief account of the incident, which convinced Det. Demma that Miss Wells was in fact a witness to the incident. Det. Demma made arrangements for Miss Wells to be interviewed in the Homicide Office later that morning.

9:00 AM

DETS. CUROLE AND Demma met and interviewed Miss Mary E. Wells (NF 10-14-51) in the Homicide Division Office. On December 6, 1984, at about 12:30 AM, she alighted from the Freret Street bus at Josephine and Dryades streets, and began walking riverbound on Josephine. Miss Wells heard someone yelling, "Here, please take my wallet, take anything you want, but please don't kill me." When she reached the corner of Baronne and Josephine, Miss Wells observed two men standing on the sidewalk next to a house in the 1700 block of Josephine. As she stood there, Miss Wells could hear one of the men, a white man, begging the other man not to shoot.

Shortly thereafter, the other man fired the first shot, which she believes struck the white man in the shoulder because she saw him immediately raise his hand to his shoulder. The white man then turned away toward Baronne Street, away from the robber. As he did, the robber continued to fire at him, aiming for his back. The white man ran almost to the corner, where he fell to the sidewalk next to the building. Miss Wells remembered hearing five shots fired.

During this period, Miss Wells observed a Negro male subject, whom she recognized as Charles Bradford, running from the scene, on Josephine Street. Miss Wells had attended Andrew J. Bell Junior High School with Mr. Bradford. Bradford continued down Josephine, crossing the street before reaching Dryades, and entering a vehicle which was parked on the western side of Josephine facing toward the river. The vehicle was a brown two-door vehicle with a white door on the passenger side and the word CUTLASS on the trunk.

Following this, Miss Wells made several calls to the police department. On one occasion she called the Crimestoppers Hotline and identified Charles Bradford as the killer of Ray Liuzza. Another time she telephoned and spoke to "Det. Leslie," to whom she gave the license number of the vehicle she had seen. She told Dets. Curole and Demma she did not give her name to Det. Leslie, who requested that Miss Wells use the name "Pam" so he could identify her in future telephone calls.

During the course of this statement, Det. Curole ran the name "Charles Bradford" in the Motion system and located a criminal record on a Charles Bradford (NM 1-8-48), last known address 2428 Erato Street, Apt. F. Det. Curole then prepared a photographic lineup consisting of photographs of suspects of similar appearance taken during that period. After viewing the photos, Miss Wells picked out the photo of Charles Bradford and positively identified him as the man she observed shooting and killing Ray Liuzza.

Det. Curole checked through his case file and located information received on the Crimestoppers Hotline on December 14, 1984, at 9:00 AM, in which the caller identified the killer of Ray Liuzza as Charles Bradford.

Dets. Curole and Demma contacted Det. Larry Leslie of the Burglary Division who confirmed that he had been speaking with a woman who provided information concerning the death of Ray Liuzza, along with the license number of the getaway vehicle. Det.

Leslie stated he asked this woman, who remained anonymous, to use the name of "Pam" so that he could identify her.

Following this, Det. Curole ran the license number through the Motion computer and found it was registered to a 1970 Oldsmobile two-door, color brown. Registered owner was Dwayne Norris Jones, residing 2407 Toledano Street. Jones had no criminal record.

3:08 PM

DETS. CUROLE AND Demma met with Criminal Court Magistrate Nils Douglas. Judge Douglas issued a warrant of arrest for Charles Bradford (NM 1-8-48) for the armed robbery murder of Ray Liuzza.

6:00 PM

DETS. CUROLE AND Demma passed the residence at 2407 Toledano Street and observed the vehicle in question parked outside. Dets. returned to the Homicide Office where they prepared an application for a warrant to search the residence at 2407 Toledano and the vehicle parked out front.

7:21 PM

DETS CUROLE AND Demma again met with Judge Nils Douglas. Judge Douglas issued two search warrants—one to search the residence at 2407 Toledano, and the second to search the vehicle bearing Louisiana license number 413B106.

8:45 PM

DETS. CUROLE AND Demma executed the search warrant at the residence at 2407 Toledano. Dets. met and interviewed Mr. Dwayne Jones (NM 11-6-60), employed as a deputy for the Orleans Parish Criminal Sheriff's Office. Mr. Jones told the Dets. he knew nothing about the murder of Ray T. Liuzza. Mr. Jones indicated the vehicle in question was owned by him, but that it had been inoperative for about three months. A search of Mr. Jones's room revealed nothing.

Dets. conducted a search of the vehicle and found no evidence. The vehicle was in fact inoperative and appeared to have been in this condition for some time.

9:20 PM

DETS RETURNED TO Miss Wells's residence and requested that she accompany them to the office. Once in the vehicle, Dets. Curole and Demma drove Miss Wells to the 2400 block of Toledano and asked her if she saw the wanted vehicle in that block. Miss Wells looked at the vehicle and adamantly denied that this was the vehicle she was referring to. It should be noted that the vehicle, and Mr. Jones's residence, is just around the corner from Miss Wells's residence, and can be plainly viewed from her front window. INVESTIGATION CONTINUING.

DECEMBER 26, 1984
2:00 PM

DETS. DEMMA AND Curole proceeded to the business office of the St. Thomas Project at 909 Felicity. The Dets. had the manager, Mr. Joseph E. Tramontano, check his records for 1814 Street Thomas, Apt. F. The apartment was occupied by Miss Ophelia Bankston, who had resided there since 1974.

2:25 PM

DETS. CUROLE AND Demma interviewed Miss Ophelia Bankston at her residence. Miss Bankston told them she does not know anyone named Charles Bradford, and had no relatives or friends by that name.

2:45 PM

DETS. MET AND interviewed Miss Frances Butler, manager for the Guste Homes at 1301 Simon Bolivar. Miss Butler checked Charles Bradford's previously listed address of 2428 Erato, Apt. F, and found that Bradford never lived there. The apartment was leased to a Miss Dorothy Varnado from 1965–1967 and to a Georgie Ricks from 1967 until the present. Both women were later interviewed by Dets., and both knew nothing of the murder of Ray Liuzza. Neither woman knew or was related to Charles Bradford. INVESTIGATION CONTINUING.

DECEMBER 27, 1984
10:00 AM

DETS. CUROLE AND Demma proceeded to Criminal Records Division of the NOPD and requested a complete search for any information pertaining to Charles Bradford. This search located an arrest report on a Charles Bradford Ricks (NM 1-8-48), residing 2428 Erato Street, Apt. A. This report, filed 11-2-68, indicated that Ricks had been arrested and charged with contributing to the delinquency of a minor. This arrest information was listed in the Motion computer under the name Charles R. Bradford. It is obvious that Charles Bradford and Charles Bradford Ricks are one and the same.

12:30 PM

DETS. CUROLE AND Demma proceeded to the Louisiana Department of Vital Statistics where they requested a search for any and all public records on file for Charles Bradford Ricks. The agency had no record of live birth on file for Charles Bradford Ricks.

2:00 PM

DETS. CUROLE AND Demma proceeded to the Andrew J. Bell Junior High School in an attempt to verify that both Charles Bradford Ricks and Miss Mary Wells attended the school during the same time period. The school was closed for the Christmas holidays and would not reopen until after New Year's. INVESTIGATION CONTINUING.

JANUARY 2, 1985
11:10 AM

DETS. CUROLE AND Demma contacted Sgt. Robert Gostle who is detailed to the Regional Transit Authority. Sgt. Gostle informed the Dets. that the Freret Street bus makes regularly scheduled stops at St. Charles and Poydras, and at Josephine and Dryades. However, he located nothing indicating the bus was delayed in any way during the late evening hours of December 5 or the early morning hours of December 6. In addition, Dets. Curole and Demma searched the Louisiana Department of Motor Vehicles and found that Charles Ricks was the registered owner of a 1978 Dodge Magnum, residence address 1818 S. Gayoso Street. The residence on Ricks's current Louisiana Driver's License is 2003 Spain Street.

9:30 PM

DETS. MET AND reinterviewed Mary Wells at her residence. Dets. questioned several points Miss Wells made in her statement, one of which was the time sequence of her bus trip to Josephine Street. Miss Wells admitted to investigators that she had lied in her initial statement to protect her boyfriend. Her boyfriend is married, and Miss Wells lied to protect his job and marriage.

On the evening prior to Liuzza's murder, Miss Wells went to see her boyfriend at his office at 7:00 PM. Miss Wells was unable to say when she left the building, other than to say it was late. Her boyfriend walked her to the bus stop at St. Charles and Poydras, where they waited for the Freret bus. When the bus arrived she boarded and rode to the intersection of Dryades and Josephine, where she debarked. Throughout this interview Miss Wells maintained that the rest of her statement was truthful, and volunteered to take a polygraph examination to prove that she witnessed Charles Ricks kill Ray T. Liuzza.

2:00 PM

DETS. CUROLE AND Demma arrived at the Andrew J. Bell Junior High School. Mary Augustus (Mary Wells) attended the junior high school in 1966, but dropped out in seventh grade. The administrator could not locate any records on Charles Ricks, but if Ricks attended a high school after graduating from Bell, his records would have been forwarded to the high school he transferred to. INVESTIGATION CONTINUING.

JANUARY 4, 1985
2:55 PM

KENNETH CARR RESIDING 1540 St. Mary Street, Apt. A, telephoned the Crimestoppers Hotline. He was inside Harry's Bar located at Euterpe and Felicity when he overheard a conversation between two Negro male subjects. The conversation was concerning the murder of Ray Liuzza.

6:00 PM

DETS. DEMMA AND Curole proceeded to 1540 St. Mary Street and interviewed Kenneth Carr. On January 1, 1985, at 1:30 AM, Kenneth Carr was inside Harry's Bar. He overheard a conversation between two Negro male subjects. One of the Negro male subjects, who was identified as "John" (alias—Nook) was very nervous while talking with a second Negro male subject, who Kenneth Carr could not identify. John was telling the second Negro male subject he didn't mean to kill the guy. The guy tried to turn on me (take the gun away), so John had to shoot the man. John was also telling the second Negro subject, he wouldn't have tried to rob the man if he had known the man's family had money. The man's family had posted a large reward for information leading to the arrest and conviction of person(s) responsible.

Kenneth Carr concluded the interview by telling Dets. that the talk on the streets is that John is responsible for the murder of Ray Liuzza.

JANUARY 5, 1985
11:26 AM

DET. DEMMA RECEIVED a telephone call from Kenneth Carr. Carr had learned that John was presently living with his grandmother at the intersection of Clio and Simon Bolivar. According to Carr, John was "hiding out" at his grandmother's because he was "hot" on the street. Dets. noted the similarity between the information from Kenneth Carr and another call received on the Crimestoppers Hotline. On December 31, 1984, at 10:30 AM, an anonymous caller gave the following information: The caller identified John Thompson (alias—Nut) (NM 23), residing 1302 Simon Bolivar, as the person who robbed and shot Ray Liuzza, while a second subject identified as Kevin Freeman (NM 24) residing 2220 Felicity, waited in a 1976 Chevy, two-door black/burgundy.

Dets. checked John Thompson and Kevin Freeman through the Motion system. Records for each man were located, and computer printouts along with Bureau of Investigation photographs of these two subjects are now contained in the case file.

JANUARY 6, 1985
9:07 PM

DETS. OBTAINED A typewritten statement from Kenneth Carr concerning the conversation he had overheard at Harry's Bar. Kenneth Carr identified John Thompson's photograph from a photo lineup as the person he initially referred to as "John." Kenneth Carr was unable to identify Kevin Freeman's photograph.

JANUARY 13, 1985
4:30 PM

DET. BRINK OF the Homicide Division received a call from Mr. Frank Maselli, owner of the property where Liuzza resided. At about 4:00 PM on Sunday, January 13, 1985, a NM subject was attempting to enter the locked iron gate in front the the apartment complex where Liuzza resided. The manager of the apartment complex, Angie Poisson, opened her door. The subject informed Angie that he knew who killed Liuzza and wanted to tell the family what he knew.

4:40 PM
DET. DEMMA TELEPHONED Angie Poisson, who related the same story.

6:00 PM
DET. DEMMA AGAIN telephoned Angie, who stated that at 5:20 PM, the subject telephoned her home. The subject stated that he knew who killed Ray Liuzza, and that the killer lived on Dryades Street. Two Negro male subjects attempted to rob Liuzza, and during the robbery attempt, one of the subjects shot the victim. When the first subject began shooting, the second subject fled the scene. The subject who shot Liuzza stole his wallet, which contained no money but several credit cards, a watch, and a ring. The man who shot Liuzza was now planning to kill his accomplice because he was afraid he would talk. This killing was supposed to take place on New Year's Eve, but for some reason it did not take place.

Angie asked the Negro male subject why he didn't want to give this information to the police. The subject told Angie he had spoken with Homicide detectives, but the detectives thought the subject was not telling the truth and was only interested in the reward. He advised Angie he would call her back to ascertain whether or not Angie had gotten in touch with Liuzza's family. He then hung up.

MONDAY, JANUARY 14, 1985
11:58 AM
DET. DEMMA RECEIVED a telephone call in the Homocide Office from Angie Poisson. She had received another call from the Negro male at 11:50 AM, who stated he would meet with Liuzza's family at the International Hotel at 4:00 PM this day. The subject repeatedly voiced his concern that Angie would notify the police of the meeting, and he again asked that Angie not call the police on him before hanging up.

3:00 PM

DETS. CUROLE AND Demma arrived at the International Hotel and spoke with the security manager, Mr. Bill Brown. Mr. Brown agreed to meet with the Negro male subject in place of Mr. Liuzza. Mr. Brown also agreed to have a recording device installed in the office where the meeting was scheduled.

THE LAST TWO pages of the dailies largely restated Perkins's sworn statement to the police, and his testimony at trial, with one notable exception: "Freeman told Perkins that a WOMAN saw him driving away from the scene." The "WOMAN" must have made an impression on Curole and Demma, because they had capitalized it in the report.

Michael looked in the envelope to see if he'd missed anything. He wanted to see how the story ended, but there was nothing more. Michael guessed that from the time Curole followed up on Funk's tip to find J.R., the summary police report would have been the same as the dailies. There was only one more day of activity, and that was the day that they got the search warrants for J.R. and Jessie Harrison, and found the murder weapon. From there, they got Dubclier to give them the arrest warrants for Thompson and Freeman, and it only took them a few hours to find both men on the streets.

So the summary police report was all they'd have to go on for the final day, but Michael was energized. He looked down at the notepad where he'd been jotting down his thoughts as he read:

- *Ronald Robertson, ID'd by white man (Schliffka?) and white woman—WHO? Description: six feet, but too short to be the shooter.*
- *$$$ reward from family known as early as 12/14, known to Curole as well.*
- *Mary Wells—worth follow-up?*

- *Compare Ken Carr's statement to police 1/4/85 with statement at trial.*
- *Perkins quote: "He had spoken to Homicide, but the detectives thought the subject was not telling the truth and was only interested in the reward." = BRADY??*
- *Perkins statement = other statements? Cops, Grand Jury, Trial?*
- *Perkins statement: "Freeman also told Perkins that a WOMAN saw him driving away from the scene." = NOT Schliffka.*

Michael reread his last note. Kevin Freeman said a *woman* saw him. And Curole's report said there was a woman along with Paul Schliffka who looked at Ron Robertson that night.

There's another witness, he thought. Someone who had never testified at trial, and who Couhig and Fanning hadn't known about, or hadn't ever told him and Gordon about. Michael didn't know who she was, but he knew how he thought they'd find her. He picked up the phone and called Maureen Kelleher, asked her to locate anyone named in these reports, and learn as much as she could. Maybe after all this time, someone who wasn't a cop could shake loose something new.

43

BACK AT OPP

MAY 15, 2000

JOHN WAS IN his cell, with a magazine open on his lap, but his mind was wandering. He was thinking about one of the guards at Angola. John had just received a stay, postponing his date. The guard came and stood in front of his cell, a little grin on his face. He said, "J.T., you just like us again."

"What?"

"You just like us again."

"What you mean?"

The guard grinned, warming to his punch line. "You just like us. You still gonna die. Only now, you just don't know what day."

John laughed at that.

In some ways, life in OPP was harder than it had been on death row. John spent most of each day worrying and wondering about his case. When he was at Angola, he thought about it, but somehow there wasn't as much riding on it then. He was already dead; they just hadn't carried out the sentence yet.

Now he was alive and so close to freedom he could taste it. But he was stuck. He knew he was going to get out now; he absolutely believed that. Gordon and Michael and Robert said that if they could get Quinlan to order a new trial, they might convince Connick not to retry the case, and to just let John out on time served. John wasn't so sure about that; he remembered the way Connick had kept going after Curtis Kyles. Connick had done five trials of Curtis. Two hung juries, then they convicted him on the third try. Then Curtis won the appeal because of *Brady* evidence withheld by Jim Williams again, and then Connick tried again twice more, each time with another hung jury, before he finally said, enough is enough. A man like that might not let John go without another trial. Still, before they got there, they needed to get that new trial.

Still, he couldn't stop thinking about what he would do when he got out. It was a dangerous way to think. It exposed him to daily frustration and potentially horrible disappointment. Michael had told him several times that it was too early to think like that, and John knew on one level that Michael was right, but Michael was outside. He'd tell John that he liked their arguments, but trials were funny. Even if they got the retrial, there was no guarantee they would win. He'd remind John, "You know, you lost last time, and the evidence is the same now."

That was true, but John felt sure that a new jury would find him free of any guilt. When he started contemplating stepping foot outside OPP, though, he had a frightening thought: *What then?*

For most of the men around him, being outside prison was like a vacation from their career, which was being in prison. All they knew was how to be a criminal. They'd get out, do something stupid, get caught, and come back in. They'd hang out with old friends, people they were criminals with, and fall back into the old habits. Or they'd go to a party to welcome them home and somebody would bring drugs to celebrate. They'd get hooked again, go and rob or steal or shoot somebody. Next thing, they'd be right back in OPP.

John didn't want that future. He needed a plan for when he got out, and he needed to follow it. He never wanted to risk coming back to prison. After fifteen years inside, he knew freedom was too precious, too valuable, to be taken for granted. He needed to remember that the freedom was the important thing, that he could live without fancy clothes, cars, jewelry, women, money—all the material things that can lead people to other problems. He'd need the basics, of course, but that was all he wanted to focus on— nothing else that could lead him back toward the path he'd been on earlier in life. The world had changed in fifteen years, and people would be doing things differently, and he'd have to understand that. He'd have to accept what God gave him, enjoy his freedom, and not push to have more than He wanted John to have.

John had discussed this with Gordon and Michael, who had similar concerns. John told them he was interested in becoming a chef, and his lawyers had said they would be willing to finance a course that would give John a chef certification. It would be a start. Still, he would need a place to stay and a way to put a little money in his pocket while taking the cooking course.

Of course, all these plans didn't mean anything unless he got out, and that wasn't happening anytime soon. The DAs were delaying everything. Quinlan told the DAs he wanted an answer to Michael and Gordon's request for a new trial, but then he'd grant them extensions to send in their answer. It seemed that now, as John and his lawyers showed the world that the DA's office might have done wrong, the DAs were moving slower and slower.

First death row; now this. Believe it, John thought.

44

NO NEW TRIAL

JOHN KNEW SOMETHING important was happening when the guards came to get him. He figured it must be something new in his case. He had been putting calls in to Gordon and Michael whenever he could, trying to get a sense of when things would start moving faster. Quinlan had been pretty angry at Harry Connick at the retrial hearing. He had been in a bunch of hearings with the judge since 1984, and he had never seen Quinlan get angry like that before.

After the hearing, John had thought, *Now he's gotta know I'm innocent. He's gonna tell them, "Let this man out of jail—let him out of this setup from the DAs all those years ago."* That's what he wanted to hear when he picked up the phone and heard Michael and Gordon on the other line.

When Michael started by hesitating, considering how he was going to proceed, John knew that he wouldn't be getting any news of his freedom.

Michael and Gordon had finally received Quinlan's ruling on the new trial. The good news—and the bad news—was that he appeared, once again, to have sided with the DA's office. Quinlan had set aside John's death sentence, meaning that John would never be sent back to death row. He had agreed with Harry Connick, however, that whatever improprieties had happened in John's armed robbery trial with the blood evidence, they were separate, and had no material impact on the murder trial. As a result, he had rejected John's request for a new murder trial.

John didn't say anything for a few seconds. Michael and Gordon were silent on their side of the phone as well. None of them knew exactly how to react. They had achieved the impossible—they had gotten John off death row. It was an amazing accomplishment, and all three men knew it. Still, this result, unthinkable in 1988 was unsatisfactory now. How could Quinlan think it was fair for John to stay in OPP for the rest of his life, with the knowledge of how John had been framed?

John quickly became frustrated and angry. Michael tried to calm him, explaining that this was not an unexpected result. His tone of voice only made John angrier. John wasn't interested in being told why it was all right that he was still in prison for life. All of his patience, all of his belief, his hope—and this was the result? How could Quinlan not see that John was innocent? How could he not apply the frame-up of the armed robbery and see that John was also innocent of the murder?

Michael could tell he was irritating John, so Gordon took over. Gordon said that he had reviewed the opinion, and he thought they could get it overturned by an appeals court. Gordon believed that Quinlan had incorrectly defined the rule about when a new trial should be granted, and that he'd also misapplied the facts of John's case to the law.

John heard Gordon's voice, but he wasn't listening. *I don't know how much more of this I can do*, he thought.

Michael tried to tell John not to get discouraged. They were going to appeal, and Michael thought they had a good chance of winning. In Michael's view, Quinlan had made a political decision, not a legal one. Rather than confront the DA's office and the Liuzza family, Quinlan had constructed a rationale that enforced the murder trial and left the issue to someone else to decide.

"John, it's what we thought from the beginning. Quinlan's not gonna overturn himself. This was his first murder trial, and he doesn't want to admit that the wrong result was reached in his courtroom in 1985."

It was the first thing that Michael had said that made sense to John. All of this, everything they did in front of Quinlan, was just a waste of time.

Michael called it a "minor setback," and said that the appeals court would make it right. He told John to "keep the faith."

John was sure that Michael was right. After all, Michael and Gordon had gotten him off death row, a miracle in itself. And he knew that he needed to keep his lawyers motivated, had to keep them energized to fight for him. God knew he couldn't do this alone. He dropped his voice and calmed himself down, told Michael and Gordon how much he appreciated their work. He told them every-thing was all right, that he believed in them and the new trial. Then he hung up the phone and let the guard take him back to his cell.

He said all the things he needed to say, but what John was thinking was that he was never going to get out. He thought about Tiger and Dedric, about his grandmother and mother, about how he would spend the rest of his life in prison, when five minutes ago he had the stupidity to think they might let a black man go free.

John was thinking that it didn't matter whether he died in OPP or Angola. Prison was prison. And he was thinking that he didn't know how long he'd live, but if he was in prison, it probably wouldn't be long.

QUINLAN'S OPINION HAD been characteristically short. Michael and Gordon, with help from Maureen, had compiled mountains of evi-dence, meticulously organizing it for maximum persuasiveness. They had spent months preparing new witnesses, not available to Couhig and Fanning because they had never seen the dailies—people who had traveled from thousands of miles away to tell Quinlan that they didn't think John Thompson had murdered Ray Liuzza sixteen years ago.

Quinlan had listened, raged at the DAs, made a number of public pronouncements for righteousness in the courtroom, waited seven months, and then waved them away in less than two and a half double-spaced, poorly reasoned pages.

Although Michael had been calm on the phone with John, he was as angry as he'd ever been. The preparations for the new trial had convinced Michael of something he had hoped was true for sixteen years, but that he didn't really ever accept before: John was innocent. He didn't kill Ray Liuzza. All of this was a frame-up job.

They had discussed it since day one—how the key to John's freedom would be convincing others of his innocence—even as they had all thought John was probably guilty.

The only person who thought John was guilty now was Judge Quinlan. *The only thing right in this opinion*, Michael thought, *is that we had five claims.* That was Quinlan's first sentence. From there, everything else was wrong. He reduced their arguments to the statement that John deserved a new trial in the murder because of the reversal of the armed robbery. Certainly that was a component of their argument—and it should have been enough to get John a new trial all by itself—but the judge's opinion completely ignored all the new testimony they had gathered: Steve McAllister and Rosemarie Cash McAllister, Sheri (Hartman) Kelly, all the information John could have provided in his own defense, Funk Perkins's lies—all of it.

The judge claimed that he had "painstakingly reviewed the entire record in the matter," but he clearly had disregarded anything new. He even said that "the court is convinced that such testimony would have had no effect on the outcome of the trial." *Why even have a jury system?* Michael thought.

The opinion stated that Couhig and Fanning didn't call John's mother or stepfather as witnesses, despite the fact that they were listed as alibi witnesses and could have testified as to his whereabouts. Michael wondered at that. Was there a jury on earth that would be thinking, "Well, since his mother didn't testify, he must have killed the man"?

The more he read, the more astonished Michael became. He had always thought that Quinlan was a pretty fair guy, but his misreading of the impact of the armed robbery on John's murder trial seemed almost willful, like he was determined not to look at it from any perspective other than the DA's. The law said that a new trial should be granted if the error at trial was "material." "Material" meant that it was more likely than not that a jury could have reached a different conclusion if the error had not been made—if things had been done properly. How could Quinlan not see that preventing John from testifying in his own defense was a structural error, one that would fundamentally change the nature of the trial in the jury's eyes? The test wasn't whether it convinced Quinlan—it was whether it reasonably could have affected a jury's decision.

Even so, Quinlan had written, "This court was indeed surprised to learn from petitioner at the post-conviction hearing that he had no recollection of where he was on the night of the murder." This seemed ridiculous, since John had been saying that since day one. How could the fact that John never had an alibi be used to refuse him a retrial after a decade and a half of imprisonment?

The judge continued, "Nothing in the testimony presented convinces this court that the outcome of the trial would have been different had [the new witnesses] testified. Instead, this court finds more telling the testimony of Richard Perkins at the hearing." *Unbelievable,* Michael thought. *Quinlan thought Funk was the most credible witness? He's said something different at every appearance.* Quinlan said that Funk "has remained consistent in each of these appearances, and in each of these appearances, he leaves no doubt that John Thompson is responsible for the death of Mr. Liuzza."

Michael's anger reached a boiling point. He didn't even realize he was speaking out loud as he said, "Consistent? The man's story changes every time he opens his mouth! Quinlan has no doubt?

None? Perkins wasn't an eyewitness and his story, every time, was based at least in part on testimony from Kevin Freeman, who was copping a plea! Funk knew he was going to get paid when he stepped forward! No doubt? What planet is this guy on?"

Michael shook his head. He and Gordon had done what they set out to do. They had saved the life of a death row inmate. They had struck a blow against the death penalty, and they'd done it from within the system, using strong advocacy and immaculate ethics to get the job done.

Now, though, they realized that it wasn't nearly enough.

This isn't finished, he thought.

45

VISUAL AIDS

FEBRUARY 22, 2002

Michael and Gordon sat down in the conference room at their office. They were appealing Judge Quinlan's rejection to the Louisiana 4th Circuit Court of Appeals, and both men knew that this new brief was John's last real chance at freedom.

It was ironic how the stakes had changed. If the DA's office in 1988 had offered Michael a deal where John was removed from death row and delivered to OPP for a life sentence, Michael and Gordon, and probably John, would have taken that deal in a heartbeat.

Not anymore.

The case they had put before Quinlan in their motion for retrial was solid, but it had failed to carry the day. Their investigation of the dailies had opened up new avenues, avenues that Maureen Kelleher had exploited to turn up new witnesses and new evidence supporting their case. They had evidence—some old, some new—of prosecutorial misconduct in both the armed robbery and murder cases. They had the fact that the DAs had deliberately accelerated the armed robbery case to facilitate the murder prosecution, a strategy admitted to by Dubelier and Williams.

Given that, anything less than John Thompson's freedom was simply unacceptable.

To rule the way Quinlan did, the judge had to believe that the armed robbery conviction was not considered by the jury in the guilt phase, and that it wasn't a reason for keeping John off the stand in the murder trial. On top of that, Quinlan had to believe that all of the people identified in the "newly discovered" police dailies either should or could have been known to John's lawyers in 1984, despite Dubelier's failure to disclose them in discovery requests. And finally, he had to believe that the combined testimony of the new witnesses couldn't have changed the outcome of the trial.

The 4th Circuit was their best—and maybe their only real—shot to get Quinlan's verdict overturned. The farther away from Quinlan's courtroom their appeal went, the more likely that the appeals courts would support Quinlan's result, on the grounds that Quinlan had seen and heard the testimony and was entitled to that deference. Unlike their previous case, they had no real issues of constitutional import that would conceivably lead to a U.S. Supreme Court review. To get around Quinlan, and keep John from cracking, they had to get a new trial, and they had to do it immediately.

Of course, even if they did get a new trial, *winning* it was something else altogether. Trials were inherently risky, flimsy, and unpredictable. No matter what the lawyers thought, losing a new murder trial was definitely possible—and the only thing more soul-crushing than not getting a new trial would be getting one and then losing it.

Michael was excited about the new brief they were drafting, though. Their argument that John had been deprived of his right to testify in his own defense was strong, but even better, this brief marked the first time that their defense of John didn't rest on cool legal detachment and objectivity. It was not burdened with the need to justify a reversal despite John's action, and his guilt. Now, just as Andy Leipold had predicted at the outset, their arguments were fueled by the righteousness of an innocent man wronged, rather than an intellectual advocacy that favored adherence to legal process even if the end result was freeing a guilty man.

As with any argument, the key would be asking the right question to the 4th Circuit. The way they wanted to phrase the question was with astonishment: *How on earth could Quinlan not grant John Thompson a new trial with all this evidence?* Using the conference room's omnipresent flip pad, Michael and Gordon outlined all the things that might be argued in a new trial.

"We've got all the facts we need," Gordon said. "With the armed robbery conviction gone, John can take the stand and testify for the first time in his own defense. We've got new witnesses to the crime and crime scene; we've got Freeman's conflicting statements, impeached by the audiotapes and other new documents in a way Couhig couldn't have done in 1985; and we've got Funk's testimony from the 2000 reward hearing, unknown in 1985, that Dubelier actively encouraged him and Freeman to collude against John. You add that to all the previously known evidence about the reward, and you've got a pretty compelling case for a new trial. At the same time, Quinlan's opinion will get deference from the higher court. We can't just put all the statements from Perkins or Ken Carr or Kevin Freeman together and count on the appeals court to rule our way."

Michael agreed. "How would you juice it up? It's hard to put a creative writing exercise in an appellate brief."

Gordon considered that. "Well . . ." Gordon looked at his friend over the polished oak table while he doodled on his notepad. "You know what we need? Visual aids," he said. "We need to tell John's story in pictures, and we can attach the pictures as appendices. Those pictures won't be quite as restricted if we use them as an argument in the brief itself."

Gordon leaned forward, flipping to a new page on his pad and drawing as he talked. "Here's Josephine Street. This line down here, this is Carondelet. And this, up here, this is Dryades. Draw Liuzza's body here on the sidewalk, you know, like a chalk outline?" Gordon drew the outline of a body on the sidewalk.

Michael followed the thought. "I like it," he said. "And we can color-code different pictures, with explanations. Quinlan said that he thought Funk Perkins was so credible? Maybe we put the different versions of his stories, or Kevin Freeman's stories, in different colors. Or we can show the difference between what Kevin Freeman testified to and what other witnesses heard or saw by outlining the stories, each in a different color."

Gordon was getting excited. "We put this in the appendix, with the red showing the new information we didn't have before, and the 4th Circuit judges have a picture of how the new information totally changes the story told at trial. They can't possibly see it as immaterial."

Then Gordon sat back, his eyes widening. He smiled. "Michael, you're a genius."

"What?"

"The colors. We can use it in the argument."

"What do you mean?"

"The colors." He leaned forward and said, "What if we give them our closing argument now? To show the 4th Circuit we deserve a new trial, we've basically got to show that we'd win if they gave it to us. So we might as well give them our closing argument today. We write it out, we show them the closing argument we *could* have used in 1984 if we had known then what we know now. And then we use your colors. We color the actual text in the brief, showing the sentences that are only known to us now in red, and we leave the old argument portions black. We can even translate that to a map with one story in red and the other in a different color, if we need to. They'll see the materiality of the facts—the judges will see just how much the closing argument changes, right there, in black and, well, red."

Michael sat back, put his pen down, and grabbed his cup of coffee, taking a sip and realizing that it had gotten cold while they had been drafting. Gordon's idea was exactly the opposite of every trial lawyer's standard gut instinct. No trial lawyer wanted his or her closing argument to be known to the other side. Showing their hand that early would give the DAs plenty of time to craft responses. Still, it wasn't like their arguments would be surprising to Solino. And now, with John's future on the line, was the perfect time to put their best arguments forward. Plus, if Connick knew how powerful their closing argument would be, maybe he'd think it wasn't a battle worth fighting. The man was nothing if not pragmatic.

"I think it's a great idea. Let's do it."

The decision galvanized both men. They divided up the issues, each man returning to his office and typing furiously on his computer. The entire closing argument was written in less than two hours. They sent it to word processing with new evidence underlined and instructions to turn those sentences red.

The next day, they reviewed the final draft. Both men agreed that the colored text was even more persuasive than they had hoped. The lines of red filled up the pages, translating a pedantic "materiality" argument into a powerful, visceral statement. Some pages had only one line of black text amid all the red, as the defense arguments shifted completely from legal minutiae and pleas for compassion to outrage at a travesty of justice, a fraud perpetrated in Quinlan's court and the jury by unethical and unscrupulous DAs.

Still, Michael was worried. As he looked at the arguments, at the red text and the green-and-red map, questions gnawed at him: Would the 4th Circuit agree that the truth as it could have been known to a jury in 1985 was different than the truth that could be known to a jury today? Would they see Funk Perkins and Kevin Freeman as liars, or as imperfect witnesses telling the truth?

Michael didn't know how the 4th Circuit would rule, but he knew that they had made a strong case for how they *should* rule. The answers, all their facts, all their arguments, they were all there. He signed the bottom of the last page, certifying his agreement to the truth of the brief, and walked it over to his paralegal. His eyes followed her as she walked down the hall to mail the brief to New Orleans.

If this doesn't work, he thought, *nothing will.*

46

WISHES GRANTED

JULY 17, 2002

MICHAEL WAS ON the phone with opposing counsel for a different case when he received a call from a reporter at the *Times-Picayune*.

The reporter told him, "I'm reading the decision in your case from the 4th Circuit and was wondering what your reaction to it was, and whether you could tell me anything about it for a story."

"Decision?"

"You mean you haven't seen it?"

Michael was confused. "I don't think so. What decision?"

"The decision I just got over the wire from the Louisiana 4th Circuit Court of Appeal in New Orleans. I just assumed that if I had it . . ."

"What does it say?" He was clenching the phone so hard his fist hurt. There was no immediate answer. He said, "Can you hear me? What does it say?"

"Well, that's what I'm trying to figure out."

Michael sat back down, looking at the clock on his wall. It was after five in the evening in New Orleans. "I don't suppose you could fax it to me?"

"Absolutely."

"Let's do that. For now, though, flip to the back page. Can you read me what it says there?"

"Well, the last page has signatures and service stuff. But the page before that says, in all capital letters, 'WRIT APPLICATION GRANTED: JUDGMENT DENYING APPLICATION FOR POST-CONVICTION RELIEF REVERSED,' and after that, it says, 'CONVICTION AND SENTENCE REVERSED AND THE CASE IS REMANDED.'"

Michael didn't answer for a few seconds. He was too busy jumping around his office and pumping his fists.

"Michael? Are you still there?"

"Yeah, I'm here. This is terrific news. I don't know exactly what it means, but I know it's good news. Do me a favor—fax it to me, let me discuss it with Gordon, and then we'll call you back."

THE FAX CAME through about fifteen minutes later. By this time, Michael, Gordon, various junior lawyers and paralegals who had worked on the case, and an assortment of other colleagues were standing around the fax machine, waiting.

The hugging, hand-shaking, and backslapping started as Michael read the first page aloud. It was a complete and total victory. The 4th Circuit had granted their writ, reversing Quinlan's opinion that John was not entitled to a new trial. They had set aside his murder conviction. No longer was John Thompson presumed guilty. For the first time since April of 1985, he was considered innocent until proven otherwise. At last, the burden of proof was back on Connick's office.

Gordon and Michael embraced, slapping each other on the back. Amid the impromptu celebration, they read the rest of the opinion. It was a unanimous decision, which was good. Even better was that it responded to their arguments, rather than ignoring them. The appeals court found that there was no question that John didn't take the stand in the murder trial because of the armed robbery, and agreed that once the armed robbery was thrown out, the failure to grant John a new trial had deprived him of his constitutional rights to due process of law, the privilege against self-incrimination, and the right to compulsory process, in violation of both the United States and Louisiana State constitutions.

Gordon's one disappointment was that the Court had not expressly addressed the issue of prosecutorial misconduct or whether the DAs had violated *Brady*. It wasn't absolutely necessary in order to give John his victory, but it would have fanned the flames of public outrage against Dubelier and his henchmen. Still, the result was a good one. John Thompson was an innocent man.

For now that was enough, maybe more than enough. Gordon turned to the group. "Four Seasons—drinks are on me."

47

AGGRAVATED ASSAULT AND BATTERY

OCTOBER 26, 2002

JOHN SAT IN an interrogation room at OPP, holding his head with his hands, feeling it swell. He tried not to think about the new charges that the police were sure to file against him now, or what they would do to his retrial. He was alive, and it would be a while before anyone could beat on him again.

At first, he had thought that OPP was different than his last time there, in 1986. But then he decided that it wasn't OPP that was different, it was him. OPP had always been a horrible, overcrowded, filthy, smelly place on Perdido Street. What was different was John, who knew things now, like *perdido* meant "lost" in Spanish.

The differences in John translated to his environment in surprising ways. He knew a lot of the men he was incarcerated with, either directly or through their families, and he hadn't been around on the streets to be part of the silly arguments and insults that led to prison fights. And the senior guards, the captains and lieutenants, they had been junior guards when John was young. All of them—the ones the young men called "old school"—they had survived by figuring out a different way of doing things. One of them had even asked John to be the tier rep for the inmates, helping the guards keep order, which presumably meant the guards would give John more respect in return.

In prison, like anywhere else, respect was the coin of the realm. If the guards wanted John to help keep the peace on the tier, he could do that, but he needed some reason to do it for them, something that showed respect to him.

That's what had really started things off on the wrong foot that morning. A different guard, one John didn't know well, had come on the tier. The dude was huge, probably four-hundred-plus pounds. John had seen him before and knew the man was on the "go get 'em squad"—OPP's shakedown squad. They would come into cells from time to time and turn them upside down or harass the prisoners in other ways to make sure they weren't getting too comfortable.

You didn't last long in prison if you didn't learn how to sense where your next threat was coming from, and John knew something bad was going to happen when the guard called roll for breakfast. He came in the tier, leaving the door open behind him, and started calling roll like any other day. The guard moved down the hall calling names as he went. By the time he got to John, he was standing with his clipboard in the hall just outside John's cell. John walked out, but he couldn't get past the guard, who was taking up most of the space in the hallway. John was having trouble figuring out how to get past him. He needed the guard to turn sideways, but the guard didn't want a prisoner to make him move. So John stood, waiting, and he and the guard just looked at each other for a few seconds. Slowly, the guard turned and put his back against the wall so John could walk by, but John knew from the look on the guard's face that he was pretty angry about that. Perhaps he thought John was making fun of him.

After breakfast, the inmates went to the group area on the tier to walk around or clean up things. The doors to the cells were open but the tier was locked down, so people were milling about, showering, cleaning, chatting. John was standing in the doorway to his cell, in the back of the tier, talking to another inmate.

The guard from the morning was back, standing outside the locked door to the tier. He was clearly irritated about something. John heard him say, in a loud voice, "Say you." John ignored it, but the guard said it a couple more times. John hadn't moved or acknowledged the guard in any way, but he assumed that the guard was actually yelling "Say you" to get his attention.

You know who I am, motherfucker, John thought. *I'm the tier rep, and you just called the roll, and I'm in a cell by my damn self—you ain't got to call no "Say you."* So John decided to pretend he hadn't heard the guard and kept on talking.

John heard the guard yell, "I know you hear me," but he kept on talking. Behind him, he heard the guard grab another inmate and send him over, saying, "Yo, tell me what his name is, tell him to come here."

The other inmate walked over to John and said, "Uh, yo, John, the man want you to come over." John decided he was going to ignore that too. *Man wants me, he can figure out my name and ask me by name.*

The guard opened the door to the tier and bellowed at the top of his voice, "Come *here!*" pointing down at his feet. It was loud enough that everything stopped.

John turned and looked at the guard. "Who?"

"You."

"*Who?*" John was playing with him now. He wasn't going to answer to "you" any more than he would answer to "boy" or "nigger."

Eventually John started walking over to the guard, taking his time. The guard took one step into the tier, saying, "Oh, no, you ain't got to come now, you ain't got to come."

"What you mean—you callin' me over, now you sayin' I ain't got to come over?"

"No, I got something for your ass—you ain't got to come."

John shrugged. "Fuck you then." He turned his back on the guard and walked back to his cell and his conversation.

That got him. The guard started screaming again. "Get your ass over here—right now!"

John could see the guard was getting a little too upset, so he walked over but stayed quiet, and stood calmly in front of the guard. "You think I'm a new jack?" the guard asked.

John kept his voice low. "Man, what you think I am? Callin' me 'you' like that. You know my name; it ain't hard to figure it out, it's on the roll. You know I'm the tier rep. You got it right there in front of you. I don't know what all this is about, you know? What you supposed to be doin' to me? What I'm supposed to let you do to me, better yet?"

The guard looked at John. "You a *bad* motherfucker, man, you got to talk *plain shit*, huh?"

The two men were standing alone in the doorway to the tier, out of earshot of the other inmates if they spoke quietly, so John said, "Man, fuck you, you stupid ass." If it was a case of his word against this guard, John knew he had other ranking guards who would make sure nothing too bad happened to him. They'd pull him aside, tell him, *John, yo, man, don't disrespect him none. Don't do that no more.* And he would agree. But right then, John thought, *This motherfucker needs to know I'm a human bein'. He's gonna address me, he can address me right.*

The guard had a different plan in mind. He was waving John out of the tier door. John knew that was dangerous. He would be exposed out there, with no one to see what might happen to him.

John said, a little more loudly to attract attention, "Man, you bring your fat ass in here. I try goin' out there and you want me to come out there so you can say I started somethin'."

The guard said, "Come on, punk." John didn't have a choice, so he stepped through the door past the guard, who locked the door behind them. John kept moving past him, wanting to be out of fighting range, but the guard said, "Hold up, hold up, let me lock the door." He turned the key quickly, turned to John, and said "Come on, let's go."

As John turned to walk down the hall the guard hit him in the back of the head, knocking him forward through a doorway to the stairs and into the stairway railing. John was able to grab the railing and keep from flipping over it as he sprawled. He pulled himself back and put his hand to his head, feeling the place where he had been hit. Then instinct took over, and so he turned and rushed right at the guard, whose open hands met John's charge and pushed him down on the ground. John rolled and fell into a pile of tin food trays from breakfast, sending them crashing and clattering around.

John jumped to his feet, picked up one of the pans, and tried to hit the guard. The pan was dirty and slippery, and the guard partly blocked it with one hand as it flew out of John's grip and clanged down the stairs.

That sound probably saved his life, because the guards upstairs and downstairs were alerted to something going on. It was a race to see whether they would arrive in time, since the guard was advancing on John and he had nothing to fight with.

John was backed into a corner and the guard put his hands around John's neck, choking him. John had managed to keep his chin down so the guard couldn't get a firm grip all the way around his throat, but the guard gave him nowhere to go, no way to escape.

The taller guard kept choking John, whose legs gave way as he thrashed under the guard's grip. As John fell to the ground, the guard's own girth blocked him from keeping his killer grip. The guard's weight became his enemy, as he couldn't get his arms down to keep choking John. The guard was panting with the exertion, repeating, "I'm gonna kill you, I'm gonna kill you" through panting breaths.

John had the opening he needed. Slowly fighting the guard's hands away, John worked himself feet first along the floor between the legs of the squatting guard, a place where he could stay out of the way of the guard's fists and arms. It worked, John pulling on the guard's ankles to get himself behind the guard, and to keep the guard from turning around easily, the movement breaking the death grip on his neck.

John got behind the guard and reached up, grabbing the guard's handcuffs from his belt. He kept trying to push the guard over, but had almost no leverage. He stood up quickly and turned around, and before the guard could spin around, John hit him in the back of the head with the handcuffs, as hard as he could.

The guard staggered forward into the wall, then turned and sat down, his hand on his head and blood going everywhere. John thought he might have killed the man.

Instead, the man got up and came at John again. John swung the cuffs like brass knuckles and hit him again, and it was over. The guard was down, holding his head. The whole fight had probably taken less than thirty seconds.

John was bleeding, too, down his neck from his eye or his head. Two other guards arrived, their billy clubs out, and John stepped back. He said to the guards, "Better get his fat ass," looking at the guard. John was exhausted, but still angry.

The guard still didn't know what he'd been hit with. He was on one knee, his hand on the back of his head covering the place where John had hit him. There was a *lot* of blood. He was telling the other guards that John was armed. "He got to have something, he got to have something," he panted, the guard trying to hold onto the railing as blood kept gushing out. John held his hands out with the handcuffs in one hand, saying, "Yeah, I got something; run your ass over here again."

The other two guards were surveying the situation, trying not to touch John. One of them had known John for a long time. He said, in that calm prison-guard way, like he was almost sorry for John, "What'd you do, son? Give me those cuffs."

John was outside the tier, by himself, with a bleeding guard and two others in front of him. He knew if he gave the cuffs up, he would be beaten to within an inch of his life, and maybe further. He refused to give up the cuffs, and the men were at a standoff.

He heard the tier door open behind him and backed up. Somehow, when the guard had turned the key, he must not have locked the door. John saw other inmates behind it. With the door open, they all could see and hear what was going on, and that was his lifeline. He said to the guards, "Y'all can go and call whoever else you need to call. I'm gonna stay RIGHT HERE. I ain't gonna go anywhere."

The guard who'd attacked him was still saying "I'm'a kill you, motherfucker, I'm'a kill you."

John's shirt was torn, and his eye was swelling and bleeding. There was blood going down his neck from a scratch on his head, and the blood was soaking into his collar. He could feel scratches from the guard's fingernails on his cheeks.

The standoff continued until a senior guard, a rank, came up the steps. He looked up at John and exhaled, a cross between a sigh and a sneer. "John, what the fuck you done did now?" John was starting to calm down, and he looked at the bleeding guard, thinking, *Man was right. What did I do here?*

"Boy, you just got yourself a new trial, too. What are you thinking about?"

The fat guard was still saying, "I'm'a kill you." *Man, please.*

John handed the cuffs over to the rank. They took him from the tier, walked him downstairs. John knew he was at risk now. Once he was off the tier, anything they wanted to do to him, they could. He knew that any beatings they wanted to administer would go on his report as having happened during the fight, a fight he had started.

But John's backup security rule saved him. It had happened once in Angola too, Andy Leipold getting a call from another New Orleans lawyer after John had absorbed a beating from one of the guards. John gave different people on the tier a phone number to call if anything happened to him. This time, one of the inmates called that number, and Robert Glass answered. He was downstairs before John even was. Robert stood right outside and the guards couldn't do much without his knowing about it. The guards knew they had to make John available to the lawyer once he'd arrived, and once Robert saw him, he'd know what injuries John had suffered, so they couldn't rough him up much more.

They didn't really let Robert talk to John, only a quick "Are you all right?" John responded, "Yeah."

They took John to the infirmary and dressed his wounds, ignored his requests to file charges, told him they'd be filing their own charges, and that his actions were considered aggravated assault and battery.

John sat on that hospital bed and wondered if he'd just thrown away his new trial and his freedom because some fat guard had refused to call him by name.

48

PLEA BARGAIN

FEBRUARY 20, 2003

THE MORE THEY learned from Maureen, the more Michael and Gordon liked their chances at trial. The granting of a new trial completely reset their case and took away all the facts that had been established by the jury in 1985. That took away perhaps their biggest roadblock—Judge Quinlan. Since the trial, Quinlan had enforced the jury's decision, a decision reached in his courtroom and under his supervision. Now, his role would be completely different. He would be an administrator in the new trial, ensuring the accurate rule of law while the jury decided who they believed.

Moreover, Maureen was turning up some interesting information based on the dailies. They had always viewed Freeman, Funk, and Carr as biased, but the more information they learned, the more they began to view them as not only biased, but completely inaccurate.

Still, no matter how good their odds were, a new trial was still a gamble. There were no certainties in a jury trial. The only way to guarantee victory was to settle the case first. That meant convincing the DA not to retry the case, and that was a political issue more than a legal one.

Still, the politics had recently changed. In 2002, Connick had announced his resignation as the Orleans Parish district attorney, a position he had held since 1973. His replacement was Eddie Jordan, the former U.S. Attorney for the Southern District of Louisiana, an African-American DA, and, coincidentally, the man who had recommended Robert Glass to Michael and Gordon several years before.

While Michael and Gordon held out some hope that a case like John's might get a different treatment under Jordan than it had under Connick, not much in their day-to-day work changed on the case with Connick's resignation. The career staff of the DA's office, including Val Solino, stayed in their jobs and continued to move the cases on their dockets, including the *State of Louisiana v. John Thompson*. Michael and Gordon had contacted Jordan immediately after his election, offering their congratulations, but Jordan and his team were still settling in, and there had been no time for a substantive meeting on their case.

Gordon and Michael discussed their options several times with Robert and Nick in New Orleans, trying to read the tea leaves and figure out the best way to avoid a trial. On the one hand, John's imprisonment was a political problem created by Connick's office, and Jordan might want to simply get rid of it and let John go without a retrial. On the other hand, Jordan was both new in his job and black. He might not want to be seen as either soft on crime or going easier on his own race. Of course, New Orleans was an overwhelmingly black city—but most of the fund-raisers were white.

It was Robert's view that the back-and-forth of macro-political issues like this could go on forever. The way to cut through them, he said, was to get Ray Liuzza Sr. to support letting John go without a retrial. If the father of the murder victim was supportive of leniency, no one else would argue.

Gordon agreed. If the Liuzza family agreed that John was innocent, Jordan was off the hook. He could blame Connick for the whole mess, without crossing swords with the powerful Liuzza family.

The only problem with the approach was that Ray Liuzza Sr. had quite politely declined to meet with them. Rather than contact

Mr. Liuzza directly, Michael and Gordon tried to find a representative, someone local and trusted by the older man, who could help them set up a meeting.

Their inquiries led them to Joe Maselli. Joe was a New Orleans lawyer, a close friend of the Liuzza family, and the brother of Ray Jr.'s landlord. Joe agreed to meet with them and hear them out. It was a long shot, but they had nothing to lose, so Gordon flew down to New Orleans for the meeting.

GORDON AND ROBERT walked into Joe Maselli's office, located in a high-rise overlooking Canal Street. They were shown into a conference room where Maselli was waiting. He introduced them to John Finkbeiner, another lawyer, who had recently married Ray Liuzza Sr.'s daughter.

"First of all, I want to thank you for agreeing to meet with us," Gordon stated. "I know that this topic carries an awful lot of emotion for you and for your families, and that you came to believe that John Thompson murdered Ray Liuzza. He must be a hated man to you and to Mr. Liuzza, and I want you to know that we appreciate your being here in an open-minded way.

"Over the fifteen years that I have been involved in this case, a lot has gone on, and we've learned a lot of things about what happened that night. Recently, we've discovered new evidence that suggests that despite the first trial's verdict, John Thompson did not murder Ray, and that, in fact, John's an innocent man. We want to make sure the Liuzza family has all of this evidence, because we actually think that we might be on the same side—we want the truth to be known so that hopefully the family can close the book on this horrible event and move on."

Gordon laid out everything they knew, speaking virtually without interruption for about forty-five minutes, watching Maselli and Finkbeiner for reactions.

Maselli's reactions were quiet and measured. It was hard to tell whether he believed Gordon or not. Finkbeiner was easier to read—rolling his eyes, gasping in amazement, and generally expressing scorn and outright personal distaste for Gordon.

At the end, Joe Maselli said, "Mr. Cooney, thank you for your time and for laying this all out for us. What would you like us to do?"

Gordon explained the status of their discussions with the DA and their efforts to have the charges against John dropped. While they thought they would be successful with that approach, they still would prefer to avoid the expense, uncertainty, and stress of a retrial. "Our first obligation is to represent John, but we also believe that a retrial will simply create more pain and anguish for the Liuzzas, and we see no reason to put them through that. We'd just ask that you communicate these facts to Mr. Liuzza and keep them in mind as these discussions evolve."

Maselli rose and extended his hand. "Very well, Mr. Cooney, we will do that. I should tell you, though, that as of now, the Liuzza family is content with the legal process that convicted John Thompson for Ray's murder, and they believe that the trial reached the correct conclusion."

Gordon nodded. There was nothing more to do but hope that they had planted a seed that would soon sprout.

APRIL 28, 2003

GORDON SAT IN Robert's conference room, surrounded by a mass of documents. Michael was out of town on one of his other cases, and Gordon was gearing up for the series of preliminary motions on the new trial that would be decided over the next two days.

These *in limine* motions were important. The structure of the trial was coming together, and the motions were John's legal arguments setting forth what he thought should or should not be allowed at the trial. Would the DA be able to flash a gun around in the courtroom when the actual weapon had been lost or destroyed? How would they deal with the testimony of Kevin Freeman, given the new information they had discovered? What about Paul Schliffka, who had recently died and could not reprise his testimony from 1985? Dozens of issues like these had emerged, and Quinlan would need to hear arguments from Solino and Gordon to sort through them and make rulings, each impacting the case that both sides could put on at trial.

Gordon sipped from a cup of stale coffee as he edited multiple motions, his red pen making precise notations. He evaluated dozens of potential witnesses and hundreds of trial exhibits. He wrote lists of the topics they would cover in voir dire, and reviewed drafts of the opening statement and closing argument. In short, he reviewed anything and everything that could happen during their three- or four-day trial. The amount of work they had to do in the next ten days was immense.

Some of the research and preparation could be delegated to junior lawyers and paralegals, but only some. He and Michael had to know everything cold. Trials were chaotic, and they had to run the plays and call the audibles on the field. And the stakes—*Well,* Gordon thought, *let's just say the stakes are kind of high.*

Stupid case shouldn't even go to trial, Gordon thought. They had asked Solino repeatedly for an audience with Eddie Jordan to ask that proceedings be dropped. Each time, they had been stonewalled: Mr. Jordan was busy with his transition and couldn't discuss the matter right now. *He better turn his attention to it soon,* Gordon thought, *or it'll all be over, one way or the other.*

Until Jordan granted them an audience, their best defense would be a good offense. If Jordon thought he might lose the retrial, he'd be more inclined to offer a deal. He could easily save face with the family. Why dredge up all of the emotions of the Liuzza shooting again when he could sidestep them? Why accept the blot on the Connick DA's office and extend it into the Jordan era by retrying John?

For now, though, their game of legal chicken continued, so Gordon, Michael, and Robert divided the witnesses and the caseload. Michael would be responsible for questioning the NOPD officers involved—Curole, Demma, Carter, Cusimano, as well as Sheri Hartman—now Sheri Kelly—the new eyewitness disclosed in the police dailies. Gordon would handle Ken Carr, if Carr appeared, as well as Otto Stubbs, the NOPD ballistics expert, and the McAllisters, their new "earwitnesses" who had lived across the intersection from the shooting. And the main witnesses, Funk and John, would be examined by Robert Glass.

When Gordon told his colleagues at work that Robert was examining the marquee witnesses, they were surprised. It was a risk for lawyers as talented in the courtroom as Michael and Gordon to give up control of key elements in the case. As Gordon saw it, though, Robert was far more experienced at criminal defense than both he and Michael combined, and would know how to handle the job. Plus, they couldn't run the risk that their very out-of-town presence in the courtroom would take away John's credibility on the stand. And Robert was locked in, still steaming after his tangle with Funk in Quinlan's courtroom in 2001. If he could expose Funk as not credible in front of the jury, they had a great chance at winning the case.

Gordon snapped himself out of his daydreaming. *If you don't pay attention to these motions,* he chided, *there won't be a case to try.* He turned back to the outlines.

APRIL 29, 2003

GORDON AND ROBERT sat in the waiting area outside the DA's office, talking quietly. They had walked back with Solino from the hearing on the motions *in limine*. It had been a fairly discouraging, though not totally surprising day. Quinlan was still an ex-DA, and he ruled in favor of the prosecution on several issues that could have gone either way. He had ruled against Gordon—against John—to permit

Solino to wave around a gun that matched the murder weapon. The fact that it had been the NOPD's job to retain the evidence and it had failed, or the concern that the gun might be unfairly persuasive to the jury, didn't dissuade Quinlan at all.

More troubling, Quinlan was going to allow all of Kevin Freeman's testimony from the first trial to be used in the new trial. As Solino had pointed out, Freeman was his key witness, and the testimony had been admitted under oath in the previous trial. With Freeman dead, the use of his prior testimony was necessary for the government's case.

Gordon had argued that in 1985, during John's murder trial, the DA's office had documents in its possession that would have called into question the truthfulness of Freeman's testimony at trial. To allow Solino to use the "sanitized" trial transcript without the other statements would effectively mean that there was no cross-examination of John's key accuser.

Quinlan realized that without Freeman, the DA's case was severely damaged, so he allowed Freeman's testimony—but he was clearly concerned about Gordon's argument. "I can't not allow the existing testimony to be used if the witness is unavailable to testify. If you can find a way to address your concerns, Mr. Cooney, I'll listen to it." Michael had told Gordon it was a victory to have kept the issue alive at all, but it didn't feel like a win to either man.

After the hearing, Solino said he had something new to give them, so they had followed him to the DA's office. Gordon looked up as Solino walked through the door, a photo in his hand, another man one step behind him.

For fifteen years, the only photo of John that Michael and Gordon had was one taken after John's arrest in January, 1985, six weeks after the murder. They had believed that there was another mug shot from mid-December, 1984, only a week or so after the Liuzza murder. John had been arrested and held for a week on a charge totally unrelated to both the murder and the Lagarde carjacking: unpaid parking tickets. It was almost comical, given his other charges.

They had asked for the photo when they first took the case over but had never received it. Now, Solino had found it in some old file folder in the DA's office while preparing for trial.

Val's comrade spoke, "Mr. Cooney, I'm Francis Reed, First Assistant District Attorney."

Gordon shook his hand.

"Let me get right to the point. Val obviously has kept me and Mr. Jordan informed of this case and its progress. We understand the situation that we find ourselves in, and that Mr. Thompson finds himself in. What do you think it would take to make this case go away?"

Gordon looked at Mr. Reed, surprised. "Well, it seems that that's totally within your control. All you have to do is drop the charges against our client, and your problem goes away immediately."

Reed gave Gordon a smile. It was the expected answer. "Yes, I know, we can simply give in, of course," he said. "But seriously. Is there a deal that we can make here to save everybody some time and some stress? The Liuzza family is behind retrying Mr. Thompson, and as a political matter, we've got to move the case forward. That said, I'm sure you understand Mr. Jordan has no personal ax to grind on Mr. Thompson. Can anything be done?"

"We certainly appreciate the position you and Mr. Jordan are in. We can't accept anything less than Mr. Thompson's immediate release. What terms could you give us that would have that result?"

Reed pulled his hand down his chin, an act to suggest that he was considering it for the first time. "Well . . . let's say we offer accessory after the fact to the murder and let him go with time served?"

Robert chimed in. "Would you accept an *Alford* plea?"

Gordon watched Reed closely. In their internal talks about plea bargains, John had stated vigorously and repeatedly that he was not going to plead guilty just to get out of prison. "I didn't do it," he said. "I ain't never said I did it, and I ain't gonna start now. They want me to plead guilty, fuck 'em. Let's go to trial and do it that way, then."

Gordon, Michael, and Robert all agreed that the DA would want a guilty plea, both to satisfy the Liuzza family and because an innocent man might sue for unjust imprisonment. They all knew, though, that convincing John to plead guilty was unlikely. The man didn't survive death row without being pretty stubborn, after all.

Robert's idea for breaking through the stalemate was an *Alford* plea, named after the Supreme Court case that allowed its use, similar to a "no contest" plea. John would not admit that he was the murderer and would continue to assert his innocence. He would admit, though, that the DA had enough compelling evidence that a jury could find him guilty. The plea amounted to "I didn't do it, but I know I might lose at trial, so let's concede that and move on." The courts treated an *Alford* plea as a type of guilty plea, and it was used the same way for sentencing and other purposes.

If John agreed, he wouldn't formally plead guilty, and the DA would avoid criticism for jailing a man who had been formally acquitted in a jury trial. John would get his freedom, and Jordan and his office could tell the Liuzza family truthfully that they had won a guilty plea and had freed John because of the previous administration's ethical lapses. Everyone got something.

Reed put his hands in his pockets and looked down for a few seconds, thinking. "The judge has got to go along with it, but if Mr. Thompson and Judge Quinlan agree to an *Alford* plea, I can deliver Mr. Jordan."

"Well, I can ask my client," Gordon said. "He was very opposed to pleading guilty. *Alford* might be acceptable to him, if he would be immediately released from prison."

"We would be willing to release him as soon as they can turn the paperwork."

"I suspect John is still back in the judge's chambers after today's hearing. We'll go back there right now and see what we can do on both of those issues." He shook Reed's hand, and the first assistant turned and walked back through the secure doors into the office, leaving Gordon and Robert with Solino.

"Sounds like you guys might not need this, but since it's what you came over here for, here you go." He handed Gordon the photo.

Gordon was astonished.

The *Times-Picayune* photo of John, the January mug shot, had shown him with an unkempt, bushy Afro extending three or four inches from his head. He looked like Don King. It was enough to indicate that when Paul Schliffka saw the shooter running away at a distance of six feet, he wouldn't have called John's hair "close-cropped."

This picture from mid-December, however, was something else altogether.

Gordon glared at Val and held the picture up, facing Val, letting him get a good look. "How long have you known you had this? You guys have been advancing the 'close-cropped hair' thing when you knew he looked like *this*? This thing is *huge*. This Afro must be, I don't know, seven, eight inches out? Are you serious, Val?"

Val's jaw set a little, enough for Gordon to get the message.

"First of all, we've never used it before. I told you about it when I found it."

"Come on, Val. How many more newly discovered files are there going to be? How many abandoned warehouses do you have behind that door? We've been at this for a while, and you've always been above that 'If we don't use it, it's not something we have to disclose' thing."

Val glared at Gordon and said, "Second of all, it doesn't change anything."

"Doesn't change anything? Have you *looked* at this? How are you going to say that *this* guy with *this* Afro"—Gordon held the photo up to Val—"had 'close-cropped hair'?"

"It doesn't. It doesn't change anything. He had an Afro in December, he had an Afro in January, he had an Afro. Schliffka could never positively ID Thompson anyway. It doesn't matter. I can only give you what I know about. And what I know, you know."

GORDON SAT IN the bar in the InterContinental, the late edition of *SportsCenter* playing on the bar TV above him as he sipped a Maker's Mark on the rocks. It had been quite a day.

After a great deal of patient cajoling and persuading, John had agreed to accept the *Alford* plea. It hadn't been easy. As they'd expected, he had been vehemently opposed to any kind of plea bargain. It had taken them more than an hour to convince him otherwise.

"Come on, man, we been through this a hundred times already," John had said when they gave him the DA's offer. "We got the new trial, we oughtta use it. I ain't pleadin' guilty to no fuckin' thing. I know what I did and didn't do, and I didn't do this murder, and that's that. You and Michael and Robert, you guys gonna win the trial, so why am I gonna plead any sort of guilty plea, *Alford* or whatever it's called, or not? It's a guilty plea—doesn't matter how you dress it up. Why I'm gonna do that? No."

Again, Gordon tried to explain to John the unpredictability of trials. He pointed out that John had thought he would win this case in 1985.

"John, you do this deal, you're out of prison. We agree to this, they let you out, and *you are out*. You're free. Things happen at trial. We can't tell you who the jury will be or what they'll see. One of them doesn't like you because you've got a funny expression, or you smile at the wrong moment, or he had a friend who got killed in a holdup three years ago, or you wore a red tie and he hates red, and then that guy convinces the rest of them you're guilty, and you're gone forever. You'll die in prison. That's a tough chance to take."

John rocked back in his chair. "When do I get out if we take the plea?"

"Tomorrow. Thursday, latest."

"And I'm not admitting I'm guilty?"

"Technically, no. Not if it's an *Alford* plea," Robert answered.

They waited for his answer.

"All right," John said. "Take the deal."

With John's agreement, Gordon and Robert had walked into Quinlan's chambers and explained the story to the judge. Quinlan thought the arrangement was reasonable and said that he would allow the settlement if both parties agreed.

Gordon called Michael in Chicago, on his way back to Philadelphia.

"It's a no-brainer," Michael said. "Take it. Call Reed back and take it, and I'll come down to New Orleans tomorrow and we can wrap this up."

With everyone aligned, Gordon called the DA's office. He was patched through to Reed. "Mr. Reed, I've got Mr. Thompson's and Judge Quinlan's agreement. From our side, from our perspective, we have a deal. Mr. Thompson will file an *Alford* plea to accessory after the fact to first-degree murder, and you'll agree to have Mr. Thompson released immediately for time served."

It was almost 7:00 PM when Gordon's cell rang. It was Reed. "I've spoken to Mr. Jordan, and it appears we have a deal. Mr. Jordan has suggested that we enter the plea with Judge Quinlan on Thursday, to give us a day to explain the situation to the Liuzza family."

Gordon hesitated. "Does the family have a say in this? This doesn't change anything, does it?"

"No, it doesn't change anything. We've got a deal. But this is a delicate matter, and Mr. Jordan wants to tell the family before the plea, rather than after."

It was a reasonable request, respecting the family by telling them the news before it was made public. Gordon agreed. He hung up the phone and called Michael, then Robert. "Well," he said to each of them, "John gets out of prison on Thursday."

Michael's voice had the same mix of happiness and relief that Gordon was feeling. Believing this was the right result was one thing—realizing it was completely different. He said, "Now all we have to do is figure out between now and Thursday how to support John once he's out, and make sure he doesn't do something that sends him back in."

It was this thought that had brought Gordon down to the hotel bar. His room was too confining, his thoughts and emotions roaming all over the place. He was exultant one minute, disappointed the next. A plea bargain was a sure result, a win on points that got John his freedom. The trial lawyer in him wanted total vindication for John, and the *Alford* plea wouldn't give them that. The advocate in him hated the thought of John pleading guilty, but the sentimentalist in him loved thinking about John's freedom.

But Michael was right: What would that freedom be like for John? Gordon didn't know the statistics for recidivist crimes for guys like John, but he knew they were pretty grim. John would be coming out of prison penniless, jobless, and homeless. His only dealings in the past—well, for his whole life—had been either with criminals on the street or with criminals in prison. There was no doubt he was a different guy than when he went in—but how would he get by on the outside? Who would he turn to for help? Gordon and Michael had agreed to sponsor John in a chef's course, and they'd do whatever they could do, but at some point, they would have to move on to the next case. They'd help John start to build roots, talk to him periodically, but they couldn't be with him late at night, every night. They couldn't live his life for him.

He had thought the task of obtaining John's freedom was Herculean. As it turned out, it was Sisyphean. Their representation of John hadn't ended with his release from death row, and it wouldn't end with his release from prison. Instead, they'd need to stay close to John, perhaps even closer than they had been up to this point, to solve the new challenges posed by his freedom.

APRIL 30, 2003

As HE HAD been doing the whole day, Gordon was working the phones from Robert's conference room. Michael was in the air, on his way down from Philadelphia to accept the plea. Gordon was talking to the Delancey Street Foundation, a group in San Francisco dedicated to helping released ex-cons build the life skills they needed to avoid returning to the criminal life and prison. It was hard to do on twenty-four hours' notice, but he thought they were going to make room for John in their program.

He looked up when Robert came into the room. "What's wrong?" he said.

Robert looked like a dead man. There was no color in his face. He quietly said, "Val Solino called. They just pulled the deal."

Gordon felt his stomach collapse in on itself. "They just *what?*"

"They just pulled the deal. Jordan talked to the family and changed his mind. There's no plea bargain."

Gordon jumped out of his chair, slapping his palms on the desk. "What do you mean, there's no plea bargain? Francis Reed told me himself it didn't matter what the family said, we had a deal. They can't pull the deal. Quinlan agreed, Reed agreed, Jordan agreed, John agreed—we all agreed."

"I know."

Gordon grabbed the receiver and punched at the phone. Solino answered. "What the hell is going on?" He listened. "No, Val. No. That is bullshit, and you know it. We had a deal." He listened again. "Francis Reed told me personally that this was a *courtesy* to the Liuzza family. They don't get a vote here, Val. You can't pull this. We've already gone to the judge." He waited again. "If that's how this is, then I want to talk to Mr. Jordan. This is ridiculous. Of all the shit you guys have pulled, making us lose two days of trial prep this close to trial—for God's sake, Val, John Thompson thinks he's getting out of jail tomorrow! How the hell can you guys—"

Gordon stopped, trying to compose himself. "Look. I want to hear it from Jordan himself. I think that's quite literally the least you can do." He hung up and turned to Robert. "Solino's going to get Jordan to call us back. Can they do this? Can they pull the plea?"

Robert nodded. "Short answer is yes. If it's not entered, it's not entered."

Gordon sat back down. Michael was on a plane; John was waiting to be released. The trial was back on for Tuesday, and they had spent the past two days working on settlement and post-release issues instead of getting ready for a trial that was now only six days away.

His cell phone rang, and he snatched it open.

Solino said, "I spoke to Mr. Jordan and conveyed to him your request to speak with him. I was instructed to inform you that Mr. Jordan has nothing to say to you."

"He has nothing to say to me? Are you kidding me, Val?"

Solino said nothing.

"He has nothing to say to me. Beautiful. You guys are going to regret this. Mark my words." He hung up the phone before Val could say anything else.

After all of their efforts convincing John of the riskiness of going to trial, that was exactly where they were going.

Gordon got up from the desk and walked out of Robert's office with a sideways glance at Robert, feeling in his pocket for the rental car key. He had to go get Michael from the airport, and then, Jesus, they'd have to go tell John.

It was after dark, and after visiting hours, when they finally made it to OPP. "Gordon Cooney and Michael Banks, to see our client, John Thompson. It's urgent."

"What's this about, sir?"

"I need to see my client, Mr. John Thompson. We had the DA renege on a settlement—a plea bargain—and Mr. Thompson is expecting to be released from prison tomorrow after eighteen years in. I need to tell him what has happened."

"Well, Mr., uh—Cooney," the guard said, looking at his Pennsylvania Bar ID card, "you're not a Louisiana lawyer?" The guard said this as if perhaps it was news to Gordon.

"No, sir, I'm not."

"Well, I'm afraid you can't do anything tonight, then."

Michael, standing behind Gordon, threw up his hands with a grunt of disgust. Gordon had greeted him at baggage claim and brought him up to speed, and this was just the final indignity. All the things they had to force their way through, and now this.

Gordon, his voice vibrating in anger, said, "Sir, are you the senior member of the staff on duty?"

"No, sir, I'm not."

Gordon stepped closer to the guard. "Well, unless you want to be named in a civil rights lawsuit and have your name on the front page of tomorrow's newspaper, I want you to get me someone, right now, who has the authority to unlock that door over there and let us in to see our client."

The guard looked at Gordon's face and retreated into the office. A few minutes later an older guard came out, holding Gordon's IDs. "What's the problem here?"

Whatever Gordon's restraint had been, it was gone now. "The problem? The problem is that our client, John Thompson, has been on death row in Angola since 1984 for a murder he didn't commit. We got him a new trial, and your fantastic district attorney, Eddie Jordan, agreed to a plea bargain under which Mr. Thompson was going to be released from prison after *eighteen years* tomorrow morning. Mr. Thompson has gone to bed tonight thinking that tomorrow, he's a free man. All we want to do is walk through that door there so that we can have the pleasure of informing Mr. Thompson that Eddie Jordan has revoked his plea bargain, meaning that our client will have to stand trial again, a *second* time, for a crime that he didn't commit in the *first* place, because the victim's white family is in denial and the DA has no balls. And your officer here won't let us in to see our client and deliver this lousy message because my Bar card happens to say *Pennsylvania* instead of *Louisiana*."

Whatever the senior guard had been told in the back room, he clearly had not been prepared for this. After looking at their IDs again, the guard shook his head in amazement. "Goddamn," he said, pushing a button under his desk that unlocked the door. "I'll show you to a room and we'll get your client."

They were led through several doors, down a long, straight hallway. Every few feet, a set of double doors opened from the center and closed quickly behind them. At the end of the hall, they were led into a small meeting room.

John came in a few minutes later, looking nervous. "What's up?"

He probably thought we were coming to release him a night early, Gordon thought, as he told John the story.

John sat down across the table as Gordon was talking. His head dropped for a moment as he heard the news, but it bounced up quickly. "Hell, you know, I didn't want to give no guilty plea anyhow, you know? This way, we're gonna win legit. We're gonna go in there, we're gonna win. You're gonna tell everyone I'm innocent, and the world is gonna know what Dubelier and Williams and Connie done did to me."

John looked at them, smiled, and said, "Hell, I don't even want to talk about this. You see the Sixers playing the Hornets tonight? I want to talk about those *playoffs,* man. This trial, I know you guys saying it's risky, but I really don't agree."

"John, I'm just really sorry about this," Michael said. "The DA's office . . . we had no idea this would happen. Reed told Gordon we had a deal."

"Yeah, I know," John said. "Ain't nothin' new. I told you guys from the beginning. No matter who it is, you just can't trust the DA."

"There's one other thing, John," Gordon said. "We've lost about three days of trial prep at a bad time. The one thing Solino did say to me was that he'd let us move for a continuance, let us start the trial later, so this doesn't hurt our case. Robert thinks that's a good idea, but we want your input. If we're going to do this, we don't want to go in underprepared."

John shook his head. "Uh-uh. No. We aren't underprepared. You aren't underprepared. We're gonna be ready. I'm ready right now, and you guys, you know what to do and how to do it. You been livin' the case for fifteen years. Besides, I'm ready to be out of here, man. This a crazy place. Crazy shit going on in here, no doubt. Let's keep the date and let's roll with it, and get me on up out of here next week."

"John, we'll run it that way, if that's what you want. But if we're going to do that, Gordon and I better go and get back to work."

John smiled. "Yeah, you do that. Get back to work. Get back to the work of gettin' my ass out of prison. I'll see you two soon." He shook their hands and sat back down to wait for the guard to return him to his cell.

They left John in the room, the door open, and walked back down the hall. Gordon was amazed at John's strength and mood. He didn't seem shaken at all by the news. *Maybe after eighteen years he's already prepared for the worst,* Gordon thought.

Near the first set of double doors segmenting the hallway, Gordon looked back. John was sitting behind the table, slumped over, head in his hands, his body recoiling in silent sobs.

Gordon thought about walking back to John, but knew that John would be embarrassed if he did. He took a long look, then turned and walked back down the hallway they had come in.

49

KEVIN FREEMAN

GORDON, MICHAEL, AND Robert entered Judge Quinlan's chambers for their status conference. The DAs were already there, of course—they always had to get in their unsupervised time alone with the judge. They exchanged terse courtesies with Val and his junior colleague, Shary Scott, eyeing each other like boxers bumping fists before a fight. Everyone sat down—John's team on the right, the DAs on the left—facing Quinlan across his large mahogany desk.

The meeting had been requested by Gordon, who had reminded Quinlan of his promise to listen to any defense requests on how to handle Kevin Freeman's testimony in a way that was equitable to both sides, given that Freeman was dead. He had been shot and killed in 1995 while trying to steal a car from an off-duty sheriff.

Gordon knew that the lawyers on both sides would have preferred to have Kevin Freeman appear in court to give his testimony and be questioned and cross-examined. He was the only person who claimed to have actually seen John Thompson pull the trigger and shoot Ray Liuzza. Solino wanted him because the impact of Freeman saying he saw the crime would be more powerful than having his testimony read to a jury, and Gordon and Michael wanted him because they wanted to cross-examine him in person. But Solino could get by with just the transcript from the last trial, whereas without the chance to cross-examine Freeman, the jury wouldn't hear a number of statements Freeman had made to the cops and in the audiotapes that hadn't been known to Couhig and Fanning in 1985. The jury would be deprived of seeing Freeman's reaction to that new evidence, and wouldn't be able to hear his voice or read his body language to help them frame their own opinions as to his credibility.

Gordon was also concerned that since Freeman's testimony was being read into the record from the previous trial, it would be given a presumption of truth from the jury's perspective, resulting in undue credibility.

Last, and most important, the new witnesses that Maureen had interviewed created a number of questions that Gordon and Michael would have wanted to ask Freeman that would directly attack his previous testimony. It was possible, after all, that Freeman had simply made the whole story up. John had always said that he wasn't anywhere near the scene of the crime on December 6, 1984—what if, after all these years, he was telling the truth? To simply enter Freeman's previous testimony into the record of the new trial without answering these questions, Gordon argued, would be a grave injustice to John. He mentioned as an aside to the judge that such a result would violate, among other things, John's Sixth Amendment right to confront his accusers. They wanted to make it clear to Quinlan that if they lost on this argument, they would appeal to a higher court.

Quinlan listened to all of these arguments and turned to Solino for his response.

Solino had let Gordon speak without interruption, but he was ready, sliding forward in his chair. He agreed that Kevin Freeman was his key witness. He was the only eyewitness and provided motive and location. He had been credible enough that the jury believed him in 1985, when he testified under oath. Without Freeman's testimony, Solino's case would be dealt a severe blow. Solino argued that there were a lot of reasons John Thompson might be released from prison after the trial, but one bad reason would be that there was no case because Kevin Freeman could not reiterate testimony that he provided within the rules of evidence under oath in 1985. He reminded the judge that Freeman's plea bargain had been clear for everyone to consider at the first trial, and it had been validated several times in multiple appeals since.

Solino's argument was balanced and persuasive that Freeman's testimony should be read into the record of the new trial. He respected the right of Gordon and Michael to find other witnesses who would tell different stories and poke holes in Freeman's testimony. "Your Honor, Kevin Freeman wouldn't change his story if he were here today, and we need to go with what we've got."

Quinlan looked back at Gordon. "Mr. Cooney?"

Gordon knew the argument rested on what he said next. Solino had been fair, practical, and compelling, and Gordon said as much to Quinlan. It was the same argument Gordon would have made if he had been in Solino's shoes. Gordon didn't think that he would be successful in convincing Quinlan to exclude Freeman's testimony altogether, so he decided to move to a more moderate position.

Gordon argued that if the Court was going to permit Freeman's testimony to be read into the record, something would be needed to balance the scales. He proposed that the judge permit the defense lawyers to read to the jury the questions that they would have been able to ask Freeman if he were alive. Gordon pointed out that this was a fair compromise—Solino would get the benefit of Freeman's prior testimony, and John's lawyers would be able to question Freeman's credibility in front of the jury at the same time. While it would be impossible for John to literally "confront his accuser," at least the jury would know that there were additional questions that deserved answers.

Solino almost jumped out of his chair at Gordon's suggestion. His voice was higher and louder than normal as he protested that asking questions with no answers would completely undermine Freeman's testimony.

Gordon, sensing that the judge was actually considering the request, jumped in to address Solino's concerns. He reassured the judge that they would gladly give Solino time in advance to review the questions, and that they would share the questions with the judge as well to ensure that they were appropriate and objective, and not prejudicial to the prosecution's case.

Amazingly, it worked. Gordon had hidden his attack as a compromise, and Quinlan was convinced. He agreed to allow the prosecution to read Mr. Freeman's testimony into the record and to allow the defense to read a list of questions they would have asked Mr. Freeman in response.

With that, the hearing was over, and Gordon, Michael, and Robert went to write their list of questions for the ghost that had haunted John Thompson for a decade and a half.

50

RETRIAL

DAY 1: MAY 7, 2003

THE ALARM CLOCK blared, preset by a previous user of the hotel room to some country music station. It woke Michael up with a start, even though it was probably more accurate to say that he'd never really gone to sleep. He put on his robe and started brushing his teeth, and was spitting into the sink when room service knocked.

He didn't generally rely on room service when he traveled. It was a lot more fun to find a decent greasy spoon near the hotel in whatever town he was in, and here, with Mother's right around the corner, why would you go anywhere else? But when he was on trial, he ate in his room. In the quiet, he could collect his thoughts and run the future proceedings through his head. He wanted to be perfect, precise. He wanted their presentation to be so perfect, so ingrained, that it was memorized without being scripted or stilted.

He ate his food without tasting it. Robert was going to give the opening, mapping their strategy for the jury, showing the jury what really happened to Ray Liuzza Jr. on December 6, 1984. Michael kept the lesson of John's first murder trial firmly in mind: It would not be enough to simply claim that John was innocent. *Innocent until proven guilty* was a nice idea, but juries didn't necessarily share that view. No; they needed to help the jury believe that someone else was Ray Liuzza's murderer. While Michael didn't often use Perry Mason as an example of great courtroom technique, they definitely wanted that kind of flair here. Perry Mason never just got the accused off; he also solved the murder. Juries needed that. They needed a believable killer, an alternative, to make sure justice was done.

Robert had managed the jury selection yesterday, and his voir dire had been masterful, weeding out problematic jurors while making their philosophy of the case clear: *The New Orleans DA screwed up this case eighteen years ago, and they are still at it today. The main witness is dead, and there's no scientific evidence. Given all of that, can you find it within yourself to possibly find in favor of the defendant?*

Michael glanced at the clock—6:15 AM. He took off the hotel robe, pulled on a T-shirt, a pair of shorts, and his Sauconys, and took the elevator down to the lobby, where Gordon was waiting. They nodded at each other, neither man feeling particularly talkative, walked out the front door, and broke into a jog, turning toward the river, past Harrah's and across Canal, down to the water. They stayed near the train tracks, looking across the river at the tugs and barges as the morning gray turned gradually into day.

It was a familiar route, built over the past fifteen years, but today they dropped their usual conversation. Michael's senses felt heightened, like he was straining to pick up any signal New Orleans wanted to send him. Right now, along the riverbank, the city seemed groggy and sweaty, waking up from its hangover. But it *would* wake up, and it would take stock of them and their work. He hoped they were ready for it when it came.

BACK AT THE hotel, Michael showered and shaved. He cut himself a little, pulled out a styptic pencil, and stopped the bleeding. He put on a dark blue suit, a blue shirt, and a yellow tie. It was his standard "first day of trial" outfit. He usually counted on the government to wear a blue suit, red tie, and white shirt—to basically wrap themselves in the flag. Michael kept the blue suit, which projected trustworthiness and dependability, and combined it with a blue shirt and yellow tie for a controlled, clean, businesslike look that would distinguish him from the prosecution.

Michael knotted the tie, grabbed his briefcase, and walked downstairs. Gordon was already there. The two men walked out the door and into a cab for the short drive to the courthouse at Broad and Tulane.

They arrived around 8:30. Robert was already there, as was Nick, and several younger Morgan, Lewis lawyers providing document and exhibit support. One of the junior associates walked up to them, smiling. He said, "Good omen. I drove up here in the cab and the cabbie asked me, was I a lawyer? I told him yes, and he said, 'But you're not from around here.' I told him no, we had local counsel, Robert Glass. The cabbie, he starts laughing. He says, 'Robert Glass—you in luck, boy! He gets *everyone* off!' "

Michael grinned. "That's why he's our guy." He walked over to Robert, busy sifting through his papers. "Hear you've got quite a reputation in the public transportation community."

Robert nodded. "They are all my people, straining under the yoke of the State."

Michael patted the older man on his thin shoulder. "Let's chalk another one up for individual liberty today, shall we?" He left Robert to his preparation and looked around.

Solino and Shary Scott came into the courtroom. Val put his briefcase down and came over to say hello. While Val was not smiling, he was at least polite—Shary Scott, on the other hand, was downright unpleasant. She was clearly not interested in shaking their hands. *We've got a true believer there,* Michael thought. That was scary. How could anyone be a true believer in *this* case? Probably good for the defense, though—true believers could have their emotions exploited.

The judge's clerks and the courtroom staff were circulating as the bailiff brought in John. Michael walked over and hugged him warmly. He stood back, holding John's shoulders and clapping him on the arm. "You dress up good, my man."

John was wearing a new suit that Michael and Gordon had bought him, a light tan suit with a shirt and tie. His head was shaved, a grooming decision that John had made years ago as his hair loss had become more and more pronounced. It meant that the jury would have no trouble seeing him as a "man with close-cropped hair," which the prosecution would use, but the fact was that growing an Afro was no longer an option available to John. Better to look clean cut for the jury.

The anticipation in John's eyes was unmistakable. Prison had given him a self-conscious shuffle, brought his posture down, hunched his shoulders a little, like he knew he was being watched and he wanted to make himself invisible. There were flecks of gray in his nicely trimmed mustache and goatee. He wore the suit awkwardly. But Michael couldn't stay away from his eyes. They were a little red, probably from lack of sleep, but alert and focused.

One of Quinlan's clerks opened the door from the judge's chambers and said, "All rise." The courtroom had filled with lawyers, family, friends of both sides, and reporters, all rising in unison. Quinlan came in, walking confidently, but, Michael thought, somewhat gingerly, to the bench.

As much as John had changed in the past fifteen years, it was possible that Quinlan had changed more. He was a tall man, but his height was even more apparent given his considerable weight loss. The bear of a man Michael had met in 1989 was now slender, almost gaunt, his skin pale and hair almost all gray. He'd had a bout with cancer a few years ago. The cancer was gone now, Michael had heard, but not without taking its toll (and as it turned out, this would be the last case Quinlan heard before passing away). He sat down and watched the jury as Quinlan spoke, searching for anything he could get, any edge, any clue.

The jury was silent, expectant, waiting for the show to begin.

When Quinlan was done, Solino stood up, buttoned his jacket, and walked to the podium. He nodded to the jury and began: "Eighteen years ago, five months almost to the day, December 6, 1984. John Thompson, the man seated right over there"—he pointed at John—"snuck up on Ray Liuzza as Ray was coming home from a date in the middle of the night, 12:30 AM, and snuffed out his life over a wallet full of credit cards, a watch, and a ring.

"Why you are here today and what we will be doing the rest of the day today is telling you the story of Ray's last day on this Earth, and the efforts in the community and the police department to bring this case to justice—justice that eighteen years, five months later is still waiting to be served.

"We will prove to you today that on that night, John Thompson saw Ray Liuzza, went up to Ray Liuzza with a gun, tried to rob him, and shot and killed him. Those are the elements of second-degree murder: a person killed during the course of a robbery or attempted armed robbery. The person on trial pulled the trigger and killed the deceased. That's what we will prove to you today."

As Solino explained to the jury that many of his witnesses would be drug dealers and criminals, Michael watched him closely, focusing on his speech patterns and movements more than the content. Solino was a stander, not a pacer, and seemed to be reading his notes, not using them as guides. To Michael, it sounded a little rehearsed, and Val's posture was stiff, not relaxed and authoritative. Still, the man had clearly tried a lot of cases and knew what he was doing. He was reading, but with feeling and careful intonation, speaking pretty quickly—maybe still working the butterflies out, using up his nervous energy and getting adjusted to the jury.

"What Richard Perkins will tell you is as follows." Michael leaned forward a little as Solino introduced one of the trial's mini battles—the credibility of Perkins. Michael, Gordon, and Robert would spend a lot of time convincing the jury that Funk Perkins was not credible, that his story changed every time he told it. It would be complicated by the eighteen-year interval between crime and trial, but it was essential to their success.

Solino continued on with a workmanlike explanation of Funk's story: Funk was given the murder weapon by John and told to go and sell it. He also saw John sell the ring that had belonged to Ray Liuzza on the street. Later, he was told by Kevin Freeman that John had used the same gun to kill Ray Liuzza. Funk, upset that he was now linked to a murder weapon, decided to tell the police what he knew.

Solino traced the gun from Perkins to Junior Lee Harris, then to Jessie Harrison, where it was found by Detective Donald Curole of the NOPD. He described Curole's discovery of the ring on Junior's hand. He told the jury they would *hear testimony* from Harris and Harrison, instead of telling the jury that Harris or Harrison *would tell them* anything, since they wouldn't actually appear at trial, neither man responding to Quinlan's subpoenas.

Solino's opening was a credible, straightforward, factual presentation that lacked any soul or emotional hook to really grab the jury. While he described the five bullets entering Ray's body, he didn't make the jury agonize about Ray pleading for his life, or transmit any outrage at the fact that Ray was unarmed and unthreatening to the shooter when he fired.

In fact, Michael was almost lulled to sleep with repetitive statements: "You'll hear Kevin Freeman say . . ." was the first sentence of every paragraph for the next several minutes, as Solino went through the events leading up to Ray Liuzza's death.

Solino closed with a sideways swipe at Michael and Gordon's case, telling the jury, "You will hear during the course of this trial that there are inconsistencies, sometimes conflicts, as to collateral extraneous issues." Even this, to Michael's ears, had some problems. Solino was trying to tell the jury that Thompson's case had holes and inconsistencies, but words like "collateral" and "extraneous" were not jury-friendly words. Michael recalled advice he'd gotten from his father years ago: *Never make a jury think.*

Robert Glass stood up. As it had been the day before, during jury selection, the differences between Solino's style and Robert's were immediately felt. Like Solino, Robert held a pad of paper in his hand. While Solino's pad of notes was a firm reading guide, Robert used his as a prop, something to do with his hands while his brain thought of the next place to go and how to get there. More telling were the differences in their voices: Solino projected his voice to the back row in an authoritative tone, while Robert spoke so softly that the jurors were forced to lean in to hear. Robert spoke in a conversational tone that engaged individual jurors, like he was telling stories to his best friends.

"Ladies and gentlemen of the jury, Mr. Solino started off by saying that this is a case for you to bring to justice. Really, this is a case to *avoid* an *in*justice, an injustice to John Thompson. John Thompson is absolutely innocent. The murder was committed alone by Kevin Freeman on that street in the early morning in December of 1984. It was an ugly, unnecessary murder by a single man—Kevin Freeman—a man who speaks out of both sides of his mouth. Kevin Freeman will tell you through his transcript that he picked up John Thompson on Prytania and Josephine as John was walking toward his home across St. Charles. Speaking out of the other side of his mouth, he told Richard Perkins that John had gone to his house and that Kevin Freeman and John Thompson had left Kevin Freeman's house together.

"Kevin Freeman will say through his transcript that he ran out of gas on Josephine Street on the way home before he got to Baronne Street where Mr. Liuzza was. But speaking out of the other side of his mouth, he told Richard Perkins that he hadn't run out of gas, that he had crossed Baronne Street, that he had parked at Katie's Beauty Salon, and that he walked back—back toward Mr. Liuzza in order to rob him.

"Kevin Freeman, through his transcript, will tell you that he ran off after the shooting, ran home because his car was out of gas. Richard Perkins will report him speaking out of the other side of his mouth. Kevin Freeman told Perkins that he ran to his car and drove off to go home.

"Kevin Freeman had every motive to lie about the circumstances upon which he put off on John Thompson. He sold his story for his life to the police, and then to the State, because he was first charged, too, with capital murder. In exchange for his testimony he was given a minor plea, accessory after the fact, going down from life or death to just one year in prison.

"Mr. Solino will bring you Richard Perkins, who will tell you that John Thompson confessed to him about the murder. He will come to you today as a person who has been convicted four times of drugs, of PCP or cocaine. He is doing fifteen years flat as a multiple offender. That is who you have to believe.

"You have to believe someone who will admit to you that during this entire period of time he was high on PCP and his mind was not right. And ultimately he will tell you that he didn't care about John, because in his words, 'He tried to frame me in it, and I needed to clear myself and I could get a reward for it, so hey, that's what I did.'

"That's who the State will ask you to rely on. But we ask you to rely on the neighbors. The people who had no ax to grind; the people who had nothing, absolutely nothing to get out of this. Three witnesses will testify with no biases. These witnesses will tell you that the man with the gun, the robber, the only person on the scene, had close-cropped hair, was not shortish like John Thompson, at five feet, eight inches, but taller, like Kevin Freeman, at five feet, eleven and one half inches. And that the man, the robber, had close-cropped hair. When John Thompson went to jail on December 12th, six days after the robbery and awful killing of Ray Liuzza, he had a big Afro, not close-cropped hair."

Richard's voice increased in volume a notch. "There will be—except for Kevin Freeman's transcript testimony to you, and Richard Perkins's testimony to you—*no corroboration whatsoever* that John Thompson was responsible in any way, was around at any point, was there and involved at all with the killing by Mr. Kevin Freeman of Mr. Ray Liuzza. It's been a long time coming, but this is a case to bring to justice. This is a case to avoid an injustice. This is a case where you have an innocent man here, and only a jury can say to that innocent man, finally, 'Go home.' "

Robert held the jury's gaze for a long moment, compelling them to look at him as his last words echoed in the courtroom. He turned and walked back to counsel's table.

Michael looked at Gordon, who gave a little nod. Round one to Robert Glass.

They won round two almost immediately after Solino stood to inform Judge Quinlan and the jury that the murder weapon and two bullets had been lost or destroyed by the Criminal District Court Property and Evidence Room. If Solino had no murder weapon to wave around in the courtroom, the jury would want to know why.

Shary Scott rose and said, "Your Honor, State calls Richard Perkins."

Michael and Gordon glanced at each other, eyebrows going up. Was the junior attorney going to examine Funk?

She was. Perhaps it was the knowledge that anything Funk said could be impeached by any of his five previous statements, or perhaps it was inexperience. Regardless, her questions seemed designed to elicit as few new statements as possible. Funk described John giving him a gun to sell, described waiting outside J.R.'s house as Funk sold him the gun for twenty-five bucks and some drugs. He described John's confession to the murder, at the end of a PCP-fueled night. Even here, even after clearly being coached, Michael thought Funk's description rang false. It was in the details he used—details that no confessing murderer would have told. When Scott asked, "Did John tell you how many times he shot the victim, Ray Liuzza?" Perkins's reply was, "I don't remember whether he told me or Kevin told me. I think it was four times. And one entered the wall or something." Michael thought, *John Thompson shoots and kills a man and while stoned on PCP, he tells Funk Perkins that one of the shots entered a wall?*

Scott pulled out the Big Daddy Red letter: "Mr. Perkins, have you seen this before?"

"Yes," said Funk.

"And where have you seen it before?"

"Red gave it to me," Funk replied.

Michael thought about objecting, thought about showing the jury Connick's op-ed piece in the *Times-Picayune* saying that the OPP censors and DA had intercepted the letter, but decided against it. They'd have time to bring that up later, if they wanted. For now, it was good to have that in their back pocket.

Scott continued: "Mr. Perkins, were you aware that there was a reward being offered in this case?" Funk admitted hearing this on TV, and stated that he had actually received a $10,500 reward, but that none of it was collected before testimony. *Perfect,* thought Michael. Funk knew of the reward beforehand, and also knew that if he didn't testify, he wouldn't get the money.

With that, Scott sat down, and Robert stood up. If Michael hadn't seen Robert and Funk go after each other before, at the hearing in 2000, he might have missed the signs of Robert's intensity, his voice a little louder, his cadence more clipped. The calmness and the Southern gentility were still there, but underneath was a new hostility. Robert was not in a mood to play games.

"Mr. Perkins, let's start off with this gun," Robert said. "You said that you didn't sell it on your own, but that you sold it for John Thompson?"

"Yeah."

"And what you got for it was some money and some drugs?"

Perkins nodded.

Robert said, politely but firmly, "Tell the jury, you know, in words."

"Yeah. Money and drugs," Funk said, looking over at the jury.

"And you gave it all to John Thompson?"

"Yeah."

"But didn't you tell the police in your statement that you gave them, after you told your story to the Liuzzas, 'I gave it all to him; I don't know what he did with it'?"

Perkins had seen Robert before, too, of course. "I told you the same thing," he said, almost spitting out *you* and *same*. "I gave it all to him and we did the drugs."

"I see," said Robert. He feigned skepticism, though in truth, he couldn't have cared less. Either Perkins was a drug user under the influence, or he was a liar for money. Either way, Robert won. "You were lying even there, weren't you?"

Perkins looked up at that, a little startled. "I was lying?"

"Weren't you?"

"What I got to lie for?"

Robert smiled, benevolent and calm. "Let's talk about what you've got to lie for. At the time that you talked to the police, you knew that the gun was implicated in the murder of Mr. Liuzza, didn't you?"

"At the time I talked to him? After I sold the gun I found out later that it was involved with a murder."

"Correct," Robert said. "So you knew that you had sold a murder weapon?"

Funk hesitated. "After—after I sold it. That's implicating me in something I wasn't implicated in."

"Absolutely. And so you were angry at John Thompson, were you not?"

"I ain't going to say I was angry with him, but I was upset. He put me in something he ain't had no business."

"You were upset at John Thompson?"

"That's what you claim for me to be. I wasn't upset with him. I ain't appreciated what he did. He had to be framing me in it."

"So as far as you were concerned, your old buddy, John Thompson, was your enemy?"

"He wasn't no buddy. He was my brother-in-law. I was messing with his sister."

Robert nodded, sagely. "I see. I see. Your former acquaintance, John Thompson, known through his sister, was now your enemy?"

"He still ain't my enemy. I'm doing my time for what I'm doing mine for."

Robert agreed. "You sure are, aren't you? Well, let's tell the jury what—at the time you went to Mr. Liuzza—and it was Mr. Liuzza you went to, not the police, right?"

"Yeah."

"At that time you didn't have any other convictions?"

"No."

"You were messing with drugs, weren't you?"

"Yeah."

"You were buying drugs, selling drugs . . ."

Shary Scott stood up and objected at the same time Funk said, "What all that got to do with this here?"

Quinlan overruled both of them.

Robert continued. "Shortly after this, you got your first drug conviction for cocaine?"

"Probably so."

"And then followed shortly by a conviction for PCP?"

"Yep."

"Followed by a conviction for possessing with intent to distribute cocaine?"

"Yep. That should tell you I'm a drug dealer not no thief."

It was a good answer, but Robert was unfazed. "You got fifteen years?"

"I got a double fifteen—that's thirty."

"You have to do fifteen, is that correct?"

"Yeah."

"And of course, if you came in here today and told this jury the stuff that I said about John Thompson was a lie, you open yourself up. You want to get out of jail, don't you?"

"Man, I done been now on nine years of fifteen flat. Six more ain't going to kill me."

"But another five on top of that would?"

Move on, Michael thought. They had talked about this in their trial prep. The plan was to lead Funk along, letting Funk's own words portray him as deceptive, confused, and not credible. Instead, Robert was trying to beat Funk up, trying to expose him as a liar. He was trying to pick Funk apart. Michael didn't want to turn Funk into a sympathetic figure, the uneducated inner-city man getting bullied by the well-to-do white lawyer. As he and Perkins circled each other, Robert focusing on the confusion, Funk's answers grew increasingly opaque. It all played poorly for their case.

Trying to parse Funk's words took Robert out of his earlier momentum. He spent ten more painful minutes trying to paint Funk as a liar, something Funk would never agree to, while jurors shifted uncomfortably in their seats. Finally, Robert turned to the reward issue. "By the first time you testified in the court in this case, you knew that you had earned the reward, didn't you, if there was a conviction? You knew that?"

"Yeah."

"Somebody told you that you had earned the reward?"

"Yeah."

"And you did get the reward, didn't you?"

"I told you. You still trying to make me say I'm lying about this trial. What I told you happened, it happened."

"Well, let's talk about lying in this case. Didn't you lie about how you first came in contact with the police?"

Michael frowned, his pen scratching absently on his notepad. Robert was taking too long. If he was going to go after Perkins, he needed to hit him fast. Otherwise, it looked like empty posturing. Juries are unpredictable, but they have remarkably sophisticated bullshit detectors. Robert was getting close to the line.

Robert pulled out the transcript from one of the hearings. He said to Funk, "Did you not say in 1985, 'Ain't nobody sent me to the police when they come see me, I just went down by myself. Come looking for me and I just went down.' Right there, on page sixty-one—didn't you say that?"

"Yeah, if it's wrote down there I did."

"But that's absolutely untrue, isn't it?"

Finally, Robert had scored. Funk got angry. He raised his voice and said, "Well, show me what do you remember twenty years ago right off the top of your head?"

Quinlan leaned forward, said, "Mr. Perkins, just stay cool." Funk glared at the judge, then caught himself and nodded. Robert kept going, going after Perkins on his conflicting statements. Robert had abandoned any subtlety. His goal now was to break Perkins, make him tell the jury that he hadn't told the truth. It was a waste of time and momentum, Perkins wriggling free of the questions, bending facts around and around until he felt that he had brought them into agreement. *We've got to move on,* Michael thought.

Robert kept at it for another thirty minutes, though—telling Perkins he was a liar, Perkins being defiant that he was not, even as every statement he made was rebutted by Robert with transcripts that were eighteen years old. In previous tellings, Funk had known J.R. had the ring before Funk's trip to the International Hotel. Today in court, he claimed otherwise. He told the police in 1985 that Kevin Freeman told him a lady had seen Freeman run away from the scene, which was different than his 1985 trial testimony. Today, he didn't know why Freeman was called Kojak, but in 1985, he knew that Freeman was nicknamed Kojak for his short hair in a neighborhood full of Afros.

It was all accurate, but it was all confusing as hell, even to Michael. *To the jury,* Michael thought, *it must be incomprehensible.*

Robert said, "You had no reason to lie on John who had framed you in the murder?"

"He ain't framed me in the murder. He implicated me in it."

"And you had no reason to lie on John in order to get ten thousand five hundred dollars?"

"That ain't no reason just to do it. No."

Robert was aggressive, challenging. "When have you seen ten thousand five hundred dollars in your life?"

Shary Scott was on her feet, objecting, but Perkins answered anyway. "Everybody wasn't born with no silver spoon in their mouth like you. I know what Kevin Freeman told me. They probably was mixing their stories up. I know what they both told me."

Michael was screaming inside. Robert's condescension was not scoring them any points. *Move on,* he thought, *just move on.*

"All right. So you didn't know he was speaking out of two sides of his mouth, did you, or three sides, or four sides? You just didn't know?"

Perkins shook his head, like he felt sorry for Robert. "He ain't doing no more than what you doing."

It rang true, thought Michael. Everything Funk said, Robert threw back a conflicting statement, but it wasn't scoring points.

Finally, Robert changed tack. "Just before you came to court, the DAs you were working with in 1985 were Mr. Williams and Mr. Dubelier, correct?"

"You said I was working with them."

"Yeah. And before you took the witness stand, you went over to the DA's office?"

"Yeah."

"And lo and behold, also at the DA's office was Kevin Freeman?"

"Yeah, he was in there."

"And one of the DAs at the time, Mr. Dubelier, said something to you and Mr. Freeman, put you all together, right?"

"We was in the office together."

"And Mr. Dubelier said to you, 'Looks like the evidence is pointing to the two of you,' didn't he say that?"

"Something like that."

"And then he did something interesting. He didn't stay the whole time, did he?"

"No. He had another guy with him."

"And they left out of the office?"

"Stepped right outside the room."

"And left you alone with whom?"

"Kevin."

"With an instruction to do what?"

"Instructed me to get our story together, what's going on."

"And you got your stories together and you got your reward, didn't you?" Perkins didn't answer. The silence grew thick in the courtroom, until Robert finally broke it, saying, "Nothing further, Your Honor." He turned and walked back to the counsel table.

Michael considered what he had just seen. Robert had regained control at the end and ended on a high note, but Michael believed it was essential to hammer things home for the jury, and he was concerned that Robert's ending was too subtle. Would the jury understand that Dubelier had put Perkins, a drug dealer who couldn't keep his story straight, in a room with Freeman, the man they believed was the actual killer, and told them to get their stories straight so that they could convict John? Did they understand that the DA's office was complicit in John's situation? The jury had never seen or heard of Dubelier, and they wouldn't meet him during the trial. He'd get credit, in their eyes, because he was a DA, while John was a street thug at best. Would they see Funk Perkins, drug addict and repeat felon, telling lies to save his own skin, or would they be so confused, or so bored, that they simply disengaged and followed the DA's road map?

Shary Scott walked up to the podium again. Given the chance to rebut Robert's examination, she took advantage. "Mr. Perkins, when you gave your statement to the police, they asked you what was the last school you attended, what level of education, do you remember your response?"

"Special ed, tenth grade."

"Mr. Perkins, did you sell a story for ten thousand five hundred dollars?"

"It wasn't no story. I didn't sell it. That's what I got."

"And did you sell the gun that John Thompson gave you to Junior?"

"Yes, ma'am."

"Your Honor, nothing further."

Funk Perkins stepped down, glaring at Robert Glass and walking away in the care of the bailiff. Michael called it a draw—Robert had described the facts they wanted to present to the jury, but he hadn't shown Perkins to be clearly dishonest. Still, the DAs wouldn't have anyone else more credible testifying, and the defense still had John.

With the overview of John's guilt—the gun, the ring, the Big Daddy Red letter, and his confession to Perkins—now introduced to the jury, Solino called David Carter, the police officer who had been first to the scene in 1984. He was now a sergeant, a decorated veteran of twenty-three years with the NOPD. He told the story of that night, seeing the bullet holes in Liuzza's back, trying to comfort Ray Liuzza as he pleaded for Carter to drive him to the hospital, asking, "Why? Why did he have to shoot me?" while his blood ran into the grass and sidewalk.

Solino showed Carter pictures of the scene and asked what description Carter had been given for the suspected shooter. "It was a black male described to me as being six feet tall, approximately six feet tall, dark-complected; he was wearing a—it was a black jacket and dark pants, as was described to me. That is what we put on the police radio."

"Did anybody indicate to you that they had seen a vehicle?"

"No, sir."

"Did anybody indicate to you that they had heard a vehicle screeching away from the scene?"

"No, sir."

"No other questions. Thank you, Sergeant."

Michael said a silent prayer of thanks as he rose for his first appearance before the jury. Sergeant David Carter, in what he hadn't said, had just given him the greatest gift his cross-examination could have asked for.

"The first thing you did, when you got there, you went to help Mr. Liuzza, right?"

"Yes, sir."

"After the EMTs took Mr. Liuzza away, your focus became the crime scene, right?"

"Yes, sir."

"When you got to the scene, there was already a man trying to help? Paul Schliffka, a white man? He was there when you arrived?"

"Yes, sir, I believe he was."

"I think you said before that you got a description of the perpetrator that was broadcast to other units?"

"Yes, sir."

"And that description came from Paul Schliffka?"

"Yes, sir."

Michael's rhythm controlled the witness, Carter falling in to Michael's questions, following his cadence and giving the answers Michael expected.

"There were some other people walking around that area, but no one else told you that he'd seen the shooter running away?"

"That's correct."

"Schliffka was the only person who you talked to who said, 'Yes, I saw the man who shot Ray Liuzza and ran away'?"

"Me, personally, yes, sir."

"That description is very important, isn't it?"

"I would think so, yes, sir. Other units patrolling could possibly spot the suspect in a certain area, or maybe if he's involved in another incident, it's good for the police out there to know what we're looking for."

"And Mr. Schliffka told you that the suspect, the man he saw running by him, had a big gun in his right hand?"

"I don't recall him saying he was right by him. I—"

"You *do* recall him saying, though, that the man he saw running had a gun in his hand?"

"Yes, sir, I do."

"So now we're at a six-foot-tall black man, dark jacket, dark pants, gun in hand, right?"

"Yes, sir."

"Whatever Schliffka told you, that was broadcast."

"Yes, sir, it was broadcast."

Michael paused for show, considering this, his chin on his hand, his arms crossed. "If he told you something material and important in helping to identify a man running down the street with a gun who just shot someone else, you wouldn't hold that back from your description?"

"Absolutely not."

Gotcha. Michael said, "Well, but Schliffka told you, though, that the man who ran by him was a black male, six feet tall, dark jacket, dark pants, gun in hand, *and close-cropped hair*, didn't he?"

Carter nodded, slowly. "Best I can recall, that is correct."

"Well, when you just gave your description a moment ago to Mr. Solino and then to me, you left out the 'close-cropped hair' part?"

"And the gun."

"Yeah. Were you deliberately trying to hide the fact that the man Mr. Schliffka described to you had close-cropped hair?" Michael felt like a spider with a fly in his web. "You remember testifying here, on this witness stand, in 1985? Let me try and show you some of your prior testimony when you were asked what Mr. Schliffka told you, of the description of the perpetrator that you had broadcast. He asked you, 'Do you recall the description given to you?' and you said 'Yes, sir, I do. It was a black male. He was described as being about six feet tall; he was wearing a black leather jacket and dark pants. He was dark-complected.' That was the answer you gave at the time, right?"

"Uh-huh."

"And he asked you, 'Was any further description given to you of the perpetrator by Mr. Schliffka?' And you said, 'No, sir.' That's right?"

"If that's what it says."

"Would it surprise you to learn that before you got on the stand to testify eighteen years ago, you looked at a report that was prepared by officers Curole and Demma, two investigation detectives?" Michael shot the jury a look, making sure they were engaged. "There was a discussion about the police report, and you were asked to step off of the witness stand and to walk over to where Mr. Dubelier's table was and to look at the police report. Do you remember that?" Michael was walking around the courtroom, acting out Carter's motions for him and to show the jury.

"If you say so."

"The court reporter typed, 'The witness stepped down from the witness stand and went to the prosecutor's table to review the police report.' "

"That's correct."

"And then the question to you was, 'Describe the hair.' And your answer was, 'Okay. It was black and short, Afro style.' Did you see those words, *Afro style*, on the police report, or were you just making it up?"

"No, that's part of the police report."

"Well, let's look at the police report." Michael held it up in front of the jury, then put it in front of Carter. "Turn to page seven, where Mr. Schliffka provided the description of the suspect. 'Afro' wasn't in there, was it?"

"It was part of the description written on the form that you check out the style of hair. One of them has 'Afro,' and that's what I checked off."

"Were you trying to make the fleeing suspect sound more like Mr. Thompson when you didn't mention the hair, and then when you said he had an Afro?"

"No, sir."

Michael stopped, looked hard at Carter, and waited, letting his silence draw the jury in. "Are you sure about that?" He waited again.

Carter's voice was clear, but quiet. "Yes, sir, I am."

"Well, now that you've gotten your recollection back, though, you'd agree with me that what Schliffka told you is that the one perpetrator, the one fleeing man, the one man with a gun in his hand, had close-cropped hair? You recall that?"

"The suspect that he described to me, yes, sir, that was correct."

"Thank you, sir."

Solino was already up as Michael sat down and was almost running to the podium to rehab his witness. "Sergeant Carter," he began, emphasis on *Sergeant,* "in December of 1984, did you know who John Thompson was?"

"No, sir."

"Did you know what he looked like?"

"No, sir."

"So any suggestion that you would be trying to fabricate something to plant against John Thompson would be, in your opinion, what?"

"Ludicrous."

"In fact, you would have completed a report that indicated the perpetrator seen fleeing had short black hair?"

"Short black hair only."

"No further questions."

Michael watched Carter walk out of the courtroom. Michael glanced at Gordon, who nodded in satisfaction. Michael nodded back as Judge Quinlan told the jury that lunch was waiting in the jury room.

They left John with the bailiff and walked over to the New Orleans version of the all-American diner across the street from the courthouse.

SHARY SCOTT STARTED the afternoon session by calling Anthony Cusimano, the crime scene technician on duty in December, 1984, to the stand. Cusimano's testimony was no secret. He was an important foundational witness for the DA to set the stage that this was a murder/robbery, and he would testify to the crime scene and the evidence he found there. Michael and Gordon weren't really worried about him; he couldn't really hurt their case because there was no forensic or other evidence that John had committed the murder.

Someone had killed Ray, but Anthony Cusimano couldn't prove it was John. Still, Gordon listened closely as Scott began her questioning.

She had Cusimano describe the bullets he collected. For whatever reason, Cusimano called them "pellets" instead of bullets. Gordon thought it sounded like something you'd feed to a deer, not like something you'd use to shoot a guy in cold blood. Minimizing the chaos and brutality of the crime scene was doing the defense a favor.

Still, it was a credible examination. Scott pulled out Cusimano's crime scene report and walked "pellet" by "pellet" through each of the five shots taken by Ray Liuzza's killer. She showed the jury Cusimano's photos of the crime scene. Gordon thought of Ray Liuzza

Sr. behind him, wondered how the jury was feeling about the obviously grief-stricken father, clearly visible from their vantage point. Scott held the pictures up for everyone to see, the blood lying on top of the ground.

It was a hit they knew they were going to take, and so Gordon took it calmly. He rose to question Cusimano, knowing he wasn't going to go anywhere near the crime scene. Instead, he wanted to trace the gun and bullets from the crime scene and Cusimano's plastic bags to the NOPD's Central Property and Evidence, where Cusimano left them. "Do you know whether they're still down there?"

"I have no knowledge of that," Cusimano said.

Gordon nodded, an "of course you don't" sort of a nod for the jury's benefit. "When you surveyed the scene of the crime, did you locate any blood or tissue evidence from the perpetrator of the crime?"

"Not to my knowledge, no."

"So there was nothing that you found there that could either identify or exonerate somebody of the crime, is that correct?"

"I wouldn't have that knowledge from the scene."

Gordon sat down.

The next witness for the DAs was Donald Curole. Carter and Cusimano had established that a murder had happened; now Curole would connect the dots and make John Thompson the lead suspect.

Curole was a problematic witness for John's case in that, other than being a cop, he didn't have an obvious bias against John. There was no reward, reprieve, or plea bargain. Curole seemed like he was just a guy who had done his job.

Solino knew this, and he knew that Curole, a twenty-three-year veteran of the NOPD, would know how to talk to a jury under direct examination. He gave his witness room to run, asking open questions and letting Curole set the stage.

Curole started at Junior Harris's house, where he had been sent by Perkins. Curole talked like a cop—in his depiction, he didn't "go in the house," he "gained entrance to the residence"—but he knew his facts and what he needed to show. He laid the necessary legal foundation, explaining that Perkins's credible informant testimony had gotten them a search warrant for Harris's house.

"As I walked through into the front room of the apartment, one of the detectives was talking with Mr. Harris. And as he was talking he was moving his hands, and I noticed a ring on his finger that fit the description of the ring that we were looking for that was stolen from Mr. Liuzza during the robbery."

John snorted a little bit, shaking his head and drawing a sharp look from Michael. Juries see *everything*. They would see him snicker and think he was arrogant—and that arrogance could cost him in the deliberation room. Michael knew John's belief that the identification of the ring was totally made up, that there were hundreds just like it, and that Junior Lee Harris's ring with an "L" almost certainly was not Ray Liuzza's ring, and they had the dailies where Curole had once referred to it as a ring with an "R" instead of an "L," but neither was a fight worth starting. In the first place, the "R" was probably a typo. In the second place, they couldn't prove anything about the ring one way or another. In the third place, why would Junior Harris wear a ring with an "L" on it? Trying to make any of these points, which were easily countered, would look desperate and petulant to the jury, and they'd lose credibility with the jury if they fought it.

Michael looked at John, held the gaze for a second.

If John was sorry, he didn't show it.

"Did you ask him about a weapon?" Solino asked Curole.

"Yes, we did. He told us that he did in fact have it at one time, but that he sold it to a person named 'Brother' who lived on MLK. Mr. Harris subsequently took us to Brother's apartment and we were able to retrieve the weapon."

Solino walked over and grabbed a gun from his table, waved it around. It wasn't the murder weapon, but Michael kept quiet, given Quinlan's pretrial ruling.

It was a tidy story, Curole laying it out piece by piece. Perkins led them to Harris and they found the ring. Harris led them to Harrison and they found the gun. Harris tracked the gun back to Perkins and the ring back to Thompson. Perkins tracked the gun from him back to Thompson. Solino had gotten what he wanted, and turned to shore up a weakness in his case. "Detective Curole, do you have any information concerning a reward in this case that was offered?"

"There was a reward, yes. As far as I know, though, no money was paid before trial." Curole described the meeting, after John's conviction, to decide who got what share of the $15,000. He looked at the jury, talking to them straight up. "My recommendation was that the information we had gotten from Richard Perkins was the most significant."

Curole said, "Nothing further, Your Honor."

As he rose, Michael gave Solino a little internal tip of his cap, Solino actually using the reward payment to bolster Perkins's credibility, using the policeman to argue that Perkins got the reward because he was credible and helpful, instead of the defense's portrayal of Perkins as a rat and a liar.

Michael walked to the podium, rested his hands on it comfortably. Curole stiffened a little, both men knowing what was coming. "You were aware the reward was paid to Mr. Perkins, not before the trial but after?"

"I was told he was paid after, yes."

"No reward was paid or promised before the trial, correct?"

"That's correct."

"So, in other words, it would have been very clear to Perkins that unless he came into court and told the story that got John Thompson convicted, he wasn't going to get his ten thousand five hundred dollars, was he?"

As he had in 1995, Curole admitted that the reward was set up as a fifty-fifty split on arrest and conviction, but that Perkins had not received any of it until after the trial.

"Let's turn to Funk Perkins. Funk Perkins first came forward by going to the Liuzza family, didn't he?"

"Yes."

"He didn't come to the police?"

"No."

"You didn't go to him?"

"No."

"So he comes forward to the Liuzza family. They didn't have the authority to protect Funk Perkins if he was afraid for his life, or to arrest anyone. But they did have the power and authority to pay the reward?"

"Yes."

"Let's turn to the investigation itself. You got to the crime scene and there were already a lot of police there?"

"No. They were all gone, as far as I remember. We interviewed some residents in that neighborhood early the next morning after sunup."

Michael pulled out the police daily reports, all written and signed by Curole. "Would you read me the description that you wrote in there of the man who was wanted for the murder of Ray Liuzza?"

"'Unknown Negro male, six foot, close-cut hair, black jacket, black jeans.'"

He showed Curole the picture of John from one week after the robbery, the one they'd gotten from Solino only a week before. "And Kevin Freeman, he had a bald head, right? And his nickname was Kojak? You're only a couple of years older than I am. You remember the TV show, *Kojak*? What was unique about Kojak?" Michael didn't wait for Curole to answer. "He had a bald head.

"Let's go back to Richard Perkins." Michael put a map on an easel in front of the jury. "You interviewed him, and Perkins told you some things about what Freeman told him, right? And you wrote that up in your police report? I mean, Perkins told you that Freeman parked up here on Josephine, between Baronne and Dryades, right?" He put a sticker on the map a block above the murder scene as Curole agreed. "And according to Perkins, Freeman ran before the shooting, jumped in this car, and drove away?"

"Yes."

"Are you aware that Freeman testified that his car was parked all the way down here on Josephine and Carondelet?" Michael put a sticker two blocks below the murder scene.

"I'm not aware of what he testified to, but I know he did say that, yes."

"And did you know Freeman also testified that he ran away; he didn't run to his car and drive away, because his car had run out of gas at Josephine and Carondelet?"

"Yes."

"That's what Freeman testified to. Different from what Perkins told you?"

"Yes."

"Perkins told you that Freeman was seen by a woman, right?"

Curole hesitated. "Uh, yes. I believe he did."

"Schliffka wasn't a woman?"

"No."

"So there was *another witness* who saw the perpetrator run away?"

"Yes, there was."

Michael smiled. In a pleasant voice, he said, "Well, we'll hold off on that until she testifies. Thank you, Captain."

Solino came forward on redirect. He asked Curole, were eyewitnesses often off on height descriptions by a few inches? Absolutely; frequently. And would it be more likely or less likely that, in his experience, somebody with a full head of hair would be nicknamed after a bald guy? "It could happen," said Curole. "It could certainly happen."

Solino called Otto Stubbs to the stand. Stubbs, the ballistics expert who had declared the gun from Jessie Harrison's house to be the murder weapon in 1985, was there to link the "pellets" collected by Cusimano with the gun recovered by Curole.

Now with St. Tammany Parish after nineteen years with the NOPD, Stubbs repeated his 1985 trial testimony, comparing bullets recovered from the scene to the gun recovered by Curole from Jessie Harrison, giving his professional conclusion that the recovered gun was the murder weapon.

Stubbs was another witness on Gordon's list. "Mr. Stubbs, I take it first of all that you're not offering any professional opinion today about who shot the gun that you tested, are you?"

"No, sir."

"How many tests have you performed?"

"Hundreds."

"And today, sitting here today, do you have any specific recollection about testing the particular .357 magnum that was involved in this particular case?"

"It's been twenty years; I can't tell you that."

"Sir, are you aware of where the gun in question is today?"

"I have no idea, sir. It was turned over to Central Evidence and Property."

"Would you agree with me that without the gun and the bullets, it would be impossible today to conduct the kind of comparison that you made eighteen years ago?"

"I couldn't. I don't know if anybody else could."

Junior Lee Harris had successfully avoided his subpoena and had not come to court, so Solino read Harris's testimony from 1985 into the record, confirming Curole's account of how the gun was found. According to the transcript, in 1985 Harris had stated that he knew John Thompson by his street name, Nut, and that he'd bought a ring, a gold ring with an "L" on it, from Nut. Cost him six dollars.

He wore the ring, and when the cops came looking for the gun, they saw it, and took it.

Solino also read Couhig's cross-examination of Harris into the record and established that it wasn't uncommon for John to sell stuff to Harris. He also pointed out the curious coincidence that Harris had been arrested on March 3, 1985, and held in custody until just before trial, when he was released and the charges against him dismissed.

When Harris's transcript testimony had been read completely to the jury, Quinlan stopped the day's proceedings. Reading testimony into the record wasn't a rhetorical high point for either side, but it was after 5:00 PM, and they had to be mindful of the jury's time.

As the jury filed out of the room, John and his lawyers stood up, showing their respect for the jurors' attention and work. Michael scanned their faces, as he did every time they walked in or out of the room, and thousands of times in between, for clues as to how they were doing. As usual, he didn't get many signals, and he didn't trust the ones he got. It was enough to make anyone crazy, the unpredictability of a trial and of a jury.

After the jury had left, Michael turned to John, who had to leave and return to OPP for the night. He told John to stay encouraged, and stated how pleased he was about how the day had gone. The DA had put almost all of its case on, and none of their witnesses had gotten away untouched. So far, things were going as well as they could have hoped.

Then Michael turned his attention to Judge Quinlan, still looking at papers on his desk. "Thank you, Your Honor. Have a good night."

The judge returned the courtesy, then stood and left the bench.

Have a good night, Michael thought. *Someone should.*

For his part, Michael doubted he'd sleep at all. Tomorrow, they were going to put John on the stand, in open court, and let him tell his story to a jury for the first time. If he did it well, he could walk out of prison after eighteen years. Or the jury could focus on something, anything, and decide he was guilty, just like that, and he'd spend the rest of his life in OPP.

Even if they were perfect, they might not win.

DAY 2: MAY 8, 2003

QUINLAN LED OFF the morning with an instruction to the jury: "As I'm sure some of you might have picked up yesterday from testimony, there—it did come from the witness stand that in fact, there has been a previous trial in this case, and the defendant was convicted. The matter has been reviewed by higher courts and the Court, not just for technical reasons, but the higher courts have decided that Mr. Thompson's guilt or innocence should be determined upon all the evidence presented to y'all, to a new jury. And that's the reason that your decision has to be made on what you've heard and seen here, not what the news media might have said, not what your brother-in-law might have said, or not what might have happened by twelve—what twelve other people might have said when they heard some of the evidence in this case."

The lawyers had discussed this with Judge Quinlan in chambers before the day officially began, and he had informed them that he was going to make this statement. Listening to it, Gordon thought it was about the best they could have hoped for. Quinlan's statement that John's conviction was reversed, "not for technical reasons," clearly indicated that this new trial was not due to some lawyer's trick—it was something real and substantial. Gordon's hope was that the jurors would conclude that the "something real" could only be one thing—innocence. Of course, it would only work if the jurors were paying as close attention to Quinlan's words as he was. As he scanned the jury, some looked confused, others bored. Juror Eight looked serious, like she was getting it. *Well, we've got one, at least*, he thought. On the other hand, Juror Two was looking sour. *Or maybe sour is just her normal look*, he thought.

The judge continued. "One of the first things that'll happen this morning is Kevin Freeman's testimony. As you know, this State's witness is deceased. His testimony is going to be read to you as it was given back in 1985. There will be some questions that the defense will read to you that they would have asked Kevin Freeman if he were here today and were testifying. There obviously won't be any answers, but it will be just something for you to consider. But once again, like I said, it wasn't in any attempt to hide anything from you. It's just that the law really does want a total emphasis on the fact that we want the judgment of the twelve of you on this evidence.

"With that, the State is ready to call their next witness."

Val Solino stood up and got ready to have the clerk read Kevin Freeman's testimony. While he did, Gordon put up the map they had used yesterday, showing the jury a physical representation of Freeman's story at trial. Solino had seen and agreed to this before trial, letting the jury see where Kevin Freeman was on the night of December 6, 1984, in his own words.

Having the clerk read Freeman's transcript was as painful to Michael now as it had been in 2001, when they had argued about Connick's motion to dismiss the armed robbery conviction. Michael felt like he was watching the recording of a nonfiction book on tape, done by a talentless amateur. The clerk read like he had social anxiety disorder, with his head down, his voice a deep monotone that was so quiet Judge Quinlan had to interrupt and bring him closer to the microphone. Michael's familiarity with the transcript made the clerk's rendition even more excruciating, the emotionless drone interrupting his own mental reading of the text.

As the clerk described Freeman's version of the story, Gordon walked over to the chart and pushed a pin in to the place where Freeman had said he was.

The clerk read, "I was coming from my sister's house from out of St. Thomas Project when I saw John. I was coming up Josephine when I seen Nut, and Nut stopped me. I told him I'm trying to get home because I'm about to run out of gas. Nut stopped me and asked for a ride. So we rides and gets over on the other side of St. Charles and Carondelet when my car went to spitting gas. I know it was going to run out of gas, so I parked it in the middle of the block of Carondelet."

Gordon pushed a car-shaped pin into the board at Josephine and Carondelet.

The clerk continued, telling the jury about Freeman picking up John Thompson, ignorant of the gun John carried with him. "When the white guy pulled up, Nut said, 'I'm going to hit him.' I said, 'Go ahead, I'm going.' So when Nut said he was going to hit that white guy, the white guy got out of the car and walked across the street. By the time he decided to go hit the white guy, the white guy had done got out the car and walked across the street—not right across the street—excuse me, I messed up. Could I go back?"

At the time, Eric Dubelier had said, "Sure." The clerk repeated this assurance. Michael and Gordon had agreed not to object to this—after all, Couhig had not objected to it in 1985—but they were still appalled. Michael thought, *I messed that up. Are you kidding? Freeman was coached by Dubelier. He messed up because he went off of the police/DA script. Get your stories straight, Dubelier had said.*

"When I seen Nut pull the pistol from his pants, he ran across the street and grabbed the white guy behind his back and throw him on the ground.

"Then I heard some more shots. I was running into Saratoga when I seen Nut running into Dryades." Gordon put a red pin shaped like a runner down near Saratoga and a second one at Josephine and Dryades. The clerk read Eric Dubelier's questions from 1985: What was John Thompson wearing on that night? "He was wearing a big, black heavy jacket with—I think he was wearing jeans that night." What kind of shoes? "Tennis shoes."

"Do you remember an occasion where you were scheduled to come to court and you were on the docks in the back with John Thompson?"

"Yeah, I remember we was on the docks that once. He told me that he was going to give the gun to a dude. He sold the gun to a dude that he didn't like, you know, to go sell it to him. That's all he was talking about."

"Kevin, what were you wearing that evening?"

"A white shirt with a pair of slacks with a pair of tennis shoes."

Rob Couhig had chimed in at this point: "Mr. Freeman, we've never met, but I've been given a copy of the statement you gave to the police. I'd like to ask you a few questions, sir. That particular evening, you were wearing a white shirt and long sleeves. And slacks and tennis shoes? Your hair, was it about like it is today?"

"Yes, sir."

"How tall are you?"

"About six feet."

"You parked your car on Carondelet? So if someone said you parked on Baronne Street, that would be an error? If someone said that you parked between Baronne Street and then were walking back toward St. Charles Avenue, would that be true?"

"No, sir, that wouldn't be true. The white guy was on the left-hand side of the street, and I never went to the right-hand side of the street. When he ran over here and grabbed him, I was about on the other side of Baronne Street, about in the middle down the block toward Dryades Street."

"You saw John grab this fellow? Grabbed him around the neck? And throw him to the ground? And John went over with him?"

"No, he didn't go down with him."

"You saw them wrestling?"

"Well, that's what was told to me."

"Oh, no. Not what was told to you, sir. I want what you saw."

"I seen them wrestling."

"Did you tell police officers that you saw them wrestling?"

"Yes, sir."

"Did you see them wrestling or not, sir?"

"Yeah, I seen them wrestling."

"Fine. And when you saw these people wrestling from three-quarters of a block away, or beyond Baronne and halfway toward Dryades, is that when the gun went off?"

"Yes, sir. About three seconds, then the other shots, boom, boom, boom."

"You said that when you got to Saratoga you turned around and you looked back, and you saw John running?"

"Running into Dryades."

"Tell the jury how many blocks it was you had to look back at that point and see John."

"Two."

The clerk read through the rest of the testimony. When he finally stopped reading, Robert Glass got up and took the podium. His job was to bring the glassy-eyed jury back from the past and into the present, to focus them on his cross-examination—the questioning of Kevin Freeman that John had deserved to hear for the past eighteen years.

Robert stood at the podium, not moving. He stared for a long moment at the empty witness stand, his eyes focused on the back of the chair. Michael watched as well. While not generally given to great fits of spirituality, Michael realized that Robert was, in a sense, conjuring for the jury a vision of Kevin Freeman. That imagined person was in some ways more powerful to everyone in the room than if Kevin Freeman had actually been sitting in front of them. Michael had never been to a séance, but if this was what they felt like, he could see how people could be swayed.

Robert said to the empty chair, "You claimed in your testimony that you just happened to pick John Thompson up in the street?

The ghost sat in the chair, sullen and defiant, saying nothing.

"Isn't it true, however, that you told Funk Perkins that you met John Thompson in your home?

Nothing.

"You told the jury in your testimony you didn't know that John Thompson was going to rob someone until after he got out of your car?" Robert waited, just an extra beat. *Answer me.* There was no reply.

"Isn't it true, however, that you told Funk Perkins that you set out to rob someone?

"You told the jury in your testimony you ran out of gas and parked the car for that reason.

"Isn't it true, however, that you told Funk Perkins you parked the car in that particular area because rich people lived there, and it would be a good idea to rob someone?

"You told the jury in your testimony you parked the car near Carondelet Street. Isn't it true, however, that you told Funk Perkins you parked your car lakeside by Katie's Beauty Salon?"

Michael looked at the jury. It was working. They had been so focused on the conversation unfolding between Robert and "Kevin Freeman" in the empty chair that some of them actually flinched as Gordon placed a green car-shaped pin on the map where Katie's was, blocks away from the red car.

"You said in your testimony that you ran away when you realized Mr. Thompson was going to rob Mr. Liuzza?

"You said in your testimony that you were half a block away—a half blosck away from Dryades Street when the property was taken from Mr. Liuzza?

"You suggested in your testimony that you stole nothing from him at all? But you were lying. Shortly after the killing you admitted stealing Mr. Liuzza's wallet?"

Michael looked at the jury, at the doubt in their faces. He saw some of them wondering, *How did Kevin Freeman get the wallet?*

"In fact, you admitted to Funk Perkins you stole Mr. Liuzza's wallet? In fact, you stole all of Mr. Liuzza's property?"

Robert was picking up steam, his voice rising, filling the courtroom with a volume the jury hadn't heard from him before. He engaged the ghost on the stand, freeing the jury, Judge Quinlan, the ADAs, the audience—maybe even the Liuzza family—from the lies that had been adopted as truth in 1985 and never corrected.

"Isn't it true you told Funk Perkins that you ran to your car and drove away that same night? And isn't it true you told Funk Perkins that you were seen leaving the scene the night of the killing by a woman?

"Isn't it true the reason you claim your car was parked on Carondelet Street was because you were concerned that if you said the car was by Katie's Beauty Salon, the woman who saw you would have identified you as the murderer?"

Robert paused and lowered his voice. "Isn't it true you killed Ray Liuzza?"

He paused again, summoning up all of his moral dignity. Robert said to the ghost, "Isn't it true you did this alone?"

Robert stood, silently, demanding an answer for several seconds. When none came, he said, "I have nothing further, Your Honor." There was no sound until he turned and walked back from the podium, his steps echoing off the courtroom's high ceiling.

Solino called Jessie Harrison to the stand as quickly as he could, and Shary Scott almost sprinted up to take down the map, getting the picture and its stickers out of the sight of the jury.

Michael was ecstatic. It had worked even better than they had hoped. The jury could not deny the power of that "examination." They were right where they wanted to be. The jury wouldn't believe Freeman, and he didn't think they would believe Funk.

If you believe John, we win, Michael thought. *If.*

QUINLAN TURNED TO John's table. "Is the defense ready to proceed?"

Michael and Robert rose together, each buttoning his jacket reflexively. "We are, Your Honor," they said.

"Call your first witness."

Robert sat down, and Michael said, "The defense calls Sheri Kelly." It was time to show the jury some new facts.

Michael set their blow-up map of Josephine and Baronne on the easel again, putting a pin on Sheri Kelly's apartment. He asked her a few easy questions, getting Sheri comfortable on the stand, letting her butterflies out. They had practiced, so this wasn't entirely new to her, but it was always different in front of a jury. She fielded the introductory questions well, not stuttering, not hesitating, just telling her story and answering what was asked of her.

That confidence was good, because Sheri was the mysterious female eyewitness named in the dailies. Her testimony would be supported by the McAllisters, but if the jury believed Sheri, Michael thought, they would agree with him that Kevin Freeman had killed Ray Liuzza Jr.

IN OCTOBER, 1984, Sheri Kelly, then Sheri Hartman, moved into a second-floor apartment at the intersection of Josephine and Baronne streets, on the north side of Baronne across from Ray Liuzza's building. The apartment had an ornate wrought-iron balcony on the street side, looking down Baronne onto the street area where Ray Liuzza had bled to death. Now, eighteen years later, Sheri showed the jury the location of her apartment on the map, and Michael drew an "SK" on the spot.

Sheri described the layout of the apartment—balcony, kitchen/living room, and the bedroom in the back—and then Michael brought her back to the night of December 6, 1984, at 12:30 AM.

"Where were you that night, ma'am?"

"I was in my bed reading. I heard an argument, or what sounded like an argument."

"Was there anything about that argument that caught your attention?"

"The yelling, the intensity. It was loud." Sheri shifted on the witness stand and continued. "When I realized I was hearing a very loud discussion, argument, I sat up, turned my light off, and was going through my living room to see if I could see what was going on."

"Why did you turn the lights off?"

"I didn't want to be seen. I was afraid of bullets. I didn't know what to expect."

Michael lowered his voice. "Did you see bullets?"

"I did hear bullets. I heard two bullets—two shots, and then a series of shots a split second later."

"Could you actually see the shooter firing a shot?"

"No, sir."

"After you heard the shots, where did you go?"

"I was on the balcony at that point, after the shots."

Michael walked over to stand near the jury box, the better to focus their attention on what he was going to ask next. "Ms. Kelly, what's the first thing you remember seeing after you heard the shots?"

"I saw two things at the same time. I saw someone laying across the street on the sidewalk, and I saw someone else running."

Michael pointed to the "X" on the map, the spot marking the location where Ray Liuzza had been shot. "Is that about where you saw a man lying on the sidewalk?"

"Yes, sir."

"Okay. Now, you said you also saw a man running? Were you on the balcony at the time?"

"Yes, sir."

"Where was he when you first saw him?"

"He was going toward Dryades. He was approaching the curb, or had stepped up on the curb." Michael handed her a pointer, and she pointed to the north side of Baronne, away from the murder scene.

"What did you see next?"

"I looked back and saw that someone was with the person on the ground, and then I looked back at the runner."

"Where were you?"

"I was at the very edge of my balcony facing Baronne."

"How close was the runner?"

"Maybe within ten feet."

"Looking down at the man from the balcony, could you tell exactly how tall he was?"

"No, no. I was looking down from above. But he appeared to be taller than I was, and I'm five-six."

"Is there anything you did see about him, though, from where you were? Could you describe what you saw?"

"The gentleman that I saw appeared to be stocky and he had short hair. It was close-cropped hair that fit the shape of his head. He was wearing dark clothes. And he looked up and he saw me."

"You thought the man saw you?"

"Yes, sir. I wasn't quiet when I came out on the balcony. And as I looked, he looked up. I just know that he saw me. I couldn't clearly see his eyes but it bothered me greatly. He had probably just shot someone and I was fearful. He knew where I lived."

Michael moved now to Sheri's discussions with the police. Sheri had spoken to them that night, and described her view, which had been faithfully reprised in the dailies, though not in Curole's summary police report. And she had spoken to them a few days later, when they asked her to look at mug-shot books. She didn't see a picture of the man who had run past her balcony, but she knew he was out there somewhere, and he scared her enough that she moved out of her brand-new apartment less than two weeks afterward.

What Sheri had given Michael was a second disinterested witness, along with Paul Schliffka from the original trial, at the scene.

Both witnesses told the same story from different locations—a single black man in dark clothes with short hair running north from the shooting, up Josephine toward the river. This contradicted Kevin Freeman's trial testimony, in which he said that he'd gone in the opposite direction, but it made sense if one believed Funk Perkins's original story, told at the International Hotel and captured on the audiotapes—that Freeman had confessed to Perkins that he'd robbed a man and that a woman had seen him.

There was one more piece that Michael needed from her. "Ms. Kelly, I'd like to show you an exhibit I've marked as D7. It's an article from the New Orleans *Times-Picayune*, with a photograph from January 18, 1985. Have you seen this before?"

Michael handed her the copy of the *Times-Picayune* article trumpeting John's arrest, including his photo, the one taken December 12, 1984.

"Yes, sir. I was a passenger in a car being driven down St. Charles when I first saw this article."

"What was you reaction when you saw this photograph of Mr. Thompson?"

"My initial reaction was, 'This is not the man that I saw.' "

"Did that reaction ever change?"

"No, sir."

With that, he had all the facts he needed. Now he had to make the fact that she'd kept quiet about this for more than a decade somehow sympathetic to the jury. Michael said, gently, "Ms. Kelly, is this the first time you've been in court in front of a jury testifying in this case?"

Sheri answered, "Yes," and Michael gave the floor to Solino. Michael had done his best to prepare Sheri for what was coming. He expected Solino to make Sheri look bad by asking why, if she knew John Thompson wasn't the murderer, she had kept quiet for so many years.

Solino took his time getting to it, showing a few pictures of Sheri's apartment, showing the jury where she had been in relation to the shooting. "When you're looking out onto Josephine Street, what is it that you see?"

Sheri straightened up and answered the way she and Michael had discussed it. "Being there were no leaves on the tree, there was a pretty bright streetlight where the victim was. What could I see or what did I see?"

"Well, let me ask it a different way. If you were standing on your balcony looking across the street, what is in your line of vision?"

"If I'm on my balcony looking across the street, I would see the street corner right here." She pointed to the map.

"Would you see back down Josephine as well?"

"No."

"The man you saw running away—you saw him run and jump in a car?" Michael wrote *McAllisters* on the pad of paper in front of him and slid it in front of Gordon, who nodded. Solino wasn't focused on discrediting her. Instead, he was laying a foundation to go after the McAllisters, new "earwitnesses" who had not been used by Couhig or Fanning in the first trial.

"No, sir."

"Did you hear tires squealing away?"

"No, sir."

"From the time you heard the last shot till the time you assumed your position out on the balcony, how much time elapsed?"

"Two seconds."

Solino looked up at her, surprised. "Two seconds?"

"It wasn't long."

"Two seconds to hop down, get the window up, and jump out on the balcony? If I understand you correctly, you have to raise the window, exit out on the balcony, get your bearings, and then see what you saw?"

"I can't give you a specific time, but it wasn't any time at all, it seemed."

"You lived in that area for two months. I take it you crossed Baronne Street from time to time? How long would it take to walk from one side of Baronne to the other, just crossing the street?"

"Maybe five seconds."

"How long would it take to run?"

"Two seconds."

"Two seconds." Solino said it like a victory. "Yet you're saying today that the shots ended, you squatted down, opened up the window, got out onto the balcony, walked to the position you were in, established the position, all in time to see the person—*after* the shots had been fired—run across the street, stop, look up at you, and then take off and run again?"

Sheri was a little flustered, but she held her ground. "I didn't see him run across the street. I saw him as he was getting to the curb on my street. And he didn't stop."

Solino said, "He did not *stop*?"

"No, sir."

"He looked up?"

"Yes, he did. I wasn't quiet."

"What does that mean?"

She smiled a little, back under control. "I slammed that window open."

"Did you tell the police that when you first heard the sounds of the man pleading for his life, or the argument that called your attention to something happening on the street, that you first went to look out your window?"

"No, sir."

"Do you have a specific recollection of telling the police what it is you had to say that was relevant to this matter?"

"No, sir."

"But you do have a specific recollection of repeating it to your sister?"

"Yes, sir."

"From the time this incident happened, or from the time you said you came to be aware that Mr. Thompson was arrested, until October of 2000, who in authority did you call and tell that they had the wrong person in custody?"

"I didn't call anyone."

"Someone sought you out in 2000, right, and asked you to come be a witness?"

"Yes."

"And what was it you told them?"

"What I've said here today—that the man I saw was not the man whose picture was in the paper."

"Is that all you told them?"

"I told them everything I've told here. But they asked questions too."

"And you specifically remember that, but you don't specifically remember what you told the police the night this happened?"

"It's more closer in my memory."

"Uh-huh. Did they tell *you* anything?"

"They told me that they were going to perhaps see what could be done, and they needed to know if I had anything to share. I don't remember."

Solino held up the photo of John Thompson from the *Times-Picayune*. "The basis for your conclusion that the man you saw was not John Thompson had nothing to do with what the man you saw that night looked like, though—because you didn't see his face, correct?"

"I saw his build and his outline."

"You saw his build and his outline." Solino's voice was marinated in skepticism. "Well, let me ask you this question. You see this picture here today displays from the chin down. And you even said, did you not, that this man here appears to be more slim?"

"Yes, sir."

"But when you made your identification, you didn't have a picture of John Thompson from the chin down; true or false?"

"I did not have a picture from the chin down."

"All you had was a head shot?"

"Yes, sir."

"Isn't it a fact that what you're stating here today is in the final result based on the fact that the man's hair looks to be picked out in this photograph in the newspapers?"

"That isn't true," Sheri protested. "The build is different."

"The build is different. How can you tell that from this photograph?" He shook the picture, pointing at it with his other hand.

"The man I saw appeared almost to have no neck. He was muscular, he was heavier. The hair and the build."

"And the man you saw running away you saw for how long? Seconds, right?"

"A split second, yeah."

"Dark, 12:30 at night?"

"It was light enough."

"Would it be fair to say you were in an excited state? Excited enough that you knocked the lights off in your apartment?"

"No, I turned them off."

"Because you were afraid, didn't you say that? So you were in an excited state?"

"I was not excited. I was interested and curious."

Michael tensed a little in his chair. Sheri was parsing her words, something that always looked defensive in front of a jury.

"You were interested and curious." Solino ran his fingers through his hair, sighing audibly for the jury. "Would it be fair to say that the hairstyle played a big role in this—that the hairstyle doesn't fit the man you saw running away?"

"Yes."

Solino was jamming their argument right back up their noses, Michael thought. They had made a big deal about close-cropped hair. Solino was poking holes at that and would move on to tell the jury that whatever the McAllisters heard, Sheri Kelly didn't hear anything. It wasn't a bad argument, he thought glumly.

"When you're standing on that balcony and there's no other noise, and it's quiet, if there were a car parked directly across the street, and it started its engines and squealed away, would you think it would be reasonable that you could hear it?"

"If I were on the balcony I possibly could have, yes."

"You would expect that a normal person could hear it, would you not?"

"Yes."

"Did *you* hear a car squeal away that night?"

"No."

"No other questions."

Michael stood up. Sheri had stood her ground pretty well, but he needed to build her back up on the car squealing away. He walked to her, his voice unconcerned and his tone pleasant.

"Ms. Kelly, I think you said before, correct me if I'm wrong, that after you saw the man with the close-cut hair run by you when you were on the balcony, your attention then went to Mr. Liuzza who was in the street?"

Sheri looked at him, and they connected. She smiled a little, nodded, and said, "Yes."

"And you looked out there for, I don't know, a second or two or something?"

"Yes."

"To try to figure out what had happened?"

"Yes."

"And then you went downstairs to go out into the street, right?"

"I went back into my apartment and put a sweater or something on."

"So you had to go back inside away from the balcony and away from the window, right?"

"And I was running."

"So you went back in, you had a sweater in a what, a closet or a drawer?"

Sheri smiled. "Most likely laying on the back of the couch."

"Sounds like my house. You went in, got the sweater off the back of the couch, you put it on, and then you had to go to the stairs somewhere, right?"

"Mm-hmm."

"The stairs weren't on a window that faced Josephine?"

"No."

"This was like an internal stairwell as opposed to, like, a fire escape?"

Sheri's eyes got big as she got it, where Michael was going. "Yes, sir."

"And there are windows from the stairs facing on Josephine?"

"No, sir."

"Would this have made it easier or harder to hear what was going on on Josephine Street?"

"Harder, and I was clattering down wooden steps, too."

Attagirl, Michael thought.

"Between 1985 and 2000, did anyone—anyone who represented Mr. Thompson, any police officer, any detective, anyone from the court—try to find you to your knowledge to ask you what you saw the night of Mr. Liuzza's murder?"

"No, sir."

"When you saw the photo of Mr. Thompson in 1985, Mr. Solino asked you whether you called the police and told them?"

"Yes, sir."

"You didn't."

"No, sir."

Michael stopped and looked at her, palms out. "Why not?"

"I was afraid. I knew that the man I saw was not the man in that paper, and he had seen where I lived. And I was afraid. I moved. I was afraid."

"Why did you come in in 2000 as opposed to January of 1985?"

"I wanted to do the right thing. I carried a burden for years, and I just needed to do the right thing."

Michael turned to the jury, making a little "see?" shrug with his hands. *She was afraid. That's all. You would have been, too.* He turned back to Judge Quinlan. "Your Honor, we have nothing further for this witness."

Quinlan called for the lunch recess. The morning was over. They had half a day left to prove John's innocence.

AFTER LUNCH, MICHAEL gave the golden-throated clerk of the court another transcript-reading assignment—this time, the testimony of Pat Jordan, Sheri Kelly's sister. Pat had come from Tennessee in 2000 to testify at the motion for a new trial, but her health was bad, and she couldn't make the trip to New Orleans to testify now. Still, Michael wanted Pat's testimony to bolster Sheri's.

Pat's story was identical to her sister's, for the parts she knew. While she had an obvious bias, she corroborated Sheri's claims with a real-time account of the story, which helped minimize the damage caused by Sheri's admitted inability to remember what she had told police that evening.

"Sheri told me that she heard the shouts—that she heard the gunshots, that she ran out on her balcony, and that she saw a man running away. And she told me that he stopped and looked up at her. And my response was, 'My God, Sheri, if you saw him, then he saw you. You've got to get out of there and you've got to get away.' She told me about his short hair, shortly cut hair. And she told me of hearing the feet, the heels, the clicking of the shoes."

This was the first time the jury had heard anything about hard-soled shoes. It contrasted with Kevin Freeman's own testimony that he had been wearing sneakers. It was probably too subtle to hope that the jury got that, but juries were smart, and you never knew what would strike a chord with them.

They were moving into the home stretch. Michael leaned over

to Gordon and murmured, "We'll get through all of this today, at this pace."

"I think you're right. All we have left is to place Freeman north of Baronne and driving away from the scene, use the unbiased witnesses to separate Freeman from John, and bring John in for the big finale."

Michael patted Gordon on the shoulder. "Go get 'em."

Gordon rose and called Stephen McAllister to the stand. The McAllisters had moved to Massachusetts a few years earlier but had traveled to Louisiana to help John's case.

Gordon kept the map of Josephine and Baronne close to the jury and used it to illustrate the progress of the shooter, now firmly identified by them as Kevin Freeman. It was a subtle advantage for the defense—Solino couldn't refer to the shooter as John Thompson without getting a mistrial, since that hadn't been proven, but Gordon and Michael could continue to suggest that Freeman was the shooter based on the difference between his testimony and the facts that each of their witnesses had stated.

Stephen described for the jury the layout of his apartment—the large bed against the wall, in a big room with a high ceiling—a place where sound traveled well. They had an iron balcony, with windows facing south, kitty-corner across the intersection from the spot Ray Liuzza was shot. From there, they could hear everything happening on the corner. When the shooting happened, he and Rose had been in bed, "not completely asleep, but in bed for some time."

Stephen was a precise man, an architect, articulate and calm with a matter-of-fact tone. "I heard what sounded like an argument between two men. There were two distinct voices. One was muffled and low, the other one was higher-pitched. The voices—you know—they escalated. We were not unused to hearing things outside, but this was—this was different. This was an argument, a confrontation of some kind. And I began to wake up to it. It escalated in intensity, and then I heard this series of popping sounds. After the first one or two I recognized it as a pistol firing. That woke me right up."

"After you heard those sounds, Mr. McAllister, what did you do?" Gordon waited.

"I got up and went to the window, in the corner facing out onto Baronne, and I looked out. There was a streetlight, I think, a single streetlight that lit up the intersection. I was looking through the slats of the blinds, and I saw a man, a person, lying here." Stephen was using a pointer to indicate locations on the map for the jurors. "There was a man lying right at that location where the 'X' is.

"There was some activity over here," he continued, pointing further south, toward Carondelet and away from the intersection, "and it may have been another person headed over there. Other than that, I didn't see anything really specific, except it's very clear in my mind that someone had been shot—that person had been shot. It was very clear to me."

Gordon nodded. "After you saw what we now know to be Mr. Liuzza lying on the street, did you hear anything?"

"Yes, I did. As I got to the window and looked out, someone came along the street here"—Stephen pointed to the Josephine side of his apartment—"and got into a car. I heard a car door open, heard it shut, car started up, and in haste, took off this way"—now pointing northbound, away from the shooting, toward the lake— "and I made a mental note that it went this way on Josephine toward the lake because, I thought, that may be important to know. I mean, 'they went that-a-way,' you know."

Gordon held up his hand to stop Stephen. "I want to make sure I'm clear on what you heard. You heard a car door open, a car door shut, and the car drive away?" Stephen nodded. "How many sets of car doors did you hear?"

"One."

"This happened eighteen years ago. How can you be so clear about that sitting here today?"

Stephen looked at Gordon like Gordon had a third head. "It's unforgettable when you hear, you know, pistol shots in the night and you look out and you realize someone's been shot and you hear a car, you know, hear someone get in a car and drive off. That's unforgettable. That's, I guess, why I'm clear on it. I don't claim to remember every single detail in the world, but there are some things I won't forget. And I won't forget them in another eighteen years, either."

Gordon nodded, not letting his face betray his pleasure over the answer and its certainty. "Can you tell the general direction the car is traveling in when it pulls away, Mr. McAllister?"

"Well, it was heading down toward the lake, along here." Stephen pointed up Josephine, away from Liuzza's bleeding body. "It accelerated to a pretty high rate of speed and—it wasn't like, you know peeling out so hard as to draw a lot of attention, but definitely in a hurry to get out of there. Maybe some squealing of tires. Not sustained but, you know, *eeerrrh!* Gone. I was, and remain, convinced that whoever did that shooting got in that car and drove off."

"Did you call the police that night?"

"Yes."

"Do you remember what, if anything, you told them?"

"I do. I told them what I had seen when I looked out and what I heard at the same time."

"Thank you, Mr. McAllister. No further questions."

Despite his setup questions with Sheri Kelly, Gordon had a hard time seeing how Solino could really attack the McAllisters. They had no apparent bias or reason to testify other than to tell the truth, and they had traveled a hell of a long way to be here. A better plan for Solino would be to wait until closing arguments, then make the point that McAllister was a useless witness. If he hadn't seen anything, who's to say it wasn't John Thompson who ran and got into a car and drove away? For that matter, who's to say the car driving away was even connected to the murder? Maybe someone was getting in his or her car and heard the shots and decided to get the hell out of there. That didn't mean McAllister was lying—but John Thompson was implicated by his own statements to Funk and to Kevin Freeman, and by having the ring and the murder weapon in his possession.

Solino didn't disappoint, standing up and down in one motion while saying, "No questions, Your Honor."

Rose McAllister took her husband's place on the witness stand. Like her husband, she had been drifting off to sleep, she said, "when I heard some shouting, some, you know, rumblings of, you know, men's voices. I'm a light sleeper, so I heard them; it woke me up. And then I heard gunshots and I was fully awake."

"When the gunshots rang out, what did you do?"

"From my bed, which is right by the window, I just dove to the floor because that was very frightening to hear the gunshots."

"Do you remember what your husband did?"

"Yeah. He jumped out of bed and ran to the front window."

"Did you go to the window or look out?"

Rose shook her head, quickly, almost defiantly. "Not at all. I was next to my bed on the floor below a window. I was under cover there. Then after the gunshots I shouted to Steve, or told Steve, you know, 'Don't go to the window,' and I heard footsteps running."

"Okay. There should be a pointer up there, Ms. McAllister. Can you show the jury the general direction you sensed the footsteps to be running in?"

Rose grabbed the pointer and waved it toward the lake. "They were running this way, toward the lake. They were hasty, running, and, you know, maybe a sole-footed shoe, not a soft sneaker, because I don't think I would have heard it. It was a definite *chk, chk, chk*."

"What did you hear after that?"

"I heard—I heard a car door slam. I heard a car start up and then a quick acceleration. Not a long screechy peeling out, just a *tcheerch*. From the sound of it, it was up toward the lake."

"Did you form any connection between the car leaving the scene and the shooting?"

Rose considered that, briefly. "I never thought it would be *dis*-connected. Shooting, running footsteps, car starting and going; to me it all seemed connected."

Gordon nodded. "One last question—did you testify in a trial in 1985?"

"No, sir. I did not."

Again, Solino had no questions.

Gordon looked at Michael and Robert and arched his eyebrows. *This is it.* Michael shrugged a little and nodded. They both looked at John. Michael leaned over, whispering in John's ear. "Time for your big moment."

John nodded but didn't say anything. Michael said, "Here we go. Stay calm, answer the questions, tell the truth, and we'll be all set."

Robert stood up, saying, "If Your Honor pleases, the defense calls John Thompson."

"Come on up, Mr. Thompson," Quinlan invited, and Gordon was struck by the familiarity and level of comfort in his tone. Quinlan addressed John like an old classmate, someone not necessarily liked but whose presence was comfortable by its familiarity alone. After eighteen years together, the men were inescapably linked, their lives forever intertwined. Gordon didn't think of Quinlan as a romantic, but he could have sworn he detected a hint of nostalgia in the judge's voice, inviting his first murder defendant to the stand—his first murder convict—the case still going on after all these years.

As frustrating as this case had been to the defense, Quinlan had never displayed any self-doubt or introspection as he had made his rulings, including some Gordon had agreed with and a good many he hadn't. Still, he knew Quinlan was thoughtful enough that he must have spent time reflecting on the case, especially after the blood evidence was revealed. Had he been naive? Had he been duped by Dubelier and Williams? How had his role affected the lives of John Thompson and his family?

Gordon had had similar thoughts—thoughts about what might have happened for John if he had told the truth in 1985 instead of taking the rap. In a world where John was released and Kevin Freeman got the death sentence, would John have become the career criminal that Dubelier and Williams described at his murder trial? Would all roads eventually have led to Angola for John, regardless?

For that matter, what if Dubelier hadn't framed the armed robbery case to get the death penalty? On the lesser charge of second-degree murder, without the exacerbating factor of the carjacking, John might have been convicted anyway and placed in the main prison population at OPP. He would have been eligible for parole. He wouldn't have had the time or the isolation to read and reflect, and wouldn't have had the incentive to change his view of the world and how he was going to live in it.

Was it a stretch to say that the death penalty had ultimately saved John Thompson's life? Did his time in solitary confinement protect him physically, and challenge him mentally and emotionally to examine his life, his path, and his purpose on the planet in a way that even regular prison would not have?

Gordon hoped so, and he hoped that the time to reflect, the time to read and write letters, and the time to think had given John an ability to express himself that would endear him to the jury now. The big risk in John's testimony was whether he could tell his story in a way that rang true, a way that would make him sympathetic to the jury. It required a delicate display of controlled emotion, which was not necessarily John's strength. John hadn't survived eighteen years in OPP and in Angola by putting his emotions on display, after all. In fact, his survival had depended in large part on his ability to *not* show people that he cared about anything at all. Now he had to undo all of that in public, in front of strangers. Michael and Gordon had worked with him, but they were concerned that his incarceration would come through and count as a strike against him—that he would not be capable of infusing his story with enough sympathy to win over the jury. Had death row hardened him so much that he wouldn't be able to be credible on the stand?

Michael fidgeted, uncomfortable with being a spectator during this key phase of the trial. But they had decided that Robert's softer style and his familiar Delta twang had the best chance of pulling a sympathetic, honest story out of John, one that explained how he'd gotten mixed up in Ray Liuzza's murder without having anything whatsoever to do with the actual crime. *Come on, John,* Michael thought. *Bring it home.*

Michael looked to his right at Gordon, who looked energized, agonized, and nauseated all at once. He realized that the courtroom was pulsing as well, with every person riveted to the witness stand. This was the defining moment of everything they had worked for: John's guilt, his life, and their careers—everything.

Robert started slowly, letting John adjust to the courtroom, the microphone, and the jury. He needed to get John past the wooden answer phase and into a more comfortable, natural voice. John could be tremendously charming, and if Robert could tap into that, they'd be halfway home.

"Good afternoon, John," Robert said calmly.

"Good afternoon," John said, his voice lower, with more of a Cajun mumble to it.

"Is it all right to call you John?" Robert asked.

"Yes, sir."

"Tell the jury where you've been these last eighteen years."

"Angola."

Michael thought it was maybe the single greatest understatement he'd ever heard in his life.

"What were you in Angola for?"

"Murder of a Mr. Ray Liuzza." John was hunched over, his thin frame seeming even smaller behind the microphone. He looked frail and uncertain.

"Did you commit the murder of Ray Liuzza?" Robert had apparently decided that John was comfortable enough.

"No, sir."

"Were you around when it was committed?"

"No, sir."

"Did you see anything involving the killing?"

"No, sir."

With that done, Robert moved straight to the unpleasant stuff. They wanted to show the jury early on that John had been a drug dealer and a fence. It was important to be direct and truthful about that up front. "How old were you when you were convicted?"

"Twenny-two."

"What were you doing for money then?"

John tilted his head, smiled a little rueful smile. "I'm not proud if it, but I was sellin' drugs and workin' here and there and buyin' hot things, hot merchandise."

"All right. And as a result of that, did you have a couple of misdemeanor convictions?"

"Yes. Possession of marijuana, and I think it was a firearm; yeah, a gun."

Robert knew the answer, helped John out a little. "A concealed weapon?"

John nodded. "Carryin' a concealed weapon, yeah."

"Back in 1984, how did you wear your hair?"

John straightened up at this a little. "A bush; an Afro."

Robert held up the December 1984 Bureau of Investigation photo. "Is this what your hair looked like in December of 1984?"

John nodded, "Yes, sir."

"So in 1984, did you do any business with Kevin Freeman?"

"Yes, sir."

"And describe what that was to the jury."

John leaned forward to the microphone, turning a little so he was facing the jury, talking to them. He had been coached on this—look into their eyes, don't spend too much time on any one person, try to connect as you're talking, show them you're telling the truth as you go. Don't worry if they aren't looking back or if they're making faces—you tell your story. They'll believe it if you're not afraid of them. "Well, around our house we got a little condo where we call the Set, that's more what they call it around the 'hood. That's on Euterpe and Saratoga.

"Like I said, I'd sell drugs. So I'd be there. And that's where everybody came to get drugs from. When Kevin came around, they had a few of them I used to give drugs to sell for me, to stop me from having to be out there all the time.

"So Kevin came around lookin' for some drugs. I didn't have none to give to him because I was runnin' out. He said he have a gun to sell. I said, 'Go get the gun and let me see it.' He brought the gun to me and I gave him some clickems."

Michael looked at the jury. It was the first time the word *clickems* had been used, but the jury didn't look confused.

"What did you do with the gun?"

"I wound up givin' it to Funk Perkins. He come around me lookin' for drugs too. It was, like I said, I have five or six of them that I knew, and they used to be out in the clubs around our house at night. They'd be out there, so I'd give them the drugs and let them sell so I wouldn't be there. So Funk come over and is lookin' for drugs. I was like, I had the drug but I ain't had the marijuana. You know, clickems is two different kind of drugs: You need to pull the weed, the marijuana—clickem juice on the marijuana leaves."

"That's what PCP is?"

"That's the PCP. Yeah, so one without the other is no good. So I had ran out of weed and I just said I wasn't goin' to mess with nothin' more tonight. He said, 'Man, I just have to make some

441

money tonight, I don't have no money.' I said, 'Well, look, only thing I can do, I got this gun, you want to go sell it?' He said yeah, so I said, 'Well, look, just give me what I paid for it back.' "

"Did you give him the gun?"

"Yeah."

"What did you do after that?"

"I left."

"At the time you got the gun from Kevin Freeman, did you know anything about Kevin Freeman being involved in a shooting of Ray Liuzza?"

"No, sir." It was an artful question. They hadn't proved that Freeman was actually the shooter, but Robert strengthened their case by asking John this question now, as if it were an established fact.

"When was the next time you saw Kevin Freeman?"

"It was a day or two after my son's birthday, which is December the 18th."

"Tell the jury where you saw him and what you did with him."

John turned toward the jury again. "I seen Freeman at Saratoga and Euterpe."

"Did anybody else see you there?"

"Yeah. Big Daddy Red."

"All right. And what happened?"

"Once again, he came around me to buy some drugs. He came around me to buy some, and I ain't had nothin' but a few. He said, 'I got a ring.' He ain't had no money so I just said, 'Well, give me the ring,' just transferred the drugs for the ring."

"Do you mean the ring that's been produced in this court with the 'L' on it?"

"Yes, sir."

"The ring that came from Mr. Liuzza?"

"Yes, sir."

"Did you know it had come from—through the killing of Mr. Liuzza?"

John shook his head. "I mean, I didn't know about Mr. Liuzza being dead at the time."

"And what did you do with the ring?"

"Put it on."

"Did you have the ring for a long time?" John shook his head again. "What did you do with it?"

"I wound up giving it to J.R."

"That's Junior Lee Harris?" Robert was helping the jury connect the dots. John agreed. "Why were you with Junior Lee Harris?"

"I was trying to purchase me some marijuana. Because I had the PCP and didn't have the marijuana. And he had the marijuana."

"Did you have enough money for the marijuana?"

"No."

"So what happened?"

"Well, basically, I told him I needed two ounces. Two ounces covered a bottle. He tell me about how the weed is cased, they don't have that much weed around there right now. So he tryin' to charge me these ridiculous prices for it. Well, I'm like tellin' him, 'I only have nothin' but a hundred dollar.' Back then you might could get an ounce of weed for like fifty-five, forty-five dollars an ounce. He tryin' to charge me like a hundred and twenty dollars for two ounces. After he seen the ring, he said, 'Well, give me somethin' for collateral.' I said, 'Well, here, take the ring and give me the weed.' He took the money and the ring for the weed. I told him I'm goin' to bring his money back for the ring."

"Did you know that he had gotten the gun, that Richard Perkins had sold him the gun?"

"No, sir." John paused, and Robert let him continue. "Next night, I'm out at the Set. Once they hear that I'm out there, they come, because they know I'm goin' to either give them somethin' to sell or smoke somethin' with them, whatever, somethin' of that nature. Funk came around, and the first thing I thought about is the money he owed me from the gun that I give him. So I'm like, 'Where's my money?' And he said, 'Well, hold on, bruh.' I think he give me like ten dollars or somethin' like that."

John continued: "He said, 'Let me make it up to you.' He said, 'Give me somethin' to go sell and I'll bring back more than I normally bring back,' so I'm like, all right, I'm thinkin' about it. He says, 'Man, you heard what Kevin Freeman did?' He said, 'Man, he talkin' about he killed that white man.' He said, that's what the poster rewards that—they had them around our house, all on the, what they call it, electric poles. They had them stamped all around there, all around the stores around our house. All these little signs with the reward.

"While he's saying it, I'm thinkin', I'm sayin' to him, 'Man, I bought a gun from Kevin. I wonder if that's the gun he used to do that, if he did it?' It was just me and him talkin', he be tellin' me about it, and I just basically said it just like that.

"He all like, 'What gun?' and I said, 'The gun I gave you to sell.' He said, 'Oh, man, what you mean?' Me and him went to arguin' about it. He like, 'What kind of games y'all playin'? You tryin' to set me up or whatever?' I don't know that it been committed to a murder till he just now told me, you know. So it got kind of hostile, really."

"How did it end?" Robert asked.

"It ended when I had to just get up and walk away because it was getting to the point of, I don't know whether he was goin' to do somethin' to me or I was goin' to do somethin' to him, but I know it just got bad, and I had drugs on me, so I ain't want to cause no heat out there. So I just was really going to walk around the corner."

"Were you able to convince him that you had not been trying to set him up?"

"I did not even see him again since that day."

Robert turned and walked back to the counsel table. He pulled out the Big Daddy Red letter, the letter Jim Williams in 1995 had called "the most damning piece of evidence I've ever seen in all my years as a prosecutor." He held it up for the jury, saying, "Who's that addressed to?"

"Big Daddy Red."

"Where were you when you wrote that letter?"

"In jail back there, OPP."

"It says, 'I need your help like I never needed before.' Why did you need his help?"

"Meant he was going to come and testify and say what he seen took place."

Robert looked at the letter. "It says, 'I want you to come to court on the 21st of the month to tell them that you seen Kevin give me a ring around December 21st or later in the month.' Why did you tell him that?"

John shifted in his seat a little, uncomfortable. "Well, it was like, at this time I been down four months or so. I know Red smoked them drugs, too, so I'm, like tryin' to make him remember, just reach out some of his memories if I can."

Robert continued: "And then you say, 'If you can find it in your heart to do that for me I'll be glad; just say we was on Euterpe Street when you seen him give me the ring and don't change your statement.' Why would you say that in there?"

"That was our sct. When we selling drugs, we on Euterpe and Saratoga. When we just chillin' out, we on Terpsichore and Saratoga, a block away."

"So why are you telling him Euterpe?"

"I'm just trying to reach all his memory. I'm trying to make him remember where we was at when it happened."

Robert was still holding the letter, almost like a trophy, showing the jury that John wasn't running from it or embarrassed about it. "Now a little later in the letter you say, 'Do you see Funk anywhere? If you do, tell him if he come to court we's going to tell on each other. He know what I'm talking about. Please find him and tell him that.' What are you talking about here?"

"He had a little clique. They little clique, what they do is they burglarize all them little stores around Dryades Street, and that was their thing, they out there hustlin'. They was goin' in and breakin' in little shops, and they would come and try to sell their hot stuff. I used to buy some of it. So I know he did all these crimes. I'm sayin', 'If you come in here lyin' on me and tryin' to get me stuck up, I'm goin' to tell somethin' that I know is the truth on you, and I know if they go and check it, they goin' to see that I know what I'm talkin' about.' That's basically all—I was tryin' to really scare him."

Robert looked at John, serious now. "Were you trying—in *any* way—to threaten him against coming to court?"

"I just mad that he was lyin'," John said. "I gave him the gun. I was sayin', 'Yeah, all right, say that, I did do that. I'm not trying to hide that. I did give you the gun. But don't go and tell them people I told you I shot this man, I did this, because I didn't do that.' That's all I was sayin'."

"And when you're asking Big Daddy Red to just come to court for you, why do you think you have to convince him? Why wouldn't an ordinary subpoena be good enough for him?"

"Red was a street dude. He, I think they call him now, he's a hustler, a gangster, or whatever, like that, and that type. He ain't goin' to come to court on nobody, it would be like rattin'."

Robert wanted to be clear. "He wouldn't be ratting on you—"

"He'd be telling the truth on me but he'd be ratting on Freeman if he come forth and say that he seen Freeman givin' me the ring. That's rattin'. That ain't how they live out there."

Robert held up another picture, this one of John and his son, the proud papa smiling at the camera, John still in his Afro. "Is that a picture of you?"

John nodded. "Me and my son, John."

"When was this taken?"

"Probably November of '84, October or November."

"So this is a picture of you with your hair as it was before December 6th?" John's Afro reached out a good three inches from his head. He nodded. Robert held up the mug shot they had gotten from Solino: "And this is a picture of you as your hair was after December 6th?" John nodded again. "Was that your son who was in here yesterday with your mama?"

"Yeah, he right there." John pointed to John Jr. in the benches behind Michael and Gordon.

"What's he doing now?"

John threw his shoulders back a little. "He in college." His pride shone through.

Robert put the photos away, let a couple of moments pass in silence. "John." He paused again. "Tell the jury. Were you any-place around Josephine and Baronne on the early morning hours of December 6, 1984?"

"No, sir." John's voice was definite, confident.

"Did you see Kevin Freeman, or anybody else, shoot Mr. Liuzza?"

"No, sir."

"Did you have *anything whatsoever* to do with that man's death?"

"Nothing at all, other than buying some property that they said was his."

"Thank you."

Robert sat down. Michael and Gordon looked at each other. Robert had managed a good direct, but neither man was calm. That had been the easy part. Now they had to pray that they had prepped John for the unexpected. Solino was going to hit him with everything he had. John could be a fiery guy. Prison hadn't taken the street out of him; it had only driven home the importance of respect and insisting on respect from others. Solino's job was expressly not to give John that respect.

Solino walked up to the podium confidently. He could easily exploit parts of John's story, most notably the convenience that John's primary defense was to blame the murder on a dead man. In 1985, when Freeman was alive, John hadn't taken the stand. Now, in 2003, with Freeman dead, John was on the stand and pointing an incriminating finger at a man no longer alive to defend himself.

But Solino had to watch his step, too. Just like Robert's cross of Funk Perkins, Solino could use too big a stick in attacking John, and it could backfire. If the jury decided that John had been railroaded in 1985, having that reinforced by having the white DA beating John up on the stand would help John far more than it would help the DA's office.

"Mr. Thompson, Kevin gave you the gun, right? And you gave it to Richard?"

"Yes, sir."

"And when Richard found out what was up, he was upset? But he was upset because the gun was hot, right, from the Liuzza murder?"

"I'm assumin', yeah." John was clearly wary. He'd seen Solino work over other witnesses on two different occasions now, and he didn't want to concede anything that could come back to haunt him.

"But you weren't upset that Kevin laid it off on you?"

John thought about that for a second, like they had told him. Good. Gordon and Michael had worked with him on that, telling him not to respond quickly when he was emotional. *Take a breath, count to three after each question, and think about your answer before you speak.* "When I was talkin' to Richard, it had just hit me at that moment. Yeah, I was mad after. But at that moment, right then and there, maybe, I didn't know that Kevin killed nobody, so how can I get upset? I just was goin' off of what Perkins had just told me."

Val opened his hands, straightened a little. "Well, would you think he'd be upset for no reason?"

"No. I was upset once it really dawned on me. I'm not sayin' that, you know, he was wrong from bein' upset. I'm saying that he just had found out that moment."

"How much money were you making from him?"

John shook his head. "I was a little dealer, man. I just get a little somethin'. Wasn't like no major dealer in the city or nothin' like that."

"You had enough to get by."

"Exactly."

"But when you went to see Junior, you didn't have enough to buy from him?"

"I had just got out of jail."

Val acted surprised, like he'd never heard this before. "You just got out of jail?"

"Yeah."

"What for?"

"Misdemeanor, city court charge. I can't even recall what it was. I had an attachment and the police stopped me and they ran my name and took me to jail."

"I see. And the first thing you did when you got out of jail, you ran over to Junior and lost the ring."

Solino was trying to make John look defensive and guilty, but Michael thought it was a shortsighted argument. How hard was it to lose a ring? If you were worried the ring was hot and linked to a murder, would you flash it around, sell it to another dealer? Of course, criminals did stupid stuff all the time—that's how they got caught.

John's response was even, calm, and reasonable: "First thing I did when I got out of jail was I went home. I got some drugs and then I went to see J.R. Might have been the next day, the day after. I don't recall."

"Let me get all this straight: Kevin gave you the gun. Was that before or after you went to jail?"

449

"Before I went to jail."

"You gave the gun to Richard, Funk Perkins, before or after you went to jail?"

"Before I went to jail."

"Richard came to you and told you what he knew about Kevin and what Kevin was running his mouth about before or after you went to jail?"

"After I come out of jail."

"After. You got the ring from Kevin before or after you went to jail?"

"I got that right from Kevin after I come home from jail."

"You talked to Richard before or after you got the ring from Kevin?"

John was surprised. "Huh?" He considered this. "No, I got the ring from Kevin. I talked to Richard after I got rid of the ring. Once I had sold the ring, that's when Richard came to me. That's when Richard told me about the killin'."

Michael breathed a little sigh of relief. The questioning could be confusing, and consistency between the cross and the direct exam was crucial. John had testified for Robert that he had sold the ring to get the weed, and then Funk had told him about Freeman's confession to the Liuzza murder. But Solino's questions were in a different order, designed to confuse. So far, John was hanging tough.

"So everything was out of your hands before you knew it was involved in a murder, is that what I'm hearing today?" The *today* was a nice touch, Michael thought. Val had never heard anything different from John, but the *today* made it sound different.

John seemed unperturbed. "When you sellin' drugs, you buy things, you know it's hot nine times out of ten. So you buyin' it from people that's out there buyin' drugs. So you know they hot so you ain't gonna keep it. You get it and you sell it. That's the whole point. I'm not proud of it, but that's the way it was."

Michael felt a nudge and looked over at the white notepad Gordon was holding. In Gordon's pristine handwriting it said, *Great answer*. Michael nodded.

"Why did Kevin want to give you the ring?"

"He wanted to score some drugs."

"And, of course, because of what happened with Funk Perkins, you obviously were aware that you were implicated in it now too?"

"No, because—"

Solino cut him off. "Well, you didn't think Funk· had anything to do with it, did you? Because you said the only reason Funk was upset was because he thought that you laid the gun off on him from Kevin?"

"Exactly."

"So·why weren't you thinking the same thing? The gun was in your hands, right?"

John raised his voice now, a little, trying to get through to this man. It was effective. His hands waved in the air, his voice saying loudly, "Because I know I ain't killed nobody. I know the most I could do is say where I got the gun from."

"But the ring was in your hands, too, right?"

John was calmer now. "I didn't know that was the ring at the time," he said.

"And after you found out, are you sitting here telling everybody you weren't thinking the same thing that Funk was, that I got the murder gun, ring from the robbery in my hand, I might have to worry about something?"

"Well, I was sorry that the man got killed, and I try to think of what I'm goin' to do if somethin' happen, if they come down to it, if the police come. But nine times out of ten, just like—just think about it. Look how many hands that gun changed in what, a month? It changed like five different people hand in that month period of time. So I looked for the same thing to happen. I just hoped it would never come back to say that John did it, or John had anything to do with it, that's all."

"So you were thinking it might happen?"

"Not necessarily. I'm just tryin' to show you that once you do this, wasn't nothin' I could do about it. I didn't see Perkins no more to ask him what he did or what he wasn't goin' to do. I don't know what was goin' on."

"Did you, at any time, try and think to come up with an explanation as to where you would have been the night of the Liuzza murder?"

Michael waited. He had known this question would come. It had to. It came from their friends, their parents, their colleagues, and total strangers. At the end of the day, it was really the only question. *Did he do it?* All the bullshit, the DA games, the evidence hiding, the *Brady* evidence, and it all came down to this. *Did you do it, John? How do we know you didn't?*

Michael thought back to his first meeting with John, the interview room in Angola. It was the same answer John had given then. He didn't have an alibi. He had never had one, and he would never have one. To Michael, the fact that John's alibi was constantly missing made it true. If he had suddenly come up with one, or if he had started with one and dropped it, Michael would have known— *he's not innocent.* But John had never used an alibi or an excuse, not even during their first meeting in Angola. "Why would I need an alibi? I wasn't there."

Michael had been John's defender for fifteen years. He had dedicated his professional reputation, his oath to the Bar, to protect John to the best of his ability, whether John was telling the truth or not. He now believed John after fifteen years of periodic bouts of doubt, and wanted to convince others that John was telling the truth.

This jury had known John for two days.

Solino asked again, "Did you, at any time, try and think to come up with an explanation as to where you would have been the night of the Liuzza murder?"

"No."

"Do you know where you were that night?"

"Probably club hopping."

"You were club hopping that night?"

"Probably. I don't know where I was at."

Solino stopped and looked at John, his head cocked at an angle, his posture projecting an *I can't believe what I'm hearing* stance. He lowered his voice, spoke more slowly, getting the jury to lean in to hear him. "Well, you had eighteen and a half years to think about it, is that true?"

"Yeah."

"You remember all those details about Euterpe and Saratoga and Kevin Freeman, Kevin Freeman and Richard Perkins—is that true?"

"Yeah."

"You remember all this stuff about J.R.—is that true?"

"Yeah."

"Now you're telling this jury you knew a murder weapon, a ring, all got laid off on you; your buddies are telling you that somebody you know that you got it from is going around the neighborhood telling people you did it—and you never thought about where you were that night in order to come up with an explanation?"

John shrugged. "No."

"You never bothered to *think* about it?"

Michael scanned the jury. For his part, though, John stayed calm. "No. I probably was club hopping. I couldn't tell you where I was at. I used to go out and hang out in the clubs at night. That was my thing."

Solino shook his head in disbelief, but he had scored his points and it was time to move on. "You were present at your last trial, right? You heard Kevin Freeman's testimony today, didn't you?"

"Yeah, I heard, they read it to us."

"Did you hear any questions directed to Mr. Freeman by your attorneys concerning the ring?"

"No."

"Were your attorneys aware that Kevin Freeman gave you that—sold you the ring or traded that ring with you?"

"I can't say. I wasn't really talking to my attorneys at that time."

"You weren't . . . you weren't talking to your attorneys at that time?"

"My communications with my attorneys weren't much good, no."

Solino shook his head. He turned to Judge Quinlan and said, "I don't have any other questions."

Solino went back to his table. He had scored some points, Michael thought, no doubt about it. But they would have the last word, as Robert rose to redirect.

"John, how many times did your lawyers come to see you in jail?" Robert asked.

"I can't really—maybe two, three times, somewhere up in that nature."

"Over the course of how many months? January to May?"

"January to May, yeah."

"Were you represented by any of us in 1985?"

"No."

"Now, why did you feel you had to write a letter to Big Daddy Red? You had lawyers."

Michael saw the light go on in John's head as he figured out where Robert was going. He turned to the jury: "I needed help, and I know it wouldn't been hard for him even if my lawyer would have been willing to go out there, to go in a black neighborhood, a white man asking questions. It just wasn't going to happen to talk about it."

Robert went back to John's drug dealing. "You told us some unpleasant stuff about what you were doing back then."

"Yes, sir. I'm not proud of it."

"Did you like what you were doing back then?"

"No, sir."

"You want your son to do that kind of thing?"

"No, that's why he in college. No, sir."

"And John—what you were doing for money is one thing. Did you have anything, anything to do with the killing of Ray Liuzza?"

"No, sir."

It was done. They had tried to show John as calm and reasonable, emphasizing his role as a parent. They wanted the jury to see him as a regular guy, a guy trying to get by—a guy with flaws, to be sure, but not a murderer. Still, Michael had to admit that Solino's questions were reasonable ones. John was tied to the gun and the ring, no doubt about that. Different people could read the Big Daddy Red letter in different ways, and could certainly take a different view than the one they had put forward in John's defense. And John still had no alibi for where he'd been on the night of December 6, 1984.

So it was done. Michael hated this feeling. It was as if he had bet his life savings on a single roll of the dice. The dice had left his hand and were bouncing on the felt, and he was stuck permanently in the moment where the dice were bouncing, caught suspended in the air so that he couldn't see whether he'd won or lost.

Judge Quinlan let John step down. For the fiftieth time that day, Michael scanned the jurors, looking for facial expressions, posture, anything to give away what they were thinking. He got nothing.

John got off the stand and walked back past the jury to the counsel table. While Gordon stood up and shook John's hand, pulling John's chair out for him and whispering congratulations into his ear, Michael stayed seated. He waited for John to look at him and nodded shortly, his lips pursed. There was a shakiness in John's demeanor that hadn't been there before.

John kept on whispering to Gordon and Robert as Michael stood and said, "Your Honor, the defense rests."

Quinlan announced a ten-minute break to give the jury a rest before letting Solino provide any rebuttal that his case required. The jury rose together and filed out, carefully avoiding eye contact with all the lawyers, and with John. They walked into the jury chamber, the bailiff closing the door behind them.

As the jury door closed and the audience, sitting in the seats behind them, stirred, Gordon rose. "Your Honor, may we approach?" Michael looked over at Gordon, surprised. What the hell was going on? Quinlan waved them up, and all the lawyers approached the bench. Robert said, "Your Honor, if you please, we'd ask that the court microphone be turned off."

Quinlan pushed a button in front of him. "Continue."

"Your Honor, while Mr. Thompson was on the witness stand, he could look out into the audience. In the audience, there are a number of members of the Liuzza family. I could not see this, as my back was turned at the time, but according to Mr. Thompson, Mr. Liuzza's son-in-law, Mr. Finkbeiner, was mouthing the words, 'I'm going to kill you,' as John testified. And he was making gestures, including pointing a gun to his head."

Quinlan looked at them all. "We're going to turn the microphones back on, and then you're all going to say all of this again." The court reporter nodded and got ready to type. Quinlan pressed the button again, and said, "We're now outside the presence of the jury, and counsel for defense has requested a sidebar."

Robert repeated the statements, and added, "Your Honor, this is Mr. Thompson saying this. I'd like to hear Mr. Finkbeiner."

Quinlan shook his head, certain. He spoke as much for the recording as for the lawyers before him: "This Court is going to deny the request. The Court, for the record, was viewing the courtroom. We have a number of people here. Obviously I didn't see everything that everybody was doing the entire time Mr. Thompson was testifying. But the Court did look specifically a number of times at the Liuzza family, including the gentleman you're talking about, and the Court did not see any improper actions. Court will keep an eye on it for the rest of the trial."

Robert said, "Judge, it's the intimidation while he was on the witness stand and how Mr. Thompson was reacting during the questioning, and whether he was tight or loose or how he appeared in his body language to the jury. I understand that the Court is denying our request for a hearing." He took a deep breath and a calculated risk. "We would, based on what we know now, move for a mistrial."

Quinlan said, "Well, if the Court thought there was any basis in fact for it, the Court would conduct a hearing. But the Court does conduct its own view of the courtroom proceedings as we go along, and the Court did not see anything that the Court felt was unruly."

Robert nodded. "Understood."

"Your objection will be noted for the record."

They walked back to their table. With the jury still out of the room, and the audience, including Finkbeiner, at ease during the court's recess, Michael turned to John. "You all right?"

John looked at Michael. "How you think I should be?"

Michael grinned. "I don't know, John. I can't even imagine right now. You did an incredible job up there. Finkbeiner, he's not going to ruin it for you. I didn't see any of that, but I saw you, and I saw that jury. We're doing fine."

Michael was amazed how much he almost believed that.

MICHAEL SPENT THE remainder of the recess wrestling with who would do the closing argument. Originally, they had planned for Robert to do it, but Michael had been unsure of that decision since the trial started. Robert had done a fine job, and Michael certainly didn't want to suggest otherwise. Robert had more than lived up to his reputation. Even so, the case was too close for Michael to be completely comfortable with the close.

Robert was a New Orleans local, the criminal defense expert, the one they had hired when they needed someone whose experience was better than theirs. Changing horses now could backfire on them. On the other hand, Robert hadn't lived and breathed this case for the last fifteen years.

You should do the close, Michael told himself.

And then he countered, *Don't let your ego ruin this case.*

It's not just ego. This case needs an aggressive close, Michael thought. *Solino has left openings. Their case has weaknesses. That suits your style, not Robert's calm gentility. We can attack. They could take it right to the DAs. We can give it back to the man,* he thought.

Yet, at the same time, he thought, *You don't want to change on the fly here. John's life is in the balance. You all decided the New Orleans voice would be more persuasive to the jury than the carpet-bagging northeastern Jew.*

Michael turned, looked at Gordon. "What do you think?"

"The close?" He looked at Michael, considering. "We could go either way." He paused. "I think you should ask John. He's seen the whole trial."

"I don't want to put him on the spot."

"Michael, he's been on the spot for the past day and a half, to say nothing of the last eighteen years."

He's right, Michael thought. He turned to John. He motioned to the bailiff that he was going to move John away from the counsel table, and the bailiff followed them into the hall, staying a respectful distance away.

"John, look," Michael said. "I need to know who you want to do the closing argument. I think Robert would do a fine job, but I think there might be a few things I can do that I wouldn't want to ask Robert to do, since he's newer on the case and hasn't lived it all this time. Robert got us this far, and he's the criminal defense expert—the New Orleans expert. You say you want him, we'll go with that." He waited.

John nodded. He thought for a few seconds before speaking. "Michael, man, you been with me, you stood by me when nobody else would, when I was writin' three hundred letters every month to every lawyer in that magazine they let us see on death row. No lawyer ever responded to my letters, and then you come in. You been fightin' for me ever since. I'm'a stay with you, do what you tell me. You got me this far."

"John, that's the point. If I, if anyone, screws up this close, doesn't do the best job that can be done, you could go back to prison. And you won't get another shot like this. This isn't just about loyalty; that's not the issue here. The issue here is who's going to get you your freedom. I know how loyal you are, and I appreciate it, but it's not disloyal to say you want Robert to close. It might be the best way to go to get you your freedom."

John smiled. "No, sir. It's all about loyalty. It's all about loyalty. And I trust you. You do what you think is best for the case. You got me this far. I trust you. I'm gonna go with what you say, and no regrets."

Michael looked at John. He wasn't lying. "Okay, then."

Michael opened the door for John and followed him into the courtroom, where Robert was preparing his thoughts. He put his hand on Robert's shoulder and whispered into the older man's ear. Robert nodded, putting the cap on his pen as he said, "It's your case. Always has been." He asked if Michael wanted to run through it in the moments they had left. Michael smiled and squeezed Robert's shoulder, about to say *No thanks*, but before he could respond, Judge Quinlan entered the courtroom and called for the jury.

MICHAEL WAS SO involved in making sure his close was organized properly that he didn't realize that Shary Scott was standing up to deliver the prosecution's closing argument. This was not as unusual as it might have appeared, as it was standard operating procedure for the New Orleans DA to use the closing argument as a teaching moment for the junior prosecutor. It was a little bit of a trap for unsuspecting defense counsel as well. Michael expected Shary would give a fact-based argument articulating the legal standard for second-degree murder and then would sit down. Many lawyers would simply address the closing argument, leaving the field wide open for Solino to come in and deliver the real close as part of his rebuttal, the last word.

In general, Michael disagreed with the strategy. In the first trial, with Williams and Dubelier both experienced trial lawyers, it made more sense; here, Michael thought it might backfire. Scott was energetic, for sure, and her every move through the trial had indicated that she truly believed John was guilty. But she was young and inexperienced, and emotional at a time when she needed to be dispassionate. Convicting a man, sentencing him to life in prison, was hard for a jury to do. John's testimony on the stand virtually ensured that while the jurors might not believe him, they wouldn't hate him. Given that, Scott had to rely on the jurors' sense of responsibility and sense of duty rather than their anger and outrage. It was a lot to ask of a junior lawyer.

Scott led off cautiously, defining the crime. "Second-degree murder is murder in the perpetration of a felony. The felony in question is armed robbery, defined as taking something of value from another person with force or intimidation while armed with a dangerous weapon." She was clearly nervous, standing stiffly at the podium, holding the sides tightly, her speech stilted and swift.

"Ray Liuzza is no longer with us. On December 6th, at 12:30 at night, he was walking to the safety of his home when he was robbed and shot. As a result of being shot, one of the five bullets that penetrated his body was what killed him. That was what killed him. That one shot out of five.

"So the only question we're left with at this point, is not that someone died and not that there was an armed robbery, but who did it. And the answer is John Thompson.

"Richard Perkins came in here and sat in that chair, and what did he tell you? He learned that he had sold the murder weapon, and he sold it to Junior Harris, J.R. After that, you learn that Perkins goes to Mr. Liuzza. He goes to Mr. Liuzza and tells him the same thing. Shortly thereafter he tells the police, Detective Curole.

"What happens then? They get a search warrant and go over to Junior's house, and they find that Junior sold the gun to Jessie Harrison. And then what do they do? Get a search warrant and they go to Jessie Harrison's house. And what do they find? A .357 Taurus revolver, blue steel. None of that is in dispute."

Of course, none of it puts the gun in John's hand when the shots are fired, Michael thought, jotting down additional notes for his closing.

"Another thing is the ring. Same thing. Perkins came in and sat here and he told y'all that John told him he got a watch, a ring, and a wallet. The watch and wallet were never recovered. The ring was recovered. And as I told you, while the police were investigating the gun, what did they find on Junior's hand? The 'L' gold ring that belonged to Mr. Liuzza. And who did J.R. say he got that ring from? He got that ring from John Thompson.

"John Thompson was desperate for money, and John Thompson shot Mr. Liuzza.

"If you're still not convinced of what you've heard through the testimony of the witnesses here, from the detectives, Mr. Perkins, and everyone else, what else do we have? We have the Big Daddy Red letter. Determine for yourself what that letter meant. You know, his defense attorneys could put any spin that they want to put on that letter and try to sell it to you. What I want you to know is what's in your heart when you read that letter, what is it that you determined that it meant.

"He says, 'Don't change your statement.' First he's telling him what to say, and then he's telling him not to change it. Is this the letter of someone who's begging for help? Is this a letter from an innocent man saying, you know, they think I framed somebody, they think I did this murder?

"That's not what this letter says. And Big Daddy Red didn't come in here. He didn't tell you that John Thompson got that ring from Kevin Freeman.

"John Thompson is guilty of second-degree murder for the killing of Ray Liuzza. Thank you."

Michael looked at Gordon, and at John. Was it over, just like that? He watched Scott walk back to her chair and sit down, surprised. He'd been waiting for the crescendo, the knockout punch. She was done, and he was still waiting.

Michael's heart was racing and his throat was dry, but he was ready.

He didn't hear a sound as he walked up to the podium, though at that moment, he wouldn't have heard mortars exploding in the courtroom. He had tried to explain to other people what it was like to stand in front of a jury, but every description he gave was inadequate. He couldn't convey it: the conflict of having to be at once completely within yourself to persuade the jury, and at the same time stepping outside of yourself so that you knew how the jury saw you, so that you could make adjustments, make sure you were hitting the right tone, striking the right notes.

Every movement was important to him how. He looked into the eyes of each juror, trying to connect with them emotionally, not just verbally. *Slow down*, he thought. His adrenaline would speed everything up for him but not for them. The jury wouldn't be ready for his uptick in speed and forcefulness, and he'd sound panicked.

He was tempted to attack Scott's close, but she was just a diversion. Solino was waiting in the wings with the last word, hoping he'd just counterpunch. No, he needed to dispense with Scott and prepare for Solino.

Michael turned again to John and smiled, knowing he was being watched.

He turned to the jurors, breathed in, and began.

"Six feet tall, close-cropped hair. Five-foot-eight, big bushy Afro. I didn't hear anything from Ms. Scott about that. I don't get it. I don't understand why the State is still pretending that height and hair have nothing to do with this when the only two eyewitnesses we heard from make it very clear.

"Paul Schliffka is crying out to you from his grave that the man he saw running by with a gun in his hand was six feet tall with closely cropped hair.

"Sheri Kelly, who drove nine hours in 2000 to come in and tell her story for the first time in this court, and appeared before a jury for the first time today, told you as clearly as possible that this was not the man—John Thompson was not the man who ran by her. He was not the man with close-cropped hair. She knew it the minute she saw his photograph in the newspaper, and she knows it today.

"Maybe Tuesday seems like a long time ago. A lot's happened since then. But when we were here on Tuesday going through jury selection, remember Mr. Solino told you there were some problems with the State's case. That was good, that was candid. But there *were* problems.

"They're trying to take John Thompson and put him in jail for the rest of his life after spending eighteen years there for something that he didn't do. They're trying to tell you they can prove it beyond a reasonable doubt. They have big problems in their case.

"The first problem is, it's eighteen years later. Eighteen years between the time of the crime and when Mr. Thompson's finally going to get a fair trial, with Sheri Kelly, Mr. and Mrs. McAllister, and John himself as witnesses.

"The second problem is the physical evidence. You see, the gun they say is the murder weapon, bullets, in the State's custody, all of that was destroyed. Imagine that. Something as important as an alleged or supposed murder weapon, and when they try to prove guilt beyond a reasonable doubt, they want you to take the word of the New Orleans Police Department.

"There are some very fine officers in the NOPD. But can we sit here and send a man to jail for the rest of his life because they say, well, at one point he had a gun, and at one point we tested it. You, Mr. Banks, or you, Mr. Cooney, or you, Mr. Glass, you can't test it. Trust us. We're the *police department*."

Michael nodded to the jury, pursing his lips, holding his arms up, palms out. *Don't overdo it*, he told himself.

"That's the second problem. The third problem they told you about was Mr. Freeman. I almost don't need to say anything on the man with close-cropped hair, Mr. Freeman. A rat telling a story to save his skin. Their case hinges on a man who was trying to save his own skin with a deal. A rotten one.

"You need to remember Mr. Freeman's testimony as it was read to you. He said he was told in this rotten deal, he'd stand trial for second-degree murder instead of first, or plead guilty to accessory after the fact and go to jail for how many years? *Five* years. Remember that?"

Michael looked around at the jury. He had their attention, if not their allegiance.

Michael was used to moving around the courtroom when he was examining a witness or arguing a point. Some people found it distracting, but the movement helped him structure his arguments and gave his energy an outlet. He thought it also gave a physical presence to his words. Today, though, he stood still. Somehow, it felt right not to move, to calmly speak, to let the words carry the emotion instead of backing it up with movement. It was a simple argument. His passion and John's credibility would take them home.

"We're up to three problems; how about four? Freeman's dead. It's not our fault, or his fault, but he's dead. They want to send Mr. Thompson away and prove guilt beyond a reasonable doubt. Well, we would have loved to question Mr. Freeman on the stand the way you heard Mr. Glass do it today.

"You remember those questions he read? Those were good questions. They must—*we* must—want answers to those questions. But because Freeman's dead and it's eighteen years later, we don't get any. And they," he pointed at Val Solino, "they want Mr. Thompson to pay for that.

"The fifth problem, and this just goes without saying: Funk Perkins, four-time felon. A man who came here in chains right from the middle of his fifteen-year sentence. A man whose brain was so fried on PCP in the mid-1980s, he couldn't tell which way was up. He's the 'show me the money' man. A big piece of their case is a man who came forward not to the police but for ten thousand five hundred reasons—the money.

"I'd say those are problems, big problems in a case where they have to prove guilt *beyond . . . a . . . reasonable . . . doubt*."

Michael lowered his volume a notch. He wanted the jury to strain to hear what he had to say next. "And yet, with all those problems they listed, they left the biggest problem out. This is the biggest problem right here, and it's real."

He stepped sideways, away from the security and protection of the podium. He took two steps toward the jurors and held up one finger. "With the exception of Kevin Freeman, any witness who saw or heard something told you *one* perpetrator. Every police officer said they were looking for *one* man. What was the man they were looking for based on? Eyewitness descriptions. Six feet tall, close-cropped hair. That's what Schliffka said. Could not have been more clear. And the State's running from it.

"Captain Curole and Officer Carter, they ran from it too. Do you remember their testimony? I read it to you from 1985. Can you believe that in 1985 Carter gets up and says on the witness stand, knowing the defense doesn't have all the evidence, knowing they don't have a police report, he said the description I got from

Schliffka was six feet tall, Negro, gun in hand, dark jacket, dark pants. He left something out, didn't he? Do you think that was an accident?

"How about Curole, when he testified in 1985? He had a simple question put to him: 'Isn't it true, sir, that after the shooting the man the police was looking for was six feet tall with close-cropped hair, Negro male, dark hair, dark jacket?' His answer, do you remember? It was no. Then I read to him from his own report: 'Wanted, Negro male, six feet tall, close-cropped hair, dark jacket, dark pants.' They were trying very, very hard to keep anyone's attention from the truth.

"It's about the truth. And the truth comes out of people like Paul Schliffka, Rosemary McAllister, Stephen McAllister, Sheri Kelly, Pat Jordan. I guess they were trying to suggest to you that Sheri Kelly made this up. Wasn't it interesting, though, how her sister said exactly the same thing? Pat Jordan told you clear as day that Sheri Kelly said the same thing to her in 1985, eighteen years ago. Sheri Kelly swore to you, with absolute conviction and utter confidence, that this man, John Thompson, was not the man she saw running by.

"Now, we've heard the facts presented in a little bit of a disjointed way; you know, that's the way a trial works. Different witnesses have different pieces. But I think we need to go back and review." Michael turned to the easel with his pointer.

"Mr. Liuzza got out of his car a little after midnight on December the 6th. At the same time, Mr. Freeman's car was parked up here." He pointed above Baronne. "We know this from Mr. Freeman, what he told Mr. Perkins, and what Captain Curole told us. We also know it from the McAllisters.

"Freeman walked toward Liuzza, he saw a man to rob, to get some money. He approached Mr. Liuzza, stole his watch, his wallet, and an initial ring. Shot him dead, five times. An utterly despicable and heinous act. He ran back to his car, slammed the door, and drove away fast. No doubt about it.

"But there were some problems for Freeman. He knew that a woman saw him. You heard that. Very interesting. Remember the testimony of Captain Curole when Freeman said a woman saw him? Because if the State's trying to suggest that she's making it up, but he said a *woman* saw him, we heard the *woman* come in and say who she saw. Right?

"So Freeman knew he had a problem. He was seen by a woman, plus he ran right by Paul Schliffka, who was getting into his own car. So later he changed his story.

"By the time Freeman got to trial we heard a whole different story. At trial, Freeman said his car was parked all the way down here," moving the pointer south two blocks, "on Carondelet. He said he didn't run to his car and get in and drive away; he just ran home. He didn't want to be tied to the car.

"What he first told Richard Perkins was different, remember? He told Perkins his car was here," the pointer hit the easel above Baronne, "and he ran to it and drove away. More important, what he told Perkins was a lie. He told Perkins that he and Thompson set out to rob someone. They saw Liuzza and they both walked over, and Freeman got the wallet. He blamed the killing on Thompson and ran away.

"Why would he change his story at trial? Why go from what he told Perkins, the first lie, to a different lie about where he parked? It's really very simple.

"Perkins came to Thompson and asked about the gun. They talked about the gun. Thompson explained he had gotten it from Freeman. Perkins heard on the street that Freeman was a murderer. So he went to Freeman and said, 'Hey, what's going on here?'

"Freeman realized, 'Uh-oh, somebody knows,' and it's not just the woman who saw him run by. So he made up a story: 'It wasn't really me, it was John.' John was the easy guy to blame it on, right? Because Perkins had already gotten the gun from John. So that was the story he told—it was John.

"But then after they arrested him, after Perkins went to the Liuzza family for the reward, Freeman had to tell a different story. He realized, 'Wait a minute—the lie I told Perkins wasn't going to work. Because that puts me in an armed robbery. They're going to send me to jail for the rest of my life whether I pulled the trigger or not.' So he made up lie number two, a completely different story. Now he's parked way down here, on Carondelet. He took himself out of the armed robbery.

"You know how we know that story is a lie, other than the ridiculousness of it? The cops didn't believe it either. And the DAs didn't believe it. Let's think for a minute about why that might be. Freeman's story at trial was, 'I didn't do anything wrong.' His story at trial was, he was driving down the street with John. 'I see John Thompson; I pick him up. We run out of gas. Thompson says, "I got the heat, let's go rob someone." ' That's according to Freeman. Not the truth—just according to Freeman. Freeman goes, 'Oh, no, he has a gun.' He turns and runs away. He didn't do anything wrong.

"So picture yourself: If the DAs believed that, why would they charge him with first-degree murder? Why would they tell him he had to make a deal? Why tell him his choices were to either go to jail for life or plead guilty to accessory after the fact and take five years, when he told them he did absolutely nothing wrong?

"You know why? Because it's the way deals work. They were squeezing him. They were squeezing him to tell a story that they didn't buy for a minute because this was a highly publicized murder and they had to put someone away. Whether it was Thompson, whether it was Freeman, they didn't care. They wanted a conviction, like Richard Perkins did so he could get his ten thousand five hundred dollars.

"Now, you may be asking yourself, if this is all so clear, why are we even here? Why was John Thompson even charged with the murder? Come on, Mr. Banks, why was he charged? It's clear now: John bought the gun and the ring at two different times from Kevin Freeman. That moment they had a man, they had a guy in possession.

"When John figured it out, he couldn't go to the police and tell them. What was he doing with the gun? He traded it for drugs. He was a drug dealer—a small-time drug dealer. He couldn't go to the police.

"Now, I'm not making excuses for the drug dealing. And I'm sure you're not either. And John's not either. It's eighteen years ago, John was twenty-two, and that's what he did to survive. He's not proud of it. He's not a murderer; he's not a violent felon. But that's what he did, and he came in and admitted it. He came in and told you about the gun and the ring.

"The State, and Ms. Scott, make a very big deal of his letter to Big Daddy Red. You just had some of it read to you, the letter that John, while he was in jail—falsely accused—wrote to Big Daddy Red on March 7, 1985. You may be asking yourselves, why did he write that?

"Well, he wrote that letter because, while his lawyer was doing nothing, John needed witnesses. He needed someone to come in and tell the truth. To say that he saw John buy the ring from Kevin Freeman.

"You might think of the letter as a jailhouse subpoena. Lawyers like me and Mr. Glass and Mr. Cooney, we might come in and ask Judge Quinlan, 'Give us a subpoena to find someone.' But John's lawyer wasn't doing anything. So he had to write Big Daddy Red. He didn't say 'Lie;' he said, 'Come in and say you seen Kevin give me a ring around December 21st.' John's already admitted that he had that ring. He bought it; he admitted that. But he needed to make it clear that it came from Kevin."

Michael paused, took a sip from his water bottle. "You know how we know the letter's true? There's actually a little clue in the letter itself. Not in what it says, but in what it *doesn't* say.

Remember, there were two pieces of physical evidence—the ring and the gun. If Big Daddy Red comes in for John and says he saw John buy the ring, it doesn't solve John's problem *because the cops still have the gun.* If John was asking Big Daddy Red to come in and lie to get him off, he'd say, 'Red, I need you to come in to Court and say you saw me buy the ring—*and the gun*—from Kevin Freeman.'

"He didn't do that. You know why? Because *that wasn't true.* John had bought the gun a few days before from Freeman, and Red wouldn't have known anything about that. John wanted Big Daddy Red to come in and put the truth out there, so he asked for that. *Tell them about the ring.* Not tell them about both and get me out of trouble.

"Ladies and gentlemen, this letter is not what Mr. Solino has told you it is, and it's not what Ms. Scott has told you it is. It's a plea for a witness to come in because people like Big Daddy Red who sell drugs and buy drugs, they don't like coming in to court and ratting on someone. He had to ask him special to come in."

Michael saw the jurors' eyes, saw the wheels turning. They were thinking, and thinking meant they were not yet convinced. But not convinced meant reasonable doubt, and reasonable doubt meant John won. He needed to remind them of that.

"When I'm done—and don't worry, it's coming soon—Mr. Solino gets to talk. I don't get to go again. This is it. You might think that's unfair that the State goes first and last, but it's not. It's fair. The reason it's fair is that *they* had the burden of proof, not us. It's a big burden of proof—*big* burden—proof *beyond a reasonable doubt.*

"They are asking you to throw John in jail for another forty years, the rest of his life, beyond the eighteen he's already served. To do that they can't just come in and say, *maybe* John Thompson murdered Ray Liuzza. That's not enough. They can't show it's possible, or even likely. They have to show you that that's what happened *beyond a reasonable doubt*. What that means is if you have *any doubt at all*, no matter how small—if it's a doubt that is reasonable in your own mind—you *have* to acquit John Thompson. Listen to that, because that's what Judge Quinlan is going to tell you. If you are not convinced of the guilt of the defendant, Mr. Thompson, beyond a reasonable doubt, you *must* find him not guilty. *Must*. It's the law, and it's what's right.

"You're going to go back into that jury room and you'll weigh things in your mind. You'll weigh what Mr. Perkins told you and what you think about Mr. Freeman, the dead man with close-cropped hair, and you'll think about the money. I hope what you'll do is weigh that against what you heard from people who had no interest in the outcome of this case. No bias, nothing to gain or lose, other than the truth—Steve McAllister, Rose McAllister, Sheri Kelly, Pat Jordan.

"And John Thompson—I hope you'll listen to what he had to say, because it's time for justice. It's time to realize that it was one perpetrator, one man who was six feet tall with close-cropped hair. No one came forward with anything different. No one saw or heard anything different.

"Folks, Kevin Freeman is dead. We can't punish him anymore for Mr. Liuzza's murder. All we can do now is to give justice to John Thompson. For the first time in eighteen years, we can give him justice."

Michael walked back to the podium, scanning his outline one more time before ending. "We all have to do the right thing. I'm asking you to go back and do the right thing and find John Thompson *not* guilty in the murder of Ray Liuzza."

It was done. Michael exhaled, looking at the jury one last time. He nodded, picked up his pad, and walked back to the table.

Val Solino stepped forward. He was confident, his voice strong and resonant, delivering all of the credibility inherent in the district attorney's office. He said, "Eighteen years, five months is a long time to wait. But it's not too long to do justice. That's what I'm going to ask everybody here. Do the best you can to decide this case on the evidence. The evidence you hear from the witness stand and the evidence you are to view, not on slick tricks and deceptions.

"What I heard today, in this argument just a few minutes ago, was let John Thompson walk because everybody in this case other than John Thompson is at fault. His lawyer was a bum, didn't do anything. Kevin Freeman's a bum, he lied. Perkins lied. Everybody lied. Detective Curole didn't do his job right. Well, everybody has to stand accountable for something, and I'm asking you to hold John Thompson accountable for what happened eighteen years, five months ago. The man who had the ring. The man who had the gun. The man who told Richard Perkins what he did."

Solino moved over to the map that Michael had used. "Let's look at this poster here. Don't believe Kevin Freeman, they say, because Kevin told Funk that he parked the car down by Katie's Beauty Salon. Nobody else said that, and Kevin didn't say that himself. He said he parked the car over here at Carondelet. The defense said that's important because Kevin wants to put the car away from the scene because he knows a woman saw him running away."

Solino sounded exasperated, his tone saying, *Any idiot could see through this.* "Well, use your common sense and your experiences. If Kevin Freeman is going to lie about his participation in this, is he going to tell you that he runs right by the place where someone claims to have seen him but put the car at the other end of the street? Or is he going to tell you, 'I booked out of there and I ran down to the car and I don't know what happened'?

"Everything you heard a few minutes ago was defense speculation as to what happened. Well, what really did happen that night? Let's see if this fits the facts. Kevin is driving home, picks John up. Kevin's old junky car starts spitting, running out of gas. Because remember what you're dealing with. John Thompson, he's a small-time drug dealer, you heard him say it. So hard up he's got to go trade the ring to get himself some weed because he can't even come up with a few bucks to go buy it.

"So does it surprise you that these guys are driving around with a dollar or two of gas in the car? The car runs out of gas, dies on Carondelet. These guys are walking, okay, and here comes poor Mr. Liuzza. He parks his car here, up near Josephine and Baronne.

"Ray gets out of the car and walks around the back of his trunk and starts to head to his driveway. They ain't got no money. Thompson says, 'Oooh, crime of opportunity.' Pulls the gun out and goes toward Ray.

"Kevin's thinking to himself, 'I don't want any part of this. I'm a small-time drug dealer—maybe hustler—never been in any serious trouble,' and he books out. Thompson grabs Ray before he gets to the door, they struggle up the block, and Ray gets killed. Kevin turns around and sees it.

"The point of all of this is, What story makes sense? Does it make sense that somebody drives a car, parks it here above Baronne, a block and a half away from where Ray Liuzza is, and decides to run back and rob Ray? Why are they walking down the street and away from their homes? How do they know what time Ray's coming home, to be laying in wait and to have a getaway car parked down the block? That makes no sense. No sense.

"The only thing that makes sense is that they ran out of gas and Ray had the poor unfortunate luck of coming up to his driveway just about the time they were getting there and Thompson decided to do something about it."

Michael watched the jury impassively, composed as his thoughts raced. *Freeman acted alone. He saw Liuzza, parked, came back, shot him, ran away, and built the story to include John later. It's even simpler than Solino's story, and it fits the witnesses and the bias issues. You've got to see this. Don't you?*

Solino continued. "Look at this photo of John Thompson that they showed you. Ask yourselves, can somebody who sees this man running for a few seconds in the middle of the night, under highly charged circumstances, tell if this hairstyle cannot be described as a short Afro? You heard the first words out of Mr. Banks's mouth, that Paul Schliffka said, 'It wasn't a large picked-out Afro, it was close to the head and it was straight back.' How can you let somebody go based upon somebody saying that?

"You know, I could sit here and waste your time, and I could tell you it's almost a standard part of a defense. You got a dead guy, you blame it on the dead guy. Those people can't come in here and speak for themselves. But you heard what Kevin said and you heard what Funk said. What did they tell you? That John Thompson did it.

"Let's get to a few other things. Paul Schliffka, no one disputes what he said. He's outside his house, he moves toward the corner. Did Paul testify to a man running to a car and jumping in it? You didn't hear that. Look where he was. You could probably throw a nickel from where Schliffka was to where the McAllisters say the car had to have been parked. If there was a car there, use your common sense and ask yourselves if Paul would have seen it?

"Sheri Kelly, ask yourself whether she could have gotten up out of her bed, turned her light off, looked out her window, run to the front, opened the window, run out on the balcony, assumed the position to look, all in the few seconds it took the shooter of Ray Liuzza to hightail it across a city street. And even if she did see somebody, she didn't see any facial features. By her own estimation, maybe two seconds, she saw a profile. She saw nothing. There's nothing in Ms. Hartman's testimony that's worthy of belief."

Solino paused. "I know it's been a long day. Eighteen years, five months is long. I'm not going to keep you but another five seconds. All I ask you to do is remember a man was killed, a man who was shot dead with a gun in the course of an armed robbery. We've shown that the gun and the loot from the robbery were directly in his hands. He's admitted that. He comes to court and says that other people laid it off on him. He writes a letter to his buddy. You read that letter, you know what that letter is. That's not a street subpoena.

"Ask yourselves why Big Daddy Red didn't come testify. Ask yourselves if that letter is anything other than what it is—an admission of guilt and an attempt to wiggle out of something he knew he couldn't get out of.

"Go back and think about all of this and ask yourselves who came to court and put the cards on the table, engaged in no deception, no cheap tricks, no attempt to trick people on the witness stand. Stand by your oath and exercise your oath as you see fit to judge all of the witnesses based upon their testimony. When you do that, I'm sure, you will conclude that beyond a reasonable doubt we have not only proven that John Thompson is guilty, but we have proven to you that a slick deceptive defense that has been presented to you today is a bunch of hot air and does not make sense. Thank you very much."

Solino took his papers and walked back to his table, his steps echoing against the high ceiling.

51

THE VERDICT

MICHAEL, GORDON, ROBERT, and John stood in the hall. The wait was agonizing.

There was nothing for them to say to one another, nothing they could say or do to change the jury's deliberations at this point, and nothing that could stop them from thinking about it, envisioning the discussions, worrying about the mistakes they had made, what the jury might be focused on, and what they might have missed.

Michael walked to the men's room, to the water fountain, back and forth, up and down the hall, just to be in motion. Gordon typed e-mails to colleagues on his BlackBerry, grateful for reminders of his other cases to distract him. Robert and John huddled, comforting each other with small successes during the trial, missteps by the DA, or moments where they had scored points.

It was impossible to know how long a jury would deliberate. They might be out in the hall for five minutes, or they could get sent home overnight with the jury still deliberating. In a civil case, Michael would have left the courthouse, gotten some physical separation, leaving a junior lawyer there to call him when the jury was ready. They couldn't make John wait alone, though, so they stayed.

The bailiff came out from the courtroom and motioned to John. Worried, Gordon walked with him. John turned to Gordon, saying, "It's okay, man. Me and him, we went to school together."

Gordon must have made a face, because John smiled. "Man, I'm'a tell you all my secrets?" He turned to the bailiff, shaking the uniformed man's hand. "A'right, man. How you doing? What you think?"

"Man, I don't know," the sheriff replied.

Gordon had never seen John more relaxed. John actually laughed and said, "You don't know? What you mean you don't know? You got to know, man. This is my life here!"

"I know, man, I know. Here's the thing: Not all of them jurors is even paying attention, man. The ones is paying attention, the comments they make? Based on that, you all good, man. They don't think you did it. But as I'm taking them back there just now, one of them says to the other one, 'I don't know why we've got much to talk about. It's obvious he did it,' some shit like that. The other woman with her said, 'You really think he did it?' so I'm assuming, you know, that she thinks you're innocent. But I just don't know. I thought you were good, man, and the jury was all nodding their heads at you, man. So I think you're good, but I just don't know."

John nodded. "A'right. Thanks." They shook hands and rejoined the others.

They all resumed their vigil, passing time with awkward conversations, steering randomly from topic to topic. The world was standing still.

THE BAILIFF OPENED the door and found them all in the hall. "They're coming back in."

Michael looked at his watch. What had felt like hours had only been thirty-five minutes. He looked at Gordon. "It's got to be good," Gordon said. Inside, though, Michael thought, *Or very, very bad. They couldn't convict that fast, could they?* He started thinking of all the things he could have or should have said differently, all the points he could have made better, things that Solino and Scott said that had resonated.

Judge Quinlan entered the courtroom and sat down. If he had any idea what the verdict was, he didn't show it. Michael wondered, with the trial now over, whether Quinlan still thought John was guilty.

For fifteen years, Michael had tried to convince Pat Quinlan of John Thompson's innocence. Now, in what was literally the moment of truth, it turned out Quinlan was as powerless as anyone else. *Still*, Michael thought, *you've gotta tip your hat to the guy, all in all*. He had run a fair trial, perhaps more than fair as far as John was concerned. If they lost this trial, it wouldn't be because of Quinlan. They couldn't ask for more than that.

Quinlan looked at everyone in the courtroom, the room choking in anticipation. He leaned into his microphone and spoke strongly and clearly. "The jury is about to come in here and deliver a verdict. This courtroom will remain in control after that verdict is read, *no matter what the outcome is*. If there is anyone here who does not think they can contain their emotion and will have to say something or make a response when the verdict is read, you must leave this courtroom right now. I will hold anyone who reacts in contempt of court. This is your chance—leave now."

Not a single person moved.

The door opened and the jury walked in, silent and single file.

Not one of the jurors looked at the defense table.

Eighteen years, thousands of letters, dozens of phone calls, hundreds of motions, thousands of hours, millions of dollars, and two jury trials had brought them to this moment—to a declaration of the truth of what happened in the early morning hours of December 6, 1984, at the intersection of Josephine and Baronne.

The jury took their seats, and the room stood still. Quinlan turned to the foreman and said, "Ladies and gentlemen, have you reached a verdict?"

"We have."

"Would you hand it to the clerk, please?"

The foreman handed a piece of paper to the clerk of court. The paper, John's destiny, moved from juror to clerk and then three steps away to the judge. Quinlan unfolded and read the piece of paper. He sighed deeply, then handed it to the clerk, and said, "Please read the verdict."

Did the sigh mean he was content or resigned? Did it mean John was innocent or guilty? Michael felt as if everything was moving in slow motion. It was driving him crazy.

For his part, Gordon had made his prediction while waiting for the jury to file in. He typed the e-mail addresses of several close friends into his BlackBerry and put NOT GUILTY in the text field. *No sense in projecting negative energy,* he thought, though he couldn't help reminding himself not to hit "send" if the verdict didn't go their way. He placed the BlackBerry on the counsel table, ready to hit the SEND button when the jury returned. Both Gordon and Michael put their arms around John's waist, as much to steady themselves as to support John.

Michael found himself trying to talk to God. He wasn't really praying to any specific god as much as he was pleading with all of them, any that would listen, whatever force that runs the universe, that sees to it that good things happen to good people. He needed that to happen now.

The clerk opened the paper himself and read aloud, "We, the jury, find the defendant, John Thompson, *not guilty.*"

The crowd buckled, letting out a collective exhalation of the relief, joy, frustration, and agony that had built up. Gordon threw both his arms around John and whispered in his ear, "Congratulations, John. You did it."

He reached for his BlackBerry and hit SEND.

Michael's head had been lowered, eyes closed as the verdict was read. He pumped his fists silently as the verdict was read, lifting his eyes to the ceiling. *Thank you,* he thought, to no one and everyone. He turned to John, still in Gordon's embrace, and slapped him on the back. He looked over Gordon's shoulder and reached out to grab Robert Glass, then turned around to face Nick Trenticosta in the front row of benches behind them. He nodded at him and looked at John's mother. She was positively vibrating in her seat, tears streaming from her eyes as she looked at Michael. He held her gaze as she said, "Thank you, thank you, thank you," then nodded and turned back.

The Liuzza family had gathered around each other, turned inward around Ray's father, no one saying a word, their backs keeping the rest of the world at bay. Michael felt sympathy for them for a brief moment, but then turned and focused on his client, his friend, as John wrapped his arms around his son, hugging his child as an innocent man, for the first time in John Jr.'s memory.

VAL REACHED THE defense table, shook Michael's hand and the hands of the other lawyers. He looked at John and nodded.

Judge Quinlan was speaking now, though no one was listening. "For the record, the verdict's eleven to one if anybody wants to see it."

Michael and Val walked up to the judge. They had discussed how to handle this moment. Solino spoke first: "Your Honor, there is the matter of Mr. Thompson's continued incarceration or release. As you know, Mr. Thompson is under arrest and awaiting a trial for the alleged aggravated assault and battery of an Orleans Parish Prison guard. However, under the circumstances, the State and the defense have agreed that the State would request that Mr. Thompson be immediately released on his own recognizance, based on defense counsel's representation that defendant has no plans to leave the New Orleans area."

Quinlan shook his head. "Court will deny that request and set bail at ten thousand dollars."

Michael couldn't help himself. "Your Honor—," he started.

Quinlan cut him off. "John Thompson may not be guilty of the murder of Ray Liuzza, but this court isn't going to do him any favors. Bail is set at ten thousand dollars." Quinlan's tone told Michael the discussion was over, so he turned and walked back to counsel's table.

"What'd he say?" Gordon asked.

"Bail's set on the prison guard at ten grand."

"You're kidding."

"Wish I was," said Michael, packing up his things. He turned to Solino. "Val, we're going to get the bail money, and we'll be back. Don't let anyone leave for the night, okay?"

Val nodded.

They left John with Nick and Robert and walked outside the courtroom, down the stairs, and across the street to Tommy's Bail Bonds. The bond for $10,000 bail was $1,200. They walked out the door and to the ATM machine helpfully installed next to Tommy's, and each man drew $600 out of his personal checking account.

Bond in hand, they walked back up the stairs to the courtroom. The clerk of court brought Quinlan back in from his chambers.

Quinlan was clearly surprised, but he said nothing. He signed the papers and said to the lawyers, "You can pick him up tomorrow." Turning to John, Quinlan said, "Mr. Thompson?"

"Yes?"

"Mr. Thompson, your lawyers have paid your bail. You will be released tomorrow once your paperwork has been processed at OPP." Quinlan paused. "Most lawyers would not put their own money up on a bail bond for a client in this manner. I hope they see their money again."

52

RELEASE

MAY 10, 2003

JOHN WOKE UP, brushed his teeth, and got dressed. When it was time, a guard came and opened the door to his cell. John walked out into the hall, turned, and walked toward the tier exit. The guards were still talking to him, like they did most days, but already it was different. The tone was completely different. It was what he'd wanted for as long as he could remember, before he was imprisoned, before he was arrested, before his earliest memory. It was two boxers looking at each other after a hard fight, or a linebacker helping a running back stand up after a brutal tackle.

It was respect.

Funny, John thought. *I'm not a different person than I was yesterday.*

Or maybe I am.

There was, as always, paperwork that had to be processed. He had to sign a form to get the things back that he had worn to OPP in 1985. He had only had the clothes on his back, so there wasn't much for them to give back worth anything, but they gave him the same clothes he'd been wearing when they arrested him in 1985.

His pants still fit. *They still fit, you motherfuckers. What do you think of that?* Eighteen years later, and his clothes still fit.

The cop processing him gave him a small bag of things that had been in his pockets, and they gave him $10. John looked at it and then back at the guard.

"For bus fare," he said.

How about that, John thought.

He was forty years old, and had spent his entire adult life trying to get out of prison. Most of the people he knew were either in Angola or in OPP, and they weren't going anywhere. Some had gotten out for a little while, but most all of those had done something else on the outside to find their way back to jail.

People had said to him, "John, it's a different world out there now, man." He knew that was true. He had kept up with some of it. He knew that cell phones had taken over, and he knew about the Internet. He even had a friend who'd made him a Web site at one point. But there was bound to be more. People told him they got cash from computers outside the bank now, instead of having to go inside during banking hours. One guy had come back to OPP, and he told John that what amazed him most was how the soda machines had changed. *Soda machines. Imagine that.*

He already knew that Louisiana didn't compensate exonerated prisoners for their time, which is why all he had was the small bag and a $10 bill. If he had been improperly imprisoned in California, he'd have a couple million bucks in his pocket after eighteen years.

Could be worse, he thought.

He wondered again how he would stay outside OPP for good. He had started by asking Gordon and Michael to find him a place that wasn't in the neighborhood with his family yet. Connick, Jordan, the cop—they would probably be watching him closely. John knew that if he went back to the neighborhood before he was ready, or right now when everybody was all excited about his release, they would all want to celebrate. That meant booze and drugs, and John knew he had to steer clear of all that. *Can't go runnin' back into that on the first day out, get my ass thrown back in jail tomorrow,* he decided.

He needed to find a job, too. John had asked the warden at OPP about what they do for prisoners who get out. The warden replied that none of the prison's post-conviction outreach or support programs applied to John because he was not a convict. He was an exoneree.

If you're innocent and you're in prison, they don't help you reintegrate. They only help you if you did the crime. John chuckled to himself.

Michael and Gordon had reserved him a hotel room for a week or so, to give him some time to adjust. Nick had told John he'd have a job for him at the Center for Equal Justice. John could help represent other death row inmates. Who would know better what those guys were going through? Who else could they trust to really tell the truth?

As he walked down the hall toward the prison exit, he knew that Michael, Gordon, and Robert were waiting for him. He passed through the last set of double doors and the room was suddenly full of smiles and handshakes and hugs and backslapping. John smiled, too, but he wasn't really sure if elation was the emotion he was really feeling.

John thought, *I'm gonna walk out that door right there, and then what?* Michael and Gordon told him that the press was outside there, with cameramen and reporters who would ask John lots of questions. Michael told John he would help field questions, and he cautioned John not to say anything bad about the State or the City of New Orleans, but just to talk about how happy he was to be out.

The last part was easy. He *was* happy to be out. No matter what the free world was like, he most certainly didn't want to be in prison anymore.

Michael pushed one door open and held it for him, and Gordon opened the other. They walked out the door and the light and the noise from all those reporters hit John like a train. They were all shouting at him, wanting to know how he felt.

John told them he wanted to thank God that he was alive, that he had a chance to get his life back.

One of the reporters asked John if he was bitter. He tried to explain it. "Bitter" wasn't the word. He had lost a lot of time, including all the time he had for bitterness. Bitterness wouldn't get his time back. He had to look forward.

The reporters wanted to know where he was going, so he told them he was going to find his boys and spend as much time with them as he could. Then Michael and Gordon cut off the questions and helped John into Michael's car. They drove to his hotel room. It wasn't anything special, but it was four times the size of his cell.

A junior lawyer took John shopping after they'd checked in to the hotel. They got some new clothes on Canal, then went out on Bourbon Street. John remembered that. It was like being a kid again, walking among all of these people looking for a party, looking to get drunk or high and run around and hook up with women and dance.

John bought a disposable camera at one of the shops and walked around, trying to get his head around where he was. He could go anywhere now, do whatever he wanted. *Turns out what I want to do right now is walk around Bourbon Street taking pictures of women's asses and drinking a beer*, he thought.

By late afternoon, his boys had joined him. The look in their eyes—the way they held him as tightly as he held them—John never wanted that moment to end. He felt that if he never let them go, everything would be all right, and the time he was away wouldn't really matter anymore. Dedric, he was twenty-four now, and Tiger was twenty-two. They were grown men. Tiger was in college but was thinking of leaving and joining the army. Dedric was more like his father had been, a high school dropout mixed up in the streets. He hadn't done anything violent yet, but had the beginnings of a record, an arrest, and was on probation for cocaine possession.

John blamed himself for a lot of his sons' troubles. If he had been with them, instead of behind bars, he could have helped them more, no question about it. He had a lot of lost time to make up for. Still, looking at them both, seeing them, although he realized they were grown men, it was as if he hadn't skipped a day, his heart soaring as they smiled and joked, just like when they were children.

Michael and Gordon had left after dropping John off, and said they'd come back in a few hours. They had made reservations at Pascal's Manale to celebrate. After eighteen years in jail, crowds made John uncomfortable. He wouldn't tell Michael and Gordon that, but he wasn't going to the restaurant. He'd find another, quieter way to celebrate.

John put on the swim trunks he had bought that afternoon. His boys had brought theirs, and the three men went down to the pool at the hotel. John put his towel on the chair and all three of them got into the pool and start horsing around. Whatever Dubelier, Williams, and Connick had taken from John—his time, his pride, his freedom, his family—he was out now, and he was regaining possession of his life. John had learned how to live in the here and now, and here and now he had his boys. And Dedric was finding out that the old man was still tough enough to dunk him under the water.

EPILOGUE

JOHN LEFT PRISON on May 10, 2003, eighteen years after his conviction. He immediately began putting in place his plan for staying out of prison. He moved in with his mother, and, knowing he needed God around him, he started going to church. A woman at his mother's church, Laverne, heard John's story on TV and remembered him from elementary school. She asked John's mother to introduce them.

Six weeks later, John and Laverne were married, and they remain married to this day.

John went to work with Nick Trenticosta, at the Loyola Death Penalty Resource Center, acting as a paralegal on cases just like his. On one occasion, he attempted to go back to Angola to meet with the Center's clients. Ironically enough, the prison that previously had kept John now refused to admit him, on the grounds that he lacked a high school diploma or GED, and thus could not possibly be there on an appropriate visit.

The Resource Center had offices in a church next to Loyola Law School. Another organization in the church was Habitat for Humanity, which encouraged John to submit an application for housing. Not long afterward, John learned that Habitat had selected him to be the recipient of a new house. He and Laverne moved into their own home, a modest two-bedroom, one-story house in New Orleans's Eighth Ward, in 2004.

In 2005, Hurricane Katrina swept through New Orleans. John and Laverne evacuated, and spent several weeks in Baton Rouge. Thankfully, their home escaped serious damage.

MICHAEL BANKS AND Gordon Cooney continue to practice law at Morgan, Lewis & Bockius. They estimate that over 175 attorneys and staff spent tens of thousands of hours representing John's death penalty challenge, at a cost to Morgan, Lewis in the millions of dollars in foregone legal fees. It is safe to assume that without a representation of this quality and magnitude, John Thompson would be dead today.

Michael, Gordon, and Morgan, Lewis continue to represent John in court. In 2003, they filed a lawsuit on John's behalf against the Orleans Parish district attorney's office and Harry Connick, Eddie Jordan, Eric Dubelier, and Jim Williams, arguing that John's civil rights had been violated due to the failure of Harry Connick to implement adequate training measures for his assistant DAs on the law surrounding the landmark case of *Brady v. Maryland*. Many observers assumed the civil lawsuit would quickly be dismissed, believing that John and his attorneys would be unable to meet the very narrow grounds for overcoming prosecutorial immunity and recovering damages from a municipal defendant for civil rights violations by prosecutors in a criminal trial.

Instead, in 2007, Judge Carl J. Barbier presided over a trial at which Harry Connick, Jerry Glas, Tim McElroy, Eric Dubelier, Jim Williams, and others were called to testify about the events that took place leading to John's convictions, the revelation of the blood evidence, and the actions of the Orleans Parish district attorney's office. A jury concluded that under Harry Connick's leadership, the DA's office had failed to create and administer policies and procedures regarding the obligation to produce exculpatory evidence, and that a failure to train and oversee prosecutors caused John's wrongful conviction and imprisonment. The jury awarded John $14 million. Judge Barbier upheld the verdict and ordered the payment of legal fees incurred by Morgan, Lewis in the civil lawsuit.

To date, neither the judgment in John's favor nor the legal fees have been paid. Lawyers representing Orleans Parish have appealed the decision, losing in appeals to the 5th Circuit Court of Appeals and then again to a special *en banc* session of the 5th Circuit. They are now seeking review of the $14 million judgment by the Supreme Court of the United States.

As JOHN WORKED through his transition from imprisonment to freedom, he spoke often with everyone he could about the challenges that all men face after their release, and how to cure recidivism. These conversations led him to found an organization called Resurrection After Exoneration (RAE), dedicated to helping exonerated men adjust to life after prison.

Louisiana has the highest exoneration rate in the country, as well as the highest rate of per capita incarceration and prisoners serving life without parole in the world. Almost half (48.6 percent) of the 14,000 prisoners annually paroled or released return to prison. Recidivism is a special concern among exonerated men, who have wrongfully spent multiple years in prison and are financially, professionally, and spiritually impoverished. The need is even greater in New Orleans, where essential resources and support for reentry are virtually nonexistent in the aftermath of Hurricane Katrina.

RAE is working to transform the experience of exonerated men and returning long-term prisoners by creating social leaders where there currently exists a cycle of recidivism, desperation, and poverty. With seed funding from the Echoing Green Foundation, RAE has purchased and completed renovations on a transitional housing facility that several exonerees currently call home. Run by exonerees for exonerees, this home is the first of its kind. Thompson has plans for a business that sustains the home and provides RAE with leadership and entrepreneurial skills.

RAE's exonerees regularly participate in individual and group counseling, have access to educational opportunities, and receive financial, literacy, and computer literacy training. Instead of working for free in the prison system, exonerees work together to help each other, thus building solidarity. RAE positions exonerees as advocates for criminal justice reform, speaking about their experiences at events and venues nationwide.

Donations to RAE are gratefully accepted and can be made online from the RAE Web site, www.r-a-e.org.